Schmidt / Hübener

New Digital Markets Act

New Digital Markets Act

A Practitioner's Guide

edited by

Jens Peter Schmidt
Fabian Hübener

2023

BECK · HART · NOMOS

Published by
Nomos Verlagsgesellschaft mbH & Co. KG, Waldseestraße 3-5, 76530 Baden-Baden, Germany,
email: vertrieb@nomos.de

Co-published by
Verlag C.H.Beck oHG, Wilhelmstraße 9, 80801 München, Germany,
email: bestellung@beck.de

and

Hart Publishing, Kemp House, Chawley Park, Cumnor Hill, Oxford, OX2 9PH, United Kingdom,
online at: www.hartpub.co.uk

Published in North America by Hart Publishing,
An Imprint of Bloomsbury Publishing 1385 Broadway, New York, NY 10018, USA
email: mail@hartpub.co.uk

ISBN Print 978 3 7560 0317 4 (NOMOS)
ISBN E-Book 978 3 7489 3706 7 (NOMOS)
ISBN Print 978 3 406 80469 4 (C.H.BECK)
ISBN Print 978 1 5099 7420 7 (HART)

First Edition 2023

Preface

The European Commission is determined to turn the coming decade into Europe's Digital Decade. Using the slogan 'A Europe fit for the digital age', the authority in Brussels is bundling measures designed to expand digital sovereignty and set its own standards.

The Digital Markets Act (DMA), which came into force on 1.11.2022, is a milestone for EU legislation in the field of the digital economy and, together with the Digital Services Act, is one of the core elements of the EU's Digital Strategy. Adopted in record time, the DMA aims to counter unfair practices by large online platforms that provide business users with key access to consumers. Platforms covered by the DMA are subject to a number of obligations designed to ensure fair and open digital markets.

This Practitioner's Guide provides a comprehensive user-friendly introduction to a complex subject. It explores the background and objectives of the DMA and sets out the extensive prohibitions and requirements that online platforms, identified as 'gatekeepers' under the DMA, have to comply with. The rights of business users and end users of digital platforms are addressed from a hands-on perspective, as are the investigative and enforcement powers of the European Commission and the role of the Member States' authorities. Covering a number of EU Member States, the book explains and assesses the role of national courts, whose importance for the future private enforcement of the DMA cannot be overestimated.

The editors would like to express their sincere thanks to all the co-authors for their work.

Brussels, July 2023

Jens Peter Schmidt *Fabian Hübener*

Contents

CHAPTER 4
DESIGNATION AS A GATEKEEPER (ART. 3 DMA)

Markus Brösamle/Johanna Krauskopf

CHAPTER 5
REVIEW BY THE EUROPEAN COMMISSION (ART. 4 DMA)

Markus Brösamle/Miriam Swamy-von Zastrow

CHAPTER 6
CONDUCT OBLIGATIONS FOR GATEKEEPERS (ART. 5–7 DMA)

Lucas Gasser/Jochen Hegener

CHAPTER 11
ROLE OF NATIONAL AUTHORITIES AND COURTS

Markus Brösamle/Emilia Etz

CHAPTER 12
THIRD-PARTY RIGHTS BEFORE THE EUROPEAN COMMISSION AND NATIONAL AUTHORITIES

Jens Peter Schmidt

CHAPTER 13
THE DMA AS THE SUBJECT MATTER OF PRIVATE ENFORCEMENT

Authors

Franck Audran

Franck Audran is a lawyer specialising in French and EU competition law (cartels, dominant positions, merger control). He has extensive experience in antitrust litigation before the French Competition Authority and in private enforcement before the commercial court. He holds a post-graduate degree (DEA) in business law and economics from the University of Paris I Panthéon-Sorbonne (2005) and a Master's degree in European law from the University of Erlangen, Germany (2004).

Markus Brösamle

Markus Brösamle advises in all areas of German and European antitrust law. He is active in the area of cartel damages, in all aspects of antitrust law in the context of M&A projects, and he also advises on all aspects of antitrust matters in the operative business (e.g. cooperation between competitors; abuse of market power; vertical cooperation; antitrust compliance). He further represents companies in antitrust investigations.

Prof. Dr. Oliver Budzinski

Oliver Budzinski is Professor of Economic Theory and Director of the Institute of Economics at Ilmenau University of Technology, Germany. He holds a Ph.D. from the Leibniz-University of Hanover, Germany. Former post-doc and professor positions include Marburg University, Germany, New York University, USA, and University of Southern Denmark, Campus Esbjerg. Oliver Budzinski specialises in competition economics as well as in media and sports economics. In these fields he has published more than 70 articles in academic journals, more than 60 chapters in collected volumes and handbooks, as well as authored or edited eight books.

Rob Corbet

Rob Corbet is a partner at Arthur Cox in Dublin. He is head of the technology & innovation team which is consistently rated as Ireland's market leading team in the TMT and digital regulation sectors.

Rick Cornelissen

Rick Cornelissen is litigation partner at Houthoff, Amsterdam, heading the firm's competition litigation team. His practice focuses on follow-on and standalone cartel damages and abuse of dominance damages claims, DMA-related issues and commercial disputes regarding distribution and other types of vertical agreements. Rick Cornelissen is a lecturer at the postgraduate program 'undertaking & liability' of the Grotius Academy and is a member of the Dutch European Law Association (NVER) and the Dutch Competition Law Association (VvM).

Emilia Etz, Maître en Droit

Emilia Etz is an international competition and trade lawyer. She focuses on European antitrust and competition matters and has successfully represented clients in merger control proceedings before the European Commission. In parallel, she advises on all aspects of international and EU trade, including sanctions and export control, customs and market access and investment control.

Pablo Figueroa, LL.M. (Cornell Law School and College of Europe)

Pablo Figueroa is partner in competition and EU law at Pérez-Llorca, where he joined in 2021. He has over fifteen years of experience in competition law, EU law and foreign direct investment. Throughout his career he has advised major clients on anti-competitive agreements, merger control, unilateral conduct and dominant positions, antitrust litigation, State aid, distribution and cooperation agreements and defence against the imposition of fines by competition authorities. He is also a visiting lecturer on competition law at Queen Mary University (London, United Kingdom) and is a regular contributor to leading European and international competition law journals, as well as editor of the leading journal 'World Competition'.

Dr. Lucas Gasser

Lucas Gasser advises on all aspects of German and European antitrust and competition law. This includes merger control proceedings, cartel and abuse of market power proceedings before the German Federal Cartel Office and the European Commission as well as before German and European courts. Another focus of his work covers EU State aid law. In that concern Lucas Gasser supports clients in notification proceedings with the European Commission as well as before European courts. Further, Lucas Gasser also supports clients regarding antitrust and EU State aid law related compliance issues and internal investigations.

Dr. Jochen Hegener, LL.M. (Columbia University)

Jochen Hegener advises on all aspects of German and European antitrust and competition law with a particular focus on the intersection to intellectual property law and on digital business models. His advice covers fields such as investigations and fine proceedings by the competition authorities (European Commission and the German Federal Cartel Office), competition litigation, antitrust and competition-related compliance topics and merger control proceedings. He is admitted to practice law in Germany as well as the state of New York, USA.

Dr. Fabian Hübener, LL.M. (Georgetown)

Fabian Hübener advises on European and German antitrust and competition matters. He has successfully represented several clients in referral proceedings before the European Court of Justice and antitrust and merger proceedings before the European Commission and national competition authorities. He also advises on the antitrust assessment of distribution models, particularly in the automotive industry, and digital business models.

Johanna Krauskopf, LL.M. (Universiteit van Amsterdam)

Johanna Krauskopf advises on European and German antitrust and competition matters. She holds an LL.M. degree from the Universiteit van Amsterdam in competition law and regulation. She is associate lawyer at Noerr, with a particular focus on antitrust damages litigation, M&A merger control and abuse of dominance matters.

Gonçalo Machado Borges, LL.M.

Gonçalo Machado Borges is counsel at CS'Associados, in Lisbon, where he heads the EU and competition practice area. Until recently, he was with Morais Leitão, where he worked in competition and TMT matters.

Elsa Mandel, LL.M. (NYU School of Law)

Elsa Mandel is a lawyer admitted to practice in Paris and New York. Her work focuses on competition law, especially private enforcement matters, as well as commercial litigation.

Leonor Martins Machado

Leonor Martins Machado works as a managing associate at the Portuguese law firm Morais Leitão. She is part of the litigation team. Leonor Martins Machado has a vast experience in national and international arbitrations and in civil cases concerning several industry sectors, with emphasis in corporate and, more recently, in private enforcement cases.

Jorge Masía, LL.M. (Northwestern University School of Law, Chicago)

Jorge Masía is counsel in antritrust litigation and economist at Pérez- Llorca, where he joined in 2020. He has 20 years of experience in complex litigation, particularly in matters involving competition. In addition, he has advised on litigation, specifically in the energy, financial and telecommunications sectors, as well as on corporate governance matters. Furthermore, he is an experienced advisor on franchising, joint ventures, strategic alliances, other competition matters and in IP litigation sectors, as well as a regular lecturer on competition and commercial law in IE University.

Jun.-Prof. Dr. Juliane Mendelsohn

Juliane Mendelsohn is Junior Professor of Law and Economics of Digitization at the Institute of Law and Institute of Economics at the Ilmenau University of Technology, Germany. She holds a Ph.D. from the Free University of Berlin, Germany, which looks at systemic risk in the banking sector. Before joining the Ilmenau University of Technology, she served as academic director of the Master of Business, Competition and Regulatory Law (MBL-FU) at the Freie Universität Berlin. Juliane Mendelsohn is a legal scholar by training and specialises on EU competition/antitrust and regulatory law and on German private law.

Robert Pahlen

Robert Pahlen advises German and international clients on all issues of German and European competition and antitrust law, especially in antitrust, abuse and merger control proceedings by Germany's Federal Cartel Office and the European Commission, as well as in filing and defending against antitrust damage claims (private enforcement). Robert Pahlen also has extensive experience in supporting companies during internal investigations and antitrust compliance programmes.

Dr. Ana Parés

Ana Parés is senior associate in antitrust litigation with a doctorate in law at Pérez-Llorca since 2021. She has over 12 years of experience in litigation, especially in the field of competition law. She has also advised on conflicts of jurisdiction and transnational regulatory disputes, as well as on cartel and damages claim proceedings in the energy, media agencies, transport as well as in IP litigation sectors. She is a lecturer at Universidad Complutense.

Dr. Raphael Reims, LL.M. (LSE)

Raphael Reims is an inhouse lawyer in Munich. Prior to that, he was a senior associated lawyer at Noerr in Munich and an associated lawyer at Willkie Farr & Gallagher in Brussels and London. He holds a Ph.D. from the University of Münster and an LL.M. degree from the London School of Economics. He is specialised in European and German antitrust law and commercial criminal law.

Dr. Edoardo Ricci, LL.M. (Université libre de Bruxelles)

Edoardo Ricci is a lawyer specialised in EU law and admitted to the bar in Italy. He has significant experience advising on the DMA, having worked both in private practice (associate at the Brussels office of Gianni & Origoni) and the European Commission (DG COMP's unit in charge of antitrust enforcement in the digital and electronic communications markets).

Dr. Francesco Maria Salerno

Francesco Maria Salerno is a practising competition lawyer with a Ph.D. from the London School of Economics in telecoms regulation. Francesco Maria Salerno has several years of experience advising clients in the digital sector before the European Commission and the Courts in Luxembourg. He has published several articles on interactions between competition law and regulation.

Dr. Henner Schläfke

Henner Schläfke is partner at Noerr, Berlin, and has extensive practical experience as a trial lawyer. He heads Noerr's class and mass action defense practice. He specialises in antitrust damages litigation and is defending clients against follow-on claims including collective actions.

Dr. Jens Peter Schmidt

Jens Peter Schmidt is an antitrust partner at Noerr and heads the firm's Brussels office. He advises on European and German antitrust and competition matters. The focus of his counseling concerns M&A merger control, foreign direct investment control and foreign subsidy risk assessments and complex merger and FDI notifications; he extensively advises on digital antitrust matters, such as the DMA. Prior to joining Noerr, he was the Brussels office managing partner and co-head of the European antitrust practice of an international US law firm.

Immo Schuler, LL.M. (Univ. of North Carolina)

Immo Schuler is partner at trustberg. in Munich, Germany. Before joining trustberg., he worked for almost ten years as an antitrust law lawyer at law firms such as Latham & Watkins, Buntscheck and Noerr.

Miriam Swamy-von Zastrow

Miriam Swamy-von Zastrow is an associate lawyer at Noerr. She focuses on private antitrust enforcement, merger control, and antitrust and market abuse proceedings of the German Federal Cartel Office and the European Commission, as well as on State aid law issues and support in antitrust compliance and internal investigations.

Lumine van Uden, LL.M

Lumine van Uden is a senior associate in Houthoff's litigation and arbitration team. She specialises in competition and commercial litigation, with a focus on follow-on cartel damages claims, damages claims relating to abuse of dominance and enforcement of the DMA. She also has a broad experience in EU and Dutch competition law, handling cases relating to the cartel prohibition, abuse of dominance and merger control. Lumine van Uden is a member of the Dutch Competition Law Association (VvM) and the International Association of Young Lawyers (AIJA).

Sofia Vaz Sampaio

Sofia Vaz Sampaio is a litigation partner at the Portuguese law firm Morais Leitão. She has been involved throughout the years in some of the most high-profile commercial and civil judicial and arbitration cases in Portugal, including in recent high-value class actions. Sofia Vaz Sampaio teaches in postgraduate studies in arbitration and civil procedural law and is a regular speaker at conferences.

Richard Willis

Richard Willis is a partner in the litigation, dispute resolution and investigations group at Arthur Cox in Dublin. He advises clients on investigations and commercial disputes focusing on the technology, financial, entertainment and sports sectors.

Abbreviations

AcP	Archiv für die civilistische Praxis (journal)
AG	Advocate General
AI	Artificial Intelligence
alt.	alternative
API	application programming interface
Art.	Article(s)
BB	Betriebs-Berater (journal)
BeckRS	beck-online.RECHTSPRECHUNG (database)
BEREC	Body of European Regulators for Electronic Communications
BGB	Bürgerliches Gesetzbuch (German Civil Code)
BGH	Bundesgerichtshof (German Federal Court of Justice)
BMWK	Bundesministerium für Wirtschaft und Klimaschutz (German Federal Ministry for Economic Affairs and Climate Action)
BoR	Board of Regulators
BT	Bundestag (German Federal Parliament)
BT-Drs.	Bundestags-Drucksache (German Federal Parliament Document)
CC	Código Civil (Spanish Civil Code)
CCiv	Código Civil (Portuguese Civil Code)
CCPC	Irish Competition and Consumer Protection Commission
cf.	compare
CFR	Charter of Fundamental Rights of the European Union
Ch.	Chapter
CJEU	Court of Justice of the European Union
CMA	Competition and Markets Authority
CMLR	Common Market Law Review
CPI	Código da Propriedade Industrial (Portuguese Industrial Property Code)
CPS	core platform service
DB	Der Betrieb (journal)
DCC	Dutch Civil Code
DCCP	Dutch Code of Civil Procedure
DG COMP	Directorate-General Competition
DG Connect	Directorate-General Communications Networks, Content and Technology
Dir.	Directive
e.g.	for example
EC	European Community
ECJ	European Court of Justice
ECLI	European Case Law Identifier
ECN	European Competition Network

ed(s)	editor(s)
edn	edition
EGC	European General Court
ELR	European Law Review
EnWZ	Zeitschrift für das gesamte Recht der Energiewirtschaft (journal)
EP	European Parliament
et al.	and others
et seq./et seqq.	following
etc.	and so forth
EU	European Union
EuCML	Journal of European Consumer and Market Law
EUR	Euro
EuR	Europarecht (journal)
EuZW	Europäische Zeitschrift für Wirtschaftsrecht (journal)
fn	footnote
FordhamLRev	Fordham Law Review
FS	Festschrift (Liber Amicorum)
GAFMA/GAFAM	Google, Apple, Facebook, Microsoft and Amazon
GLTR	Georgetown Law Technology Review
GRUR	Gewerblicher Rechtsschutz und Urheberrecht (journal)
GRUR-Int	Gewerblicher Rechtsschutz und Urheberrecht – International (journal)
GWB	Gesetz gegen Wettbewerbsbeschränkungen (German Competition Act)
GWR	Gesellschafts- und Wirtschaftsrecht (journal)
HdB	Handbuch (handbook)
i.e.	that is
ICC	Italian Civil Code
IIC	International Review of Intellectual Property and Competition Law
infra	below
IoT	Internet of Things
JBL	Journal of Business Law
JECLAP	Journal of European Competition Law & Practice
JIPITEC	Journal of Intellectual Property, Information Technology and Electronic Commerce Law
JIPLP	Journal of Intellectual Property Law and Practice
JLE	Journal of Law and Economics
JLS	Journal of Legal Studies
JREG	Yale Journal on Regulation
JTÖR	Junge Tagung Öffentliches Recht
LEC	Ley de Enjuiciamiento Civil (Spanish Civil Procedural Act)
lit.	littera

M&A	Mergers & Acquisitions
MLR	Modern Law Review
MMR	Multimedia und Recht (journal)
mn.	margin number(s)
N&R	Netzwirtschaften und Recht (journal)
NFC	near field communication
NJOZ	Neue Juristische Online-Zeitschrift (journal)
NJW	Neue Juristische Wochenschrift (journal)
no.	number(s)
NYUJLL	NYU Journal of Law & Liberty
NZA	Neue Zeitschrift für Arbeits- und Sozialrecht (journal)
NZI	Neue Zeitschrift für das Recht der Insolvenz und Sanierung (journal)
NZKart	Neue Zeitschrift für Kartellrecht (journal)
NZWiSt	Neue Zeitschrift für Wirtschafts-, Steuer- und Unternehmensstrafrecht (journal)
OJ	Official Journal
OLG	Oberlandesgericht (German Higher Regional Court)
ORDO	ORDO – Jahrbuch für die Ordnung von Wirtschaft und Gesellschaft (journal)
p.	page(s)
para.	paragraph(s)
PHi	Produkthaftpflicht international (journal)
PIMS	personal information management system
PRC	pratiques restrictives de concurrence (restrictive practices)
RDi	Recht Digital (journal)
RdZ	Recht der Zahlungsdienste (journal)
rec.	recital(s)
Reg.	Regulation(s)
RFI	request for information
sent.	sentence(s)
subpara.	subparagraph(s)
supra	above
TEU	Treaty on European Union
TFEU	Treaty on the Functioning of the European Union
UWG	Gesetz gegen den unlauteren Wettbewerb (German Act against Unfair Competition)
v	versus
VO	Verordnung (Regulation)
VuR	Verbraucher und Recht (journal)
WAMCA	Wet afwikkeling massaschade in collectieve actie (Dutch Act on Damages Claims in a Collective Action)
WM	Wertpapier-Mitteilungen (journal)

WRP	Wettbewerb in Recht und Praxis (journal)
WuW	Wirtschaft und Wettbewerb (journal)
YaleLJ	Yale Law Journal
ZAG	Zahlungsdiensteaufsichtsgesetz (German Payment Services Oversight Act)
ZD	Zeitschrift für Datenschutz (journal)
ZEuP	Zeitschrift für Europäisches Privatrecht (journal)
ZfDR	Zeitschrift für Digitalisierung und Recht (journal)
ZHR	Zeitschrift für das gesamte Handels- und Wirtschaftsrecht (journal)
ZPO	Zivilprozessordnung (German Code of Civil Procedure)
ZUM	Zeitschrift für Urheber- und Medienrecht (journal)
ZWeR	Zeitschrift für Wettbewerbsrecht (journal)

General bibliography

Auer-Reinsdorff/Conrad IT- und DatenschutzR-HdB	Auer-Reinsdorff/Conrad (eds), Handbuch IT- und Datenschutzrecht, 3rd edn, Munich 2019
Bechtold/Bosch	Bechtold/Bosch, Gesetz gegen Wettbewerbsbeschränkungen: GWB, 10th edn, Munich 2021
BeckOK BGB	Hau/Poseck (eds), Beck'scher Online-Kommentar BGB, 66th edn, Munich 1.5.2023
BKKKO 10. GWB-Novelle	Bien/Käseberg/Klumpe/Körber/Ost (eds), Die 10. GWB-Novelle, Munich 2021
Bunte	Bunte (ed), Kartellrecht, 14th edn, Cologne 2021
Calliess/Ruffert	Calliess/Ruffert (eds), EUV/AEUV – Das Verfassungsrecht der Europäischen Union mit Europäischer Grundrechtecharta, 6th edn, Munich 2022
Federal Cartel Office Background Paper DMA	Bundeskartellamt, Digital Markets Act: Perspektiven des (inter)nationalen Wettbewerbsrechts. Tagung des Arbeitskreises Kartellrecht. Hintergrundpapier (7.10.2021) <https://www.bundeskartellamt.de/SharedDocs/Publikation/DE/Diskussions_Hintergrundpapier/AK_Kartellrecht_2021_Hintergrundpapier.pdf> (last accessed: 12.7.2023)
Fezer/Büscher/Obergfell	Fezer/Büscher/Obergfell, Lauterkeitsrecht: UWG, 3rd edn, Munich 2016
FK-KartellR	Jaeger/Kokott/Pohlmann/Schroeder/Kulka, Frankfurter Kommentar zum Kartellrecht, 105th edn, Cologne May 2023
Grabitz/Hilf/Nettesheim	Grabitz/Hilf/Nettesheim (eds), Das Recht der Europäischen Union, 78th edn, Munich January 2023
Grützner/Jakob Compliance A–Z	Grützner/Jakob, Compliance von A–Z, 2nd edn, Munich 2015
HK-DMA	Podszun (ed), Digital Markets Act, Baden-Baden 2023
Hoeren/Sieber/Holznagel MMR-HdB	Hoeren/Sieber/Holznagel (eds), Handbuch Multimedia-Recht, 58th edn, Munich March 2022
Immenga/Mestmäcker	Immenga/Mestmäcker (eds), Wettbewerbsrecht, 6th edn, Munich 2019–2022
Jarass GRCh	Jarass, Charta der Grundrechte der Europäischen Union: GRCh, 4th edn, Munich 2021
Kersting/Podszun 9. GWB-Novelle	Kersting/Podszun (eds), Die 9. GWB-Novelle, Munich 2017

Köhler/Bornkamm/Feddersen	Köhler/Bornkamm/Feddersen, Gesetz gegen den unlauteren Wettbewerb: UWG, 41st edn, Munich 2023
Leupold/Wiebe/Glossner IT-R	Leupold/Wiebe/Glossner, IT-Recht, 4th edn, Munich 2021
LMRKM	Loewenheim/Meessen/Riesenkampff/Kersting/Meyer-Lindemann (eds), Kartellrecht, 4th edn, Munich 2020
MHdB GesR I	Gummert/Weipert (eds), Münchener Handbuch des Gesellschaftsrechts, Band 1: BGB-Gesellschaft, Offene Handelsgesellschaft, Partnerschaftsgesellschaft, Partenreederei, EWIV, 5th edn, Munich 2019
MüKoBGB	Säcker/Rixecker/Oetker/Limperg (eds), Münchener Kommentar zum Bürgerlichen Gesetzbuch, 9th edn, Munich 2021
MüKoUWG	Heermann/Schlingloff (eds), Münchener Kommentar zum Lauterkeitsrecht, 3rd edn, Munich 2020/2022
MüKoWettbR	Säcker/Bien/Meier-Beck/Montag/Bardong (eds), Münchener Kommentar zum Wettbewerbsrecht, Band 1: Europäisches Wettbewerbsrecht, 3rd edn, Munich 2020
	Bien/Meier-Beck/Montag/Säcker (eds), Münchener Kommentar zum Wettbewerbsrecht, Band 2, 3, 4, 5, 4th edn, Munich 2022
MüKoZPO	Krüger/Rauscher (eds), Münchener Kommentar zur ZPO, 6th edn, Munich 2020/2022
Musielak/Voit	Musielak/Voit (eds), Zivilprozessordnung: ZPO, 20th edn, Munich 2023
Ohly/Sosnitza	Ohly/Sosnitza, Gesetz gegen den unlauteren Wettbewerb: UWG, 8th edn, Munich 2016
Staudinger	Staudinger, Bürgerliches Gesetzbuch: BGB – J. von Staudingers Kommentar zum Bürgerlichen Gesetzbuch mit Einführungsgesetz, 18th edn, Berlin 2018
Streinz	Streinz (ed), Vertrag über die Europäische Union (EUV), Vertrag über die Arbeitsweise der Europäischen Union (AEUV), Charta der Grundrechte der Europäischen Union, 3rd edn, Munich 2018
Vögele Immaterielle Werte	Vögele (ed), Intangibles – Immaterielle Werte, 2nd edn, Munich 2021
von der Groeben/Schwarze/Hatje	von der Groeben/Schwarze/Hatje (eds), Europäisches Unionsrecht, 7th edn, Baden-Baden 2015
Wiedemann KartellR-HdB	Wiedemann, Handbuch des Kartellrechts, 4th edn, Munich 2020

Legal acts

Damages Directive	Directive 2014/104/EU of the European Parliament and of the Council of 26 November 2014 on certain rules governing actions for damages under national law for infringements of the competition law provisions of the Member States and of the European Union (OJ 2014 L 349, 1)
DMA	Regulation (EU) 2022/1925 of the European Parliament and of the Council of 14 September 2022 on contestable and fair markets in the digital sector and amending Directives (EU) 2019/1937 and (EU) 2020/1828 (Digital Markets Act) (OJ 2022 L 265, 1)
DSA	Regulation (EU) 2022/2065 of the European Parliament and of the Council of 19 October 2022 on a Single Market for Digital Services and amending Directive 2000/31/EC (Digital Services Act) (OJ 2022 L 277, 1)
ECMR/FKVO	Council Regulation (EC) No 139/2004 of 20 January 2004 on the control of concentrations between undertakings (the EC Merger Regulation) (OJ 2004 L 24, 1)/ Verordnung (EG) Nr. 139/2004 des Rates vom 20. Januar 2004 über die Kontrolle von Unternehmenszusammenschlüssen (EG-Fusionskontrollverordnung) (OJ 2004 L 24, 1)
ePrivacy Directive	Directive 2002/58/EC of the European Parliament and of the Council of 12 July 2002 concerning the processing of personal data and the protection of privacy in the electronic communications sector (Directive on privacy and electronic communications) (OJ 2002 L 201, 37)
GDPR	Regulation (EU) 2016/679 of the European Parliament and of the Council of 27 April 2016 on the protection of natural persons with regard to the processing of personal data and on the free movement of such data, and repealing Directive 95/46/EC (General Data Protection Regulation) (OJ 2016 L 119, 1)
Implementing Regulation	Commission Implementing Regulation (EU) 2023/814 of 14 April 2023 on detailed arrangements for the conduct of certain proceedings by the Commission pursuant to Regulation (EU) 2022/1925 of the European Parliament and of the Council (OJ 2023 L 102, 6)
P2B Regulation	Regulation (EU) 2019/1150 of the European Parliament and of the Council of 20 June 2019 on promoting fairness and transparency for business users of online intermediation services (OJ 2019 L 186, 57)

RAD	Directive (EU) 2020/1828 of the European Parliament and of the Council of 25 November 2020 on representative actions for the protection of the collective interests of consumers and repealing Directive 2009/22/EC (OJ 2020 L 409, 1)
Recast Brussels I Regulation	Regulation (EU) No 1215/2012 of the European Parliament and of the Council of 12 December 2012 on jurisdiction and the recognition and enforcement of judgments in civil and commercial matters (recast) (OJ 2012 L 351, 1)
Reg. (EC) No 1/2003	Council Regulation (EC) No 1/2003 of 16 December 2002 on the implementation of the rules on competition laid down in Articles 81 and 82 of the Treaty (OJ 2003 L 1, 1)
UCP Directive	Directive 2005/29/EC of the European Parliament and of the Council of 11 May 2005 concerning unfair business-to-consumer commercial practices in the internal market and amending Council Directive 84/450/EEC, Directives 97/7/EC, 98/27/EC and 2002/65/EC of the European Parliament and of the Council and Regulation (EC) No 2006/2004 of the European Parliament and of the Council ('Unfair Commercial Practices Directive') (OJ 2005 L 149, 22)

Glossary

Robert Pahlen/Markus Brösamle

A. Definition of key terms in connection with the DMA

The DMA is designed to make digital markets fair, especially digital services provided on such markets, to keep them open to new competitors and to protect consumers at the same time. Digital markets and digital services in general, and online platforms in particular, have a number of typical, characteristic features. The following terms are intended to provide an overview of the key characteristics of digital markets/digital services in the context of competition law and to serve as a reference at the same time: 1

Algorithms

Platforms process user data and, in doing so, use algorithms that influence which content is displayed to users when they use the platform. It is an automated selection process designed to identify preferences and individualise content.[1] Art. 21(1) sent. 2 DMA states that the European Commission can require companies to disclose the algorithms they use. 2

Antitrust law

The aim of antitrust law is to protect undistorted competition (in particular by preventing restraints on competition and abuse of market power (both behavioural control) as well as by merger control (structural control)) and, in doing so, to ensure the best possible allocation of resources for the supply to consumers by preventing harmful private restraints on competition, abusive practices or mergers that are detrimental to competition.[2] 3

Big data

Big data describes both large volumes of data and state-of-the-art digital processes and technologies for analysing mass data in a beneficial manner, an approach used primarily to achieve competitive advantages.[3] Big data is characterised by four key features: (i) data volume, (ii) data variety, (iii) transmission speed, and (iv) analysis.[4] 4

---

[1] Gersdorf MMR 2017, 439 (444).
[2] Säcker in MüKoWettbR 1. Teil Grundlagen mn. 3.
[3] Sarre/Pruß in Auer-Reinsdorff/Conrad IT- und DatenschutzR-HdB § 2 mn. 186 et seqq.
[4] Bodenmüller in Vögele Immaterielle Werte § 7 mn. 10.

Big tech

5 Big tech is a term used to describe companies that are particularly dominant in digital markets.[5] These are often grouped under the acronym 'GAFA' (Google/Alphabet, Apple, Facebook/Meta and Amazon)[6] or 'GAFAM' (also including Microsoft).

Bottleneck

6 Gatekeepers hold a so-called bottleneck position, i.e., they are the bottleneck and, thus, essential to operate in markets that are placed behind this bottleneck. Any undertaking that wants to operate in that or those markets must therefore pass through this bottleneck. Thus, gatekeepers control access to these markets and can determine who is 'allowed to pass through'. The DMA is intended to oblige gatekeepers to safeguard competition and facilitate or ensure fair market access.[7]

Business user

7 A business user (according to Art. 2 point (21) DMA) means any natural or legal person using platforms for the purpose of or in the course of providing goods or services to end users.

Competition

8 Competition refers to a scenario in which companies operate in the same market and offer interchangeable products or services from the point of view of consumers.[8] In digital markets, market power is usually concentrated in the hands of a small number of players, meaning that individual providers dominate the platform market concerned. A large number of users is, in turn, important for the individual user, meaning that there is often hardly any competition in winner-takes-it-all markets like these.[9] What is appealing for a specific undertaking, however, prevents competition for the specific market and for innovations. The DMA is intended to make these markets fairer and to counteract the concentration of power.[10]

Competition authority

9 The competition authorities are responsible for prosecuting infringements of competition law. At EU level, the European Commission is responsible under Art. 17 TEU via the Directorate-General (DG) for Competition (DG COMP). The national competition authorities in Germany are, for example, the Federal Cartel Office (*Bundeskartellamt*), the Federal Ministry for Economic Affairs and Climate Action (*Bundesministerium für Wirtschaft und Klimaschutz)* and the competent supreme federal State authorities (*Lan-*

[5] Gielen/Uphues EuZW 2021, 627 et seq.
[6] Grünwald MMR 2020, 822.
[7] Podszun/Bongartz/Langenstein EuCML 2021, 60 (62).
[8] Mattfeld in MHdB GesR I § 52 mn. 12.
[9] Kalbhenn ZUM 2022, 266 (276).
[10] Gielen/Uphues EuZW 2021, 627 et seq.

desbehörden) according to § 48(1) of the German Competition Act (*Gesetz gegen Wettbewerbsbeschränkungen*, GWB).[11]

Competition law

Whereas antitrust law primarily comprises the prohibition of cartels, the prohibition of abusive practices and the provisions governing merger control, competition law is the umbrella term for the legal fields of antitrust, public procurement, State aid and fair trading law.[12] **10**

Conduct obligations/dos and don'ts

If an undertaking has been designated as a gatekeeper, it is subject to specific obligations and prohibitions under Art. 5 and 6 DMA (and possibly – depending on the gatekeeper – under Art. 7 DMA) (→ Ch. 6 mn. 11 et seqq., 42 et seqq., 89 et seqq.). These conduct obligations are designed to be 'self-executing'. This means that the conduct obligations already take effect without a prior specification decision (they have an *ex ante* effect).[13] **11**

Core platform service

To be classified as a gatekeeper, the undertaking concerned must offer a core platform service, pursuant to Art. 3(1)(b) DMA, which represents crucial access to end users for other companies. **12**

Delegated act

Delegated acts are non-legislative acts designed to allow non-essential elements of a legislative act to be supplemented and amended by the European Commission (Art. 290 TFEU). This is intended to relieve the European Union legislature of the need to set out detailed regulations.[14] In Art. 12 DMA, for example, the European Commission is authorised to update the gatekeepers' obligations to be updated by way of a delegated act. **13**

Designation

Classification of an undertaking as a gatekeeper according to Art. 3 DMA is achieved by designation (→ Ch. 3 mn. 11 et seqq.). Whether an undertaking is classified as a gatekeeper depends in particular on the thresholds that are set.[15] The European Commission publishes information regarding designated Gatekeepers inter alia here: https://digital-markets-act.ec.europa.eu/index_en. **14**

---

[11] Ritter/Wirtz in Immenga/Mestmäcker VO 1/2003 Art. 35 mn. 1.
[12] Grützner/Jakob Compliance A–Z 'Kartellrecht'.
[13] Kumkar RDi 2022, 347 mn. 11.
[14] Ruffert in Calliess/Ruffert AEUV Art. 290 mn. 10.
[15] Kerber ZD 2021, 544 (545).

Digital economy

15 The digital economy comprises Internet-based trading and industrial production. This is increasingly changing consumer behaviour, in the sense that, for example, online retail is becoming more and more prevalent compared to brick-and-mortar retail.[16] The dynamics of the digital economy are shaped by digital companies, which are becoming increasingly important in economic terms.[17]

Dynamic markets

16 Digital markets feature specific and fast-moving dynamics, as they are characterised by an innovative competitive environment and interdependencies between several sides of the market. This means that innovation momentum can also pose a general threat to the position of monopolists.[18] At the same time, this makes regulation more difficult, as the market environment changes frequently.

Economies of scale

17 An economy of scale describes the relationship between the production quantity and the production factors used, and arises when the average costs are reduced the higher production quantity. The initial costs for platforms are high due to investments in hardware and software. Once, however, the platform is established in the specific market, only marginal costs are incurred and processes can be automated.[19] This is why platform operators strive to reach the critical mass of users that will allow them to recoup the high investment costs.[20]

Economies of scope

18 Economies of scope arise when users use a platform in as many ways as possible, therefore revealing data sets and valuable information on how the undertaking can become attractive to further users.[21] An undertaking can also, however, operate in several markets at the same time and feed its data supply from different sources.[22] Economies of scope work to the advantage of market-dominant competitors, meaning that these, along with network effects and economies of scale, influence how successfully a market participant can consolidate its position.[23]

Ex ante

19 The DMA sets out *ex ante* rules. *Ex ante* refers to the assessment of an event in advance. This means that the DMA imposes rules on the gatekeepers in advance –

---

[16] Wolf in MüKoWettbR AEUV Art. 101 mn. 432.
[17] Karbaum/Schulz NZKart 2022, 107 (108).
[18] Körber in Immenga/Mestmäcker FKVO Art. 2 mn. 24.
[19] Uphues in Hoeren/Sieber/Holznagel MMR-HdB Teil 15.3 mn. 12.
[20] Körber ZUM 2017, 93 (94).
[21] Weck/Fetzer NZKart 2019, 588 (589).
[22] Fuchs in Immenga/Mestmäcker GWB § 18 mn. 148b.
[23] Gerpott NZKart 2021, 273.

i.e. before an infringement occurs, or 'preventively' to some extent. The conduct obligations imposed on gatekeepers *ex ante* in the DMA are intended to ensure the proper functioning of the internal market and not merely to sanction infringements after the event (rec. 7 DMA).

Ex post

Ex post means 'after the event', or in this context, 'after the (potential) infringement'. **20**
In competition law, this term is used to describe a scenario in which prohibited conduct is only sanctioned afterwards. *Ex post* control is based on abuse control exercised by the European Commission under Art. 102 TFEU.[24] This means that unlawful conduct has already taken place or is ongoing, and is only assessed retrospectively with penalties or fines being imposed after the event, where appropriate.

Formation of opinion

Digital platforms, especially those with a focus on social media, have a considerable **21**
impact on the formation of opinions among the population due to their user numbers, which is why platforms are also said to have power over opinions. In order to contain this power, the Digital Services Act (DSA), among others, is being created in parallel to the DMA.[25]

Gatekeeper

Gatekeepers control access to very large user groups, so that the use of their services **22**
is almost inevitable for companies and consumers. A prerequisite for market access and participation in economic or social interactions is for the user concerned to be authorised by the gatekeeper.[26] Art. 2 DMA defines who is a gatekeeper (→ Ch. 3 mn. 3 et seq.).

High-level group

The high-level group established by the European Commission (Art. 40 DMA) is **23**
composed of the Body of the European Regulators for Electronic Communications, the European Data Protection Supervisor and European Data Protection Board, the European Competition Network, the Consumer Protection Cooperation Network and the European Regulatory Group of Audiovisual Media Regulators. The high-level group is designed to ensure the exchange of sector-specific expertise with the European Commission.[27]

---

[24] Jovanovic/Geiner MMR 2021, 678 (680).
[25] Gielen/Uphues EuZW 2021, 627 (632).
[26] Podszun/Bongartz/Langenstein EuCML 2021, 60 (61).
[27] Paal/Kieß ZfDR 2022, 1 (30).

Horizontal relationship

24 In contrast to a vertical relationship, companies are in a horizontal relationship with each other if they are on the same level of the production/distribution chain. Since the companies operate at the same level of the production or distribution chain, they are competitors.[28]

Implementing act

25 'Implementing powers' can be conferred on the European Commission or the Council (Art. 291(2) and (3) TFEU) where there is a need for additional control over the implementation of legally binding Union acts and uniform conditions for this. In order to implement a regulation, the European Commission can lay down uniform rules using an implementing act (Art. 291(2) TFEU). The European Commission can, for example, adopt implementing acts specifying the measures that the gatekeeper concerned is to implement in order to comply effectively with the obligations laid down in Art. 6 and 7 DMA (cf. Art. 8(2) and 13 DMA, should the gatekeeper attempt to circumvent the DMA). Similarly, the European Commission can suspend specific obligations for certain gatekeepers if required by exceptional circumstances (Art. 9(1) DMA) or public health and public security concerns (Art. 10(1) and (3) DMA).[29]

Inspection

26 Inspections (Art. 23 DMA, → Ch. 8 mn. 35) are an instrument that the European Commission can use to fulfil its tasks. For example, European Commission officials and other accompanying persons authorised by the European Commission can enter all premises of an undertaking, examine the books or obtain copies of records related to the business.[30]

Intermediation power

27 Digital platforms are also information intermediaries in that they bundle and organise the information available on the Internet for users.[31] This can give rise to considerable competitive influence by controlling access to information or sales markets.[32]

Internal market

28 According to Art. 26(2) TFEU, the European internal market comprises primarily an economic area without internal frontiers in which the free movement of goods, services and capital is ensured. This concept is also to be transferred to digital markets. A Euro-

[28] Guidelines on the applicability of Article 101 of the Treaty on the Functioning of the European Union to horizontal co-operation agreements, 14.1.2011 (OJ 2011 C 11, 1; corrected in OJ 2011 C 33, 20 and OJ 2011 C 172, 22), para. 1.

[29] Nettesheim in Grabitz/Hilf/Nettesheim AEUV Art. 291 mn. 21; further implementing acts are provided for in Art. 15, 17, 18, 24, 25, 29, 31, 38 and 46 DMA.

[30] Dannecker NZWiSt 2022, 85 (95).

[31] Bergmann/Fiedler in LMRKM AEUV Art. 102 mn. 44a.

[32] Körber in Immenga/Mestmäcker FKVO Art. 2 mn. 281.

pean digital strategy – of which the DMA is a part – aims to control the dominance of large Internet platforms.[33]

Internet of Things (IoT)

The European Commission refers to the Internet of Things (IoT) as the fourth stage in the development of the Internet.[34] This umbrella term covers all technologies that network physical and virtual systems and make them work together through information and communication technologies (such as SIM cards).[35] 29

Interoperability

Interoperability generally describes the ability of hardware or software components to exchange information and to process exchanged information, which is, in turn, made possible by support programs in the form of interfaces.[36] According to Art. 6(4) and (7) DMA, future interoperability of operating systems, hardware or software functions as well as applications is to be ensured. 30

Lock-in effect

Lock-in effects occur when, due to a lack of data portability, it is not possible for a platform user to switch to another platform and the user remains, to all intents and purposes, bound to the platform used so far (because the effort involving in switching is too high and the user tends to avoid it).[37] In turn, this makes it almost impossible for new and small providers to attract users. This could be remedied by, for example, interoperability for the exchange of user data.[38] 31

Market investigation

In the event of a systematic infringement of the provisions of the DMA and in relation to new practices that occur and have the same negative impact as the practices already caught by the DMA, the European Commission can use the well-known institute of market investigation to examine (i) the requirements for the designation as a gatekeeper (Art. 17 DMA), (ii) the suspicion of systematic non-compliance conduct (Art. 18 DMA), or (iii) the need to amend the DMA (Art. 19 DMA; cf. Art. 16 to 19 DMA, → Ch. 8 mn. 6 et. seq.). The European Commission uses the market investigation tool to arrive at a detailed and comprehensive overview of a market and, if necessary, to initiate appropriate (remedial) action.[39] 32

[33] Gielen/Uphues EuZW 2021, 627.

[34] European Commission, 'Advancing the Internet of Things in Europe (Commission Staff Working Document)', 19.4.2016, SWD(2016) 110 final, Figure 1; Wiesner in Leupold/Wiebe/Glossner IT-R Teil 10.6 mn. 1.

[35] Wiesner in Leupold/Wiebe/Glossner IT-R Teil 10.6 mn. 1 et seq.

[36] Metzger in MüKoBGB BGB § 327e mn. 16.

[37] Krause NZA 2022, 521 (533).

[38] Kalbhenn ZUM 2022, 266 (276).

[39] Zober NZKart 2021, 611 (612).

Market power (in the context of competition law)

33 In European competition law, market power refers to a specific market, and describes the circumstance that an undertaking has a dominant position in this market, which means that an undertaking either has no competitors or is not subject to significant competition, or has a superior market position compared to other competitors.[40] The question as to whether an undertaking holds a dominant position is determined by the undertaking's position on the relevant product and geographic market. Typically, this assessment of the market position refers to a defined market.[41]

Multi-homing

34 Multi-homing involves users using several similar services in parallel, for example several messenger services.[42] Multi-homing occurs mainly when platforms offer more differentiated products or services.[43]

Multi-sided markets

35 Two or multi-sided markets are characterised by so-called network effects. Multi-sided markets arise in the 'analogue world' (ad-financed advertising publications or credit cards) but are much more typical of the Internet economy.[44] A multi-sided market exists if an undertaking (e.g. an online broker) offers its products/services to two different groups of customers, i.e. creates a digital platform where 'each side' of the platform usually forms a separate market (this includes search engines, hotel booking platforms and auction platforms).[45] Usually, at least one user group receives services from the platform free of charge in monetary terms.[46]

Network effects

36 As network effects can vary in nature, a distinction is made between the following categories:

Direct network effects occur between similar users.[47] Direct network effects occur when the increase or decrease in the number of users has a direct impact (both positive and negative) on the usefulness of the product or its performance for the individual user. Since these effects affect users of one and the same group, they are direct effects.[48] This can be observed, among other things, in communication services, which become more attractive once they are able to reach more users.[49]

---

[40] Cf. Bundeszentrale für politische Bildung (bpp), 'kurz&knapp, Lexika, Das Lexikon der Wirtschaft – M – Marktmacht' <https://www.bpb.de/kurz-knapp/lexika/lexikon-der-wirtschaft/20080/marktmacht/> (last accessed: 12.7.2023).

[41] Cf. Jung in Grabitz/Hilf/Nettesheim AEUV Art. 102 mn. 33.

[42] Körber in Immenga/Mestmäcker FKVO Art. 2 mn. 24.

[43] Podszun/Schwalbe NZKart 2017, 98 (100).

[44] Immenga/Mestmäcker/Körber FKVO Art. 2 mn. 24.

[45] Bergmann/Fiedler in LMRKM AEUV Art. 102 mn. 44, 45.

[46] Körber in Immenga/Mestmäcker FKVO Art. 2 mn. 24; Kühnen in LMRKM GWB § 18 mn. 106.

[47] Wolf in MüKoWettbR GWB § 18 mn. 52.

[48] Kühnen in LMRKM GWB § 18 mn. 106.

[49] Körber in Immenga/Mestmäcker FKVO Art. 2 mn. 24.

Indirect network effects occur primarily between different user groups.[50] With indirect network effects, several user groups benefit from one another either unilaterally or reciprocally. Positive effects are also possible here, e.g., if a larger number of users (e.g. end consumers) leads to more advertisers using the search engine (advertising companies as another user group); likewise, negative indirect network effects can also occur as soon as the increasing number of advertisements limits the usefulness of the search engine for users.[51]

Open markets

Competition requires that market participants have access to the market concerned, i.e. it is open to new competitors.[52] The European Commission intends to keep digital markets open.[53] 37

Paying with data

If digital services are offered to a user group without any monetary consideration, the platform operator generally collects personal information and data which can be analysed and evaluated.[54] These are data-driven economic models that only become profitable when a large number of datasets are obtained, because, for example, this allows for personalised advertising and the data can be monetised.[55] Users are not always aware of this commercial use of their data far beyond the platform they have provided their data to, as platforms advertise 'free' services.[56] 38

Platforms

Platforms are intermediaries that enable direct interaction between two or more user sides, meaning that this term is sometimes used as a synonym for multi-sided markets.[57] The DMA requires a gatekeeper to provide a 'core platform service' (Art. 3(1) DMA) and legally defines such services (Art. 2 point (2) DMA). 39

Pressure to innovate

Digital markets are subject to fast-moving changes based, for example, on considerable advances in innovation in computing power, storage capacities, manufacturing technology and transmission capacities. Market participants are in innovation competition with each other in order to also be able to meet the changing needs of users. This has a pronounced effect on markets with free services, as price competition is irrelevant here, at least vis-à-vis one user group.[58] Pressure to innovate is characterised by the fact 40

[50] Wolf in MüKoWettbR GWB § 18 mn. 52.
[51] Schwintowski NJOZ 2018, 841 (843).
[52] Körber NZKart 2021, 379 (380).
[53] Gielen/Uphues EuZW 2021, 627 (628).
[54] Kerber GRUR-Int 2016, 639 (644).
[55] Schmitz/Buschuew MMR 2022, 171.
[56] Podszun GRUR-Int 2022, 197 (203).
[57] Uphues in Hoeren/Sieber/Holznagel MMR-HdB Teil 15.3 mn. 6.
[58] Fuchs in Immenga/Mestmäcker GWB § 18 mn. 149.

that in cases involving disruptive innovations, even superior market positions have to be re-evaluated within a short period of time and established companies can lose their market positions.[59]

Private enforcement

41 Private enforcement describes the enforcement of rights by a private plaintiff (→ Ch. 13 mn. 1), for example by way of a claim for damages brought before a civil court (e.g. if a cartel victim asserts claims for damages against the cartel members). The primary purpose of private enforcement is not the protection of effective competition, but rather the enforcement of subjective rights (especially claims for abatement or removal, injunctive relief and damages).[60] Nevertheless, private enforcement also serves to enforce the law as a whole, because companies that are faced with the risk of private lawsuits are more likely to behave in a law-abiding manner.

Public enforcement

42 Unlike private enforcement, public enforcement refers to the official prosecution and sanctioning of infringements (such as cartel offences, e.g. by the European Commission or the German Federal Cartel Office (*Bundeskartellamt*) to protect effective competition).[61]

Regulatory law

43 Regulatory law is a sub-area of competition law characterised by *ex ante* controls.[62] Regulators apply sector-specific regulatory law and not general competition law. For example, the German Federal Network Agency (*Bundesnetzagentur*) applies the relevant sector-specific regulatory law (from the postal, telecommunications, electricity or gas network, or the railway network sector).[63]

Sharing economy

44 Sharing economy generally refers to business models in which platforms provide multi-sided markets for the temporary use of goods or services. Contractual partners are often private individuals who offer temporary private accommodation or carpooling on the platforms, for example.[64] As these services can be used by consumers, their use is 'shared'.

---

[59] Fuchs in Immenga/Mestmäcker GWB § 18 mn. 149.
[60] Rec. 3 Damages Directive.
[61] Mäger NZKart 2018, 3.
[62] Säcker EnWZ 2015, 531.
[63] Bardong/Mühle in MüKoWettbR VO 1/2003 Art. 3 mn. 46.
[64] Meller-Hannich/Krausbeck/Wittke VuR 2019, 403 et seq.

Switching costs

Switching costs arise when it is difficult or even impossible to use the accumulated information and data of one network in another. This can be observed, for example, in social networks, where established contacts, messages and posts are not transferable.[65] 45

Tipping/tipping point

The tipping point describes the moment at which an undertaking achieves a certain market power that excludes further competition in the market concerned, and the market 'tips' in favour of the monopolist (tipping).[66] Other platforms are forced out of the market and the winner-takes-it-all situation means that considerable market shares go to the remaining platform.[67] Monopolisation is then maintained through economies of scope and scale.[68] 46

User data

Platforms collect data from their users, be it in the form of the data provided directly or in the form of analytics data. In particular, in Art. 5 and 6, the DMA sets out requirements and prohibitions with regard to how platforms can handle these user data.[69] 47

Vertical integration

When an undertaking joins forces with its supplier (upstream market) or customer (downstream market), it operates in two successive markets that are in a buyer/seller relationship with each other. The fact that the undertaking operates in two successive markets or intends to do so is called vertical integration. This can also arise without a merger through an undertaking taking up the activity on the upstream or downstream market itself.[70] 48

Vertical relationship

The vertical relationship describes the various levels of the production or distribution chain. Two or more companies are in a vertical relationship if they each operate at a different level of the production or distribution chain, e.g. manufacturer to wholesaler.[71] 49

Winner-takes-it-all principle

Strong market momentum in the digital economy due to economies of scale and network effects mean that a supplier (winner) who wins the (innovation) competition 50

---

[65] Podszun/Schwalbe NZKart 2017, 98 (100).
[66] Zober NZKart 2021, 611 (612).
[67] Podszun/Offergeld ZEuP 2022, 244 (255).
[68] Körber in Immenga/Mestmäcker FKVO Art. 2 mn. 24.
[69] Gielen/Uphues EuZW 2021, 627 (630).
[70] Thomas in Immenga/Mestmäcker GWB § 36 mn. 160.
[71] Art. 1(1a) Reg. (EU) 2022/720.

can often bring about a change in market leadership in a comparatively short space of time. While there may initially be intense competition in these markets, once the market position has been consolidated, the result is often a decline in the development of innovative services and an increasing collection of personal data.[72]

B. Legal definitions used in Art. 2 DMA

51 The legal definitions used in Art. 2 DMA are presented in a comprehensible manner below using the definition of the corresponding EU Regulation in those paragraphs that contain references to EU Regulations; the inserted definition is written in *italics* in each case. The original text of the DMA can be found after the definition in square brackets.

52 **Article 2**

Definitions

For the purposes of this Regulation, the following definitions apply:

[…]

53 (3) **'information society service'** *means any service normally provided for remuneration, at a distance, by electronic means and at the individual request of a recipient of services* [any service as defined in Article 1(1), point (b), of Directive (EU) 2015/1535];

[…]

54 (5) **'online intermediation services'** *means services which meet all of the following requirements:*

(a) they constitute information society services within the meaning of point (b) of Article 1(1) of Directive (EU) 2015/1535 of the European Parliament and of the Council [cf. above under (3)];

(b) they allow business users to offer goods or services to consumers, with a view to facilitating the initiating of direct transactions between those business users and consumers, irrespective of where those transactions are ultimately concluded;

(c) they are provided to business users on the basis of contractual relationships between the provider of those services and business users which offer goods or services to consumers

[online intermediation services as defined in Article 2, point (2), of Regulation (EU) 2019/1150];

55 (6) **'online search engine'** *means a digital service that allows users to input queries in order to perform searches of, in principle, all websites, or all websites in a particular language, on the basis of a query on any subject in the form of a keyword, voice request, phrase or other input, and returns results in any format in which information related to the requested content can be found* [an online search engine as defined in Article 2, point (5), of Regulation (EU) 2019/1150];

[…]

56 (8) **'video-sharing platform service'** *means a service normally provided for remuneration, insofar as it is not governed by the provisions relating to freedom of movement for goods, capital and persons [service as defined by Articles 56 and 57 of the Treaty on the Functioning of the European Union], where the principal purpose of the service or of a dissociable section thereof or an essential functionality of the service is devoted to providing programmes, user-generated videos, or both, to the general public, for*

[72] Gielen/Uphues EuZW 2021, 627 (628).

which the video-sharing platform provider does not have editorial responsibility, in order to inform, entertain or educate, by means of transmission systems and, where applicable, switching or routing equipment and other resources, including network elements which are not active, which permit the conveyance of signals by wire, radio, optical or other electromagnetic means, including satellite networks, fixed (circuit- and packet-switched, including Internet) and mobile terrestrial networks, electricity cable systems, to the extent that they are used for the purpose of transmitting signals, networks used for radio and television broadcasting, and cable television networks, irrespective of the type of information conveyed [electronic communications networks within the meaning of point (a) of Article 2 of Directive 2002/21/EC] and the organisation of which is determined by the video-sharing platform provider, including by automatic means or algorithms in particular by displaying, tagging and sequencing [a video-sharing platform service as defined in Article 1(1), point (aa), of Directive 2010/13/EU];

(9) **'number-independent interpersonal communications service'** *means a service normally provided for remuneration that enables direct interpersonal and interactive exchange of information via electronic communications networks between a finite number of persons, whereby the persons initiating or participating in the communication determine its recipient(s) and does not include services which enable interpersonal and interactive communication merely as a minor ancillary feature that is intrinsically linked to another service, which does not connect with publicly assigned numbering resources, namely, a number or numbers in national or international numbering plans, or which does not enable communication with a number or numbers in national or international numbering plans* [a number-independent interpersonal communications service as defined in Article 2, point (7), of Directive (EU) 2018/1972]; **57**

[…]

(13) **'cloud computing service'** *means a digital service that enables access to a scalable and elastic pool of shareable computing resources* [a cloud computing service as defined in Article 4, point (19), of Directive (EU) 2016/1148 of the European Parliament and of the Council]; **58**

[…]

(16) **'payment service'** *means any business activity set out in Annex I [to Directive (EU) 2015/2366]:* **59**

1. *Services enabling cash to be placed on a payment account as well as all the operations required for operating a payment account.*
2. *Services enabling cash withdrawals from a payment account as well as all the operations required for operating a payment account.*
3. *Execution of payment transactions, including transfers of funds on a payment account with the user's payment service provider or with another payment service provider:*
   - *(a) execution of direct debits, including one-off direct debits;*
   - *(b) execution of payment transactions through a payment card or a similar device;*
   - *(c) execution of credit transfers, including standing orders.*
4. *Execution of payment transactions where the funds are covered by a credit line for a payment service user:*

(a) execution of direct debits, including one-off direct debits;
(b) execution of payment transactions through a payment card or a similar device;
(c) execution of credit transfers, including standing orders.

5. Issuing of payment instruments and/or acquiring of payment transactions.
6. Money remittance.
7. Payment initiation services.
8. Account information services.

[a payment service as defined in Article 4, point (3) of Directive (EU) 2015/2366];

60 (17) **'technical service supporting payment service'** *means services provided by technical service providers, which support the provision of payment services, without them entering at any time into possession of the funds to be transferred, including processing and storage of data, trust and privacy protection services, data and entity authentication, information technology (IT) and communication network provision, provision and maintenance of terminals and devices used for payment services, with the exclusion of payment initiation services and account information services* [service within the meaning of Article 3, point (j), of Directive (EU) 2015/2366];

[...]

61 (25) **'personal data'** *means any information relating to an identified or identifiable natural person ('data subject'); an identifiable natural person is one who can be identified, directly or indirectly, in particular by reference to an identifier such as a name, an identification number, location data, an online identifier or to one or more factors specific to the physical, physiological, genetic, mental, economic, cultural or social identity of that natural person* [personal data as defined in Article 4, point (1), of Regulation (EU) 2016/679];

[...]

62 (28) **'control'** *means control constituted by rights, contracts or any other means which, either separately or in combination and having regard to the considerations of fact or law involved, confer the possibility of exercising decisive influence on an undertaking, in particular by:*

(a) ownership or the right to use all or part of the assets of an undertaking;
(b) rights or contracts which confer decisive influence on the composition, voting or decisions of the organs of an undertaking

[the possibility of exercising decisive influence on an undertaking, within the meaning of Article 3(2) of Regulation (EC) No 139/2004];

[...]

63 (30) **'turnover'** *means the amounts derived by the undertaking concerned in the preceding financial year from the sale of products and the provision of services falling within the undertakings' ordinary activities after deduction of sales rebates and of value added tax and other taxes directly related to turnover* [the amount derived by an undertaking within the meaning of Article 5(1) of Regulation (EC) No 139/2004];

64 (31) **'profiling'** *means any form of automated processing of personal data consisting of the use of personal data to evaluate certain personal aspects relating to a natural person, in particular to analyse or predict aspects concerning that natural person's performance at work, economic situation, health, personal preferences, interests, reliability, behaviour, location or movements* [profiling as defined in Article 4, point (4), of Regulation (EU) 2016/679];

(32) **'consent'** *means any freely given, specific, informed and unambiguous indication of the data subject's wishes by which he or she, by a statement or by a clear affirmative action, signifies agreement to the processing of personal data relating to him or her* [consent as defined in Article 4, point (11), of Regulation (EU) 2016/679]. **65**

CHAPTER 1
THE DMA AT A GLANCE

Jens Peter Schmidt

The Digital Markets Act (DMA[1]), together with the Digital Services Act (DSA[2]), is one of the **cornerstones** of the **European Digital Strategy**, by which the EU intends to ensure that transformation brought about by digital technologies benefits people and businesses alike, and contributes to climate neutrality. The DMA aims to ensure the **contestability** and **fairness of markets** in the **digital sector**, to promote innovation and to enhance consumer protection. The EU did not consider the existing legal instruments, namely the *ex post* abuse of dominance regime under Art. 102 TFEU, sufficient to adequately monitor the systemic online platforms of large internet companies. 1

The DMA, which was ultimately uncontroversial in political terms and was adopted swiftly, addresses the major **online platforms**, known as gatekeepers, on which new **obligations** are imposed. Gatekeepers are companies that provide core platform services which grant business users **essential access** to end users. Examples of the total of ten core platform services set out in the legislation include online search engines (Google), operating systems (Microsoft), web browsers (Explorer), virtual assistants (Alexa) and online social network services (Facebook). Gatekeepers also have a specific **size** and **importance** in the EEA, generally measured on the basis of objective quantitative parameters (e.g. turnover, number of users). It is **exclusively** up to the **European Commission** to designate a company as a gatekeeper. 2

At the heart of the DMA are 21 new **obligations** designed to prevent unfair practices or practices that limit contestability in relation to any relevant core platform service of the gatekeepers. The regulation sets out directly applicable ***ex ante*** **obligations** and **prohibitions**, as well as those that are to be defined in greater detail in the future. This means that the DMA will put the existing business models of major digital companies to the test. When determining the obligations and prohibitions, the legislator drew on the experience gleaned from the enforcement of European competition law. The obligations are supported by compliance, monitoring and reporting duties for gatekeepers. Far-reaching **investigative**, **inspection** and **decision-making powers** of the European Commission are put in place to ensure the objectives of the DMA are effective, as are the sanctions the European regulator can impose (e.g. fines corresponding to up to 20 % of global turnover or remedies). 3

The European Commission is empowered to supplement gatekeepers' obligations in certain circumstances in order to keep them 'up to date'. In addition, the European Commission can launch a **market investigation** if it wishes to (i) designate a company as a gatekeeper outside the standard procedure, (ii) investigate systematic non-compliance with the DMA obligations, or (iii) include new core platform services in the scope of the DMA. 4

National competition authorities do **not** directly enforce the DMA against gatekeepers. They are, however, called upon to cooperate and can initiate investigations against gatekeepers regarding possible infringements of the DMA obligations in the 5

[1] Regulation (EU) 2022/1925 of the European Parliament and of the Council of 14 September 2022 on contestable and fair markets in the digital sector and amending Directives (EU) 2019/1937 and (EU) 2020/1828 (Digital Markets Act) (OJ 2022 L 265, 1).

[2] Regulation (EU) 2022/2065 of the European Parliament and of the Council of 19 October 2022 on a Single Market For Digital Services and amending Directive 2000/31/EC (Digital Services Act) (OJ 2022 L 277, 1).

Member State concerned. Nevertheless, the **European Commission** – via existing resources in the Directorates-General for Competition and Connect, as well as posts yet to be filled, including that of a Chief Technology Officer – is **exclusively** competent to take decisions. **National courts** apply the DMA but avoid decisions that diverge from those of the European Commission. The DMA gives **third parties** a number of **rights of participation** and **indirect options for lodging complaints** which can be asserted before the European Commission, national competition authorities and national courts. All decisions made by the European Commission on the basis of the DMA are subject to **judicial review** – with regard to fines or periodic penalty payments as part of an unlimited review.

6 The DMA was published in the Official Journal on 12.10.2022 and came into force on 1.11.2022. The regulations set out in the DMA apply as of 2.5.2023. For core platform services existing by 2.5.2023, companies had to notify the European Commission if they meet the gatekeeper thresholds by 3.7.2023 (seven companies submitted respective notifications), and on 6.9.2023 at the latest, the European Commission will designate the gatekeepers, which in turn have to fulfil the obligations under the DMA at the latest by 6.3.2024.

CHAPTER 2
DMA: BACKGROUND, OBJECTIVES, AND ITS RELATIONSHIP TO COMPETITION LAW

Juliane Mendelsohn/Oliver Budzinski

Bibliography: Acquisti/Taylor/Wagman, 'The Economics of Privacy', Journal of Economic Literature 54 (2016), 442; Akman, 'Regulating Competition in Digital Platform Markets: A Critical Assessment of the Framework and Approach of the EU Digital Markets Act', ELR 47 (2022), 85; Aristotle, Nicomachean Ethics, transl. by J. A. K. Thomson, London 2004; Armstrong, 'Competition in Two-Sided Markets', Rand Journal of Economics 37 (2006), 668; Audretsch/Baumol/Burke, 'Competition Policy in Dynamic Markets', International Journal of Industrial Organization 19 (2001), 613; Basedow, 'Das Rad neu erfunden: Zum Vorschlag für einen Digital Markets Act', ZEuP 2021, 217; Baumol, 'Contestable Markets – An Uprising in the Theory of Industry Structure', American Economic Review 72 (1982), 1; Baumol/Panzar/Willig, Contestable Markets and the Theory of Industry Structure, New York 1982; Body of European Regulators for Electronic Communications (BEREC), 'Analysing EU consumer perceptions and behaviour on digital platforms for communication', Analysis Report (10.6.2021), BoR (21) 89; Bongs/Lehoczky-Deckers, 'The German Parliament passes the 10th amendment of the German Act against Restraints of Competition' (19.1.2021), Concurrences, e-Competitions Art. N°99351; Botta, 'Sector Regulation of Digital Platforms in Europe: Uno, Nessuno e Centomila', JECLAP 12 (2021), 500; Bougette/Budzinski/Marty, 'Exploitive Abuse and Abuse of Economic Dependence: What can we learn from an Industrial Organization Approach?', Revue d'Economie Politique 129 (2019), 261; Bougette/Budzinski/Marty, 'Self-Preferencing and Competitive Damages: A Focus on Exploitative Abuses', The Antitrust Bulletin 67 (2022), 190; Budzinski, '„Wettbewerbsfreiheit" und „More Economic Approach": Wohin steuert die europäische Wettbewerbspolitik?' in Grusevaja (ed), Quo vadis Wirtschaftspolitik? Festschrift für Norbert Eickhof, Berne 2008, p. 15; Budzinski, 'An Institutional Analysis of the Enforcement Problems in Merger Control', European Competition Journal 6 (2010), 445; Budzinski, 'Zur Bedeutung der Ordnungsökonomik für eine moderne, ökonomiebasierte Wettbewerbspolitik' in Pies (ed), Das weite Feld der Ökonomik. Festschrift zu Ehren von Karl-Hans Hartwig, Munich 2013, p. 145; Budzinski, 'Gatekeeping in the Audiovisual Sector: Economic Background, Competition, and Regulation' in Cappello (ed), Unravelling the Digital Services Act Package, Strasbourg 2021, p. 94; Budzinski, 'The Economics of International Competition Policy: New Challenges in Light of Digitization?' in Anderson/Lugard (eds), The International Competition Network at Twenty: Origins, Accomplishments and Aspirations, Paris 2022, p. 429; Budzinski, 'Lobbyismus und Medienwirtschaft – Strategische Beeinflussung von Informationsflüssen' in Mause/Polk (ed), Handbuch Lobbyismus, Berlin 2023, p. 971; Budzinski/Gaenssle/Lindstädt-Dreusicke, 'Data (R)Evolution – The Economics of Algorithmic Search & Recommender Services' in Baumann (ed), Handbook of Digital Business Ecosystems, Berlin 2022, p. 349; Budzinski/Gaenssle/Stöhr, 'Outstanding Relevance across Markets: A New Concept of Market Power?', Concurrences 17 (2020), 38; Budzinski/Kuchinke, 'Industrial Organization of Media Markets and Competition Policy' in von Rimscha (ed), Management and Economics of Communication, Berlin 2020, p. 21; Budzinski/Mendelsohn, 'Regulating Big Tech: From Competition Policy to Sector Regulation?' (Ilmenau Economics Discussion Papers 27/168, 2022) <https://ssrn.com/abstract=4248116> (last accessed: 12.7.2023); Budzinski/Noskova, 'Prospects and Limits of Merger Simulations as a Computational Antitrust Tool', Stanford Computational Antitrust Journal 2 (2022), 44; Budzinski/Stöhr, 'Competition Policy Reform in Europe and Germany – Institutional Change in the Light of Digitization', European Competition Journal 15 (2019), 15; Federal Network Agency (Bundesnetzagentur), 'Interoperabilität zwischen Messengerdiensten' (2021) <https://www.bundesnetzagentur.de/SharedDocs/Downloads/DE/Sachgebiete/Digitales/OnlineKom/diskussionspapier_IOP.pdf> (last accessed: 12.7.2023); Cabral et al., 'The Digital Markets Act: A Report from a Panel of Economic Experts' (Boston University Questrom School of Business Research Paper No. 3783436, 2021) <https://econpapers.repec.org/paper/iptiptwpa/jrc122910.htm> (last accessed: 12.7.2023); Caffarra/Scott Morton, 'The European Commission Digital Markets Act: A translation' (5.1.2021) <https://voxeu.org/article/european-commission-digital-markets-act-translation> (last accessed: 12.7.2023); Caffarra/Scott Morton, 'How Will the Digital Markets Act Regulate Big Tech?' (ProMarket, 11.1.2021) <https://www.promarket.org/2021/01/11/digital-markets-act-obligations-big-tech-uk-dmu/> (last accessed: 12.7.2023); Caillaud/Jullien, 'Chicken and Egg: Competition among Intermediation Service Providers', Rand Journal of Economics 34 (2003), 309; Canaris, 'Wandlungen des Schuldvertragsrechts – Tendenzen zu seiner „Materialisierung"', AcP 200 (2000), 273; Colangelo, 'In Fairness We (Should Not) Trust. The Duplicity of the Eu Competition Policy Mantra in Digital Markets' (ICLE white paper, 2023) <https://papers.ssrn.com/sol3/papers.cfm?abstract_id=4360057> (last accessed: 12.7.2023); Colino, 'The Antitrust F Word: Fairness Considerations in Competition Law', JBL 2019, 329; Crane, 'How much brandeis do the neo-brandeisians want?', The Antitrust Bulletin

64 (2019), 531; Crémer/de Montjoye/Schweitzer, 'Competition Policy for the Digital Era' (2019) <https://ec.europa.eu/competition/publications/reports/kd0419345enn.pdf> (last accessed: 12.7.2023); Crémer et al., 'Fairness and Contestability in the Digital Markets Act', JREG 40 (2023 forthcoming), 101; Demsetz, 'Why Regulate Utilities?', JLE 11 (1968), 55; Dunne, 'Fairness and the Challenge of Making Markets Work Better', MLR 84 (2021), 230; Eifert et al., 'Taming the Tech Giants: The DSA/DMA Package', CMLR 2021, 987; Farrell/Saloner, 'Standardization, Compatibility, and Innovation', Rand Journal of Economics 16 (1985), 70; Fox, 'Against Goals', FordhamLRev 81 (2013), 2157; Franck/Peitz, 'Digital Platforms and the new 19a Tool in the German Competition Act', JECLAP 12 (2021), 513; Furman et al., 'Unlocking Digital Competition. Report of the Digital Competition Expert Panel' (13.3.2019) <https://www.gov.uk/government/publications/unlocking-digital-competition-report-of-the-digital-competition-expert-panel> (last accessed: 12.7.2023); Gerard, 'Fairness in EU Competition Policy: Significance and Implications', JECLAP 9 (2018), 211; German Monopolies Commission (Monopolkommission), 'Special Report 82: Recommendations for an effective and efficient Digital Markets Act' (5.10.2021) <https://www.monopolkommission.de/images/PDF/SG/sr_dma_fulltext.pdf> (last accessed: 12.7.2023); Haucap/Heimeshoff, 'Google, Facebook, Amazon, eBay: Is the Internet driving competition or market monopolization?', International Economics and Economic Policy 11 (2014), 49; Haucap/Stühmeier, 'Competition and Antitrust in Internet Markets' in Bauer/Latzer (eds), Handbook on the Economics of the Internet, Cheltenham 2016, p. 183; Heinderyckx/Vos, 'Reformed Gatekeeping', Communication & Media 11 (2016), 29; Hellwig, 'Effizienz oder Wettbewerbsfreiheit? Zur normativen Grundlegung der Wirtschaftspolitik' in Engel/Möschel (eds), Recht und spontane Ordnung, Berlin 2006, p. 231; Hoffmann, 'Fairness in the Digital Markets Act' (8/1 European Papers, 2023) <https://www.europeanpapers.eu/en/europeanforum/fairness-in-digital-markets-act> (last accessed: 12.7.2023); Jacobides/Lianos, 'Regulating Platforms and Ecosystems: An introduction', Industrial and Corporate Change 30 (2021), 1199; Kades/Scott Morton, 'Interoperability as a Competition Remedy for Digital Networks' (2021) <https://papers.ssrn.com/sol3/papers.cfm?abstract_id=3808372> (last accessed: 12.7.2023); Karg, 'Marktmacht und Meinungsbildung in der Digitalindustrie', JTÖR 62 (2022), 68; Katz/Shapiro, 'Network Externalities, Competition, and Compatibility', American Economic Review 75 (1985), 424; Katz/Shapiro, 'Systems Competition and Network Effects', Journal of Economic Perspectives 8 (1994), 93; Kerber/Budzinski, 'Towards a Differentiated Analysis of Competition of Competition Laws', ZWeR 2003, 411; Kerber/Schweitzer, 'Interoperability in the Digital Economy', JIPITEC 8 (2017), 39; Khan, 'Amazon's Antitrust Paradox', YaleLJ 126 (2017), 564; Khan, 'The New Brandeis Movement: America's Antimonopoly Debate', JECLAP 9/3 (2018), 131; Lamadrid de Pablo, 'Competition Law as Fairness', JECLAP 8/3 (2017), 147; Lane, 'Distributive Justice: A Social-Psychological Perspective', American Political Science Review 80 (1986), 383; Leistner, 'The Commission's vision for Europe's digital future: Proposals for the Data Governance Act, the Digital Markets Act and the Digital Services Act – a critical primer', JIPLP 16 (2021), 778; Marsden/Podszun, 'Restoring Balance to Digital Competition – Sensible Rules, Effective Enforcement', Gutachten für die KAS (2020) <https://www.kas.de/de/einzeltitel/-/content/restoring-balance-to-digital-competition> (last accessed: 12.7.2023); Mendelsohn, Systemrisiko und Wirtschaftsordnung, Baden-Baden 2018; Mendelsohn, 'Die „normative Macht" der Plattformen – Gegenstand der zukünftigen Digitalregulierung?', MMR 2021, 857; Monti, 'The Digital Markets Act – Institutional Design and Suggestions for Improvement' (TILEC Discussion Paper No. 2021–04, 2021) <https://papers.ssrn.com/sol3/papers.cfm?abstract_id=3797730> (last accessed: 12.7.2023); Petit, 'The Proposed Digital Markets Act (DMA): A Legal and Policy Review', JECLAP 12 (2021), 529; Podszun/Brauckmann, 'Germany's Pressing Ahead: The Proposal for a Reformed Competition Act' (CPI 11, 2019) <https://www.competitionpolicyinternational.com/wp-content/uploads/2019/11/Europe-Column-November-2019-Full.pdf> (last accessed: 12.7.2023); Podszun/Bongartz/Langenstein, 'Proposals on How to Improve the Digital Markets Act' (18.2.2021) <http://dx.doi.org/10.2139/ssrn.3788571> (last accessed: 12.7.2023); Rahman, 'Infrastructure Regulation and the New Utilities', JREG 35 (2018), 911; Rahman, 'Regulating Informational Infrastructure: Internet Platforms as the New Public Utilities', GLTR 2 (2018), 234; Ritz/Weber, 'A Game Changer for Germany's Competition Practice: Compliance Defense and Sweeping New Cartel Enforcement Powers in the 10th Amendment to the German Competition Act' (CPI 02, 2021) <https://www.competitionpolicyinternational.com/wp-content/uploads/2021/02/EU-News-Column-February-2021.pdf> (last accessed: 12.7.2023); Rochet/Tirole, 'Two-sided Markets: A Progress Report', Rand Journal of Economics 37 (2006), 645; Schmidt, 'Ordnungsökonomische Wettbewerbskonzepte: Die Wettbewerbspolitik im Spannungsfeld zwischen Freiheit und Effizienz', ORDO 59 (2008), 209; Schrepel, 'Antitrust Without Romance', NYUJLL 13 (2020), 326; Schweitzer, 'The Art to make Gatekeeper Positions Contestable and the Challenge to know what is fair', ZEuP 2021, 1; Schweitzer et al., 'Modernising the Law on Abuse of Market Power: Report for the Federal Ministry for Economic Affairs and Energy (Germany) 2018' (17.9.2018) <https://dx.doi.org/10.2139/ssrn.3250742> (last accessed: 12.7.2023); Scott Morton et al., 'Committee for the Study of Digital Platforms: Market Structure and Antitrust Subcommittee Report 2019' (15.5.2019) <https://research.chicagobooth.edu/-/media/research/stigler/pdfs/market-structure---report-as-of-15-may-2019.pdf> (last accessed: 12.7.2023); Scott Morton et al., 'Equitable Interoperability: The "Super Tool" of Digital Platform Governance' (Tobin Center Policy Discussion Paper, 13.7.2021)

<https://tobin.yale.edu/digital-economy-project/policy-discussion-papers> (last accessed: 12.7.2023); Shapiro, 'Antitrust in a time of populism', International Journal of Industrial Organization 61 (2018), 714; Smith, An Inquiry into the Nature and Causes of the Wealth of Nations, London 1776; Stigler, 'The Law and Economics of Public Policy: A Plea to the Scholars', JLS 1 (1972), 1; Vanberg, 'Consumer Welfare, Total Welfare and Economic Freedom – On the Normative Foundations of Competition Policy' in Drexl/Kerber/Podszun (eds), Competition Policy and the Economic Approach, Cheltenham 2011, p. 44; Wagner-von Papp, 'Habemus Regierungsentwurf 11. GWB-Novelle', WuW 2023, 301; Wielsch, 'Private Law Regulation of Digital Intermediaries' (Tilburg Private Law Working Paper Series No. 2/2019, 2019) <https://papers.ssrn.com/sol3/papers.cfm?abstract_id=3369592> (last accessed: 12.7.2023); Wu, The Curse of Bigness, New York 2018; Yeung/Morgan, An Introduction to Regulation, Cambridge 2007; Zimmer/Göhsl, 'Vom New Competition Tool zum Digital Markets Act: Die geplante EU-Regulierung für digitale Gatekeeper', ZWeR 2021, 29.

Serving as an **introduction**, this chapter provides an overview of the economic policy 1
background to, as well as the development of, the DMA. The legal nature and objectives of the DMA and its relationship with components of the (digital) European economic system are also discussed.

A. Background

I. Digital platforms and ecosystems as a new challenge for economic policy

Digital ecosystems describe, in simplified terms, networks of various (online) mar- 2
kets that are interconnected by a digital information services market.[1] This information services market sometimes assumes the status of a **gatekeeper**. It often takes the form/business model of a platform, which, to put it simply, acts as an intermediary between

[1] Crémer/de Montjoye/Schweitzer, 'Competition Policy for the Digital Era' (2019); Jacobides/Lianos Industrial and Corporate Change 30 (2021), 1199.

different groups of players.[2] A good example is the service of providing a 'digital marketplace', which enables distributors and producers of various (physical and digital) goods (and services) to offer their goods for sale. This means that a large number of goods markets are linked via this virtual marketplace. There are also services that reduce the transaction costs of exchange on this marketplace, such as payment systems, security services, search and recommendation systems, advertising, insurance, conflict resolution and complaint services etc., which can be offered by the marketplace service provider or by third parties. Examples of large, **general digital marketplaces** include Amazon Marketplace or Ebay. **Specialised digital marketplaces** include, for example, app stores (marketplaces for smartphone software such as the Apple App Store or Google Play), streaming services (marketplaces for audio and audiovisual content such as YouTube, Netflix, Disney+, Spotify, Apple Music etc.) or services for the organisation and placement of online advertising (such as Google AdWords and AdSense). Similarly, **central search engines** (e.g. Google Search) and **communication services/social networks** (e.g. the related Facebook, Instagram and WhatsApp services), but also data networks in the Internet of Things (IoT), are referred to as digital ecosystems.

3 The definition of **digital ecosystems** is often blurred and not very precise. A common feature of many large digital ecosystems is that they are shaped by a single company that has considerable economic power within the ecosystem and also accumulates significant social power. Examples include the Alphabet Group, which dominates the search engine market in most countries across the globe with its Google Search division, sometimes with market shares of more than 80 % and 90 %.[3] With its Facebook, Instagram and WhatsApp services, the Meta Group dominates social networks and online communication networks in many places, although a new competitor, TikTok, is gaining ground here. Amazon offers by far the largest general marketplace and Apple (Apple App Store) and Alphabet (Google Play) each dominate 'their' smartphone software ecosystem, strictly segregated from each other. In some other digital ecosystems – at least up until 2023 – there is still no sign of any single company that is dominating the system. For example, there is currently intense competition in the streaming markets, and video telephony, which has recently become very popular, is also not dominated by any single provider.

4 Although the widely used services of the GAFMA companies[4] enjoyed considerable popularity for some time due to the innovative power of their offerings and their high fit with consumer preferences, growing dissatisfaction with the economic and social power of these services or companies has become apparent in recent years. This dissatisfaction relates to those companies that dominate 'their' digital ecosystems and whose position now appears virtually incontestable. As a result, both competition law proceedings against GAFMA companies and calls for **special regulation** for these platforms have increased.[5] The latter demand is also fuelled by the fact that the current options and

[2] A precise definition of the economic term 'platform' is provided in the context of a discussion on indirect network externalities (→ mn. 7). Please refer to the Glossary for definitions of DMA terms in general.

[3] Cf. European Commission 27.6.2017 – case AT.39740 para. 273 et seqq. – Google Shopping.

[4] This refers to the large digital corporations Google (Alphabet), Apple, Facebook (Meta), Microsoft and Amazon.

[5] As an example and with further literature references for the controversial discussion: Schweitzer et al., 'Modernising the Law on Abuse of Market Power: Report for the Federal Ministry for Economic Affairs and Energy (Germany) 2018' (17.9.2018); Marsden/Podszun, 'Restoring Balance to Digital Competition – Sensible Rules, Effective Enforcement' (2020); Crémer/de Montjoye/Schweitzer, 'Competition Policy for the Digital Era' (2019); Furman et al., 'Unlocking Digital Competition. Report of the Digital Competition Expert Panel' (13.3.2019).

mechanisms for intervention – primarily via competition law – are not perceived as being sufficient, because digital ecosystems have a number of special economic features that set them apart from many conventional markets. The need to either **modernise competition policy** appropriately or to create additional regulation was confirmed in a number of **expert studies**.[6]

These **special economic features**, which, however, vary in degree from digital ecosys- 5
tem to digital ecosystem and also by no means occur across the board, include the following:

First, digital ecosystems are characterised by **demand-side economies of scale** that 6
occur as direct or indirect network effects. **Direct network effects** arise when the individual utility enjoyed by the individual network user increases the more users participate in the network.[7] If, for example, a communication network is only used by a very small number of people, the individual utility of joining the network is low because it only offers the opportunity to communicate with a very small number of other users. The more network participants join, the greater both the individual utility for someone joining the network (direct network effect) and the individual utility for all network members (direct network externality). If there is no interoperability between competing networks, the largest network will enjoy economies of scale on the demand side and will continue to grow at the expense of the smaller networks, potentially to the point of establishing a monopoly. While this could be efficient in the short term, in the medium term, declining innovation and the lack of cost efficiency incentives would lead to welfare problems, as would the growing economic power of the network monopolist. In cases involving strong direct network effects, such as those that occur primarily in communication networks, sustainable competition is presumably only possible through **regulation** that ensures, by way of interoperability obligations,[8] that members of different communication networks, such as mobile telephony or messenger

[6] Without claiming to be exhaustive: Schweitzer et al., 'Modernising the Law on Abuse of Market Power: Report for the Federal Ministry for Economic Affairs and Energy (Germany) 2018' (17.9.2018); ACCC Digital Platforms Inquiry, 'Australian Competition and Consumer Commission Final Report 2019' (26.7.2019) <https://www.accc.gov.au/publications/digital-platforms-inquiry-final-report> (last accessed: 12.7.2023); German Federal Ministry for Economic Affairs and Energy (Bundesministerium für Wirtschaft und Energie), 'A New Competition Framework for the Digital Economy: Report by the Commission "Competition Law 4.0"' (3.9.2019) <https://www.bmwk.de/Redaktion/EN/Publikationen/Wirtschaft/a-new-competition-framework-for-the-digital-economy.pdf> (last accessed: 12.7.2023); Crémer/de Montjoye/Schweitzer, 'Competition Policy for the Digital Era' (2019); Furman et al., 'Unlocking Digital Competition. Report of the Digital Competition Expert Panel' (13.3.2019); Ofcom, 'Online Market Failures and Harms: An Economic Perspective on the Challenges and Opportunities in Regulating Online Services' (UK Office of Communications Report 2019, 25.3.2022) <https://www.gov.uk/find-digital-market-research/online-market-failures-and-harms-an-economic-perspective-on-the-challenges-and-opportunities-in-regulating-online-services-2019-ofcom> (last accessed: 12.7.2023); Scott Morton et al., 'Committee for the Study of Digital Platforms: Market Structure and Antitrust Subcommittee Report 2019' (15.5.2019); UK Competition and Markets Authority, 'Online Platforms and Digital Advertising, Final Report 2020' (1.7.2020) <https://www.gov.uk/cma-cases/online-platforms-and-digital-advertising-market-study> (last accessed: 12.7.2023); US Congressional Subcommittee on Antitrust, Commercial and Administrative Law, 'Investigation of Competition in Digital Markets Report 2020' (2.10.2020) <https://judiciary.house.gov/uploadedfiles/competition_in_digital_markets.pdf?utm_campaign=4493-519> (last accessed: 12.7.2023). A comparative and analytical summary is provided by Kerber, 'Updating Competition Policy for the Digital Economy? An Analysis of Recent Reports in Germany, UK, EU, and Australia' (24.10.2019) <http://dx.doi.org/10.2139/ssrn.3469624> (last accessed: 12.7.2023).

[7] Cf. for fundamental information Farrell/Saloner Rand Journal of Economics 16 (1985), 70; Katz/Shapiro American Economic Review 75 (1985), 424; Katz/Shapiro Journal of Economic Perspectives 8 (1994), 93.

[8] Scott Morton et al., 'Equitable Interoperability: The "Super Tool" of Digital Platform Governance' (Tobin Center Policy Discussion Paper, 13.7.2021).

services, can communicate with each other. This reduces the incentive to switch to the largest network. While communication networks are typically characterised by strong direct network effects, these are usually much less pronounced in general marketplaces.

7 **Indirect network effects** arise when a service provider faces at least two distinct demand groups where increased participation by one demand group leads to an increase in individual utility for participants of the other demand group.[9] For example, the provider of a payment system (e.g., a credit card) faces the distinct demand groups of consumers (who want to pay for purchases using the card) and business owners (who are to accept the card as a means of payment). The more consumers now (want to) pay using the card, the greater the benefit for the business owners to accept the card – and vice versa (two-way positive indirect network externality). This creates a characteristic chicken-and-egg problem when it comes to attracting demand from the different groups if relevant transaction costs prevent direct trade between the demand groups.[10] Services that meet these requirements are referred to as platforms in modern economics, although it is disputed whether positive indirect network effects in both directions are constitutive or whether effects in only one direction (with possibly even opposing effects in the other direction) are sufficient. **Platforms** are to be distinguished from 'normal' vertical value chains in which a distributor is also an intermediary but acts as a customer of (demand side for) its upstream suppliers. An example for a platform in the economic sense would be the offering of an online marketplace, which addresses the demand groups of (i) consumers, who search the marketplace for goods offered by retailers, and (ii) business owners, who need virtual retail space on the marketplace to offer their goods. Both demand groups can request further services from the marketplace operator or from third parties, such as payment systems, insurance services, complaint mechanisms etc. By contrast, an online retailer buys goods offered to it by suppliers and sells them to consumers – possibly in an online marketplace.[11] In addition to marketplaces, communication networks are usually also platforms in the strict economic sense. If one-sided indirect network externalities are sufficient, then services and media financed by advertising also fulfil the characteristics of a platform. Similar to direct network effects, indirect network effects also favour the largest platform in the market and drive further growth of this platform, meaning that dominant platforms may (but not necessarily must) emerge, which can, in turn, be efficient in the short term but entail welfare losses in the medium term.

8 Second, digital ecosystems can also be characterised by supply-side economies of scale. Significant supply-side economies of scale (and scope) can arise in the form of **range effects** if customers have relevant **one-stop shopping preferences**, i.e. prefer to purchase all goods from a single source. Providers that can offer the biggest range of goods benefit from these economies of scale and may continue to grow at the expense of their competitors. One-stop shopping preferences vary: while some consumers would like to purchase all goods through one marketplace, others prefer diversification and alternate between different marketplaces. Moreover, at least in the case of virtual goods, the breadth and depth of the product range of smaller providers is unlikely to be significantly inferior to that of the largest – due to the low cost of storage space.[12] On

[9] Rochet/Tirole Rand Journal of Economics 37 (2006), 645; Armstrong Rand Journal of Economics 37 (2006), 668; Budzinski/Kuchinke in v. Rimscha, p. 21.

[10] Caillaud/Jullien Rand Journal of Economics 34 (2003), 309.

[11] This means that Amazon Marketplace is a platform whereas Amazon Retail is not (instead it is one of many virtual retail shops on Amazon's marketplace).

[12] Unless other aspects – such as the availability of (streaming) rights, the existence of exclusive conditions (app stores) etc.– stand in the way of this in individual cases.

the other hand, the reduction of the **'cost of geography'** (i.e. the cost of supplying goods across long distances, such as transportation costs or cultural and language barriers) means that digital ecosystems are often intercontinental or even truly global, which may leave little room for local niches and local competition. Digital ecosystems are typically based on **data-driven business models.**[13] The availability of more (user) data allows for a superior design of data-based strategies, meaning that data-rich companies enjoy significant supply-side economies of scale. The law of diminishing marginal utility, however, also applies to the use of data, i.e. the economies of scale resulting from the availability of data are not sustainable enough in most markets to be the sole factor explaining the persistent dominance of individual companies. There is also an economically ambivalent effect of data usage effects on user privacy, which may serve as a limiting factor.[14]

The question as to whether competition between platforms and between digital ecosystems may be sustainable furthermore depends on a number of additional factors.[15] In an economic context, however, it is not just what is known as **tipping**, i.e. the monopolisation of digital ecosystems and platform markets, that is a social welfare problem. Another problem lies in the **exploitation of relative market power** or superior bargaining power, even below monopoly or dominance thresholds, by some services, platforms and companies with central positions within digital ecosystems. This exploitation of market power is seen not only in the squeezing out of actual or potential competitors (kill zones), but also in the exploitation of complementary providers within digital ecosystems that are commercially dependent on a marketplace provider, for example, or another essential/core service.[16] Providers that organise access to customers/users or their attention (which is becoming a scarce commodity in the information overload of the Internet), respectively, may act as gatekeepers. Thus, they enjoy systemic market power throughout the ecosystem even without dominant market shares in other areas of the digital ecosystem. This generates the exploitation potential that ultimately may also harm consumers and society.[17] Examples of commercially dependent complementary providers can include app developers for Apple's and Google's app stores, online shops in relation to Amazon Marketplace and its terms and conditions, or digital content providers/creators in relation to YouTube and Instagram (or their search and recommendation rankings, respectively).[18] From an economic perspective, however, such exploitation scope must be accompanied by **exploitation incentives** before a social welfare problem arises. These incentives emerge when the provider of a core service, like for instance a marketplace or a search and recommendation ranking, offers goods provided by this service itself, i.e. its own goods via its own marketplace or its own items via its own ranking service (so-called **dual role** problem). This is where the incentive for **self-preferencing** arises, which in dual role situations is detrimental to welfare.[19] The combination of **gatekeeping power and vertical integration** in the digital ecosystem thus creates a scenario in which anticompetitive actions that are detrimental to welfare become likely to occur. 9

[13] On data economics Budzinski/Kuchinke in v. Rimscha, p. 21–45; Budzinski/Gaenssle/Lindstädt-Dreusicke in Baumann, p. 349–366.

[14] Acquisti/Taylor/Wagman Journal of Economic Literature 54 (2016), 442.

[15] Haucap/Heimeshoff International Economics and Economic Policy 11 (2014), 49; Haucap/Stühmeier in Bauer/Latzer, p. 183–210; Budzinski/Kuchinke in v. Rimscha, p. 21–45.

[16] Bougette/Budzinski/Marty Revue d'Economie Politique 129 (2019), 261.

[17] Budzinski/Gaenssle/Stöhr Concurrences 17 (2020), 38.

[18] Cabral et al., 'The Digital Markets Act: A Report from a Panel of Economic Experts' (Boston University Questrom School of Business Research Paper No. 3783436, 2021), p. 17-19.

[19] Bougette/Budzinski/Marty The Antitrust Bulletin 67 (2022), 190.

10 The special economic features of digital ecosystems imply a **need for revising** the form of a regulation of platforms and services that enjoy systemic market power. This could be achieved by **reforming competition law** by expanding and re-invigorating controls on (systemic) market power below dominance thresholds and preventing the emergence of further systemic power in such digital ecosystems by re-focusing non-horizontal merger control (see also → mn. 43 et seqq.). Alternatively, it could be achieved via **specific conduct regulation** of those platforms and powerful services that dominate individual digital ecosystems as gatekeepers. Obligations regarding interoperability and the prevention of self-preferencing would need to be the focus here from an economic point of view. The further accusation that competition policy is too slow[20] is illustrated spectacularly by the Google Shopping proceedings of the European Commission, which lasted more than six years.[21] Leaving this outlier out of the equation, however, there is not much evidence to suggest that digital proceedings are systematically excessive in duration[22] – and this would presumably also be a question relating to institutional law enforcement conditions needing reform.[23]

II. Development of the DMA

11 As a result of an increasingly Big Tech-critical public opinion and political mood, as well as the expert studies cited above, a series of initiatives aimed at reforming national competition policy were launched from the mid-2010s onwards. In Germany, for example, these led to the 9th (2017),[24] 10th (2021)[25] and 11th (2023)[26] amendment of the German Competition Act (*Gesetz gegen Wettbewerbsbeschränkungen*, GWB). As their core objective, all of them seek to **improve competition rules for the digital economy** and further reform steps are already under way. In February 2020, the European Commission unveiled its ideas for a DSA package for the first time. In addition to a Digital Services Act (DSA) as a new and independent regulation, this was also to include a **New Competition Tool** (NCT) to expand competition policy. As a result of a public consultation of stakeholders and experts, the European Commission ultimately focused on creating a new type of regulation which, according to its proposal of December 2020, was to consist of a modified DSA[27] and the Digital Markets Act (DMA),[28] mixing the market-oriented parts of the original DSA and elements of the NCT. The European Parliament ultimately approved the DMA in December 2021 with significant amendments. The trilogue negotiations (between the European Commission, European Parliament and the Council) in spring 2022, in which further relevant changes were

[20] Marsden/Podszun, 'Restoring Balance to Digital Competition – Sensible Rules, Effective Enforcement' (2020), p. 31.

[21] European Commission 27.6.2017 – case AT. 39740 para. 38 et seqq. – Google Shopping.

[22] Karg JTÖR 62 (2022), 68 (80–81).

[23] Budzinski European Competition Journal 6 (2010), 445; Budzinski/Noskova Stanford Computational Antitrust Journal 2 (2022), 44.

[24] Kersting/Podszun, Die 9. GWB-Novelle, Munich 2017; Budzinski/Stöhr European Competition Journal 15 (2019), 15.

[25] Budzinski/Gaenssle/Stöhr Concurrences 17 (2020), 38; Franck/Peitz JECLAP 12 (2021), 513; Podzsun/Brauckmann, 'Germany's Pressing Ahead: The Proposal for a Reformed Competition Act' (CPI 11, 2019); Ritz/Weber, 'A Game Changer for Germany's Competition Practice: Compliance Defense and Sweeping New Cartel Enforcement Powers in the 10th Amendment to the German Competition Act' (CPI 02, 2021); Bongs/Lehoczky-Deckers Concurrences, e-Competitions Art. N° 99351.

[26] Wagner-von Papp WuW 6 (2023), 301–303.

[27] Regarding analyses, see Cappello (ed), Unravelling the Digital Services Act Package, Strasbourg 2021; Leistner JIPLP 16 (2021), 778.

[28] COM(2020) 842 final.

made, ultimately led to the final version of the DMA, which was adopted in July 2022. The DMA entered into force on 1.11.2022 and became applicable on 2.5.2023.

III. The specific approach taken by the DMA

The DMA is neither applicable to all companies in all markets (like competition law) nor is it generally applicable to a defined sector (like sector regulation). Instead, the DMA regulates **'gatekeepers'** (a novel category of regulatory addressees) that provide **'core platform services'** (which are listed in full in Art. 2 point (2) DMA) and have an established and lasting economic position with regard to their activities, or will achieve such in the near future (Art. 2 point (1), Art. 3 DMA). Turnover and market value thresholds, as well as minimum numbers of the end users and business users reached, are defined in concrete terms for this purpose. To date (on 3.7.2023) seven companies have notified the Commission that these thresholds were met: Alphabet, Amazon, Apple, ByteDance, Meta, Microsoft and Samsung.[29] This method of establishing the norm addressees, however, means that the DMA is not based on a general concept of power, markets or systems guided by economic theory. Instead, it is essentially through size, the exercise of specific 'core' services and the pursuit of a platform-based business model that a gatekeeper position is attributed to certain companies to be publicly designated by the European Commission. The gatekeeper concept therefore does not tie in with any concept commonly used in media studies and the media industry. Here, the term 'gatekeeper' is usually understood as the ability to restrict, distort, or promote information flows, creating power in the sense that gatekeepers control access to audiences in media markets.[30] Although many of the gatekeepers defined by the DMA are likely to have gatekeeping power in this sense of the term, a whole range of other companies and digital ecosystems not covered by the DMA are likely to have it as well.[31] 12

These gatekeepers as per the definition of the DMA are subjected to a series of conduct-specific obligations in the Regulation (Art. 5–7 DMA, → Ch. 6 mn. 10 et seqq.). In this context, the DMA does not contain any general clause or general prohibition formula as is customary in competition and unfair competition law. Instead, it sets out a **catalogue of more than 30 obligations** (plus sub-items) which defines prohibitions for, and obligations incumbent upon, gatekeepers that vary considerably in terms of their level of detail. While there were 18 obligations in the first draft at the end of 2020, the number of obligations – and in part also their level of detail – increased continuously (to 39) in the course of the legislative process, presumably also due to the influence of interest groups. The conduct requirements address, among other things, the granting of data access, the combination of data from different sources, strategic incompatibilities, self-preferencing, discrimination against business users, and exclusivity and bundling strategies. 13

B. Legal basis, legal nature and objectives

The Digital Markets Act aims to control the power of these gatekeepers in core platform services. In its rec. 11, the DMA states that it pursues an objective '[...] that is **complementary to, but different from** that of protecting undistorted competition on 14

[29] European Commission, Statement (4.7.2023) <https://ec.europa.eu/commission/presscorner/detail/en/STATEMENT_23_3674> (last accessed: 12.7.2023).
[30] COM(2020) 825 final; Heinderyckx/Vos Communication & Media 11 (2016), 29; Budzinski in Cappello, p. 94–109.
[31] Budzinski in Cappello, p. 94–109.

any given market, as defined in competition-law terms'. This novel focus and legal nature of the DMA is also reflected in the focus of the Regulation, the manner in which the regulatory instrument works and in the choice of legal basis and the objectives set out therein.

I. Legal basis

15 In the course of the legislative process, both Art. 103 and Art. 114 TFEU were prospective legal bases. A further development of competition law and consistency with the objectives of competition policy spoke in favour of **Art. 103 TFEU**.[32] Indeed one could argue that the closeness of the objectives to those of competition law compellingly spoke in favour of Art. 103 TFEU as the more suitable legal basis.[33] Measures that would have been adopted on the basis of Art. 103 TFEU would, however, have had to be guided by competition law, in particular, by the scope of Art. 102 TFEU. The European Commission, on the other hand, intended to create a regulatory instrument that reaches beyond the objectives set out in Art. 102 TFEU and also '[...] ensure(s) that markets where gatekeepers are present are and remain contestable and fair, independently from the actual, potential or presumed effects of the conduct of a given gatekeeper covered by this Regulation on competition on a given market' (rec. 11 DMA). Moreover, Art. 103 TFEU would have been politically sensitive because, according to Art. 103(1) TFEU, the European Parliament would only have been granted a consultative role, limiting its political influence on the legislative process.[34]

16 The European Commission justifies its choice of **Art. 114 TFEU** with the formulation of different and novel objectives and the statement that the instrument of the DMA is different from competition law, but also with the **harmonisation** function of the Regulation, which consists of ensuring the proper functioning of the (digital) internal market and protection against fragmentation (rec. 8 DMA). The harmonisation legal basis also, however, entails some restrictions and must be based on 'objective factors which are amenable to judicial review'.[35] These requirements have been criticised by authors who assign the DMA to competition policy and point out that reforms have already been adopted in some Member States and that harmonisation thus becomes more 'preventive' in nature.[36]

II. Legal nature as a regulatory instrument

17 The DMA is referred to as a form of **asymmetrical, sector-specific, self-executing *ex ante* regulation**.[37]

1. Asymmetrical regulation

18 The asymmetry is due to the realisation that an increasing number of large corporate entities are taking on key roles and dividing up digital markets among themselves. The

[32] Basedow ZEuP 2021, 217; Schweitzer ZEuP 2021, 1.

[33] Basedow ZEuP 2021, 217 (219).

[34] Eifert et al. CMLR 2021, 987 (1000).

[35] CJEU 11.6.1991 – case C-300/89, ECLI:EU:C:1991:244 para. 10 = BeckRS 2004, 76145 – Titandioxid; for a critical view, Basedow ZEuP 2021, 217 (219).

[36] Eifert et al. CMLR 2021, 987 (1001).

[37] Budzinski/Mendelsohn, 'Regulating Big Tech: From Competition Policy to Sector Regulation?' (Ilmenau Economics Discussion Papers 27/168, 2022), p. 2 et seqq.

aim of the DMA is to make these **key positions**, but also neighbouring and downstream markets, 'free' or **contestable** again and to ensure that fair conditions prevail on the platforms. There has been little criticism of the intention to subject the major GAFMA companies, in particular, to regulation.[38] This is consistent with the current development in competition policy (sometimes referred to as 'hipster antitrust'[39]), which is distancing itself from long-prevailing Chicago School doctrines and once again, like the Harvard School (USA) or Ordoliberalism (EU), turning its attention to the issue of economic power and assessing it critically.[40]

2. Sector-specific regulation

The question as to whether the DMA's regulatory approach and target group can really be described as a specific **'sector'** is disputed, and is extremely difficult to support from an economic point of view (→ mn. 2 et seqq.). Though all of the relevant services belong to the digital sector and are integrated into similar structures, such as platforms and digital ecosystems, this does not form an independent labour market or production sector.[41] Equally the DMA cannot really be described as a kind of 'utilities regulation'.[42] The regulation of traditional utility companies or infrastructures usually has a natural monopoly as its object.[43] Digital infrastructures, such as search engines, on the other hand, represent **quasi-monopolies** or monopoly-like market positions at best, despite very high market shares.[44] The DMA also assumes that even the positions of gatekeepers covered by the Regulation are not entirely incontestable (rec. 3 DMA). Another special feature of the DMA is that, although the addressees are determined in qualitative and quantitative terms, this determination is not based on market definition or market analysis, unlike in competition law. Rather, the services included in the DMA are politically hand-picked (Art. 2 point 2(a)–(j) DMA). 19

3. Ex ante regulation

The DMA imposes more or less **pre-formulated conduct obligations** on its addressees without requiring specific proof of impact or harm. These obligations relate primarily to ensuring data access and data use (Art. 5(2), (9)–(10), Art. 6(2), (8)–(11) DMA), prohibiting self-preferencing and bundling of services (Art. 5(3)–(4), (6)–(8), Art. 6(5) DMA), access based on fair and non-discriminatory conditions (Art. 6(12), (13) DMA), and the establishment of interoperability (Art. 5(5), Art. 6(3)–(4), (6)–(7) and Art. 7 DMA). This form of *ex ante* regulation is therefore also a more rule-based rather than a principle- or risk-oriented.[45] 20

---

[38] Caffarra/Scott Morton, 'The European Commission Digital Markets Act: A translation' (5.1.2021).

[39] Khan JECLAP 9 (2018), 131; crit. Shapiro International Journal of Industrial Organization 61 (2018), 714.

[40] As an example, Khan YaleLJ 126 (2017), 564; Wu, The Curse of Bigness, New York 2018; for a critical view, on the other hand, Crane The Antitrust Bulletin 64 (2019), 531; Schrepel NYUJLL 13 (2020), 326.

[41] See the definition in the dictionary of the German Federal Agency for Civic Education (Bundeszentrale für politische Bildung) <https://www.bpb.de/kurz-knapp/lexika/politiklexikon/296546/wirtschaftssektoren/> (last accessed: 12.7.2023).

[42] Cf. Rahman JREG 35 (2018), 911.

[43] Demsetz JLE 11 (1968), 55.

[44] Rahman GLTR 2 (2018), 234; crit.: Eifert et al. CMLR 2021, 987 (995).

[45] Yeung/Morgan, p. 151.

4. Self-executing regulation

21 Following the original design of the DMA, many of the obligations are self-executing.[46] The draft version to the DMA divided the obligations into those that are to be **applied without any further specification** (Art. 5) and others that can still be set out in greater detail (Art. 6). The final version maintains this distinction and adds another set of obligations that can also be further specified (Art. 7). Accordingly, the obligations under Art. 6 and 7 DMA are '**susceptible of being further specified** under Article 8'.[47] This results in the following: According to Art. 8(1) sent. 2 DMA, the measures implemented by the gatekeeper must lead to the effective achievement of the objectives of the DMA and the relevant obligation. According to Art. 8(2) DMA, the European Commission can adopt implementing acts (Art. 291 TFEU) specifying measures in the context of the above. Examples include the obligations under Art. 6(11) and (12) DMA, according to which online search engines have to (i) provide access on fair, reasonable and non-discriminatory terms to ranking, query, click and view data, and (ii) apply fair, reasonable, and non-discriminatory general conditions of access to the relevant core platform services for business users for its software applications, online search engines and online social networking services. Thus, the clarity of the promise to create self-executing obligations is likely to be blurred not only by the **implementing acts** and reviews by the European Commission (Art. 6, 7 and 8 DMA), but also by numerous ambiguities, and by requirements and terminology in need of interpretation. These inconsistencies could, in turn, compromise the promised **effectiveness** and enforcement power of the DMA.[48] Many voices would have liked to see the standardisation of higher-level principles in this Regulation.[49]

III. Objectives

22 The existing competition law and regulatory law build on concepts that have evolved since the 1950s. For a long time, the idea that the economic system could be governed by consistent fundamental principle and interlocking regulations remained prevalent. During the negotiations of the DMA this idea and the spirit of reform seemed to be overshadowed by the Commission's efforts to formulate new, albeit complementary goals, and to design a **novel regulatory instrument**. In addition to **fairness and contestability**, concepts such as transparency, neutrality, interoperability and good faith are used to cover questions to which there are still no clear answers in the digital realm.[50] The values and goals of the overall new digital legal framework are, however, currently all still unclear and vague.

---

[46] Budzinski/Mendelsohn, 'Regulating Big Tech: From Competition Policy to Sector Regulation?' (Ilmenau Economics Discussion Papers 27/168, 2022), p. 2.

[47] According to Art. 6(12) sent. 2 and 3 DMA, these conditions are to be worded and published in general terms and the European Commission is to check whether the general access conditions published meet these standards. According to Art. 8(8) DMA, the European Commission also checks whether measures ensure that there is no imbalance of rights and obligations on business users and that the measures do not confer a disproportionate advantage on the gatekeeper.

[48] Budzinski/Mendelsohn, 'Regulating Big Tech: From Competition Policy to Sector Regulation?' (Ilmenau Economics Discussion Papers 27/168, 2022), p. 10 et seqq.

[49] Petit JECLAP 12 (2021), 529; Joint position paper 'Friends of an effective Digital Markets Act' by France, the Netherlands and Germany of 27.5.2021 (Part 1) <https://www.bmwk.de/Redaktion/DE/Downloads/M-O/non-paper-friends-of-an-effective-digital-markets-act.pdf> (last accessed: 12.7.2023).

[50] Wielsch, 'Private Law Regulation of Digital Intermediaries' (Tilburg Private Law Working Paper Series No. 2/2019, 2019).

Ensuring contestability and fairness in digital platforms are the two goals of the DMA (see rec. 11 DMA). The novelty and conceptual **ambiguity** of these objectives, as well as their unclear relationship with competition law, have given rise to much confusion and sparked criticism since the publication of the draft DMA in December 2021.[51] The main problem is that these vague objectives frame obligations that are open to interpretation, giving the European Commission considerable discretion and, at the same time, giving gatekeepers scope for argumentation and influence.[52] Other authors could at least extract a **coherent message** from the DMA.[53] Few were comfortable with the terms used and the interplay between objectives and obligations.[54] 23

It can be assumed that this criticism was acknowledged by the Commission, because the final version of the DMA now contains a (negative) **definition** of fairness and a definition of contestability. In addition, numerous obligations are set out in more detail than in the first draft. With regard to the obligations for messenger services that were also added as new obligations in Art. 7 DMA, the question arises as to whether interoperability is to be considered an independent objective. The argument is supported by the importance and individual focus of the principle; it is countered by the fact that the DMA does not identify or define this as an objective. Only practice will show whether the definitions and additions are sufficient to ensure **legal certainty** and to dispel ongoing concerns. 24

1. Fairness

a) Classification

The concept of fairness is initially a very **broad term that is almost impossible to define**. In law the idea of fairness dates back to Aristotle's theory of justice and underlies the distinction between allocative and distributive justice that has prevailed since then.[55] **Allocative justice** or market justice requires a fair market process to allocate goods among private parties.[56] **Distributive justice**, which is more closely associated with public law, distributes goods according to other maxims based on public interests and also social objectives.[57] The term 'fairness' as it is now used, however, probably does not refer to the historical term, but is somewhat of a 'trend' term that can be found in various areas of commercial law. 25

This term has been reinvigorated and used, especially since the financial crisis of 2008, in an attempt to develop options for an economic and competition policy that breaks with the models found in mainstream financial market economics and competition policy at the time.[58] However, the concept of fairness also comes into play in 26

---

[51] Cf. Budzinski/Mendelsohn, 'Regulating Big Tech: From Competition Policy to Sector Regulation?' (Ilmenau Economics Discussion Papers 27/168, 2022), p. 21; Schweitzer ZEuP 2021, 1; Akman ELR 47 (2022), 85; German Monopolies Commission (Monopolkommission), 'Special Report 82: Recommendations for an effective and efficient Digital Markets Act' (5.10.2021).

[52] Budzinski/Mendelsohn, 'Regulating Big Tech: From Competition Policy to Sector Regulation?' (Ilmenau Economics Discussion Papers 27/168, 2022), p. 21 et seqq.; in conjunction with: Budzinski in Mause/Polk, p. 971 et seqq.

[53] Monti, 'The Digital Markets Act – Institutional Design and Suggestions for Improvement' (TILEC Discussion Paper No. 2021-04, 2021).

[54] For a ground-breaking view, see Podszun/Bongartz/Langenstein, 'Proposals on How to Improve the Digital Markets Act' (18.2.2021).

[55] Aristotle, mn. 1129a–1145a.

[56] Lane American Political Science Review 80 (1986), 383; Smith, An Inquiry into the Nature and Causes of the Wealth of Nations, London 1776.

[57] On the 'materialisation' of private law, see Canaris AcP 200(2000), 273.

[58] Mendelsohn, p. 38, Ch. 3.

discussions regarding the objectives of competition law.[59] While fairness has long been unpopular in competition law because of its unpredictability and was once described as 'a suitcase full of bottled ethics from which one freely chooses to blend his own type of justice',[60] it is now making a comeback as a term directed against the efficiency-oriented approach attributed to the influence of the Chicago School (and also certain interpretations of the more economic approach[61]). Proponents claim that concepts such as 'justice, fairness and equality [...] are embedded in the structure of law'[62] and that fairness can bring competition policy in line with the interests of 'society'.[63]

27 What fairness can mean in the context of the digital economy was highlighted even before the publication of the draft DMA, in particular in the study by Marsden and Podszun. The authors localise fairness concerns in the intermediation activities of gatekeepers and see **power and information asymmetries** as the cause of compensation concerns that extend beyond the efficiency of welfare production through profit maximisation.[64] The authors also note that a certain level of social trust in the system of competition and its market participants is necessary to maintain general acceptance of this system. While fairness is already the basis for rules designed to protect against unfair commercial practices and unfair contractual terms, it should accordingly also serve as the basis for 'reasonable' market rules in general.[65]

28 A new issue is the use of the concept of fairness as a normative policy objective in the context of the Digital Single Market.[66] According to empirical research,[67] the *Juncker Commission* with *Margrethe Vestager* as Commissioner for Competition started to use this term in 2015 – but only a few times. This continued in the von der Leyen Commission: the term was used more and more frequently from 2020 onwards (40–120 times from the beginning to the end of 2020). This development picked up speed with the adoption of the P2B-Regulation (Reg. (EU) 2019/1150) and the plans to introduce the DMA, the DSA and the Data Act. Between the end of 2021 and the beginning of 2022, fairness was used more than 100 times in individual drafts and other consultation documents, but remained undefined until mid-2022. One established use of the concept of fairness, which has attracted general interest in this context, can be found in the patent law requirements for **'FRAND' terms** – fair, reasonable and non-discriminatory

---

[59] Fox FordhamLRev 81 (2013), 2157.

[60] Stigler JLS 1 (1972), 1 (4).

[61] On the discussion of the more economic approach, freedom of competition and fairness, see Hellwig in Engel/Möschel, p. 231; Budzinski in FS Eickhof, p. 15; Schmidt ORDO 59 (2008), 209; Vanberg in Drexl/Kerber/Podszun, p. 44; Budzinski in FS Hartwig, p. 145.

[62] Colino JBL 2019, 329; Gerard JECLAP 9 (2018), 211.

[63] Lamadrid de Pablo JECLAP 8 (2017), 147.

[64] Marsden/Podszun, 'Restoring Balance to Digital Competition – Sensible Rules, Effective Enforcement' (2020), p. 38.

[65] Marsden/Podszun, 'Restoring Balance to Digital Competition – Sensible Rules, Effective Enforcement' (2020), p. 44. But the study on competition policy in the digital arena by Crémer, de Montjoye and Schweitzer also emphasises the importance of fairness: '[P]latforms [...] have a responsibility to ensure that competition on their platforms is fair, unbiased, and pro-users.' (Crémer/de Montjoye/Schweitzer, 'Competition Policy for the Digital Era' (2019), p. 5).

[66] Hoffmann, 'Fairness in the Digital Markets Act' (8/1 European Papers, 2023), p. 17; Crémer et al. JREG 40 (2023 forthcoming), 101; Dunne MLR 84 (2021), 230.

[67] A total of 330 documents from five European Union institutions – the European Commission, the European Parliament, the Council of the European Union, the Economic and Social Committee and the European Commission's Directorate-General for Competition – published and available in official databases were searched for the concept of fairness between 2010 and 2022. We would like to thank *Lukas Breide* for his support in this empirical research.

licensing terms and fees.[68] Similar requirements are numerous in the DMA, but also in the (draft) Data Act. In patent law, however, this term causes considerable interpretation difficulties for parties and the courts which are largely considered unresolved.[69]

b) Negative definition and localisation

The concept of fairness was defined in the course of the legislative process (or, more precisely, with the publication of the trilogue version). The DMA initially defines **'fairness'** only negatively and, in rec. 33, paraphrases 'unfair' circumstances as follows: 29

> For the purpose of this Regulation, unfairness should relate to an imbalance between the rights and obligations of business users where the gatekeeper obtains a disproportionate advantage.

This functional definition limits the broad, even boundless concept of fairness. The main issue is the **power imbalance** between gatekeepers and business users (i.e. vertical/conglomerate complementors, but also horizontal competitors), which is expressed in terms and conditions used by gatekeepers. This power imbalance is not only due to classical **'market power'** of the gatekeepers, but also to their **normative rule-making power**: the gatekeepers alone decide on the conditions and rules of the game in these structures.[70] The DMA behaves in a similar way to the P2B Regulation or the checks on general terms and conditions of business. It assumes that 'serious imbalances in bargaining power [... lead] to unfair practices and conditions for business users, as well as for end users [...]' (rec. 4 DMA). This is also strongly reminiscent of the concept of relative and superior market power in § 20 GWB.[71] Unlike competition law, however, the DMA enables intervention in market activity without there being any normative connection to the competitive activity or market conditions.[72] Also, in general, superior (bargaining) power is assumed and regulatory intervention (or the assumption of unfairness) is not limited to cases of dependency and lack of alternatives, unlike in the GWB. In addition, Crémer et al. look at 'fairness' in terms of the sharing of surpluses and rewarding users for their contribution to the success of the platform.[73] 30

Obligations related to fairness are mainly contained in Art. 5(7–10) and Art. 6(2) and (11–13) DMA. These regulations are primarily concerned with ensuring that, despite the intermediation power (see rec. 43 et seqq. DMA, cf. § 18(3b) GWB) of the gatekeepers, fair, neutral and non-self-preferencing exchange conditions prevail. Conditions and parameters are also to be handled transparently in order to reduce information asymmetries. Moreover, users and consumers are not to be exploited in terms of the use and sharing of their data. The content of a majority of these clauses has been the subject of competition proceedings against GAFMA companies in the past,[74] even though 'fairness' did not play an explicit role in these cases.[75] 31

[68] A FRAND declaration is a declaration made by the patent holder to a standardisation organisation to grant a licence to any interested party on fair, reasonable and non-discriminatory terms (FRAND).

[69] Most recently BGH 5.5.2020 – K ZR 36/17, IIC 2021, 1466 – Huawei v ZTE; ECJ 16.7.2015 – case C-170/13, ECLI:EU:C:2015:477 – Huawei Technologies v ZTE Corp.

[70] Eifert et al. CMLR 2021, 987 (991); Mendelsohn MMR 2021, 857.

[71] Regarding use in cases involving digital data (interface information): OLG Munich 25.1.2021 – 21 U 145/20, BeckRS 2021, 1051 – Fahrzeugdaten.

[72] Eifert et al. CMLR 2021, 987 (1000).

[73] Crémer et al. JREG 40 (2023 forthcoming), 101.

[74] See Caffarra/Scott Morton, 'The European Commission Digital Markets Act: A translation' (5.1.2021).

[75] See also Colangelo, 'In Fairness We (Should Not) Trust. The Duplicity of the Eu Competition Policy Mantra in Digital Markets' (ICLE white paper, 2023), p. 7.

32 The definition that now applies can be said to exemplify the fundamental **objective** of the regulation with regard to fairness. Although not markets, but rather (core) services are defined, the aim is to break up existing digital structures or quasi-monopolies where there are high barriers to market entry and no parity or non-discriminatory competition regarding terms and conditions, and to curb the power in the hands of a small number of corporations in this segment and open the core platform services and downstream markets back up to fair competition.

2. Contestability

a) Background

33 In contrast to fairness, 'contestability' was not a term commonly used in the relevant competition policy discussions before the DMA draft was published. It is best known from the field of microeconomics in the 1980s. The theory of contestable markets, as developed by **William Baumol** et al.,[76] deals with the idea that even potential competition can be sufficient to discipline a monopolist so that it behaves as if it were in competition, i.e. does not exploit market power. This means that (quasi-)monopolies do not cause any competition problems as long as the markets are contestable and instant and immediate market entry to cream off the monopolist's profits is an option. On the one hand, the **contestable markets theory** was seen as supporting the Chicago School scepticism of market intervention because it reinforced the importance of potential competition and emphasised the self-healing powers of market competition. On the other hand, Baumol's theory develops the requirements for market contestability (especially the sunk cost dilemma) very thoroughly. It turns out that the requirements for perfect contestability are highly restrictive and are rarely met in real markets. Thus, the theory of contestable markets basically reveals the limits of **potential competition** and illustrates that real markets often cannot remedy the inefficiencies of a (quasi-)monopoly.[77] Since contestability is usually imperfect in the real world, active competition policy is needed to combat anti-competitive behaviour and maintain competitive market structures.

b) Definition and localisation

34 Contestability is defined as follows in rec. 32 DMA:

> For the purpose of this Regulation, contestability should relate to the ability of undertakings to effectively overcome barriers to entry and expansion and challenge the gatekeeper on the merits of their products and services.

This definition confirms that the DMA, unlike conventional utilities regulation, does not assume that gatekeepers' market or monopoly power is completely 'incontestable' or has become so entrenched that there is no room for competition in and around the gatekeepers' market positions. Instead, the DMA assumes that gatekeepers can come under competitive pressure in principle, even if only with the help of regulation. It can, however, be inferred from the justification for the DMA that some tipping is already assumed, although it is unclear how far such a process has progressed and how much market power has become entrenched. Furthermore, the DMA cannot prevent the tipping of **future gatekeepers**.[78]

---

[76] Baumol American Economic Review 72 (1982), 1–15; Baumol/Panzar/Willig, Contestable Markets and the Theory of Industry Structure, New York 1982.

[77] Audretsch/Baumol/Burke International Journal of Industrial Organization 19 (2001), 613.

[78] Budzinski/Mendelsohn, 'Regulating Big Tech: From Competition Policy to Sector Regulation?' (Ilmenau Economics Discussion Papers 27/168, 2022), p. 18 et seqq.

The definition set out in rec. 32 DMA can also help to distinguish the objective of contestability from the usual competition law objectives. Indeed, several authors have already pointed out that the DMA is not only about protecting competition in defined markets[79] and about competition for markets or access to markets and services, but also about **competition in other, additional markets.**[80] With regard to contestability, gatekeepers are mainly considered as a 'gateway for business users to reach end users' (rec. 24 DMA). Although the DMA also wants to make the actual (core) gatekeeper services contestable, the main aim is to enable competition in further markets and for further services by opening these 'gateways'. This is also reflected in the relevant obligations. Obligations implementing contestability are primarily intended to facilitate market entry or access to data and services, to prevent gatekeepers from extending their power uncontrollably to other or neighbouring markets and to ensure that market counterparties (especially users) are able to switch smoothly between services.[81] These obligations are strongly reminiscent of the European Commission's proceedings against Google[82] and Apple[83].[84] 35

As a result, contestability is not only about protection of, but also about **creating competition** where established structures and practices do not (or no longer) produce it. Both objectives also deliberately serve to distinguish themselves first and foremost from narrow interpretations of the **consumer welfare**-oriented approach of competition law and to establish regulations that serve to open the market without this being tied to proof of direct positive effects for consumers in individual cases. 36

3. Interoperability?

The draft DMA initially only contained obligations in Art. 5 and 6. In the course of the legislative process, however, further obligations were included in Art. 7 DMA, specifically the **interoperability** obligation for number-independent interpersonal communications services. This mainly concerns **messenger services** such as WhatsApp, Facebook (Messenger) and Instagram (Direct Messenger), but also Signal/Telegram and Snapchat services and possibly competing services such as Zoom, MS Teams and MS Skype.[85] 37

In principle, greater interoperability promises significant benefits for competition and counteracts market failure in the digital arena.[86] For example, Kades and Scott Morton argue that interoperability provisions could allow network effects currently realised in individual companies to spread across the market.[87] Accordingly, (according to the proponents) 'instead of competition for the largest number of users, stronger competi- 38

[79] Zimmer/Göhsl ZWeR 2021, 29.

[80] Schweitzer ZEuP 2021, 1 (7): 'competition for the market, competition on the market and competition on other markets'.

[81] This is also, however, to be achieved on fair (FRAND) terms.

[82] European Commission 27.6.2017 – case AT.39740 – Google Shopping; European Commission 18.7.2018 – case AT.40099 – Google Android; European Commission, ongoing proceedings – case T.40670 – Google Adtech.

[83] European Commission, ongoing proceedings – cases AT.40437 and 40716 – Apple.

[84] Caffarra/Scott Morton, 'The European Commission Digital Markets Act: A translation' (5.1.2021).

[85] For an overview of relevant messenger applications, see PPMi study for the Body of European Regulators for Electronic Communications (BEREC) analysing EU consumer perceptions and behaviour on digital platforms for communication, BoR (21) 89, 35 et seqq.

[86] Scott Morton et al., 'Equitable Interoperability: The "Super Tool" of Digital Platform Governance' (Tobin Center Policy Discussion Paper, 13.7.2021); Kerber/Schweitzer JIPITEC 8 (2017), 39.

[87] Kades/Scott Morton, 'Interoperability as a Competition Remedy for Digital Networks' (2021), p. 30: 'Having a remedy in its toolkit that removes network effects at the level of the company – and instead makes them operate at the level of the market, available to all – will be of tremendous benefit to future consumers.'

tion with regard to functions or data protection levels could develop ('competition in the market instead of competition for the market').[88] As such, interoperability directly relates to the **direct network effects** present in many digital ecosystems (see AI).

39 The narrow scope of application and the fact that **interoperability** is not defined as an objective appears to argue against considering it as a **regulatory objective** of the DMA in its own right (see rec. 24 DMA); instead it also serves to promote contestability of these communication channels. Insofar as gatekeepers have to provide the necessary technical interfaces or similar solutions that facilitate interoperability, upon request, and free of charge (Art. 7(1) DMA), this also addresses a kind of fairness.

C. Context

40 Even though the **scope** of application of the DMA has a very specific focus, there are numerous interactions and interdependencies with other areas of (digital) commercial and regulatory law. The interlocking of these regulations and instruments pose a central challenge for the upcoming years of regulatory and competition law enforcement.

I. DMA as a component of the Digital Single Market

41 The special features of the digital economy have posed challenges to existing **competition regulations** and the economic regulatory framework in recent years. It has been noted in policy and academic discussions that these regulations, which have their roots in the post-war period, are no longer fit for the digital age. Accordingly, the digital economy not only needs new rules, but rather a new (regulatory) framework including new approaches and instruments.[89]

42 This need is not yet met with the DMA/DSA-package alone. In addition, there are currently numerous other regulations dedicated to the **special features of the digital economy**. These include, first and foremost, the data-related regulations – the Data Governance Act and the Data Act.[90] In addition, digital services and products (e.g. chatbots) are subjected to new transparency and explicability requirements in the AI Regulation.[91] Following the comprehensive reform of consumer private law and the introduction of the legislation for digital offerings (products, services),[92] the draft version of a new Product Liability Directive has been published.[93] In this context, it is important not to forget that conventional competition law is undergoing an innovation through a new Vertical Block Exemption Regulation.[94]

---

[88] Federal Network Agency (Bundesnetzagentur), 'Interoperabilität zwischen Messengerdiensten' (2021), p. 4.

[89] Marsden/Podszun, 'Restoring Balance to Digital Competition – Sensible Rules, Effective Enforcement' (2020), p. 16 et seqq.

[90] Proposal of the European Commission for a Regulation of the European Parliament and of the Council on European data governance (Data Governance Act), 25.11.2020, COM(2020) 767 final; Proposal of the European Commission for a Regulation of the European Parliament and of the Council on harmonised rules on fair access to and use of data (Data Act), 23.2.2022, COM(2022) 68 final.

[91] Proposal of the European Commission for a Regulation of the European Parliament and of the Council laying down harmonised rules on artificial intelligence (Artificial Intelligence Act) and amending certain Union legislative acts, 21.4.2021, COM(2021) 206 final.

[92] Dir. (EU) 2019/771 – Sale of Goods Directive; Dir. (EU) 2019/770 – Digital Content Directive.

[93] Proposal of the European Commission for a Directive of the European Parliament and of the Council on adapting non-contractual civil liability rules to artificial intelligence (AI Liability Directive), 28.9.2022, COM(2022) 496 final.

[94] Reg. (EU) 2022/720 on the application of Art. 101 TFEU to vertical agreements.

II. Relationship with European and German competition law

As the DMA arose out of the **competition policy** need for new regulations on digital matters, interaction with European and national competition law will be an important challenge. Ideally, these legal frameworks should complement or even reinforce each other – and their differences highlight where such can take place. 43

The main differences between **competition law** and the DMA are said to be the objectives (→ mn. 22 et seqq.) and the addressees (→ mn. 18) as well as the move from ***ex post*** intervention management to ***ex ante*** regulation.[95] However, competition law is itself a mixture of *ex ante* rules (ban on cartels, merger control) and *ex post* control (cartel exemptions, abuse control). Accordingly, this move refers to the prohibition of abuse of a dominant position under competition law (Art. 102 TFEU, § 19 GWB), which actually has an *ex post* effect in enforcement, i.e. a strategy of a market dominator that is being implemented is reviewed and found to be abusive (or not). By contrast, the obligations of the DMA are intended to have an *ex ante* effect for addressees, i.e. without any prior determination of unlawful conduct. Of course, *ex post* control also includes *ex ante* deterrence effects, i.e. anticompetitive strategies that are likely to be captured and effectively sanctioned by *ex post* control will probably not be conducted by companies in the first place. 44

The **disadvantage of *ex post* control** is that the abusive strategy is already being implemented and having a harmful effect before it can be stopped (and possibly sanctioned) in the course of (potentially long and complex) enforcement proceedings. This obviously poses a problem, especially if the damage to competition turns out to be irreversible. Long-winded proceedings also increase the harm and the likelihood that effects will be irreversible. The **disadvantage of *ex ante* control**, on the other hand, is that abusive strategies which have a detrimental impact on social welfare have to be recognised in advance by the regulator in order for them to be prevented. If the effects are unclear *ex ante* or if the strategy is perhaps not even known in advance, *ex ante* controls cannot work. By contrast, *ex post* control via an impact-based general clause can also combat previously unknown strategies and thus also address conduct that was not previously considered anti-competitive, but whose legal assessment changes due to new evidence and findings. The specific characteristics of *ex ante* and *ex post* control mean that *ex ante* control is advantageous when the legislator/regulators are familiar with the strategies open to companies and the competitive effects of these strategies.[96] 45

The digital economy is one of the younger and most **innovation-driven** industries in the modern economy. Its leading companies are considered particularly innovative and creative – and this applies to both pro-competitive and anti-competitive strategies. This means that, in numerous cases, neither the strategies of digital ecosystems nor their effects are known *ex ante*. It is no coincidence that the obligations set out in the DMA, on the whole, reflect precisely the strategies of gatekeepers that have recently been, or are currently, the subject of proceedings under competition law abuse control. Consequently, it is feared that the approach will prohibit soon to be outdated forms of conduct that have already been addressed, and which innovative and creative companies can easily replace with new anti-competitive forms of conduct that are not yet known.[97] If this is true, the effect of the DMA may be weakened and the main burden would still lie with 46

[95] Botta JECLAP 12 (2021), 500; Petit JECLAP 12 (2021), 529.

[96] For more details on the entire paragraph: Budzinski/Mendelsohn, 'Regulating Big Tech: From Competition Policy to Sector Regulation?' (Ilmenau Economics Discussion Papers 27/168, 2022), p. 25 et seqq.

[97] Budzinski/Mendelsohn, 'Regulating Big Tech: From Competition Policy to Sector Regulation?' (Ilmenau Economics Discussion Papers 27/168, 2022), p. 25 et seqq.; Caffarra/Scott Morton, 'How Will the Digital Markets Act Regulate Big Tech?' (ProMarket, 11.1.2021).

competition law abuse control. Although the DMA provides for the option of updating the existing catalogue of obligations (Art. 12 DMA), this is likely to involve considerable procedural effort.

47 It also remains to be seen whether *ex ante* regulation under the DMA will result in shorter proceedings than those resulting from *ex post* control under competition law. This also applies to abuse control under competition law itself, because the problems diagnosed using the previous system could possibly be reduced or eliminated by reforming abuse control. This is the approach taken so far by the German legislator, which, with both the most recent and the currently planned amendments to the German Competition Act, is attempting to improve and strengthen competition law enforcement against strategies that abuse market power in digital ecosystems. The reform initiatives also address one of the major problems of traditional competition law from an economic point of view, namely the strict requirement of traditionally defined market power in a clearly defined market: § 19a GWB now contains the concept of **paramount significance for competition across markets**, which describes a form of **systemic market power** that is particularly common in digital ecosystems. The new provision makes it possible to sanction the abuse of a position constituting paramount significance for competition across markets.[98] At the same time, the options for the authorities to control abuses of superior bargaining power in the sense of relative market power have been expanded (§ 20 GWB).[99]

48 We may have to await future competition law and regulatory practice to see which approach works better, or whether the DMA and (modernised and expanded) competition law can complement each other. Institutional competition – competition between two legal systems or approaches – can also create **regulatory knowledge**,[100] but also leads to a divergence of rules. This is reinforced by the fact that outside the EU, numerous jurisdictions are also reforming their competition law significantly in the area of abuse control and/or adding additional regulations, including in countries such as the US, Australia and the UK. As most digital ecosystems operate globally, **inconsistency in competition rules across countries** creates and reinforces friction with a negative impact on welfare, and poses new challenges to collaborative approaches and **international cooperation**.[101]

D. Summary

49 The digital economy has created large digital platforms and ecosystems. These are characterised by special economic features that have created new structures and concentrations of power and pose **new challenges** to the economic system as a whole, but especially to competition policy. Alongside the DSA, the DMA is the new market-based approach to opening up digital structures to competition and making digital services more contestable and fair in future. The DMA is **novel** in many respects. Not only the addressees ('gatekeepers' in digital services instead of companies with considerable market power), but also the objectives (**contestability and fairness**) and the asymmetrical *ex ante* approach differ from the common methods and approaches seen in European competition and regulatory law. In order to ensure the effectiveness of the DMA, its substantive provisions and objectives must be developed further and create a meaningful distinction from traditional competition law.

[98] Budzinski/Gaenssle/Stöhr Concurrences 17 (2020), 38; Franck/Peitz JECLAP 12 (2021), 513.
[99] Budzinski/Gaenssle/Stöhr Concurrences 17 (2020), 38.
[100] Kerber/Budzinski ZWeR 2003, 411.
[101] For more details, see Budzinski in Anderson/Lugard, p. 429–443.

CHAPTER 3
GATEKEEPERS (ART. 2 DMA)

Miriam Swamy-von Zastrow/Robert Pahlen

Bibliography: Achleitner, 'Digital Markets Act beschlossen: Verhaltenspflichten und Rolle nationaler Wettbewerbsbehörden', NZKart 2022, 359; Belloso, 'The EU Digital Markets Act' (18.5.2022) <https://ssrn.com/abstract=4109299> (last accessed: 12.7.2023); Caffarra/Scott Morton, 'The European Commission Digital Markets Act: A translation' (5.1.2021) <https://voxeu.org/article/european-commission-digital-markets-act-translation> (last accessed: 12.7.2023); Centre on Regulation in Europe (CERRE), 'Digital Markets Act: Making economic regulation of platforms fit for the digital age' (24.11.2020) <https://cerre.eu/publications/digital-markets-act-economic-regulation-platforms-digital-age/> (last accessed: 12.7.2023); Franck/Peitz, 'How to Challenge Big Tech' (6.9.2021) <https://verfassungsblog.de/dsa-dma-power-12/> (last accessed: 12.7.2023); Germanwatch, 'Hintergrundpapier DMA' (January 2022) <https://www.germanwatch.org/sites/default/files/digital_markets_act_hintergrundpapier.pdf> (last accessed: 12.7.2023); Gielen/Uphues, 'Digital Markets Act und Digital Services Act – Regulierung von Markt- und Meinungsmacht durch die Europäische Union', EuZW 2021, 627; Haus/Weusthof, 'The Digital Markets Act – a Gatekeeper's Nightmare?', WuW 2021, 318; Herbers, 'Der Digital Markets Act (DMA) kommt – neue Dos und Dont's für Gatekeeper in der Digitalwirtschaft', RDi 2022, 252; Jovanovic/Greiner, 'DMA: Überblick über die geplanten EU-Regulierungsrahmen für digitale Gatekeeper', MMR 2021, 678; Kuß/Lehmann, 'Digital Services Act – Entwurf eines einheitlichen Rechtsrahmens für die EU-Digitalwirtschaft', DB 2021, 605; Podszun/Bongartz/Langenstein, 'The Digital Markets Act: Moving from Competition Law to Regulation for Large Gatekeepers', EuCML 2021, 60; Rodríguez de las Heras Ballell, 'The Scope of the DMA' (30.8.2021) <https://verfassungsblog.de/power-dsa-dma-02/> (last accessed: 12.7.2023); Zimmer/Göhsl, 'Vom New Competition Tool zum Digital Markets Act: Die geplante EU-Regulierung für digitale Gatekeeper', ZWeR 2021, 29.

A. Overview

The DMA serves to regulate a number of large companies that provide core digital 1
platform services and have accumulated economic power. The concept of the **gatekeeper** is at the very heart of the DMA. In principle, these gatekeepers are the sole addressees of the DMA's special conduct obligations. It is, therefore, essential to clarify which companies are classified as gatekeepers by the DMA in the first place.

Art. 2 point (1) DMA contains the relevant definition. The concept of gatekeeper is 2
closely linked to the concept of 'core platform services' (Art. 2 point (2) DMA, → mn. 5 et seqq.). The **designation** of gatekeepers by the European Commission and the thresholds required for this purpose are governed by Art. 3 DMA (→ mn. 11 et seqq. and → Ch. 4 mn. 2 et seqq.).

B. Definition

I. Gatekeeper (Art. 2 point (1) DMA)

3 Art. 2 point (1) DMA states that the term 'gatekeeper' refers to companies that (i) provide core platform services as defined in Art. 2 point (2) DMA, and (ii) have been designated in accordance with Art. 3 DMA. These companies provide important access for business users as well as for relevant end users via their platform services, implying that they have a significant impact on the internal market.[1] Gatekeepers can control access for users to the services they provide. This gives them the opportunity to influence or even deny other participants' access to a market or a virtual space.[2] Online intermediation services can, for example, pre-select and rank (search) results to some extent via online search engines, as in the case of Google Search or Amazon Marketplace.[3] This is because the perception of website operators, for example in the case of Google Search, depends to a significant degree on website operators making it to the top of the search results in order to attract users when search queries are redirected.[4] In this context, gatekeepers are usually **online platforms** (such as the **GAFAM** companies) with considerable market power that are systemically relevant to the digital economy and in some cases dominate entire digital ecosystems (→ Ch. 2 mn. 2 et seqq.).[5] Based on Art. 2 point (1) DMA, the companies concerned do not automatically become gatekeepers; instead this requires a declaratory decision by the European Commission (Art. 3 DMA).

4 By way of comparison, § 19a German Competition Act (*Gesetz gegen Wettbewerbsbeschränkungen*, GWB), which was introduced into German law with the 10th amendment to the GWB, also addresses companies with paramount significance for competition across markets for competition in digital markets (cf. § 18(3a) GWB). In contrast to the DMA, however, § 19a GWB does not contain any specific definition of a gatekeeper, nor does it contain any threshold values.[6] Nevertheless, the German Federal Cartel Office also sees digital companies of paramount significance for competition across markets as encompassing the 'big players' addressed by the DMA, such as the **GAFAM** companies. The Federal Cartel Office has already opened proceedings on the basis of § 19a GWB against Meta/Facebook,[7] Amazon,[8] Alphabet/Google[9] and Apple;[10] it has already established that Meta/Facebook, Amazon and Alphabet/Google are of paramount significance for competition across markets as defined by § 19a(1) GWB.

1 Cf. Haus/Weusthof WuW 2021, 318 (320).

2 Cf. Germanwatch, 'Hintergrundpapier DMA' (January 2022), p. 2.

3 Gielen/Uphues EuZW 2021, 627 (628).

4 Gielen/Uphues EuZW 2021, 627 (628).

5 Kuß/Lehmann DB 2021, 605 (609).

6 Wolf in MüKoWettbR GWB § 19a mn. 14 et seq.

7 German Federal Cartel Office, press release dated 28.1.2021 <https://www.bundeskartellamt.de/SharedDocs/Meldung/EN/Pressemitteilungen/2021/28_01_2021_Facebook_Oculus.html;jsessionid=06134825702B025DCA49DD862D2CAB42.1_cid390?nn=3591568> (last accessed: 12.7.2023).

8 German Federal Cartel Office, press release dated 6.7.2022 <https://www.bundeskartellamt.de/SharedDocs/Meldung/EN/Pressemitteilungen/2022/06_07_2022_Amazon.html> (last accessed: 12.7.2023).

9 German Federal Cartel Office, press release dated 5.1.2022 <https://www.bundeskartellamt.de/SharedDocs/Meldung/EN/Pressemitteilungen/2022/05_01_2022_Google_19a.html> (last accessed: 12.7.2023).

10 German Federal Cartel Office, press release dated 21.6.2021 <https://www.bundeskartellamt.de/SharedDocs/Meldung/EN/Pressemitteilungen/2021/21_06_2021_Apple.html> (last accessed: 12.7.2023).

II. Core platform services (Art. 2 point (2) DMA)

The notion of a gatekeeper is closely linked to the notion of **core platform services** (CPS). Companies are not subject to the DMA per se and as a whole, but only in relation to the core platform services they offer, with regard to which they are designated as gatekeepers within the meaning of Art. 3 DMA. This means that providing core platform services is a necessary requirement for the designation as a gatekeeper, but not every provider of core platform services is automatically a gatekeeper as defined by the DMA.[11] 5

Art. 2 point (2) DMA does not define the term core platform service, but instead provides an exhaustive list of (virtual) services that are considered core platform services (→ mn. 8 et seq.). This serves to ensure predictability and legal certainty for providers and users of these services. However, the **lack of** an **abstract definition** of a core platform service may become problematic, as it is likely, given the rapid changes in the online market, that new offerings or services that are developed will not be captured by the list in Art. 2 point (2) DMA.[12] Further, it is questionable whether Art. 2 point (2) DMA can be applied by analogy to further, newly developed platform services. 6

The CPS must be offered to business users **based in the EU** or targeted at end users resident or located in the EU. It is irrelevant where the gatekeeper is established or located and which law is otherwise applicable to the provision of service (Art. 1(2) DMA). 7

CPS include the – in particular – **essential services offered by the GAFAM companies.**[13] The DMA lists the following services in Art. 2 point (2): 8

- online intermediation services and intermediaries[14] (e.g. Amazon Marketplace, App Store)
- online search engines[15] (e.g. Google)
- online social networking services[16] (e.g. Meta/Facebook)
- video-sharing platform services[17] (e.g. YouTube)
- number-independent interpersonal communications services (e.g. Meta/WhatsApp)[18]
- operating systems (e.g. Android, iOS)[19]
- web browsers (e.g. Chrome)[20]
- virtual assistants (e.g. Alexa, Siri)[21]

---

[11] The threshold values set out in Art. 3(2) DMA have to be reached for designation, → mn. 11 et seqq.

[12] Rodríguez de las Heras Ballell, 'The Scope of the DMA' (30.8.2021).

[13] Podszun/Bongartz/Langenstein EuCML 2021, 60 (63).

[14] According to Art. 2 point (5) DMA, the definition matches the definition set out in Art. 2 point (2) Reg. (EU) 2019/1150 (P2B Regulation).

[15] According to Art. 2 point (6) DMA, the definition here is also based on Art. 2 point (5) Reg. (EU) 2019/1150 (P2B Regulation).

[16] A platform that enables end users to connect and communicate with each other, share content and discover other users and content across multiple devices and, in particular, via chats, posts, videos and recommendations (Art. 2 point (7) DMA).

[17] According to Art. 2 point (8) DMA, the definition is based on Art. 1(1) point (aa) Dir. 2010/13/EU.

[18] According to Art. 2 point (9) DMA, the definition is based on Art. 2 point (7) Dir. (EU) 2018/1972.

[19] System software that controls the basic functions of the hardware or software and enables software applications to run on it (Art. 2 point (10) DMA).

[20] Software application that enables end users to access and interact with web content hosted on servers that are connected to networks such as the Internet, including standalone web browsers as well as web browsers integrated or embedded in software or similar (Art. 2 point (11) DMA).

[21] Software that can process demands, tasks or questions, including those based on audio, visual, written input, gestures or motions, and that, based on those demands, tasks or questions, provides access to other services or controls connected physical devices (Art. 2 point (12) DMA), in particular voice assis-

- cloud computing services (e.g. Amazon Web Services)[22]
- online advertising services (e.g. Google Ads), including any advertising networks, advertising exchanges and any other advertising intermediation services.[23]

9 These platform services are characterised by pronounced **economies of scale**, i.e. low marginal costs for acquiring additional users.[24] In particular, these effects can be observed when digital platforms are offered. While the initial creation of the platform requires considerable financial investment, the marginal costs are low if the platform is then positively accepted by users, and processes are largely automated.[25] In addition, strong network effects, a significant degree of dependency, lock-in effects, the absence of opportunities for multi-homing, vertical integration and data-based advantages are evident in connection with the platform services listed by the DMA (for a more detailed explanation of economies of scale and network effects, lock-in effects and multi-homing, → *Glossary* mn. 17, 31, 34, 36).

10 Offering even only **one of the aforementioned platform services** is sufficient for designation as a gatekeeper. The legislator thus decided against the proposal that arose in the legislative process to limit the DMA to companies that operate at least two core platform services,[26] or alternatively to apply it to the entire 'ecosystem'.[27] The platform services of web browsers and virtual assistants were also included in the final version of the DMA. Virtual assistants were included based on the preliminary report of the European Commission on the sector inquiry into the Internet of Things for consumers, in which the European Commission emphasised the particular competitive importance of these services.[28]

C. Designation (Art. 3 DMA)

I. Size, gateway and durability criterion (Art. 3(1) DMA)

11 Art. 3(1) DMA specifies a size, gateway and durability criterion for the **designation** of gatekeepers:[29] According to Art. 3(1) DMA, the undertaking concerned must have a significant impact on the internal market (a), provide a core platform service which is an important gateway for business users to reach end users (b), and enjoy an entrenched

tants. In this respect, there is an interface with the 'Internet of Things' (IoT), for which the European Commission recently published the final report of its sector inquiry into the consumer IoT <https://competition-policy.ec.europa.eu/system/files/2022-01/internet-of-things_final_report_2022_en.pdf> (last accessed: 12.7.2023).

[22] According to Art. 2 point (13) DMA, the definition is based on Art. 4 point (19) Dir. (EU) 2016/1148.

[23] For a list and examples, see Belloso, 'The EU Digital Markets Act' (18.5.2022); Achleitner NZKart 2022, 359 (360); see also Jovanovic/Greiner MMR 2021, 678 (679); Kuß/Lehmann DB 2021, 605 (610).

[24] Cf. Herbers RDi 2022, 252 (253).

[25] Uphues in Hoeren/Sieber/Holznagel MMR-HdB Part 15.3 mn. 12.

[26] Schwab, 'Draft Report on the proposal for a regulation of the European Parliament and of the Council. Contestable and fair markets in the digital sector (Digital Markets Act) (COM(2020)0842 – C9–0419/2020 – 2020/0374(COD))' (1.6.2021) <https://www.europarl.europa.eu/doceo/document/IMCO-PR-692792_EN.pdf> (last accessed: 12.7.2023), p. 79.

[27] Centre on Regulation in Europe (CERRE), 'Digital Markets Act: Making economic regulation of platforms fit for the digital age' (24.11.2020), p. 99; Zimmer/Göhsl ZWeR 2021, 29 (37); Gielen/Uphues EuZW 2021, 627 (629).

[28] Available at <https://competition-policy.ec.europa.eu/system/files/2022-01/internet-of-things_final_report_2022_en.pdf> (last accessed: 12.7.2023).

[29] Herbers RDi 2022, 252 (254).

and durable position, in its operations, or it must be foreseeable that it will enjoy such a position in the near future (c).

Gatekeepers are identified in this manner based on market power, number of users and network effects.[30] In particular, the **market power** of the major digital companies affects the way in which the market functions, because it may lead to an imbalance in bargaining power – gatekeepers can use their position to influence prices, quality, alternatives and innovation to the detriment of end users and gatekeepers' competitors.[31] 12

II. Turnover and user thresholds (Art. 3(2) DMA)

If the thresholds specified in Art. 3(2) DMA are met, there is a **rebuttable presumption** that the undertaking is a gatekeeper with a significant impact on the internal market, cf. rec. 23 DMA. In this case, there is a notification obligation on the part of the company concerned. The Implementing Regulation[32] now provides more detailed templates for undertakings to fulfil this notification obligation (see Annex I of the Implementing Regulation), including questions regarding a possible alternative delineation of a core platform service (see Annex I Section 2 of the Implementing Regulation). 13

In order to be designated as a gatekeeper, the company must first of all have a strong economic position and operate in several EU countries. The company to which the operator belongs (see the definition in Art. 2 point (27) DMA) needs to achieve an **annual turnover** of at least 7.5 billion EUR in the EU in each of the past three financial years or an **average market capitalisation** or equivalent **fair market value** in the past financial year of at least 75 billion EUR. In addition, the company must provide the same core platform service in at least **three Member States**. 14

Second, the company must also have a significant **user base** for the core platform service it operates, namely at least 45 million monthly active end users established or located in the EU and at least 10,000 yearly active business users established in the EU. This represents around 10 % of the EU population and 1 % of distributors selling via online retail.[33] This criterion also has to have been met in each of the last three financial years in accordance with Art. 3(2)(c) DMA. 15

When it comes to calculating active end users and business users of the platform service, an important reference is provided for companies in the **Annex to the DMA**, which can be updated by the European Commission (for details, → Ch. 4 mn. 10). Criticism was voiced during the legislative process as to whether the focus on a pure number of users was helpful and should not instead be based on the number of search queries.[34] The Annex to the DMA now stipulates that it is the users of the relevant (distinct) core platform service and not the provider's entire services that are relevant (for the exact definition of the relevant distinct platform services, see D. 2. of the Annex to the DMA). 16

According to rec. 23 DMA, the presumption can only be **rebutted in exceptional circumstances**. In addition, pursuant to Art. 3(8) DMA, the European Commission can designate companies that provide core platform services but do not meet the thresholds set out in Art. 3(2) DMA as gatekeepers pursuant to the procedure set out in Art. 17 17

[30] Kuß/Lehmann DB 2021, 605 (609 et seq.).
[31] Kuß/Lehmann DB 2021, 605 (610).
[32] Commission Implementing Regulation (EU) 2023/814 of 14 April 2023 on detailed arrangements for the conduct of certain proceedings by the Commission pursuant to Regulation (EU) 2022/1925 of the European Parliament and of the Council (OJ 2023 L 102, 6).
[33] Podszun/Bongartz/Langenstein EuCML 2021, 60 (63) with further substantiation.
[34] Gielen/Uphues EuZW 2021, 627 (629).

DMA (market investigation, → Ch. 8 mn. 9 et seqq.; for more detail, → Ch. 4 mn. 17 et seqq.).

D. Application cases in practice

18 The thresholds described above have been raised compared to the original draft version of the DMA. Nevertheless, the current definition covers a **large number** of – also European – digital companies. It remains to be seen whether the European Commission has sufficient capacity for enforcement and monitoring.

19 Ultimately, the DMA currently covers not only the 'Big Five' (i.e. the **GAFAM** companies, → mn. 4), but probably around 10–15 digital companies as gatekeepers.[35] The core platform services offered by the GAFAM companies were also used by the DMA legislator as a guide when listing the core platform services covered by the DMA. It is important to note that some of the digital companies offer several platform services as defined in Art. 2 point (2) DMA. Each of these services has to be reviewed to determine whether the requirements of Art. 3(1), (2) DMA are met. For example, in addition to various services offered by the GAFAM companies, Oracle, SAP, Amazon Web Services and Microsoft Azure may also fulfil the requirements specified in the DMA.[36]

20 Some platforms, on the other hand, currently meet several but not all **thresholds** (including Booking.com, Spotify, Uber, Bytedance/TikTok, Salesforce, Google Cloud, IBM Cloud). Others currently do not – yet – meet the thresholds (Twitter, AirBnB, Netflix, Bing, LinkedIn, Zoom).[37] This means that the European Commission could only designate these companies as gatekeepers pursuant to Art. 3(8) DMA, which it presumably will do in view of the considerable importance of some of these companies.

[35] Podszun/Bongartz/Langenstein EuCML 2021, 60 (64).

[36] Cf. Franck/Peitz, 'How to Challenge Big Tech' (6.9.2021).

[37] Caffarra/Scott Morton, 'The European Commission Digital Markets Act: A translation' (5.1.2021); cf. Germanwatch, 'Hintergrundpapier DMA' (January 2022), p. 11 et seq.

CHAPTER 4
DESIGNATION AS A GATEKEEPER (ART. 3 DMA)

Markus Brösamle/Johanna Krauskopf

Bibliography: De la Mano et al., 'The Digital Markets Act' (2021) <https://www.compasslexecon.com/the-proposed-dma-back-to-the-form-based-future/> (last accessed: 12.7.2023); de Streel et al., 'Making the Digital Markets Act more resilient and effective' (2021) <https://cerre.eu/publications/european-parliament-digital-markets-act-dma-resilient-effective/> (last accessed: 12.7.2023); Geradin, 'What is a digital Gatekeeper?' (2.4.2021) <https://dx.doi.org/10.2139/ssrn.3788152> (last accessed: 12.7.2023); Gielen/Uphues, 'Digital Markets Act und Digital Services Act, Regulierung von Markt- und Meinungsmacht durch die Europäische Union', EuZW 2021, 627; Haus/Weusthof, 'The Digital Markets Act – a Gatekeeper's Nightmare?', WuW 2021, 318; Herbers, 'Der Digital Markets Act (DMA) kommt – neue Dos and Don'ts für Gatekeeper in der Digitalwirtschaft', RDi 2022, 252; Körber, 'Lessons from the Hare and the Tortoise: Legally imposed self-regulation, proportionality and the right to defence under the DMA – Part 1', NZKart 2021, 379; Petit, 'The Proposed Digital Markets Act (DMA): A Legal and Policy Review', JECLAP 2021, 529; Schweitzer, 'The Art to Make Gatekeeper Positions Contestable and the Challenge to Know What Is Fair: A Discussion of the Digital Markets Act Proposal', ZEuP 2021, 503; Zimmer/Göhsl, 'Vom New Competition Tool zum Digital Markets Act: Die geplante EU-Regulierung für digitale Gatekeeper', ZWeR 2021, 29.

1 The **designation** of an undertaking as a gatekeeper is the key procedural step for applicability of the DMA's conduct obligations. At the heart of the procedure is a **quantitative presumption rule**, combined with a **self-assessment** obligation for undertakings.

A. Definition

2 The European Commission first has to designate undertakings as gatekeepers in order for them to meet the obligations of a gatekeeper as defined in the DMA (see Art. 3(10) DMA with reference to Art. 5, 6 and 7 DMA). As a result, the procedural step of **designation** is of great importance. The procedure for designation is governed by Art. 3 DMA. It is initially based on a **presumption** using **quantitative criteria**, without recourse to market definition ('technical quantitative approach').[1] Market definition is a time-consuming process and, in 'conventional' competition law, often leads to proceedings becoming complex and lasting longer. The long duration of proceedings is particularly problematic given that digital markets are so dynamic and fast-moving. Designation is, however, also possible based on criteria other than the thresholds of presumption. In such cases, the procedure is supported by a **market investigation** (Art. 3(8) and 17 DMA). The European Commission ultimately issues what is known as a **designation decision** in which the relevant core platform service or services of the gatekeeper concerned are explicitly listed (Art. 3(9) DMA).

[1] Zimmer/Göhsl ZWeR 2021, 29 (38).

B. Designation procedure

I. Presumption (Art. 3(2) DMA)

3 A provider of core platform services is designated as a gatekeeper if specific **qualitative criteria** are met (Art. 3(1) DMA), which is presumed to be the case when the quantitative thresholds set out in Art. 3(2) DMA are reached (→ Ch. 3 mn. 3 et seqq.).

4 If an undertaking providing core platform services exceeds all the **thresholds** set out in Art. 3(2) DMA, it is obliged to notify the European Commission (Art. 3(3) DMA). Undertakings are therefore required to **assess independently** the requirements of Art. 3(2) DMA. A fixed time frame is provided for this self-assessment (for more details, → mn. 24 et seqq.): The **notification** must be made without delay and in any event within two months after the thresholds are reached (Art. 3(3) subpara. 1 sent. 1 DMA). This also applies whenever a further core platform service provided by an undertaking that has previously been designated as a gatekeeper exceeds the thresholds in Art. 3(2)(b) and (2)(c) DMA (Art. 3(3) subpara. 1 sent. 3 DMA). By the deadline of 3.7.2023 the European Commission received notifications from Alphabet, Amazon, Apple, ByteDance, Meta, Microsoft and Samsung.[2] In terms of content, the notification must contain the relevant information on the quantitative thresholds pursuant to Art. 3(2) DMA for each of the core platform services provided by the undertaking that meets the thresholds in Art. 3(2)(b) DMA (Art. 3(3) subpara. 1 sent. 2 DMA).

5 On 14.4.2023, the European Commission adopted the DMA's Implementing Regulation which entered into force on 2.5.2023. The Implementing Regulation regulates inter alia the form, content and other details of notifications (Art. 1(1) Implementing Regulation). Art. 2 Implementing Regulation deals with notifications that meet the thresholds for presumption.

6 The **content required for a notification** is specified in Annex I ('Form GD (for gatekeeper designation)'). Regarding substantive elements, the information to be provided in the Form GD concerns information about core platform services (Section 2) and information relating to the quantitative thresholds in Art. 3(2) DMA (Sections 3 and 4). Under Section 2, undertakings meeting the thresholds with at least one of their core platform services must provide 'an exhaustive list of all core platform services provided by the notifying undertaking including any plausible alternative delineation'. This includes core platform services which do not meet the quantitative criteria. Sections 3 and 4 demand information on the calculation of turnover and market capitalisation, active end users and active business users.

7 The **format** and **length** of documents to be submitted under the provisions of the DMA in general are guided by Annex II of the Implementing Regulation (Art. 4 Implementing Regulation). Most notably, Annex II sets a **stringent page limit** for notifications pursuant to Art. 3(3) DMA. The maximum number of pages for the notification of each core platform service shall not exceed 50 pages and 30 pages for substantiated arguments. Documents must be submitted in a format that allows the European Commission to process them electronically. The European Commission may request undertakings to put documents in order (Art. 4(3) Implementing Regulation). Where a document does not comply with the requirements regarding format and length laid down in Annex II,

[2] European Commission, 'Potential gatekeepers notified the Commission and provided relevant information' (press release, 4.7.2023) <https://digital-markets-act.ec.europa.eu/potential-gatekeepers-notified-commission-and-provided-relevant-information-2023-07-04_en> (last accessed: 12.7.2023).

time periods shall not start running until the document is put in order in accordance with a request by the European Commission (Art. 9(3) Implementing Regulation).

Favouring a cooperative approach, the Implementing Regulation stresses the possibility for undertakings to 'engage in **pre-notification contacts**' with the European Commission (rec. 2 Implementing Regulation). 8

The DMA is applicable since 2.5.2023 (Art. 54 subpara. 2 DMA). The first potential gatekeepers notified the European Commission by 3.7.2023 (→ mn. 4). Afterwards the European Commission has 45 working days for the assessment and designation. In the event a market investigation is conducted – especially if the undertaking raises substantial doubts as to gatekeeper status – the process can even take up to an additional five months. The date of designation may be delayed if the undertaking does not initially provide all the required information. Under the Implementing Regulation the European Commission's assessment period begins only on the date on which the complete (and correct) information is received by the European Commission (Art. 3(1) sent. 2 Implementing Regulation). The risk of delays can be reduced by pre-notification. The gatekeeper must comply with the conduct obligations set out in the DMA no later than six months after its designation (Art. 3(10) DMA). 9

An important reference is provided for undertakings in the **Annex** to the DMA in order to assess whether the thresholds set out in Art. 3(2)(b) DMA are reached. The Annex sets out the methodology for identifying and calculating active end users and active business users. The terms are defined in general and specifically for each core platform service. The criteria are also explained. The calculation of active end users and business users raised many questions on the part of potential gatekeepers when the European Commission's proposal on the DMA was published and was widely debated overall (→ Ch. 3 mn. 16).[3] The Annex to the DMA now clarifies which services are considered distinctly or separately, and in which context (Annex D. 2. DMA). It also provides definitions for each category of core platform services to determine the number of active end users and active business users. If further problems in dealing with the methodology of the Annex come to light in practice, or if new core platform services are included in the DMA, the European Commission is empowered to adopt delegated acts to amend the Annex (Art. 3(7) DMA). 10

If the undertaking does not notify the European Commission that the thresholds have been reached and does not comply with a request for information from the European Commission (Art. 21 DMA), the European Commission shall be entitled to designate that undertaking as a gatekeeper based on **information available** to the European Commission (Art. 3(3) subpara. 2 DMA). 11

II. Rebuttal of presumption (Art. 3(5) DMA)

The presumption of gatekeeper status can be rebutted. For this to happen, the undertaking providing core platform services must present **sufficiently substantiated arguments** to demonstrate that, in its particular exceptional case, it does not meet the requirements set out in Art. 3(1) DMA despite meeting the quantitative thresholds (Art. 3(5) DMA). In this respect, in order to **rebut** the presumption based on quantitative criteria, it is the qualitative criteria set out in Art. 3(1) DMA that is decisive. According to the wording used alone, rebuttal of the presumption is an exception.[4] The burden 12

[3] Gielen/Uphues EuZW 2021, 627 (629).

[4] The recitals of the DMA also refer to 'exceptional circumstances' in which rebuttal is an option (rec. 23 DMA).

of adducing evidence that the presumption does not apply is therefore also borne by the undertaking (rec. 23 DMA).

13 Based on the wording, the sufficiently substantiated arguments refer to the circumstances in which the relevant core central platform service operates (Art. 3(5) subpara. 1 DMA). The standard required by the vague legal term 'sufficiently substantiated arguments' is not sufficiently specified in the DMA. In this respect, the literature calls for **clarification** in the DMA itself or in the form of guidelines in order to guarantee gatekeepers' rights of defence.[5]

14 By contrast, the DMA sets out more detailed and precise provisions on the European Commission's handling of any objections raised. It may **reject the arguments** put forward within the time limit for designation (45 working days) without conducting a market investigation (Art. 3(5) subpara. 2 DMA) if the arguments put forward are not sufficiently substantiated to clearly rebut the quantitative presumption of the thresholds. This is designed to prevent the designation process from being blocked by the option of rebuttal.[6]

15 The DMA clarifies, however, which **substantive issues** will be taken into account when assessing the evidence and arguments presented. The European Commission is only to consider those issues that relate directly to the quantitative criteria. These elements include (rec. 23 DMA):

- with regard to the size of the undertaking, 'the impact of the undertaking providing core platform services on the internal market beyond revenue or market cap, such as its size in absolute terms, and the number of Member States in which it is present',
- with regard to the position of the core platform service as a 'bottleneck', 'by how much the actual business user and end user numbers exceed the thresholds', and
- with regard to the durability criterion, 'the importance of the undertaking's core platform service considering the overall scale of activities of the respective core platform service; and the number of years for which the thresholds have been met'.

16 On the other hand, justification on **economic grounds** is not taken into account (rec. 23 DMA). A market definition is just as irrelevant as the undertaking's **efficiency gains**, as these criteria do not play any role in designation as a gatekeeper (rec. 23 DMA).

Annex II of the Implementing Regulation limits the length of documents presenting substantiated arguments to 30 pages.

III. Designation other than via presumption (Art. 3(8) DMA)

17 In addition, undertakings can also be designated as gatekeepers **other than via presumption**. The European Commission designates an undertaking as a gatekeeper if it does not exceed the thresholds set out in Art. 3(2) DMA but meets all the qualitative criteria of Art. 3(1) DMA. This affects, among others, undertakings referred to as emerging gatekeepers. Assessment is based on a **market investigation** (Art. 17 DMA, → Ch. 8 mn. 9 et seqq.).

[5] Körber NZKart 2021, 379 (384).
[6] Cf. also Herbers RDi 2022, 252 (255).

1. General

18 The DMA also sets out the elements to be taken into account for the **individual examination** by the European Commission (Art. 3(8) subpara. 2 DMA). The **elements** include, depending on their relevance to the undertaking concerned, (i) the size of the undertaking, (ii) the number of users, (iii) network effects and data driven advantages, (iv) scale and scope effects, (v) lock-in effects, (vi) conglomerate corporate structures or vertical integration of the undertaking, and (vii) other structural business or service characteristics. This gives the European Commission a very wide margin of discretion; at the same time, however, the criteria also represent decision issues that can be assessed in judicial proceedings to review the designation decision.

19 The European Commission takes into account some or all of the issues mentioned, depending on the case in hand, and also includes **foreseeable developments** in these issues in its assessment (Art. 3(8) subpara. 2 and 3 DMA). Foreseeable developments also include planned concentrations with undertakings from the digital sector or undertakings enabling the collection of data (Art. 3(8) subpara. 3 DMA).

2. Emerging gatekeepers

20 The group of undertakings designated other than via presumption also includes undertakings that do not yet hold an established position with regard to their activity, but are predicted to enjoy such a position in the near future (**emerging gatekeepers**, Art. 3(1)(c) alt. 2 DMA). This is intended to give the European Commission an opportunity to intervene before a market 'tips' (→ *Glossary* mn. 46) irreversibly (rec. 26 DMA). Unlike other cases of designation, the European Commission has to impose constitutively the application of specific conduct obligations on emerging gatekeepers. Since Art. 17(4) DMA only refers to specific conduct obligations from Art. 5 and 6 DMA, the European Commission only has this selection of dos and don'ts at its disposal for emerging gatekeepers. These are the obligations that are of particular relevance for tipping markets. The European Commission is to take into account the temporary nature of the measure and review, at a later point in time, whether the conditions for the presumption of full gatekeeper status are now met or whether these conditions have not been fulfilled, meaning that the previously imposed obligations should be lifted (rec. 74 DMA). The obligations declared to be applicable by the European Commission must be appropriate and necessary to prevent the gatekeeper concerned from achieving, by unfair means, an entrenched and durable position with its business model (Art. 17(4) sent. 2 DMA).

21 The concept of the emerging gatekeeper is not without controversy. Some Member States have already criticised the lack of a definition of the condition 'in the near future' during the legislative process and have, therefore, called for clarification.[7] Even the version of the DMA that was ultimately adopted did not provide clarity. In addition, the DMA's **advance intervention threshold** is also criticised because it is difficult to predict when markets are in danger of tipping.[8] Other opinions in the literature, on the other hand, have identified the risk that, due to the duration of market investigations, markets could already tip while the procedure is ongoing.[9]

[7] Körber NZKart 2021, 379 (383); Council of the European Union, 'Progress report', 17.5.2021, 2020/0374/(COD), para. 23.
[8] Cf. only Petit JECLAP 2021, 529 (541).
[9] Zimmer/Göhsl ZWeR 2021, 29 (44 et seq.).

IV. Procedure

22 The European Commission issues a **designation decision** (Art. 3(9) DMA) both if the presumption criteria set out in Art. 3(2) DMA are fulfilled and if designation is not based on the presumption but solely on the requirements of Art. 3(1) DMA. In its designation decision, the European Commission lists the relevant core platform services which are an important gateway – or bottleneck – for business users to reach end users.

23 The **constitutive designation** of the DMA's addressees offers increased legal certainty for (potential) gatekeepers compared to the applicability of the obligations by operation of law. Without constitutive designation, temporary changes in the relevant figures of core platform service providers would decide on whether an undertaking falls in or out of scope.[10] In contrast to merger control, which refers to a specific merger, the quantitative thresholds set out in the DMA would, in the absence of constitutive designation, have to be observed and examined throughout.[11] Nevertheless, even under the regulatory approach chosen by the EU legislator, potential gatekeepers always have to check whether the thresholds may have been reached and whether they need to notify the European Commission accordingly.

24 The procedure leading up to the issue of the designation decision is characterised by various **time limits** that are intended to allow the process to be planned in terms of timing. Undertakings that reach the presumption thresholds are obliged to notify the European Commission without delay, and in any case within two months, and to provide it with the necessary information to verify the requirements of Art. 3(2) DMA (Art. 3(3) subpara. 3 sent. 1 DMA). Undertakings already designated as gatekeepers are also obliged to notify the European Commission within two months if another core platform service reaches the presumption thresholds (Art. 3(3) subpara. 1 sent. 3 DMA). The European Commission then designates the undertaking as a gatekeeper within 45 working days of receiving the complete information (Art. 3(4) DMA).

25 If the undertaking explains why the presumption does not apply in its specific case, the European Commission can **reject** these arguments within the period of 45 working days if the arguments put forward are not sufficiently substantiated (Art. 3(5) subpara. 2 DMA). If, on the other hand, the undertaking submits sufficiently substantiated arguments to rebut the presumption, the European Commission may open a **market investigation** procedure within a period of 45 working days (Art. 3(5) subpara. 3 DMA). The market investigation should then be completed within five months (Art. 17(3) DMA). It is designed to examine thoroughly the undertaking's status as gatekeeper and ends with a decision to be published (→ Ch. 8 mn. 31 et seqq.; legal protection against designation decision, → Ch. 10 mn. 36 et seqq.).

26 The conduct obligations set out in the DMA (Art. 5, 6 and 7) must be fulfilled by the gatekeeper no later than **six months** after a core platform service has been listed in the designation decision. Overall, this means the following regarding applicability: The DMA is applicable since 2.5.2023 (Art. 54 subpara. 2 DMA; the DMA entered into force on 1.11.2022, Art. 54 subpara. 1 DMA). Designation as a gatekeeper will then, however, take around at least another four months based on the deadlines outlined. This is based on the two-month deadline for the gatekeeper to report that the thresholds have been reached and on the 45 working day period for designation as a gatekeeper by the European Commission. In the event of a market investigation, for example because the gatekeeper raises substantial doubts as to its gatekeeper status, the process may be extended

[10] Federal Cartel Office Background Paper DMA p. 5.
[11] Federal Cartel Office Background Paper DMA p. 5; Körber NZKart 2021, 379 (382).

by a further five months. Gatekeepers must comply with the conduct obligations no later than six months after their designation.

C. Evaluation

The DMA sets out detailed provision on the procedure for designation as a gatekeeper. Designation has a **crucial function** – both for gatekeepers and for companies that derive claims against gatekeepers from the DMA or are to benefit from the conduct obligations, as well as for the business users and end users that use the core platform service. The focus is on the technical quantitative approach of the **presumption rule**, which is combined with the obligation of undertakings to conduct self-assessments. The DMA is to be applied swiftly, accompanied by a **clear deadline regime**. Compared to familiar competition law procedures, in particular review of the abuse of dominance (Art. 102 TFEU), a decision has been made not to define specific markets. Likewise, the conduct obligations mean that there is no need to assess and furnish evidence of specific abusive practices. The intended **accelerating effect** of the presumption criteria was therefore already assessed as a positive issue during the legislative process.[12] The question as to whether the DMA can, in fact, respond quickly and flexibly enough to the exceptional speed seen in digital markets (→ *Glossary* mn. 15) remains to be seen. It will also be very interesting to see whether the DMA will provide undertakings with sufficient guidance for checking the thresholds for presumption or whether there is a need for adjustment, e.g. with regard to the Annex for the calculation of user numbers. 27

Even during the legislative process, criticism primarily concerned the **content of the presumption criteria**. One issue that was criticised is that turnover and user numbers are merely indications of size, but do not mean that the gatekeeper actually holds a corresponding position of power.[13] Although the number of users could indicate network effects, its informative value with regard to the competitive relationships affected could, for example, be put into perspective again by an actual option for multi-homing (→ *Glossary* mn. 34).[14] 28

So it remains to be seen whether the criteria set out in the DMA and the associated procedure will actually prove proficient to keep digital markets **fair and contestable**. Nevertheless, the DMA offers the option of taking quick and early action against undertakings – which are either already gatekeepers or will become gatekeepers in the near future – in order to counteract negative developments. 29

[12] Schweitzer ZEuP 2021, 503 (521).

[13] De la Mano et al., 'The Digital MarketsAct' (2021), para. 4.9; de Streel et al., 'Making the Digital Markets Act more resilient and effective' (2021), p. 18; Geradin, 'What is a digital Gatekeeper?' (2.4.2021), p. 15, 20; Körber NZKart 2021, 379 (382); Schweitzer ZEuP 2021, 503 (525).

[14] Haus/Weusthof WuW 2021, 318 (320); Schweitzer ZEuP 2021, 503 (525); Körber NZKart 2021, 379 (382 et seq.).

CHAPTER 5
REVIEW BY THE EUROPEAN COMMISSION (ART. 4 DMA)

Markus Brösamle/Miriam Swamy-von Zastrow

A. Overview

1 The European Commission may reconsider, amend, or repeal a decision it has adopted designating a company as a gatekeeper (pursuant to Art. 3 DMA) (→ Ch. 4 mn. 22 et seqq., Art. 4 DMA). The review is carried out **upon request** or **on its own initiative** (para. 1). This means that companies can request the amendment or repeal of their status as gatekeeper if necessary. Other than via a request, companies are also protected by the fact that the European Commission is obliged to **regularly review** designation decisions, **without this review having to be prompted by specific grounds** (para. 2).

2 The **European Commission**, however, remains solely responsible for the review. This means that it has a key role in reviewing its own decisions in accordance with Art. 3(1) DMA. The key role assigned to the European Commission is explained by the approach taken by the DMA: the main objective is to ensure fast and effective control of gatekeepers and prevention of legal fragmentation resulting from a multitude of national regulations (cf. rec. 8 DMA). Therefore, although the DMA provides for cooperation between Member States and the European Commission (rec. 90, Art. 37 et seqq. DMA), it assigns the 'leading role' clearly to the European Commission.

3 A **judicial review** of the designation decision is possible. Even though Art. 45 DMA (in conjunction with rec. 94) states that the ECJ has unlimited jurisdiction to review decisions by which the European Commission has imposed fines or periodic penalty payments, this does not mean that other decisions (not involving fines or periodic penalty payments) cannot be subject to judicial review. This only means that the scope of judicial review regarding decisions involving fines or periodic penalty payments is extended to unlimited jurisdiction (and thus not only to misuse of powers, cf. Art. 263(1), (4) TFEU). Action against the designation decision, however, does not have any suspensory effect (Art. 278 sent. 1 TFEU).

4 The European Commission is also required to publish and update a **list** of gatekeepers and core platform services that have to comply with the conduct obligations (→ Ch. 6 mn. 11 et seqq., Art. 5, 6 and 7) (Art. 4(3) DMA, → mn. 21 et seqq.) In addition to the review of its designation decisions pursuant to Art. 4 DMA, the European Commission has further specific **review options** at its disposal (→ mn. 22 et seqq.).

B. Types of review

5 Art. 4 DMA provides **two types of review**: An 'event-driven' review pursuant to para. 1 (→ mn. 6 et seqq.) and a 'regular' review pursuant to para. 2 (→ mn. 14 et seqq.).

I. Event-driven review (Art. 4(1) DMA)

6 An event-driven review can be carried out upon request or on the European Commission's own initiative (Art. 4(1) DMA). In this context, a review based on a **request** will probably be the rule due to the interest of the company concerned in losing the gatekeeper status.

7 It remains to be seen to what extent the European Commission will act **on its own initiative** in the context of Art. 4(1) DMA or will merely carry out regular reviews pursuant to Art. 4(2) DMA. Reviews on the European Commission's own initiative will probably only be performed in cases where the designation decision is evidently incorrect, because the European Commission has to use its capacities in a targeted manner. The European Commission has **discretion** as to whether to initiate a review.

1. Substantial change in the underlying facts (lit. a)

8 An event-driven review is an option if there has been a **substantial change** in any of the **facts** on which the designation decision was based (Art. 4(1)(a) DMA). Not every change in the facts is substantial, but only those aspects that lead to a change in the legal assessment with regard to the designation decision (cf. rec. 30 DMA). This means the amendment will only be necessary if the change in the facts also leads to a change in the assessment. Whether or not that is the case is to be based on a case-by-case assessment (cf. rec. 30 DMA).

2. Based on incomplete, incorrect or misleading information (lit. b)

9 An event-driven review is also an option if the designation decision is based on **incorrect, incomplete or misleading information** (Art. 4(1)(b) DMA). These terms are not defined any further in the DMA. The following definitions apply based on an understanding of these terms in the field of European merger control:

10 Therefore, **'incomplete information'** is information that does not have the scope required in the Commission's original request for information sent to the company concerned regarding the fulfilment of the latter's duties under the DMA (cf. on the fundamentally broad scope, Art. 21 DMA). Information is also incomplete if the information provided by the company does not match the legally required content (cf. Art. 3(3) DMA).[1]

11 By contrast, the term **'incorrect information'** is to be understood as an objectively incorrect communication of the facts.[2] Once again, however, it is likely to be the case that not every incorrect notification to the European Commission is covered by this term. Instead, the term only covers information that was at least partly responsible for the decision made by the European Commission to issue a designation decision pursuant to Art. 3(1) DMA (Art. 4(1)(a) DMA).[3]

[1] Cf. in the context of Art. 14(1)(a) of the EC Merger Regulation (ECMR), which is comparable in this respect, Jaeger in FK-KartellR FKVO Art. 14 mn. 12.

[2] Cf. in the context of Art. 6(3)(a) ECMR, Körber in Immenga/Mestmäcker FKVO Art. 6 mn. 87, 88.

[3] Cf. Körber in Immenga/Mestmäcker FKVO Art. 6 mn. 87.

12 **'Misleading information'** describes – at least in merger control law – a situation in which an incorrect impression has been created by an unclear presentation of the facts, or by a presentation of the facts that is otherwise difficult to understand.[4] When it comes to the assumption of misleading information, a subjective component ('intention to mislead') on the part of the company concerned is likely to be required at the point when the company submitted the relevant information to the European Commission, which, however, can (but does not have to) also apply in the case of the submission of incomplete or incorrect information.[5] In this respect, the individual elements of Art. 4(1)(a) DMA may also overlap.

3. Legal consequence of the event-driven review

13 If the Commission concludes that the original decision was incorrect, it declares the **designation decision** to be incorrect; at the same time, it amends or repeals the designation decision. The new decision must be published by the European Commission (Art. 44(1) DMA), having regard to the legitimate interest of gatekeepers or third parties in the protection of their confidential information (Art. 44(2) DMA).

II. Regular review (Art. 4(2) DMA)

14 The regular review, not prompted by any specific grounds, pursuant to Art. 4(2) DMA supplements the event-driven review (para. 1). In addition to the regular duty to **review the classification** of a company as a gatekeeper (para. 2 subpara. 1), the European Commission also has the duty to review whether **new or further companies** providing core platform services meet the requirements set out in Art. 3(1) DMA (para. 2 subpara. 2). Subpara. 1, therefore, only refers to companies that have already been designated as gatekeepers, while subpara. 2 refers to all other companies and thus also to (new) potential gatekeepers. Unlike in the context of Art. 4(1) DMA, there is **no discretion** for the European Commission to determine whether the review obligations set out in Art. 4(2) DMA should be exercised. Instead, this is a regular review obligation tied to specific time periods.

15 In this respect, the provision is an expression of the **principle of proportionality** (cf. rec. 27 DMA): The European Commission is to apply only those obligations that are necessary and proportionate to achieve the objectives of the Regulation and is to regularly review whether such obligations should be maintained, suppressed or adapted. This also serves to reassure actual or potential market participants about the contestability and fairness of the services concerned (rec. 28 DMA).

16 The obligation to conduct reviews even in the absence of specific grounds is also an expression of a **corrective** resulting from the obligatory prohibitions and obligations arising from classification as gatekeeper: Where competition law can often only be applied *ex post* and, as a result, too late to respond to what is happening in dynamic markets, the DMA already imposes obligations and prohibitions on gatekeepers without the need to prove any infringement of the law. Consequently, this 'advance effect' of the DMA requires a comprehensive obligation of the European Commission to control the classification of companies as gatekeepers.

---

[4] Cf. on Article 14(1) ECMR, Jaeger in FK-KartellR FKVO Art. 14 mn. 7.

[5] Cf. on requests for information pursuant to Art. 11 ECMR, Körber in Immenga/Mestmäcker FKVO Art. 11 mn. 23; also Jaeger in FK-KartellR FKVO Art. 14 mn. 7.

1. Routine review of gatekeeper status (para. 2 subpara. 1)

With regard to companies that have already been designated as gatekeepers, the European Commission has to review regularly, and at least every three years, whether the gatekeepers continue to satisfy the requirements laid down in Art. 3(1) DMA, and review the list of the gatekeeper's core platform services as defined by Art. 3(1)(b) (Art. 4(2) subpara. 1 DMA, see also → Ch. 3 mn. 5 et seqq., Art. 3 DMA). This review explicitly has **no suspensory effect** on the gatekeeper's obligations (Art. 4(2) sent. 3 DMA). 17

Due to the **dynamic change** in the digital sector, these regular checks have to be carried out in an appropriate time frame in order to ensure legal certainty with regard to the regulatory framework, because the actual circumstances and the market environment can change significantly within a short period of time. It is important to ensure that any practice that is likely to limit the contestability of core platform services, or is unfair, is identified (cf. rec. 77 DMA). In the event of a substantial change in the facts, however, which could mean that the requirements for classification as a gatekeeper (Art. 3(1) DMA) no longer apply, it should be assumed in any case that companies will act independently and submit a corresponding application in accordance with Art. 4(1) DMA even before the expiry of the three-year period. 18

2. Annual review of new core platform services (para. 2 subpara. 2)

In addition, the European Commission is obliged to review at least once a year whether new companies offering **core platform services** satisfy the requirements for classification as gatekeepers (Art. 4(2) subpara. 2 DMA). This supplements the obligation of companies to notify the European Commission that they have reached the gatekeeper thresholds (presumption of Art. 3(2) DMA) without delay, but in any case within two months of reaching the thresholds, and to provide the necessary information (Art. 3(3) subpara. 1 DMA, see also → Ch. 4 mn. 4 et seqq.). 19

3. Legal consequence of the regular review

The **legal consequence** of the regular review conducted by the European Commission is confirmation/issue of an initial designation decision, provided that the requirements for classification as a gatekeeper continue to be, or are, met. Otherwise, the decision shall be amended or repealed (Art. 4(2) subpara. 3 DMA). The decision must be published by the European Commission (Art. 44(1) DMA), having regard to the legitimate interest of gatekeepers or third parties in the protection of their confidential information (Art. 44(2) DMA). 20

C. Publication and updating of the gatekeeper list (Art. 4(3) DMA)

The European Commission is obliged to publish and update a list of gatekeepers and a list of the core platform services for which they need to comply with the obligations laid down in Art. 5–7 DMA (→ Ch. 6 mn. 11 et seqq.) (Art. 4(3) DMA). As the services offered in the digital sector can change within a short period of time, publication of the list is intended to ensure that potentially problematic and unfair practices of core platform services are **identified** (cf. rec. 77 DMA). As such, the publication also serves periodically to review this Regulation and closely monitor its effects on the contestability and fairness of commercial relationships in the online platform economy (rec. 105 DMA). 21

D. Further review options open to the European Commission and gatekeepers

22 In addition to the review of the designation decision within the context of Art. 4 DMA, **further specific review options** are also available to the companies concerned and the European Commission.

I. Review options for gatekeepers

23 A gatekeeper may request that the European Commission determine whether the measures it has taken effectively **achieve** the **objective of the obligations imposed on it** (Art. 8(3) sent. 1 DMA). In this respect, the European Commission has discretion in deciding whether to engage in such a process, respecting the principles of equal treatment, proportionality and good administration (Art. 8(3) sent. 2 DMA).

24 The gatekeeper may also request the **suspension** of **its obligations** in full or in part (Art. 9(1) DMA). This, however, requires the gatekeeper to demonstrate exceptional circumstances beyond the gatekeeper's control that would pose a threat to the economic viability of its operation in the European Union. Suspension is, again, at the discretion of the European Commission. In urgent cases, there is also the possibility of a provisional suspension (Art. 9(3) DMA).

25 Comparable regulations apply in cases involving an **exemption on grounds of public health or security** (Art. 10(1) DMA). The European Commission reviews this exemption once a year (Art. 10(2) DMA). Once again, a provisional exemption is possible in urgent cases (Art. 10(4) DMA).

II. Review options for, and obligations of, the European Commission

26 The review options for the European Commission within the context of a **market investigation** (Art. 17 and 18 DMA) are particularly noteworthy. In particular, designations as gatekeepers for companies that do not yet hold an entrenched and durable position in their operations (Art. 3(8) DMA) are to be reviewed by the European Commission on an event-driven and regular basis as part of the procedure pursuant to Art. 4 DMA (Art. 17(4) DMA). In addition, the European Commission regularly reviews the **remedies** imposed in the event of systematic non-compliance with the conduct obligations by a gatekeeper (Art. 18(1), (2) DMA) to ensure that the gatekeeper actually complies with its conduct obligations (Art. 5, 6 and 7 DMA) (Art. 18(8) DMA). Within the context of a mandatory review obligation, the European Commission also reviews both suspension decisions (Art. 9(2) DMA) and exemption decisions (Art. 10(2) DMA) once a year.

CHAPTER 6
CONDUCT OBLIGATIONS FOR GATEKEEPERS (ART. 5–7 DMA)

Lucas Gasser/Jochen Hegener

Bibliography: Achleitner, 'Selbstbegünstigung als Konzept des Marktmissbrauchs unter Art. 102 AEUV. Das Grundsatzurteil des EuG zu Google Shopping als Initialzündung für einen Wandel in der Digitalwirtschaft? – Anmerkung zum Urteil des EuG v. 10.11.2021, Rs. T-612/17 (Google und Alphabet/ Kommission [Google Shopping])', EuR 2022, 253; Achleitner, 'Digital Markets Act beschlossen: Verhaltenspflichten und Rolle nationaler Wettbewerbsbehörden', NZKart 2022, 359; Basedow, 'Das Rad neu erfunden: Zum Vorschlag für einen Digital Markets Act', ZEuP 2021, 217; Fiebig, 'Meistbegünstigungs- und Preisparitätsklauseln im Internetvertrieb', NZKart 2014, 122; Grünwald, 'Gekommen, um zu bleiben? – § 19a GWB im Lichte des DMA-Entwurfs', NZKart 2021, 496; Haus/Weusthof, 'The Digital Markets Act – a Gatekeeper's Nightmare?', WuW 2021, 318; Herbers, 'Der Digital Markets Act (DMA) kommt – neue Dos and Don'ts für Gatekeeper in der Digitalwirtschaft', RDi 2022, 252; Hoffer/Lehr, 'Onlineplattformen und Big Data auf dem Prüfstand – Gemeinsame Betrachtung der Fälle Amazon, Google und Facebook', NZKart 2019, 10; Khan, 'Amazon's Antitrust Paradox', YaleLJ 2017, 710; Kumkar, 'Der Digital Markets Act nach dem Trilog-Verfahren', RDi 2022, 347; Lichtenberg, 'Die Bedingungen des App Stores auf dem Prüfstand', NZKart 2021, 551; Podszun, 'The Digital Markets Act: What's in it for Consumers?', EuCML 2022, 1; Podszun, 'Should Gatekeepers Be Allowed to Combine Data? Ideas for Art. 5(a) of the Draft Digital Markets Act', GRUR-Int 2022, 197; Polley/Konrad, 'Der Digital Markets Act – Brüssels neues Regulierungskonzept für Digitale Märkte', WuW 2021, 198; Quandt, 'Der App-Store als Kartellrechtsproblem', EuZW 2021, 13; Reumann/Weber, 'Selbstbegünstigung im Kartellrecht – Marktmachtmissbrauch superdominanter Plattformen?', NZKart 2022, 314; Schweitzer, 'The Art to Make Gatekeeper Positions Contestable and the Challenge to Know What Is Fair: A Discussion of the Digital Markets Act Proposal', ZEuP 2021, 503; Völcker/Benditz, 'Die Entwicklung des europäischen Kartellrechts im Jahr 2021', EuZW 2022, 247; Westermann, 'Der geplante Digital Markets Act: Europäische Regulierung zentraler Plattformdienste außerhalb des Kartellrechts?', ZHR 186 (2022), 325; Wolf/Brüggemann, 'Der Digital Markets Act und § 19a GWB' (D-Kart, 19.7.2022) <https://www.d-kart.de/blog/2022/07/19/agenda-2025-der-digital-markets-act-und-%C2%A719a-gwb/> (last accessed: 12.7.2023); Zimmer/Göhsl, 'Vom New Competition Tool zum Digital Markets Act: Die geplante EU-Regulierung für digitale Gatekeeper', ZWeR 2021, 29.

A. Overview

1 Conduct obligations for gatekeepers are at the heart of the Digital Markets Act. The conduct obligations are intended to **restrict** companies classified as gatekeepers in their **scope of action** in such a way that they are ultimately prevented from further sealing off their positions from competition in relation to their core platform services in digital markets and from behaving unfairly towards other market participants.[1]

2 Numerous abuse proceedings initiated by the antitrust authorities against major digital companies in recent years have been aimed at classifying specific behaviour as abusive and thus implicitly anti-competitive. Regarding the conduct covered by the DMA's **catalogue of obligations**, the (usually very time-consuming) classification by the authorities as anti-competitive is to be dropped in the future. Instead, such conduct is deemed to be **anti-competitive** for all companies designated as gatekeepers (cf. Art. 3(3)–(10) DMA) ***ex ante*** (on a self-executing basis) – i.e. irrespective of official or judicial findings (→ Ch. 3 mn. 10).

3 This approach is central to the DMA: after all, whereas 'conventional' **competition law** usually required years of proceedings and litigation[2] before anti-competitive behaviour could be stopped, gatekeepers can now no longer adopt a wait-and-see approach, but must comply with the DMA's prohibitions and requirements right away.[3] This means that there is no need for any specific assessment of the **actual or likely effects** of a particular form of conduct on competition.[4]

4 This approach also explains why the European Commission did not base the DMA on Art. 103 TFEU, but instead on Art. 114 TFEU (→ Ch. 2 mn. 14). After all, it is not primarily concerned with punishing an infringement of Art. 101 et seqq. TFEU (*ex post*) – although this can admittedly be disputed[5] – but instead with ensuring the **functioning of the internal market** *ex ante* through the catalogue of conduct obligations. In this respect, the DMA is not to be understood as just another instrument of competition law, but instead as **'genuine regulatory law'**.[6]

5 The conduct obligations can essentially be divided into **dos and don'ts**. These are not general requirements applicable to a wide range of circumstances, but instead largely specific requirements for the conduct of gatekeepers in relation to a core platform service (CPS) they provide.[7] Some object to this **strongly normative approach** of

[1] Rec. 7 DMA; regarding the economic background, see rec. 2 DMA; cf. also Herbers RDi 2022, 252.

[2] One example of this is the Google Shopping case, which was initiated back in 2009 and ended (pending the outcome of an appeal) with the judgment of the EGC of 10.11.2021; cf. EGC 10.11.2021 – case T-612/17, ECLI:EU:T:2021:763 = NZKart 2021, 684 – Google Shopping.

[3] Podszun EuCML 2022, 1 (1); Kumkar RDi 2022, 347 (348).

[4] Achleitner NZKart 2022, 359 (360).

[5] For a critical view on the choice of legal basis Basedow ZEuP 2021, 217 (221); Polley/Konrad WuW 2021, 198 (199); Haus/Weusthof WuW 2021, 318 (318 et seq.); Zimmer/Göhsl ZWeR 2021, 29 (33).

[6] Kumkar RDi 2022, 347 (349); Schweitzer ZEuP 2021, 503.

[7] Herbers RDi 2022, 252 (254).

the DMA, pointing out that it also declares conduct that is not anti-competitive or anti-competitive per se to be inadmissible across the board and without considering the individual case.[8]

In the event of non-compliance with the conduct obligations, the European Commission may – in the context of issuing a non-compliance decision pursuant to Art. 29 DMA – impose **fines** pursuant to Art. 30 DMA or **periodic penalty payments** pursuant to Art. 31 DMA (→ Ch. 10 mn. 2 et seqq.). 6

The central conduct obligations for gatekeepers are set out in **Art. 5–7 DMA**.[9] All provisions are intended to be self-executing in accordance with the regulatory focus of the DMA described above. Nevertheless, the provisions **vary in their specificity**: The obligations under Art. 5 DMA are directly applicable without any further specification. The obligations under Art. 6 and 7 DMA, on the other hand, still need to be specified to some extent, primarily by the gatekeeper itself. If the European Commission finds that specification by the gatekeeper is not sufficient, it is also able to specify the obligations itself as part of a 'regulatory dialogue' (Art. 8 DMA).[10] 7

The more precisely, however, a conduct obligation is formulated, the more likely it is that it will require **further development** in the future. This is because the requirements and prohibitions set out in the DMA must be as specific as possible in order to avoid ambiguities that could only be resolved through lengthy administrative or judicial clarification. However, this 'accuracy' of the conduct obligations is often likely to prevent technical changes, which are always to be expected in highly dynamic digital markets, from being covered by the DMA. In this respect, an adjustment of the DMA's conduct obligations on the basis of the **delegated act** of the European Commission, as provided for in Art. 12 DMA following a market investigation pursuant to Art. 19 DMA, is likely and possibly necessary at regular intervals. 8

Furthermore, it remains to be seen whether the requirements of the DMA will actually be **implemented** by gatekeepers without further ado.[11] Decisions made by the European Commission on the basis of the DMA are subject to **judicial review** as a general rule; fines or periodic penalty payments are even subject to an unlimited review of the European Commission's use of discretion. Despite all the intentions of, and assurances given by, the European Commission, systematic application of the DMA in the form of self-execution will probably only be possible after a court decision. 9

Precisely in order to avoid lengthy judicial reviews before the EGC and ECJ due to legal ambiguities in the text of the Regulation, the **European Commission, as the central enforcement body**, will have to fulfil its role as guarantor of a uniform interpretation of the catalogues of obligations from the outset. In this context, cooperation with national authorities and courts is likely to become crucially important (→ Ch. 11 mn. 2). In this respect, it remains to be seen, first and foremost, to what extent the European Commission will rely on this cooperation. The same applies to the question of the extent to which infringements can lead to conflict with national law (in Germany in particular 10

[8] Cf. for example Lichtenberg NZKart 2021, 551 (554).

[9] Further procedural law conduct obligations are laid down in Art. 14 and 15 DMA, → Ch. 9 mn. 4.

[10] Kumkar RDi 2022, 347 (350).

[11] Andreas Mundt, President of the German Federal Cartel Office, recently pointed out this problem: <https://mlexmarketinsight.com/news/insight/self-enforcing-dma-provisions-will-trigger-litigation-mundt-says> (last accessed: 12.7.2023).

with § 19a GWB[12]). Another practical area of development of the DMA is likely to be how consumers can derive direct benefits from its application.[13]

B. Conduct obligations pursuant to Art. 5 DMA

I. Overview

Art. 5(2)	Prohibition of the combination of personal data
Art. 5(3)	Prohibition of the use of most-favoured nation clauses
Art. 5(4)	Obligation to allow communication to end users
Art. 5(5)	Obligation to grant end users access to services of business users
Art. 5(6)	Prohibition on restricting users' legal remedies
Art. 5(7)	Prohibition on tying
Art. 5(8)	Prohibition on requiring registration with other core platforms
Art. 5(9)	Obligation to provide advertisers with information on advertising prices
Art. 5(10)	Obligation to provide publishers with information on advertising prices

II. Prohibition of the combination of personal data (Art. 5(2) DMA)

11 Art. 5(2) DMA prohibits gatekeepers from combining personal data in four specific scenarios.[14] All four scenarios build on previously **known behaviours** of major digital companies:[15]

- using personal data for (online) advertising purposes obtained by a gatekeeper through its services for third parties (a),
- combining personal data obtained in different services of the gatekeeper (or from third parties) (b),
- using personal data from one service of the gatekeeper to offer another service of the gatekeeper (c), and
- combining personal data by signing in end users of a core platform service to another service of the gatekeeper for the purpose of combination (d).

12 The purpose of these prohibitions is to limit the advantage associated with the central position held by gatekeepers. This advantage for gatekeepers essentially consists of the opportunity, arising from their central position, to accumulate and **combine data** from **different user sources** (cf. rec. 36 DMA). Rec. 36 DMA also states that the gatekeeper should provide end users with a less personalised alternative that must not differ in quality from the service requiring consent, unless a degradation of quality is due to the reduction in the data collected (cf. also rec. 37 DMA).

[12] On the problem of the DMA in relation to § 19a GWB, cf. in particular Westermann ZHR 186 (2022), 325; Grünwald NZKart 2021, 496; Zimmer/Göhsl ZWeR 2021, 29 (57); Polley/Konrad WuW 2021, 198 (199); Wolf/Brüggemann, 'Der Digital Markets Act und § 19a GWB' (D-Kart, 19.7.2022).

[13] Podszun EuCML 2022, 1.

[14] For a critical discussion of this prohibition, cf. in particular Podszun GRUR-Int 2022, 197.

[15] Achleitner NZKart 2022, 359 (362).

In certain circumstances gatekeepers may, however, continue to combine personal data in the scenarios described. This is subject to the provision that the end user is given a **choice** and has ultimately **consented** to the relevant processing. In the event that consent is refused or withdrawn, Art. 5(2) subpara. 2 DMA stipulates that the gatekeeper shall not repeat its request for consent made to the user more than once within a period of one year. 13

Not giving consent should also not be more difficult than giving consent (cf. rec. 37 DMA).[16] In addition, when the gatekeeper requests consent from the end user, it should proactively present a **user-friendly solution** to the end user to provide, modify or withdraw consent in an explicit, clear and straightforward manner (cf. rec. 37 DMA). As to its form, consent should be given by a clear affirmative action or statement establishing a freely given, specific, informed and unambiguous indication of agreement by the end user (cf. rec. 37 DMA with reference to the GDPR). In the process of granting consent, the gatekeeper should also inform the end user that not giving consent will lead to a less personalised offer, but that the end user can still use the platform service without certain functionalities being suppressed (cf. rec. 37 DMA). It should also be as easy to **withdraw consent** as to give it (cf. rec. 37 DMA). 14

The gatekeeper's opportunity to make use of exemptions for data processing provided for in the GDPR is not affected by Art. 5(2) DMA (Art. 5(2) subpara. 3 DMA, Art. 6(1)(c), (1)(d) and (1)(e) GDPR). 15

▶ **Summary:** Users will no longer have to tolerate a gatekeeper combining personal data from different services unless the user has explicitly consented to this. 16

III. Prohibition of the use of most-favoured nation clauses (Art. 5(3) DMA)

Art. 5(3) DMA provides for a prohibition of most-favoured nation clauses. Accordingly, gatekeepers must allow their business users to offer those services which they offer through the gatekeeper also through other online intermediation services at better conditions. Most-favoured nation clauses are considered to be particularly anti-competitive, insofar as business users cannot offer the products via other platforms at conditions that are more advantageous for the market counterparty if such clauses are complied with (cf. rec. 39 DMA). This can generally hinder the **differentiation of offerings** and the **emergence of platforms competing** with the gatekeeper.[17] The prohibition should therefore have positive effects from a consumer's point of view in the form of lower prices. 17

The European Commission's decision of 4.5.2017 served as a model for this prohibition.[18] In this decision, the European Commission took the view that Amazon was abusing its dominant positions on the markets for retail distribution of English language and German language e-books, in breach of Art. 102 TFEU, by requiring e-book suppliers to notify Amazon of more favourable or alternative terms and conditions they offered elsewhere, and also to make available to Amazon terms and conditions which directly or indirectly depended on the terms and conditions offered to another e-book retailer (**parity** 18

---

[16] Regarding the characteristics of consent in relation to the General Data Protection Regulation (GDPR) and the associated problem of a possible double penalty, see also Polley/Konrad WuW 2021, 198 (202).

[17] Polley/Konrad WuW 2021, 198 (202).

[18] Case AT.40153, OJ 2017 C 264, 7 – Amazon.

clauses).[19] Another prominent case on (narrow) **best price clauses** is the Booking.com case, on which the German Federal Court of Justice (BGH) has since ruled.[20]

19 ▶ **Summary:** This means that business users can no longer be prevented by a gatekeeper from offering their products also on other platforms at better conditions.

IV. Obligation to allow communication with end users (Art. 5(4) DMA)

20 Art. 5(4) DMA prohibits gatekeepers from preventing their business users from **communicating directly** with end users. In this respect, business users can no longer be obliged to exclusively use the gatekeeper's services for communication, and consequently also for advertising their own services. In return, end users are thus also given the fundamental opportunity to obtain information, on the gatekeeper's platform, about the services offered by business users and their (potentially more favourable) offerings. In this respect, Art. 5(4) DMA gives users the opportunity to **enter into commercial relationships independently of the gatekeeper** (cf. rec. 40 DMA).

21 The provision is presumably inspired by the European Commission's case against **Apple**.[21] First, Apple had required app developers to use Apple's own in-app purchasing system for in-app purchases and had provided for commission of 30 % to be paid to Apple. Second, Apple restricted the options available to inform users about alternative purchase options.[22] This was the subject of a complaint lodged with the Commission by **Spotify**, which wanted to use the iOS app to inform its users that they could upgrade to a Spotify Premium subscription on the Spotify website.

22 ▶ **Summary:** Gatekeepers can no longer prevent business users from communicating their products and alternative ways of purchasing these products on the gatekeeper's platform. Conversely, this opens up the opportunity for end users to obtain information about suitable alternatives from the business user directly on the gatekeeper's platform.

V. Obligation to grant end users access to services of business users (Art. 5(5) DMA)

23 Supplementary to Art. 5(4) DMA, gatekeepers are obliged, in Art. 5(5) DMA, to allow end users to **access and use**, through the gatekeeper's core platform services, content, subscriptions, features or other items, by using **software applications of a business user**, including where the end users acquired such items from the relevant business user without using the core platform services of the gatekeeper.

24 End users are thus also given the opportunity to use **services offered by business users via other (cheaper) channels** than those offered by the gatekeeper. This applies even if the initial contact between the business user and the end user was established via a service offered by the gatekeeper. One example might involve users of an Apple iPhone also being able to use apps on their iPhone that they purchased in app stores other than Apple's own App Store.

---

[19] Cf. Fiebig NZKart 2014, 122 for a good overview of similar cases.

[20] BGH 18.5.2021 – KVR 54/20, GRUR 2021, 1213 – Booking.com.

[21] Case AT.40437.

[22] European Commission, 'Antitrust: Commission sends Statement of Objections to Apple on App Store rules for music streaming providers', press release, 30.4.2021, IP/21/2061.

▶ **Summary:** End users can now choose alternative ways of obtaining the services offered by a business user through a gatekeeper, but also through alternative channels. The gatekeeper can no longer categorically prevent alternative commercial relationships between its users. 25

VI. Prohibition on restricting users' legal remedies (Art. 5(6) DMA)

Art. 5(6) DMA sets out the prohibition on directly or indirectly restricting users' ability to seek legal remedies. The opportunity for business users or end users to lodge complaints with the competent administrative bodies or public authorities, including national courts, must therefore be preserved. The prohibition is intended to be **far-reaching**, meaning that ultimately any practice (e.g. an agreement on confidentiality clauses) that inhibits or hinders users in raising their concerns is prohibited (cf. rec. 42 DMA). 26

This means, for example, that gatekeepers cannot disadvantage a distributor or subject the latter to other consequences if the distributor lodges a **complaint** about (possibly) unlawful business practices of the gatekeeper with the competent authorities. The same applies to **restrictions on the place of jurisdiction**: for example, in proceedings before the German Federal Cartel Office,[23] Amazon had voluntarily agreed no longer to maintain a regulation based on which Luxembourg was the exclusive place of jurisdiction. This had made it difficult for smaller distributors, in particular, to seek legal remedies at all. 27

Measures taken by the gatekeeper to **combat illegal online content** are not, however, covered by Art. 5(6) DMA. There is also the option of agreeing on valid complaints-handling mechanisms and out-of-court **dispute settlement mechanisms** in accordance with European and national law (cf. rec. 42 DMA). 28

▶ **Summary:** Users can now ideally enforce their rights independently of contractual restrictions imposed by a gatekeeper without the risk of commercial disadvantages. 29

VII. Prohibition on tying (Art. 5(7) DMA)

Art. 5(7) DMA stipulates that gatekeepers may not **require** either business users or end users to use **specific services of the gatekeeper** (prohibition on tying). These include identification services, web browser engines, payment services or technical services of the gatekeeper. The draft version of the DMA only covered the identification service in its Art. 5(e) DMA. 30

The provision is intended to protect business users from gatekeepers imposing the use of individual products on them if they do not actively choose to use the product in question. Business users are thus protected in their **freedom of choice**. In turn, this is designed to give every provider in every market segment the same chances of winning the favour of users – regardless of their position in another market segment. It has, however, been raised as a point of criticism that the use of a **uniform identification service for all apps** could ultimately be in the end user's interest.[24] 31

[23] Case B2–88/18.
[24] See Polley/Konrad WuW 2021, 198 (203).

32 Art. 5(7) DMA prohibits a gatekeeper, for example, from making access to its app store dependent on app developers integrating the gatekeeper's own service (e.g. an **Apple ID**[25]) into their apps.

33 ▶ **Summary:** The provision thus offers users the opportunity to choose combinations of different services themselves. Consequently, a 'one-stop solution' offered by a gatekeeper for handling various interconnected services will no longer necessarily have to be used by users. Users are still free, however, to opt actively for uniform gatekeeper solutions.

VIII. Prohibition on requiring registration with other core platform services (Art. 5(8) DMA)

34 Art. 5(8) DMA supplements the tying prohibition in Art. 5(7) DMA by stipulating that neither business users nor end users can be obliged to **subscribe to, or register with, a service offered by the gatekeeper** if they actually only want to use another service of the gatekeeper. This now prohibited practice sometimes allows gatekeepers to attract new users to possibly less prominent or successful services. Even if the additional service were free of charge for users, the gatekeeper can still gain a further potential advantage through the data obtained in the process (cf. rec. 44 DMA). For example, Google can no longer require advertisers that want to run YouTube ads to also use Google's advertising platform Google Ads.

35 The provision – at least according to the wording – does not cover what are known as **single log-ins**. This means that a user that is offered the option of using several services with a single log-in cannot withdraw from this combined offer.

36 ▶ **Summary:** In the future, users will therefore have the opportunity to decide largely for themselves which services of the gatekeeper they want to register for or subscribe to. This should rule out any obligation to register for unwanted services.

IX. Obligation to provide advertisers and publishers with information on advertising prices (Art. 5(9) and (10) DMA)

37 Art. 5(9) DMA stipulates that **advertisers** for which the gatekeeper provides online advertising services must be provided, on request, with **information on a daily basis free of charge** concerning each **advertisement placed by publishers**. This information concerns

- the price and fees paid by that advertiser for each of the relevant online advertising services provided by the gatekeeper (a),
- the remuneration received by the publisher, subject to the publisher's consent (b), and
- the metrics on which each of the prices, fees and remunerations are calculated (c).

38 In the event that a publisher does not consent to the sharing of information within the meaning of Art. 5(9)(b) DMA, the gatekeeper is nevertheless obliged to provide the advertiser free of charge with information concerning the daily **average remuneration** received by that publisher, including any deductions and surcharges, for the relevant advertisements.

[25] For comprehensive information on the admissibility of the app store under competition law, see Lichtenberg NZKart 2021, 551.

The purpose of the obligation is primarily to boost **transparency** regarding the conditions and prices based on which gatekeepers offer online advertising services (adtech) to business users. This is designed, in turn, to allow advertisers to switch between companies providing online advertising services and, in doing so, find the best online advertising provider available on the market for them (cf. rec. 45 DMA). **Google** and **Facebook** have often been accused of exploiting the lack of transparency of intermediation services in the field of online advertising to enforce excessive prices.[26] In the future, a gatekeeper cannot refuse to release information about what proportion of advertising spend actually reaches publishers etc. 39

Art. 5(10) DMA extends the gatekeepers' obligation to provide information to include requests from **publishers**. 40

▶ **Summary:** Advertisers and publishers that either place advertisements with gatekeepers or display advertisements for gatekeepers have the right to request that they receive the aforementioned information from the gatekeeper, allowing them to compare different offers. 41

C. Conduct obligations pursuant to Art. 6 DMA

I. Overview

Art. 6(2)	Prohibition of data use in competition with business users
Art. 6(3)	Obligation to allow un-installation of pre-installed software and changes to default settings
Art. 6(4)	Obligation to allow the installation of third-party software
Art. 6(5)	Prohibition of self-preferencing in ranking, indexing and crawling
Art. 6(6)	Prohibition of the restriction of the ability to switch between services
Art. 6(7)	Obligation to ensure interoperability
Art. 6(8)	Obligation to provide advertisers and publishers with access to performance measuring tools
Art. 6(9)	Obligation to grant end users access to data
Art. 6(10)	Obligation to grant business users access to data
Art. 6(11)	Obligation of search engine operators to provide search data based on FRAND conditions
Art. 6(12)	Obligation to grant access to app stores, online search engines and online social network services based on FRAND conditions
Art. 6(13)	Prohibition of disproportionate conditions for termination

[26] Cf. UK Competition and Markets Authority, 'Online Platforms and Digital Advertising, Final Report 2020' (1.7.2020) <https://www.gov.uk/cma-cases/online-platforms-and-digital-advertising-market-study> (last accessed: 12.7.2023), para. 5.334 et seqq.; cf. German Federal Cartel Office, 'Sektoruntersuchung Online-Werbung, Diskussionsbericht' (29.8.2022) <https://www.bundeskartellamt.de/SharedDocs/Publikation/DE/Sektoruntersuchungen/Sektoruntersuchung_Online_Werbung_Diskussionsbericht_lang.html> (last accessed: 12.7.2023), para. 202.

II. Prohibition of data use in competition with business users (Art. 6(2) DMA)

42 Art. 6(2) DMA prohibits the use of data of business users of the gatekeeper that is not publicly available to compete with these business users on another market level or segment. This is understood to mean that gatekeepers may not use data generated on, or in connection with, their own core platform services, concerning or from business users with which they are in direct competition (on another market level or segment), to compete with those same users.[27] It is expected that this prohibition will become particularly relevant for **online marketplaces** or for data stored on **cloud computing services.**[28]

43 Art. 6(2) DMA clarifies that the prohibition refers to **data** that is **not publicly available** and can be inferred from, or collected through, the commercial activities of business users or their customers on the relevant core platform services. The regulation also covers data generated on services provided together with, or in support of, the gatekeeper's core platform services. This includes, for example, click, search, view and voice data.

44 This means, for example, that a gatekeeper must not use **data on visits to product pages, sales patterns or turnover** that it collects in its role as operator of an **online marketplace** for business users in order to then compete with these business users in its role as a product/service provider. It is precisely here that competitive problems arise in connection with the possibility of obtaining sensitive data from competitors. This can be the case especially in scenarios in which a gatekeeper provides its business users with a core platform service for the distribution of goods and at the same time also acts as a provider of goods that business users also offer (cf. rec. 46 DMA with further examples).

45 A similar scenario involving a **dual role** played by a gatekeeper is conceivable if a business user purchases online advertising services from a gatekeeper on a core platform service, but at the same time the gatekeeper itself, as a company, provides similar services or sells similar goods to the advertised services and products (rec. 47 DMA). In this respect, gatekeepers and business users are also in a **competitive relationship**. Insofar as the business user makes data relevant to competition available to the gatekeeper or generates this sort of data on the gatekeeper's core platform service, this could also result in a competitive advantage for the gatekeeper.

46 Rec. 48 DMA also clarifies that the obligation set out in Art. 6(2) DMA should also extend to data provided or generated in the context of the offering of a **cloud computing service** or a **software or app store**. Important clarification is also contained in rec. 46 DMA. According to this recital, the prohibition of data use set out in Art. 6(2) DMA applies to the gatekeeper as a whole, including but not limited to its business unit in which the gatekeeper competes with the business users of its core platform service.

47 The prohibition is based on the European Commission's proceedings on Amazon Buy Box and Facebook. The Amazon Buy Box[29] proceedings concerned, inter alia (and crucially in the present case), Amazon's alleged practice of relying on the business data provided by independent sellers to make its own retail decisions. Amazon acts in a dual capacity on its **Amazon Marketplace**: on the one hand, the company makes the marketplace available to independent sellers, but on the other hand, it also acts as a seller itself on this marketplace. By providing its core platform service to those independent sellers (= business users), Amazon has access to non-public business data of these independent sellers. This includes, for example, the number of products ordered

[27] Cf. Achleitner NZKart 2022, 359 (362).
[28] Cf. Herbers RDi 2022, 252 (256).
[29] Case AT.40703.

and delivered, revenue generated, the number of times the seller's offers are viewed or shipping data. Before the proceedings were opened, the European Commission had concluded that this data flowed into Amazon's systems automatically and was being processed there, meaning that the company could use it for its own purposes as a retailer.[30] Similar allegations have been circulating for some time in other jurisdictions, particularly in the US.[31]

Proceedings against Facebook[32] are based on a similar scenario. Specifically, Facebook makes its social network available to business users (including operators of online classifieds services) so that they can place ads. At the same time, however, the accusation has been levelled that Facebook uses the data resulting from these ads to optimise its own **Facebook Marketplace** (an online classifieds service) as a direct competitor of its business users.[33] 48

▶ **Summary:** Business users are to be protected from a gatekeeper using data resulting from the use of its core platform service by business users to compete simultaneously with these users on another market level or segment. 49

III. Obligation to allow un-installation of pre-installed software and changes to default settings (Art. 6(3) DMA)

Art. 6(3) DMA sets out the gatekeeper's obligation to allow the un-installation of pre-installed software and the modification of default settings related to the gatekeeper's products or services. A **selection screen** for the most important services (online search services, virtual assistants and web browsers) must be offered in respect of the default settings (Art. 6(3) subpara. 2 DMA).[34] By contrast, an exception to the obligation to allow un-installation is provided in Art. 6(3) subpara. 1 DMA for software applications that are **essential for the functioning** of the operating system or of the device and that cannot technically be offered on a standalone basis by third parties. 50

The obligation is derived from the decision of the European Commission of 18.7.2018 in the **Google Android** proceedings.[35] This decision imposed a fine of €4.34 billion on Google. Among other things, the European Commission criticised Google's practice of requiring all manufacturers to pre-install the 'Google Search' application and the Google browser 'Chrome' on their devices as a condition for licensing Google's own app store. In addition, payments were made by Google to specific large manufacturers and mobile network operators on condition that they exclusively pre-installed the 'Google Search' app on their devices.[36] 51

[30] Cf. Representation of the European Commission in Germany, 'EU-Kartellwächter werfen Amazon Bruch der Wettbewerbsregeln vor' (10.11.2020) <https://germany.representation.ec.europa.eu/news/eu-kartellwachter-werfen-amazon-bruch-der-wettbewerbsregeln-vor-2020-11-10_de> (last accessed: 12.7.2023); cf. also Völcker/Benditz EuZW 2022, 247.

[31] Cf. in detail Khan YaleLJ 2017, 710 (780 et seqq.).

[32] Case AT.40684.

[33] European Commission, 'Antitrust: Commission opens investigation into possible anticompetitive conduct of Facebook' (4.6.2021) <https://ec.europa.eu/commission/presscorner/detail/en/ip_21_2848> (last accessed: 12.7.2023).

[34] Cf. also rec. 49 DMA; Achleitner NZKart 2022, 359 (362).

[35] Case AT.40099.

[36] Cf. European Commission, 'Antitrust: Commission fines Google €4.34 billion for illegal practices regarding Android mobile devices to strengthen dominance of Google's search engine' (18.7.2018) <https://ec.europa.eu/commission/presscorner/detail/en/IP_18_4581> (last accessed: 12.7.2023). The European Commission's decision is currently being challenged by Google before the EGC in case T-604/18.

52 ▶ **Summary:** Gatekeepers are to be prevented from using pre-installations and default settings to attract end users to their own services, giving them an advantage over competitors.

IV. Obligation to allow the installation of third-party software (Art. 6(4) DMA)

53 Art. 6(4) DMA sets out the obligation of gatekeepers to allow and technically enable the installation of apps from other providers. Specifically, this means that the gatekeeper has to tolerate and permit the installation and use of third-party software applications (or apps) and third-party operated stores for software applications (or app stores) that use the gatekeeper's operating system or interoperate with it (for information on the **concept of interoperability**, see also Art. 6(7) and 7 DMA). In this context, pursuant to Art. 6(4) subpara. 1 sent. 2 DMA, the gatekeeper must also not prevent the downloaded third-party apps or app stores operated by third parties from prompting end users to decide whether they want to set that app or store as their default. According to Art. 6(4) subpara. 1 sent. 3 DMA, the gatekeeper must technically enable end users, who decide to set the app as their default, to carry out that change easily.

54 Pursuant to Art. 6(4) subpara. 2 DMA, the gatekeeper can only **restrict** this option to the extent that this is strictly necessary and appropriate to protect the **security and integrity of its systems**. In addition, the gatekeeper must provide sufficient justification for these measures. Pursuant to rec. 50 DMA, this is to include any design options that need to be implemented and maintained in order for the hardware or the operating system to be protected against unauthorised access, by ensuring that security controls necessary for the hardware or the operating system concerned cannot be compromised.

55 Pursuant to Art. 6(4) subpara. 3 DMA, a gatekeeper can also take measures and apply settings other than default settings to the extent that they are strictly necessary and proportionate, enabling end **users to effectively protect themselves** in relation to third-party software applications or software application stores operated by third parties. Again, these measures also must be duly justified by the gatekeeper.

56 This conduct obligation is evidently based on Apple's practice of preventing users from installing apps from third-party providers – i.e. apps independent of **Apple's own App Store**.[37]

57 ▶ **Summary:** Users are, therefore, to be provided with a wider range of possible combinations of different apps and software offerings, and third-party providers of apps and app stores are also to be protected.

V. Prohibition of self-preferencing in ranking, indexing and crawling (Art. 6(5) DMA)

58 Gatekeepers are also prohibited from any form of self-preferencing in ranking, indexing, and crawling (Art. 6(5) DMA). Self-preferencing is not permitted, neither by legal, commercial, or technical means (cf. rec. 52 DMA). **Crawling** refers to the process in which web pages are searched and analysed by what is known as a web crawler. In the

[37] Cf. European Commission, 'Antitrust: Commission opens investigations into Apple's App Store rules', press release (16.6.2020) <https://ec.europa.eu/commission/presscorner/detail/en/ip_20_1073> (last accessed: 12.7.2023); on the antitrust assessment of Apple's practice, cf. also Quandt EuZW 2021, 13; Lichtenberg NZKart 2021, 551.

context of **search engines**, the crawling results are then displayed on the results page. The crawler usually gets from one website to the next via hyperlinks and stores the results found as part of this process. The process of **indexing** goes together with crawling and refers to the inclusion of web pages in an arranged directory, the index. In both crawling and indexing, a gatekeeper can theoretically **exploit its position to favour specific content** (cf. rec. 51 DMA).

The order in which results are displayed to users after indexing is then determined by the **ranking**. In the context of the DMA, ranking covers all forms of relative prominence, including display, rating, linking or voice results and is also to include instances where a core platform service presents or communicates only one result to the end user (Art. 2 point (22) DMA; cf. also rec. 52 DMA). This ranking also has to be carried out on the basis of **transparent, fair and non-discriminatory conditions** in accordance with Art. 6(5) sent. 2 DMA. 59

The EGC's **Google Shopping** decision of 10.11.2021[38] and the prior proceedings of the European Commission[39] were certainly paradigmatic for the prohibition of self-preferencing. Google Inc. and its parent company Alphabet Inc. had, according to the European Commission's findings, placed and displayed their own price comparison service on Google's general search results pages in a more prominent position than competing price comparison services. The EGC considered this to constitute inadmissible discrimination of competitors, exploiting Google's own market power, and, as a result, an infringement of Art. 102 TFEU.[40] 60

▶ **Summary:** Gatekeepers are to be prevented from being able to favour other services of their own over competitors on the basis of offering search functions. 61

VI. Prohibition of the restriction of the ability to switch between services (Art. 6(6) DMA)

Art. 6(6) DMA sets out the prohibition on restricting, technically or otherwise, end users' ability to switch between services. This means that gatekeepers must allow end users to switch, or subscribe to, different software applications and services when they access services and applications via the gatekeeper's core platform services.[41] Pursuant to Art. 6(6) DMA, this applies for instance to the **choice of Internet access services** by end users. One example of this could be a scenario in which a gatekeeper wants to prevent its end users from switching to another service provider that is not one of the providers the gatekeeper has concluded an exclusive agreement with. 62

The purpose of this provision is to give end users a wider choice of services and thus to promote competition. It should be noted, however, that pursuant to rec. 53 DMA, the **mere offering of a given product or service** to end users by the gatekeeper, including by means of pre-installation, as well as the improvement of the offering to end users, should not be construed as constituting a prohibited barrier to switching. 63

▶ **Summary:** Consequently, this provision is consistent with the other provisions on increasing flexibility for users. As well as giving users the option to change pre-installed software and default settings and to gain effective access to offers from other providers, 64

[38] European Commission 27.6.2017 – case AT.39740 – Google Search (Shopping).

[39] Cf. also the comments in Achleitner EuR 2022, 253; Reumann/Weber NZKart 2022, 314; Hoffer/Lehr NZKart 2019, 10.

[40] A decision by the ECJ on the appeal filed by Google is still pending at this time.

[41] Cf. rec. 53 DMA; Achleitner NZKart 2022, 359 (362).

the prohibition set out in Art. 6(6) DMA also protects the actual possibility for users to switch.

VII. Obligation to ensure interoperability (Art. 6(7) DMA)

65 Art. 6(7) DMA contains a general obligation for gatekeepers to ensure interoperability. This means that a gatekeeper must allow providers of services and providers of hardware **effective interoperability** of the services or products offered with the hardware and software features of an operating system or virtual assistant offered by the gatekeeper, insofar as the gatekeeper is actually able to do so. Furthermore, the gatekeeper is to grant business users and third-party providers **effective access** to the same operating system, hardware or software features available to the gatekeeper for its own (additional) services.

66 The reason for this obligation is the limitation of competition caused by the lack of interoperability. Where alternative providers of services or hardware are prevented from accessing the same operating system, hardware or software functions available to the gatekeeper for the provision of its own complementary or supporting services or hardware, this evidently has the potential to **restrict innovation by alternative providers** (cf. rec. 57 DMA). In this respect, the prohibition against Apple preventing Spotify from using the **Siri service** when Apple Music has Siri integrated at the same time is cited as a practical example.[42]

67 Pursuant to Art. 6(7) subpara. 2 DMA, however, these provisions do not in turn prevent the gatekeeper from taking strictly necessary and proportionate measures to ensure that interoperability does not compromise the integrity of its operating system, virtual assistant, hardware or software features. In such cases, however, the gatekeeper must provide sufficient justification for these measures.

68 ▶ **Summary:** The provision therefore promotes the opportunity for other providers to compete with the gatekeeper with regard to ancillary services related to core platform services.

VIII. Obligation to provide advertisers and publishers with access to performance measuring tools (Art. 6(8) DMA)

69 The gatekeeper's obligation to provide both advertisers and publishers with access to performance measuring tools is set out in Art. 6(8) DMA. In this respect, transparency with regard to the **effect of advertisements inventory** shall be promoted: Upon request, advertisers and publishers (or third parties authorised by them) will be provided with access to the **performance measuring tools** of the gatekeeper free of charge.[43] The gatekeeper must make the data pursuant to Art. 6(8) sent. 2 DMA available in such a way that advertisers and publishers can run their own verification and measurement tools to assess the performance of the core platform services provided by gatekeepers. In this respect, this obligation is related, in substantive terms, to the requirements set out in **Art. 5(9) and (10) DMA**.

70 This provision is intended to put a stop to the often cited lack of transparency regarding the effect of advertisements.[44] According to rec. 58 DMA, **authorised third**

[42] Cf. Achleitner NZKart 2022, 359 (362).
[43] Cf. Achleitner NZKart 2022, 359 (362).
[44] Cf. the comments above on Art. 5(9) and (10) DMA; cf. also rec. 58 DMA.

parties acting on behalf of a company placing advertising (such as advertising agencies) are also to benefit from the provision.

▶ **Summary:** The aim is to ensure (as was already the case with Art. 5(9) and (10) DMA) increased options for verifying the efficiency of advertisements on gatekeepers' core platform services. 71

IX. Obligation to grant end users access to data (Art. 6(9) DMA)

Art. 6(9) DMA sets out the obligation for gatekeepers to provide end users and third parties authorised by an end user, at their request and **free of charge**, with **access to data obtained in connection with the core platform service**. Access includes data provided by the end user or generated in connection with the latter's use of the core platform service. Pursuant to rec. 59 DMA, the data is to be provided in a format that can be immediately and effectively accessed. The gatekeeper must also provide free tools (e.g. application programming interfaces, API) that facilitate effective use of this data portability. In addition, data access must be guaranteed in the form of permanent real-time access.[45] 72

The central aim of this provision is to ensure that end users can **transfer their data to other platforms** and use it there. In other words, users should no longer be prevented from switching to another provider or also from using different services (multi-homing) because they can only access specific data via the current platform service. This is designed to prevent gatekeepers from undermining the contestability of core platform services or the innovation potential of the dynamic digital sector. Facilitating switching or enabling **multi-homing** is to lead, in turn, to increased choice for end users and to act as an incentive for gatekeepers and competing business users to innovate (cf. rec. 59 DMA). 73

Criticism has been levelled that this provision could be problematic due to the fact that there is no **universally applicable format** in which the data can be made available. Moreover, it will entail considerable effort for gatekeepers to provide the data described. Additionally, gatekeepers also run the risk of disclosing **trade secrets**, because the data to be disclosed also encompasses data that gatekeepers derive from user data.[46] In this respect – as with regard to many aspects of the DMA – there is still a need for clarification of the problems resulting from the detailed requirements. 74

▶ **Summary:** Users, therefore, have a comprehensive opportunity to access the data they have provided and that has been generated by using the core platform service. This results in increased (switching) options for users. Because a gatekeeper can no longer bind users to its services solely through exclusive access to their data. 75

X. Obligation to grant business users access to data (Art. 6(10) DMA)

Art. 6(10) DMA extends the group of persons entitled to access data under para. 9 to **business users and third parties authorised** by them. The provision explicitly also concerns the right of access to the data of end users that business users reach via the core platform service. By way of limitation, sent. 2 clarifies that, with regard to **personal da-** 76

[45] In summary, the data described therefore has to be provided free of charge, effectively, in high quality and in real time. Within this context, it is sometimes noted that the DMA is also a test case for the EU Data Act, because the latter also provides for such data access rights, but for data generated by IoT devices; cf. Herbers RDi 2022, 252 (257).

[46] Polley/Konrad WuW 2021, 198 (203).

ta, the gatekeeper may only provide access to this data where the data is directly connected with use of the products or services offered by the relevant business user through the relevant core platform service. Further, end users must opt in to such sharing by giving their consent (cf. rec. 60 DMA). In all other respects, the comments on para. 9 (→ mn. 72) apply accordingly.

XI. Obligation of search engine operators to provide search data based on FRAND conditions (Art. 6(11) DMA)

77 The obligation for gatekeepers to provide access to search data based on FRAND conditions to other online search engine providers and third parties commissioned by the operator of an online search engine to process such data upon their request is found in Art. 6(11) DMA. FRAND conditions are understood to mean fair, reasonable and non-discriminatory access to data.[47] Search data includes **ranking, query, click and view data** related to unpaid and paid search results generated by end users via online search engines.

78 Regarding **personal data**, sent. 2 clarifies that this data must be anonymised. This anonymisation should not, however, degrade the quality or usefulness of the data (cf. rec. 61 DMA). Data is anonymised if it is irreversibly altered in such a way that information does not relate to an identified or identifiable natural person or where personal data is rendered anonymous in such a manner that the data subject is not or is no longer identifiable (cf. rec. 61 DMA).

79 The (lack of) access to the data described is an important barrier to entry and expansion for **providers of other online search engines** (cf. rec. 61 DMA). Data access is thus intended to enable competitors of the gatekeeper to improve their own search services by **training** with provided data, and in doing so to strengthen their role in the market.[48]

80 ▶ **Summary:** A gatekeeper, as a search engine operator, cannot deny the provider of a competing online search engine access to the query data of its own search engine if that provider makes an offer based on FRAND terms.

XII. Obligation to grant access to app stores, online search engines and online social network services based on FRAND conditions (Art. 6(12) DMA)

81 Art. 6(12) DMA obliges a gatekeeper to apply FRAND conditions[49] of **access for business users** to its app stores, online search engines and online social networking services designated by the European Commission as core platform services.

82 Compared to the draft version of 2020, the version of the DMA that came into force includes the access obligation not only for app stores, but also for online search engines and online social networking services. Moreover, the original draft did not yet refer to FRAND conditions, but only to FAND (fair and non-discriminatory) conditions. The new check on the appropriateness of access is to be carried out, among other things, by

[47] Cf. regarding requirements for FRAND terms: ECJ 16.7.2015 – case C-170/13, ECLI:EU:C:2015:477 para. 15 – Huawei/ZTE.

[48] Polley/Konrad WuW 2021, 198 (204).

[49] For information on the FRAND concept, cf. above → mn. 77.

way of a **comparison with corresponding offers** made by other providers (cf. rec. 62 DMA).

Price-related access regulations could be the focus of particular attention in the future, because the question of access conditions also includes price, according to rec. 62 DMA. However, it is precisely the amount of **commission that app store operators** charge that has often been criticised.[50] Under the DMA, these or other general access conditions are to be considered unfair if they lead to an imbalance of rights and obligations imposed on business users or confer an advantage on the gatekeeper which is disproportionate to the service provided by the gatekeeper to business users or lead to a disadvantage for business users in providing the same or similar services as the gatekeeper (cf. rec. 62 DMA). 83

Art. 6(12) subpara. 2 DMA also requires **publication** by the gatekeeper of the **general conditions of access**, including an alternative dispute settlement mechanism. The alternative dispute settlement mechanism is to be easily accessible, impartial, independent and free of charge for the business user, without prejudice to the business user's own cost and proportionate measures aimed at preventing the abuse of the dispute settlement mechanism by business users. The mechanism is also intended to be without prejudice to the right of business users to seek redress before judicial authorities (cf. rec. 62 DMA). 84

In addition, Art. 6(12) DMA stipulates in subpara. 3 that the **European Commission** is obliged to **assess** whether the published general conditions of access comply with the gatekeeper's obligation. 85

▶ **Summary:** In the future, business users will be able to gain access to gatekeeper's app stores, online search engines and online social networking services relevant to them based on FRAND conditions. 86

XIII. Prohibition of disproportionate conditions for termination (Art. 6(13) DMA)

Art. 6(13) DMA prohibits gatekeepers from imposing disproportionate conditions for the termination of use of core platform services (or deletion of an account) by business users and end users. Pursuant to Art. 6(13) sent. 2 DMA, a gatekeeper must also ensure that the conditions of termination can be exercised without undue difficulty. This refers, for example, to the period of notice, the form of termination or the grounds for termination. Overall, this should make cancelling a subscription or closing an account no more complicated than creating a profile. Gatekeepers should also not charge additional fees for termination (cf. rec. 63 DMA). 87

▶ **Summary:** Gatekeepers are to be prohibited from preventing their users from leaving a core platform service due to unreasonable effort involved in terminating or deleting an account. 88

D. Conduct obligations pursuant to Art. 7 DMA

Art. 7 DMA follows on from the **interoperability obligation** set out in Art. 6(7) DMA, but refers to interpersonal communications services that are not linked to a mobile telephone number. These include the popular messenger services such as **WhatsApp** 89

[50] Cf. the examples cited by the Dutch competition authority in Autoriteit Consument & Markt, 'Market Study into mobile app stores' (11.4.2019) <http://hbfm.link/9879> (last accessed: 12.7.2023), p. 91 et seq.

or **Signal**. At least with regard to the basic functions, gatekeepers must guarantee interoperability free of charge upon request.

90 The background to this provision is that the most important selection criterion of end users, especially for messenger services, is that of **network effects**: generally, you only use the messenger that overlaps with your own contacts the most. This leads to a preference for messenger services that have already achieved a high level of market penetration, i.e. as many users as possible.

91 To implement these requirements, the DMA requires in Art. 7(2) DMA that interoperability with regard to **basic functions** be enabled immediately after designation as a gatekeeper for a core platform service. This applies, for example, to end-to-end text messages, the transmission of images, the transmission of voice messages and the exchange of files between two individual end users. Step-by-step implementation is planned for more **complex requirements**, such as for group messages and ultimately audio and video calls. This obligation does not, however, apply to social networks.

92 With regard to practical implementation, some have already warned that the interoperability obligation could lead to a loss of **data security** for consumers, especially in cases involving messenger services. This is because it might then be the case that the functionality of specific technology – such as WhatsApp's end-to-end encryption – would no longer be guaranteed.[51] Nevertheless, the DMA creates the preconditions that have long been a matter of course in e-mail transmission: to write a message, you no longer have to use the same messenger service as the recipient of the message.

[51] Cf. Achleitner NZKart 2022, 359 (363).

CHAPTER 7
COMPLIANCE AND REPORTING OBLIGATIONS OF GATEKEEPERS

Jens Peter Schmidt

1 The DMA does not rely solely on compliance with the obligations that are directly applicable to gatekeepers; in addition to public enforcement, it relies on specific **compliance duties** and regular **reporting obligations** to the European Commission for gatekeepers. Compliance refers to the legally proper organisation of a company with the aim of avoiding civil or even criminal liability of the company and its executive bodies. The compliance organisation of a gatekeeper addressed by the DMA now has to ensure that the following functional, monitoring and reporting obligations are met.

A. Internal compliance function (Art. 28 DMA)

2 According to Art. 28(1) DMA, gatekeepers are required to introduce a **compliance function**. The provision set out in Art. 28 DMA contains detailed requirements to be complied with by gatekeepers regarding the compliance function as an organisational unit, the management of the compliance function as well as the duties of the gatekeeper's management body (e.g. Management Board).

I. Resources for the compliance function

3 Pursuant to Art. 28(1) DMA, the compliance function must be **independent** from the **operational functions** of the gatekeeper and composed of one or more **compliance officers**, including the **head** of the compliance function. The gatekeeper is obliged to ensure that the compliance function has sufficient **authority, stature and resources**, as well as **access** to its **management body** (e.g. Management Board or responsible Management Board member) to monitor compliance with the obligations arising from the DMA (Art. 28(2) DMA).

II. Tasks of the head of the compliance function

4 Pursuant to Art. 28(4) DMA, the **head** of the compliance function is assigned the task of raising **concerns** and issuing **warnings** to the gatekeeper's management body where risks of non-compliance with the DMA emerge. This also applies if there are overlaps with supervisory and managerial functions of the management body. The internal division of responsibilities is to avoid conflicts of interest and ensure the independence of the compliance function as a whole (Art. 28(7) DMA). The head of the compliance function acts as the **liaison point** between the gatekeeper and the **European Commission**,

which is why the gatekeeper must inform the European Commission of his or her name and contact details (Art. 28(6) DMA).

III. Remit of the compliance officers

5 Pursuant to Art. 28(5) DMA, the compliance function shall be assigned a **compliance officer** (or several **compliance officers**), including the head of the compliance function (→ mn. 4). The compliance officers have the following tasks:

- **organising, monitoring and supervising** the measures and activities of the gatekeepers (a);
- **informing and advising the management** and **employees** of the gatekeeper on the relevant obligations to comply with (b);
- where applicable, **monitoring compliance** with commitments made binding pursuant to Art. 25 DMA, without prejudice to the Commission being able to appoint independent external experts (c); and
- **cooperating** with the **Commission** for the purpose of the DMA (d).

IV. Remit of the management body (Management Board) of the gatekeeper

6 The head of the compliance function **reports** directly to the gatekeeper's **management body** (Art. 28(4) sent. 1 DMA). It may not be removed without prior approval of the management body (Art. 28(4) sent. 2 DMA). The management body of the gatekeeper must ensure that the head of the compliance function is an **independent senior manager** with distinct responsibility for the compliance function (Art. 28(3) sent. 2 DMA). The internal division of responsibilities and governance arrangements must be defined and overseen by the gatekeeper's management body in such a way that the **independence** of the **compliance function** is guaranteed and conflicts of interest are avoided (Art. 28(7) DMA). With regard to the compliance officers, the management body shall also ensure, pursuant to Art. 28(3) DMA, that they have the professional qualifications, knowledge, experience and ability necessary to fulfil the tasks assigned to them.

7 The DMA explicitly requires the management body to devote sufficient **attention** to management and **compliance** in order to comply with the DMA regulations (Art. 28(9) DMA). The management body is to participate actively in decisions relating to management and compliance and ensure that **adequate resources** are allocated to compliance.

8 At least once a year, the **compliance strategy** is to be reviewed and reapproved by the gatekeeper's management body (Art. 28(8) DMA). If the gatekeeper intentionally or negligently fails to introduce the **compliance function** required in Art. 28 DMA, the European Commission can impose **fines** not exceeding 1 % of the total worldwide turnover in the preceding financial year (Art. 30(3)(j) DMA).

9 Pursuant to Art. 26(1) DMA, the **European Commission** has to take the necessary actions to **monitor** effective **implementation** of, and **compliance** with, the DMA obligations by the gatekeeper. The measures that the European Commission can take to enforce compliance include the appointment of **independent external experts** and **auditors** as well as the appointment of officials from national competent **authorities of the Member States** (Art. 26(2) DMA). *Expressis verbis*, the measures pursuant to Art. 26(1) sent. 2 DMA can also include imposition of an obligation on gatekeepers to retain all documents (i.e. information and data) that the European Commission deems to be rele-

vant to assess implementation of, and compliance with, the obligations – and any decisions made by the European Commission.

B. Review and annual reporting obligation (Art. 8 and 11 DMA)

If a company has been designated as a gatekeeper pursuant to Art. 3 DMA, it must **ensure** and **demonstrate compliance** with the **obligations** laid down in Art. 5, 6 and 7 DMA pursuant to Art. 8(1) DMA. When developing the measures, gatekeepers must observe compliance with applicable law, in particular the GDPR, the ePrivacy Directive, as well as legislation on cybersecurity, consumer protection, product safety and accessibility. 10

Pursuant to Art. 11(1) DMA, gatekeepers must submit a **report** to the European Commission within six months of the designation decision, describing in a detailed and transparent manner the **measures** implemented to ensure **compliance** with the obligations laid down in Art. 5, 6 and 7 DMA. Details relating to form and content of the report as well as to other procedural issues are set out in the **Implementing Regulation**[1] (cf. Art. 8(2) sent. 2, Art. 46(1)(b) DMA). In addition, the European Commission has proposed a **template** that specifies the requirements for these compliance reports. The draft template – that as of writing of this Chapter is under public consultation – will contribute to the standardisation of the reports of the various gatekeepers and it will ideally ensure that sufficient information is provided for the European Commission and third parties to be able to **effectively verify compliance** with the DMA obligations. As it stands, the template is divided into five sections. In addition to formal information on the company (section 1) and the compliance function to be introduced (section 3), a non-confidential version (section 4) as well as a declaration that the compliance report is true, correct and complete (section 5) must be submitted. In substance, section 2 is of great relevance: it provides for an **extensive catalogue** of questions on the **details** of the **compliance measures** carried out. For example, it must be described exactly when and by which technical means which measures were taken and what effects they have. The European Commission reserves the right to further adapt the template over time and may request additional information if it is necessary to evaluate compliance. In addition, according to Art. 11(2) DMA, the gatekeeper must provide a **non-confidential summary** of the report – that is clear and comprehensible (rec. 68 DMA) – which the European Commission makes available on its **website**. This non-confidential publication aims at enabling **third parties** to assess whether gatekeepers are complying with the obligations laid down in the DMA. It will, therefore, be a **highly important** element to enable **third parties** to make their observations known to the European Commission and/or to make use of it in private enforcement actions. The European Commission makes it very clear that such summary reports must enable third parties to provide meaningful input to the Commission on the gatekeeper's compliance with its obligations under the DMA.[2] Gatekeepers are obliged to **update** the report as well as its non-confidential version at least **once a year** (Art. 11(2) sent. 2 DMA). 11

In the context of compliance with the obligations incumbent upon them under Art. 5, 6 and 7 DMA, gatekeepers may **request** the European Commission to **examine** the **ef-** 12

[1] Commission Implementing Regulation (EU) 2023/814 of 14 April 2023 on detailed arrangements for the conduct of certain proceedings by the Commission pursuant to Regulation (EU) 2022/1925 of the European Parliament and of the Council (OJ 2023 L 265, 6).

[2] European Commission consultation on the template for compliance report under the DMA, 6.6.2023 <https://ec.europa.eu/eusurvey/runner/dma_compliance> (last accessed: 12.7.2023).

fectiveness of the **measures** they plan to take or have taken (Art. 8(3) sent. 1 DMA). In this context, it is at the discretion of the European Commission to decide whether to engage in such **'regulatory dialogue'**, while respecting the principles of equal treatment, proportionality and good administration (Art. 8(3) sent. 2 DMA). Gatekeepers must attach to their request a reasoned submission to explain the measures that they intend to implement or have implemented. A **non-confidential version** of the reasoned opinion, also to be prepared by the gatekeeper, may be shared with third parties. The European Commission can be expected to enter into a regulatory dialogue with the gatekeepers regularly, in particular at the beginning of DMA enforcement where the scope and interpretation of the DMA obligations, and technical details on appropriate compliance will have to be explored. Incidentally, the **European Commission** also publishes a non-confidential version of its **preliminary assessment** on the initiation of proceedings pursuant to Art. 20 DMA in order to give **third parties** the opportunity to comment.

CHAPTER 8
MARKET INVESTIGATIONS (ART. 16–19 DMA)

Johanna Krauskopf/Markus Brösamle

Bibliography: Achleitner, 'Digital Markets Act beschlossen: Verhaltenspflichten und Rolle nationaler Wettbewerbsbehörden', NZKart 2022, 359; Bunte, 'Sektoruntersuchung im Retail-Bankgeschäft', WM 2007, 1197; de Bronett, 'Sektoruntersuchungen', WuW 2010, 258; Fletcher, 'Market Investigation for Digital Platforms: Panacea or Complement?', advance release (6.8.2020) <https://ssrn.com/abstract=3668289> (last accessed: 12.7.2023); Harta/Kulluas/Gasparotti, 'Digital Markets Act – Part II', cepAnalyse no. 15/2021 (27.7.2021) <https://www.cep.eu/en/eu-topics/details/cep/digital-markets-act-part-ii-enforcement-and-governance-ceppolicybrief-com2020-842.html> (last accessed: 12.7.2023); Motta/Peitz, 'Intervention triggers and underlying theories of harm: expert advice for the impact assessment of a new competition tool', expert study (2020) <https://data.europa.eu/doi/10.2763/487824> (last accessed: 12.7.2023); Podszun/Bongartz/Langenstein, 'The Digital Markets Act: Moving from Competition Law to Regulation for Large Gatekeepers', EuCML 2021, 60; Schweitzer, 'The new competition tool: its institutional set-up and procedural design', expert study (2020) <https://data.europa.eu/doi/10.2763/060011> (last accessed: 12.7.2023); Schweitzer, 'The Art to Make Gatekeeper Positions Contestable and the Challenge to Know What Is Fair: A Discussion of the Digital Markets Act Proposal', ZEuP 2021, 503; Zimmer/Göhsl, 'Vom New Competition Tool zum Digital Markets Act: Die geplante EU-Regulierung für digitale Gatekeeper', ZWeR 2021, 29; Zober, 'Durchsetzung des DMA-E und dessen Verhältnis zum Kartellrecht', NZKart 2021, 611.

A. Overview

1 The DMA introduces a **market investigation** as a new investigative tool that must precede specific decisions (Art. 16–19 DMA). While the DMA does not provide any definition or specific description of the term 'market investigation', it sets out comprehensive provisions on the scope of application, deadlines, and investigative and enforcement powers in relation to market investigations

2 The European Commission is to conduct market investigations to (i) **designate gatekeepers** (Art. 17 DMA), (ii) **investigate systematic non-compliance** (Art. 18 DMA) and (iii) **identify new digital services and practices to be included** (Art. 19 DMA). For this purpose, the European Commission has at its disposal the strong general investigative powers of the DMA, which are intended to ensure the effective implementation of, and compliance with, the Regulation (rec. 80 DMA). The investigative powers include rights to request information and carry out interviews (Art. 21, 22 DMA) as well as the power to conduct inspections (Art. 23 DMA).

3 The market investigation instrument originated from the reform project for the **New Competition Tool** presented by the European Commission in the summer of 2020,

which, however, was not pursued further in this form.[1] The New Competition Tool was designed – based on the **British CMA's market investigation** – to combine a form of market investigation with direct powers of intervention in the form of behavioural and/or structural measures without this being dependent on a finding of an infringement of competition law.[2] The market investigation provided for in the DMA is ultimately based on the market investigation of the CMA, but does not provide any direct, individual powers of intervention. It is therefore similar to the **sector inquiry** under Art. 17 of Regulation (EC) No 1/2003, which is familiar to European law, and similar to the sector-specific investigations also provided for in national legal systems, e.g. in Germany and the Netherlands.[3]

4 **Sector inquiries** already give the European Commission the opportunity to analyse entire economic sectors in detail and in a comprehensive manner, which is particularly important in cases involving unknown or complex markets.[4] This gives the European Commission profound insights; it is not uncommon for sector inquiries to end with specific investigation proceedings against individual undertakings. The European Commission already emphasised back in 2009 just how important sector inquiries are.[5] These broad-based investigations can be used to identify not only the behaviour of individual undertakings, but also factors such as network effects, economies of scale and scope, regulatory and structural barriers, and consumer behaviour.[6]

5 The DMA's market investigation, with its different areas of application and corresponding objectives, also extends beyond the analysis of the behaviour of individual undertakings to identify **market failures in the digital sector** and address these with appropriate solutions. Due to the narrower scope of application, however, the market investigation tool falls short of the function originally envisaged under the New Competition Tool as a catch-all solution.[7] The introduction of direct intervention powers in the DMA, for example, could not be implemented.

I. Areas of application of the market investigation

6 First, the DMA does not set out any substantive requirements for the initiation of market investigations, but rather is limited to **formal requirements** and **deadlines**. Incidentally, this is different in competition law proceedings pursuant to Art. 17 Reg. (EC) No 1/2003 where the initiation of a sector inquiry requires objective factual grounds for

[1] European Commission, 'New Competition Tool (NCT) Inception Impact Assessment', 4.6.2020, Ref. Ares(2020)2877634; Zober NZKart 2021, 611 (612); Podszun/Bongartz/Langenstein EuCML 2021, 60 (61); cf. European Commission, Directorate-General for Competition, Schweitzer, 'The new competition tool: its institutional set-up and procedural design', expert study (2020), p. 4 et seq.

[2] European Commission, 'New Competition Tool (NCT) Inception Impact Assessment', 4.6.2020, Ref. Ares(2020)2877634; Zimmer/Göhsl ZWeR 2021, 29 (49); Fletcher, 'Market Investigation for Digital Platforms: Panacea or Complement?', advance release (6.8.2020), p. 2.

[3] Zober NZKart 2021, 611 (612); Podszun/Bongartz/Langenstein EuCML 2021, 60 (61); cf. European Commission, Directorate-General for Competition, Schweitzer, 'The new competition tool: its institutional set-up and procedural design', expert study (2020), p. 4 et seq.

[4] Henning in Immenga/Mestmäcker VO (EG) Nr. 1/2003 Art. 17 mn. 5.

[5] 'Communication from the Commission to the European Parliament and the Council, Report on the functioning of Council Regulation (EC) No 1/2003', 29.4.2009, COM(2009) 206 final, para. 61.

[6] Fletcher, 'Market Investigation for Digital Platforms: Panacea or Complement?', advance release (6.8.2020), p. 4.

[7] Schweitzer ZEuP 2021, 503 (533); European Commission, 'New Competition Tool (NCT) Inception Impact Assessment', 4.6.2020, Ref. Ares(2020)2877634; European Commission, Directorate-General for Competition, Motta/Peitz, 'Intervention triggers and underlying theories of harm: expert advice for the impact assessment of a new competition tool', expert study (2020), p. 6 et seqq., 48 et seqq.

a presumption of a restriction or distortion of competition (cf. Art. 17(1) sent. 1 Reg. (EC) No 1/2003).[8] For sector inquiries under competition law, there is no case law to date that specifies concrete requirements for their initiation – the European Commission does not, at any rate, have a general right of investigation.[9]

7 Although the DMA lacks any explicit provision on substantive requirements for the initiation of a market investigation, there is good reason to suggest – also due to the **extensive investigative powers** associated with the market investigation – that there has to be sufficient initial suspicion that justifies the initiation of a market investigation.[10] This initial suspicion would then have to relate to a specific DMA issue that the European Commission wants to address by initiating the investigation, such as the suspicion that the requirements for designation as a gatekeeper (Art. 17 DMA) are met or the suspicion of systematic non-compliance conduct (Art. 18 DMA) or the need to amend the DMA (Art. 19 DMA) to avoid 'fishing expeditions'.[11] Apart from market investigations in case of systematic non-compliance with the DMA (Art. 18 DMA), however, no indications of misconduct on the part of individual undertakings are required.[12]

8 In contrast to the substantive requirements for initiating market investigations, their **areas of application** are clearly set out. Market investigations can be considered in the following cases:

1. Market investigation for designating gatekeepers (Art. 17 DMA)

9 The European Commission can use the market investigation for **designating gatekeepers**. This refers to cases in which an undertaking does not fulfil the thresholds set out in Art. 3(2) DMA but the European Commission needs to examine whether an undertaking providing core platform services should be designated as a gatekeeper, i.e. is to be appointed **other than via presumption**. The European Commission can also use the market investigation for the **identification of core platform services** to be listed in the designation decision (Art. 17(1), Art. 3(8) and (9) DMA, → Ch. 4 mn. 17 et seqq.). Also, it covers cases in which an undertaking providing core platform services presents sufficiently substantiated arguments to **rebut the presumption** (Art. 17(3), Art. 3(5) subpara. 3 and 4 DMA).

a) Designation other than via presumption

10 In the case of designation other than via presumption, the market investigation refers to the **qualitative criteria** set out in Art. 3(1) DMA (→ Ch. 4 mn. 17 et seqq.). This group of cases also covers scenarios involving **emerging gatekeepers**. An emerging gatekeeper is only expected to achieve an entrenched and durable position in its operations as a provider of core platform services in the foreseeable future. The European Commission will endeavour to conclude its market investigation within twelve months of commencing it (Art. 17(1) sent. 2 DMA). Before doing so, it will notify the undertaking con-

---

[8] Neideck in MüKoWettbR/Bischke VO (EG) Nr. 1/2003 Art. 17 mn. 3; Hennig in Immenga/Mestmäcker VO (EG) Nr. 1/2003 Art. 17 mn. 7 et seq. considers a 'certain initial suspicion' to be necessary, which, however, does not have to mean that there is a specific restriction of competition.

[9] Hennig in Immenga/Mestmäcker VO (EG) Nr. 1/2003 Art. 17 mn. 10; Barthelmeß/Rudolf in LMRKM VO (EG) Nr. 1/2003 Art. 17 mn. 7; Bischke/Neideck in MüKoWettbR VO (EG) Nr. 1/2003 Art. 17 mn. 3.

[10] Zober NZKart 2021, 611 (612 et seq.); European Commission, Directorate-General for Competition, Schweitzer, 'The new competition tool: its institutional set-up and procedural design', expert study (2020), p. 11.

[11] Zober NZKart 2021, 611 (612).

[12] Zober NZKart 2021, 611 (612); for information on the sector enquiry, cf. de Bronett WuW 2010, 258 (262).

cerned of its preliminary findings, if possible, within six months of the commencement date of the procedure, indicating whether it considers, on a provisional basis, that it is appropriate for the undertaking to be designated as a gatekeeper and which core platform services of the undertaking are covered (Art. 17(2) DMA). The undertaking concerned can comment on the European Commission's preliminary assessment within a period of at least 14 days (Art. 34(1), (2) DMA). This is an important procedural step in guaranteeing the **right to be heard** of the undertakings concerned. This means that the European Commission may only base its decisions on preliminary findings on which the undertaking has had the opportunity to comment (Art. 34(3) DMA). The European Commission shall grant access to the file upon request of the undertaking to which it has addressed preliminary findings (Art. 8(1) sent. 1 Implementing Regulation). Access to the file will not be granted prior to the notification of the preliminary findings (Art. 8(1) sent. 2 Implementing Regulation).

11 The procedure is concluded by an **implementing act** of the Commission in which it sets out its decision (Art. 17(1) sent. 3, 4 DMA). An implementing act is a non-legislative act laying down detailed rules for the uniform implementation of legally binding Union acts adopted by the European Commission subject to the control of committees (Art. 291 TFEU).[13] This means that, before a decision is issued, the **advisory procedure** must be completed with the Digital Markets Advisory Committee (Art. 17(1) sent. 4, Art. 50(2) DMA). The Advisory Committee serves to assist the European Commission and is composed of representatives of the Member States (Art. 3(2) Reg. (EU) No 182/2011); the Member States may delegate to, among others, experts from the competent authorities which hold the relevant expertise (rec. 101 DMA). Accordingly, when adopting the implementing act, the European Commission must take the utmost account of the conclusions drawn from the discussions within the committee and of the opinion delivered (Art. 4 Reg. (EU) No 182/2011).

12 In cases involving an emerging gatekeeper, the European Commission **constitutively** imposes the application of specific conduct obligations on the gatekeeper but does not have the entire catalogue of duties set out in the DMA at its disposal (→ Ch. 4 mn. 20).

b) Designation in cases involving the rebuttal of presumption

13 If, despite sufficiently substantiated arguments to rebut the presumption, the European Commission reaches the conclusion that the provider of core platform services has not provided evidence showing that the **qualitative requirements set out in Art. 3(1) DMA are not met**, it can only designate this provider as a gatekeeper after conducting a market investigation (Art. 3(5) subpara. 4, Art. 17(3) DMA). In such cases, the European Commission is to endeavour to notify the undertaking of the preliminary findings after three months at the latest and to conclude the market investigation within five months of initiating it (Art. 17(3) DMA). Again, the undertaking must be granted the right to be heard in relation to the provisional findings and can request access to the file for this purpose (Art. 8(1) Implementing Regulation). This is the **shortest period** for conducting the market investigation under the DMA, which is intended to ensure planning with regard to timing and legal certainty for the undertaking concerned.

[13] European Council, 'Implementing and Delegated Acts' (22.4.2022) <https://www.consilium.europa.eu/de/council-eu/decision-making/implementing-and-delegated-acts/> (last accessed: 12.7.2023).

2. Market investigation into systematic non-compliance (Art. 18 DMA)

In addition, the European Commission can conduct a market investigation for the purpose of examining whether a gatekeeper **has engaged in systematic non-compliance with its obligations under the DMA** (Art. 18 DMA). The market investigation in this case refers to a gatekeeper's **behaviour**. 14

The European Commission communicates to the gatekeeper its preliminary findings on whether it assumes systematic non-compliance by the gatekeeper within **six months** of initiating the investigation and which **remedy or remedies** it is considering (Art. 18(4) DMA). The gatekeeper shall be granted access to the European Commission's file upon its request (Art. 8(1) Implementing Regulation). The European Commission has twelve months from the initiation of the market investigation to conclude it (Art. 18(1) DMA). The market investigation can be **extended** both with regard to the deadline for the preliminary findings and the adoption of the final decision (Art. 18(7) DMA). The number of extensions is unlimited, but the total duration must not exceed a total period of six months. 15

Interested third parties are involved in the procedure in such a way that the preliminary findings of the European Commission are not only communicated to the gatekeeper, but also that the European Commission publishes the case and potential remedies in summary and non-confidential form (Art. 18(5) DMA). Third parties can then submit their comments within a timeframe set by the European Commission. 16

If the market investigation reveals that the gatekeeper has systematically failed to comply with its obligations and has maintained, extended or strengthened its gatekeeper position, the European Commission can impose proportionate and necessary behavioural or structural remedies (Art. 18(1) sent. 3 DMA). In this context, systematic non-compliance is **presumed** if the European Commission has issued at least **three non-compliance decisions** against the gatekeeper with respect to one of its core platform services within a period of **eight years** prior to the opening of a market investigation (Art. 18(3) DMA). The measures are to be adopted by means of an implementing act, in which the opinion of the Advisory Committee is to be considered (Art. 18(1) sent. 4 DMA, Art. 4 Reg. (EU) No 182/2011). 17

The gatekeeper can offer **commitments** during the market investigation procedure to ensure compliance with the dos and don'ts (Art. 25(1) sent. 1 DMA). It is at the discretion of the European Commission to decide whether the commitments are sufficient. If the European Commission deems the proposed commitments sufficient, it declares them binding and that there are no further grounds for action (Art. 25(1) sent. 1 DMA). If, following the market investigation, the European Commission intends to identify systematic non-compliance and declare commitments binding, it will publish a non-confidential summary of the case and the commitments so that interested third parties can also comment on them (Art. 18(6) DMA). 18

The European Commission is to regularly review the remedies that it imposes and can **modify** them if, following a new market investigation, it finds that they are not effective (Art. 18(8) DMA). 19

3. Market investigation on the inclusion of new core platform services and on new practices (Art. 19 DMA)

The European Commission can also conduct a market investigation to examine whether **new services** from the digital sector should be added to the list of core platform services pursuant to Art. 2 point (2) DMA or to detect **new practices** that are not yet effectively addressed by the conduct obligations pursuant to Art. 5–7 DMA (Art. 19(1) 20 sent. 1 DMA). This form of market investigation relates to **general information on competition**. As part of this process, the European Commission can draw on findings from proceedings under Art. 101 and 102 TFEU and consult third parties, including business users and end users (Art. 19(1) sent. 2, (2) DMA).

21 The European Commission publishes the results of its findings in a **report** within 18 months of opening the market investigation (Art. 19(3) DMA). The market investigation is designed to provide the European Commission with a solid evidentiary basis on which to initiate amendments to the DMA (rec. 77 DMA): Where appropriate, it therefore submits, together with the report, a **legislative proposal** to amend the DMA to include additional digital sector services in the list of core platform services or new dos and don'ts. Alternatively, the European Commission can also propose the **removal** of services or existing obligations (Art. 19(3) subpara. 3 DMA). In addition, the European Commission can submit a draft **delegated act** updating gatekeepers' obligations. Art. 12 DMA defines the scope of application of these delegated acts.

22 Consequently, Art. 19 DMA always combines the instrument of market investigation with an **abstract general rule** (in the form of a legislative or a delegated act). In this respect, the DMA differs from the concept originally envisaged for the New Competition Tool, but still shows 'remnants' of it.[14] The New Competition Tool was designed – as demonstrated (→ mn. 3) – to combine a form of market investigation with direct powers of intervention, modelled on regulations in the UK for specific markets.[15] While the European Commission cannot create specific individual regulations after a market investigation within the context of the DMA, it is authorised, in the area covered by Art. 12 DMA, to adopt abstract general regulations and can initiate a legislative procedure on matters that extend beyond the scope of Art. 12 DMA.

23 This means that the European Commission also has options to amend the DMA through **delegated acts** to a limited extent. It remains to be seen how much leeway the European Commission will have in this respect. Parts of the literature assume a broad discretionary basis for the European Commission; reference is made to the previous decision-making practice of the ECJ on delegated acts in scenarios characterised by rapid change and a high degree of technical complexity.[16] Compared to the original Commission proposal for the DMA, the leeway available to the European Commission has been limited because the scope of application for amending the dos and don'ts is enumerated (Art. 12(2) DMA), which was not the case in the original Commission proposal. Specifically, Art. 12(2) DMA restricts and specifies the process of updating via delegated acts to specific additions to existing obligations. In view of the primary law requirement of Art. 290(1) subpara. 2 sent. 2 TFEU, according to which legislative powers can only be transferred to the European Commission to supplement or amend specific non-essential elements of a legislative act, this restriction is to be welcomed in principle. However, the existing tension with the requirements of primary law is not eliminated by Art. 12(2) DMA and is viewed critically by many, because the conduct obligations represent the core of the DMA.[17]

---

[14] Zimmer/Göhsl ZWeR 2021, 29 (49); cf. European Commission, 'New Competition Tool (NCT) Inception Impact Assessment', 4.6.2020, Ref. Ares(2020)2877634.

[15] Zimmer/Göhsl ZWeR 2021, 29 (49); Fletcher, 'Market Investigation for Digital Platforms: Panacea or Complement?', advance release (6.8.2020), p. 2.

[16] Zimmer/Göhsl ZWeR 2021, 29 (50) with reference to ECJ 30.10.1975 – case C-23/75, ECLI:EU:C:1975:142 para. 10 et seq. = BeckRS 2004, 72456; ECJ 13.7.1995 – case C-156/93, ECLI:EU:C:1995:238 para. 18 = BeckRS 2004, 74515.

[17] Achleitner NZKart 2022, 359 (361); Harta/Kulluas/Gasparotti, 'Digital Markets Act – Part II', cep-Analyse no. 15/2021 (27.7.2021), p. 4; Podszun/Bongartz/Langenstein EuCML 2021, 60 (65).

Consequently, the list of core platform services (Art. 2 point (2) DMA) as well as adjustments to obligations that go beyond Art. 12 DMA, such as the addition of new obligations, can only be made, after a market investigation has been conducted via an **amendment to the DMA** and not by means of delegated acts. Given that a market investigation can last up to 18 months (Art. 19(3) DMA) and given the subsequent legislative procedure of the European Union (Art. 294 TFEU), which takes an average of 22 months, it is expected to take a considerable period of time before amendments to the DMA enter into force.[18] As a result, the combination of a market investigation and legislative procedure, which leads to a long **duration of the procedure**, is often criticised.[19] 24

Against this backdrop, some literature calls for the European Commission to be **empowered** to add new services to the list of core platform services if the market investigation indicates relevant market tipping and if specific characteristics of digital platforms emerge that typically give rise to competition concerns, such as a strong intermediation position.[20] This approach would, however, require an abstract definition of the term 'core platform services'.[21] 25

II. Procedure

The European Commission initiates market investigations with a **decision**. When implementing the investigation, it has extensive **investigative powers**, in particular in the form of requests for information, and the power to carry out interviews and conduct inspections (Art. 21–23 DMA). The powers mentioned largely correspond to the investigative powers of the European Commission in sector inquiries (cf. Art. 17 et seqq. Reg. (EC) No 1/2003).[22] Market investigations end with a decision that is to be published. In addition, the European Commission can issue more detailed provisions on practical arrangements for market investigation proceedings by means of implementing acts, specifying the practical implementation of the instrument (Art. 46(1)(i) DMA). 26

1. Opening of a market investigation

Art. 16 DMA sets out uniform provisions governing the **opening** of a market investigation for all cases of application. The European Commission opens a market investigation by adopting a **decision** (Art. 16(1) DMA). The decision is to specify the date of opening of the market investigation as well as the issue to which the market investigation relates and the investigation's purpose (Art. 16(3) DMA). The decision to initiate a sector inquiry pursuant to Art. 17 of Regulation (EC) No 1/2003 also has to state the reason why the inquiry is being initiated.[23] There are concerns that the European Commission's practice of often wording its opening decisions in very general terms will also become established in the context of the market investigation under the DMA.[24] 27

---

[18] Zimmer/Göhsl ZWeR 2021, 29 (39) with reference to the Guide of the Directorate-General for Internal Policies of the Union to how the European Parliament co-legislates of November 2017, 'Handbook on the Ordinary Legislative Procedure', PE 608.827, <https://www.europarl.europa.eu/cmsdata/215107/OLP_2020_EN.pdf> (last accessed: 12.7.2023), p. 63.

[19] Schweitzer ZEuP 2021, 503 (521); Zimmer/Göhsl ZWeR 2021, 29 (39 et seq.).

[20] Schweitzer ZEuP 2021, 503 (521); with reference to the proposal for the rewording of Art. 2 point (2) DMA by Zimmer/Göhsl ZWeR 2021, 29 (40).

[21] Schweitzer ZEuP 2021, 503 (521).

[22] Zober NZKart 2021, 611 (613).

[23] Henning in Immenga/Mestmäcker VO (EG) Nr. 1/2003 Art. 17 mn. 22.

[24] Zober NZKart 2021, 611 (613); for a critical view of the usually very general wording used in opening decisions under Art. 17 Reg. (EC) No 1/2003 Bunte WM 2007, 1197.

28 When deciding whether to open an investigation, the European Commission does not have to involve **third parties** – such as the **high-level group**, a specifically established advisory body of experts (Art. 40 DMA). The European Commission can, however, draw on the expertise and advice of the high-level group (Art. 40(5) DMA).

29 In this respect, only the **Member States** are granted rights about the opening of a market investigation subject to specific conditions. If, in the view of the Member States, there are reasonable grounds for opening a market investigation, they can ask the European Commission to open one (Art. 41 DMA). This applies to all areas of application of the market investigation. With regard to market investigations under Art. 17 DMA (i.e. for designation as gatekeepers) and Art. 19 DMA (i.e. in relation to new services and practices), at least three Member States must request the opening of the investigation; whereas under Art. 18 DMA (i.e. for systematic non-compliance with the DMA's conduct obligations), a request by one Member State is sufficient. The Member States are to submit evidence in support of their requests (Art. 41(4) DMA). Even if the request is submitted by the required number of Member States, this does not necessarily lead to the market investigation being carried out. The European Commission is still responsible for examining and deciding whether there are reasonable grounds to open a market investigation (Art. 41(5) DMA).

30 The decision to open proceedings must be **published**, naming the parties involved and the main content (Art. 44(1) DMA).

2. Conducting the market investigation

31 The European Commission is granted extensive **(enforcement and) investigative powers** in the context of market investigations (cf. rec. 80 DMA). It can exercise its investigative powers even before issuing a decision to open a market investigation (Art. 16(2) DMA). Furthermore, the European Commission can ask **national competent authorities** to assist it in its market investigation (Art. 16(5), Art. 38(6) DMA). Some national competition authorities, including the German Federal Cartel Office, have already declared their intention to support the European Commission in enforcing the DMA.

32 While Chapter IV of the DMA ('Market investigation') does not explicitly address the investigative powers of the European Commission, their scope is derived from **Art. 21 et seqq. DMA**, according to which the European Commission can exercise powers to fulfil its tasks under the DMA. Investigative measures can also be directed against **third companies** and not only against the gatekeeper. Accordingly, the European Commission's investigative powers include requests for information, including the power to carry out interviews and take statements, and the power to conduct inspections. The powers are largely based on the powers for **sector inquiries** under Art. 18–20 Reg. (EC) No 1/2003.[25] As with sector inquiries, further informal and formal investigations are available to the European Commission due to the wording of the investigative powers as 'permissive provisions'.[26] In compliance with the general legal principle of proportionality, the European Commission chooses which investigative instruments to use at its discretion.

33 As part of its **request for information**, the European Commission can – by simple request or by decision – require undertakings to provide all necessary information (Art. 21(1) sent. 1 DMA). This includes access to all relevant data and algorithms of undertakings and the power to request information about testing, as well as explanations of

[25] Zober NZKart 2021, 611 (613); Schweitzer ZEuP 2021, 503 (532).
[26] De Bronett WuW 2010, 258 (265).

them (Art. 21(1) sent. 2 DMA). **Access to data and algorithms** is an important new feature compared to the investigation options set out in Regulation (EC) No 1/2003.[27] It does not matter who possesses such information, its form or format, storage medium, or the place where it is stored (rec. 81 DMA). The European Commission can also query the information available to the Member States (Art. 21(5) DMA).

The European Commission's **right to carry out interviews** is limited to the extent that natural or legal persons that may have relevant information must consent to being interviewed (Art. 22(1) DMA). As these are voluntary statements, the European Commission cannot enforce them and cannot impose sanctions for incorrect or inaccurate information.[28] 34

Art. 23 DMA grants the European Commission the power to conduct **inspections** (dawn raids) on undertakings. In contrast to the powers for sector inquiries, the European Commission can demand access to, and explanations on, undertaking algorithms and databases (Art. 23(2)(d) DMA) and involve experts and auditors in the inspection (Art. 23(4) DMA). 35

Conduct of the market investigation, like the Commission's other investigative powers, is subject to the **fundamental rights** of the parties involved.[29] For further specification of procedural rights in the context of market investigations, it should be possible to rely on the case law on Reg. (EC) No 1/2003.[30] Criminal law principles also have to be taken into account because under Art. 18 DMA, there is the threat of a fine and also, under Art. 17 and 19 DMA, the findings may be used in other proceedings under the DMA such as in investigations of non-compliance with the DMA's conduct obligations (Art. 36 DMA). This means that the same rights as those guaranteed in any fine proceedings must already be guaranteed as part of the market investigation.[31] Prior to adoption of a decision pursuant to Art. 17 or 18 DMA, the undertaking concerned can comment on the assessment and the measures envisaged by the European Commission (Art. 34(1) DMA). In addition, Art. 34(4) DMA sets out explicit provisions on the right to access files. 36

The proceedings again end with a **decision** that is to be published (Art. 44(1) DMA). If there has been a material change in any of the facts on which a decision was based after it is adopted, or if the decision is based on incomplete, incorrect or misleading information, the European Commission can reopen a market investigation that it has previously closed (Art. 16(4) DMA). 37

In its annual **report** to the European Parliament and the Council, the European Commission also provides a summary of ongoing market investigations (Art. 35(2)(a) DMA). Once again, the European Commission can adopt implementing acts laying down detailed practical arrangements of the proceedings concerning the market investigations (Art. 46(1)(i) DMA). 38

---

[27] Zober NZKart 2021, 611 (617).

[28] Cf. Art. 31 DMA, which does not refer to Art. 22 DMA, and parallels with sector inquiries: Sura in Bunte VO (EG) Nr. 1/2003 Art. 19 mn. 7; Hennig in Immenga/Mestmäcker VO (EG) Nr. 1/2003 Art. 19 mn. 2.

[29] Art. 34(4) sent. 1 DMA: 'The rights of defence of the gatekeeper, undertaking or association of undertakings concerned shall be fully respected in any proceedings'; cf. also rec. 80 DMA; COM(2020) 842 final, 13.

[30] Zober NZKart 2021, 611 (613).

[31] Cf. de Bronett WuW 2010, 258 (266), also on sector inquiries; Hennig in Immenga/Mestmäcker VO (EG) Nr. 1/2003 Art. 17 mn. 40 et seq. with further substantiation.

B. Evaluation

39 The option of conducting market investigations gives the European Commission a **powerful tool** that it can use to systematically investigate the highly dynamic markets of the digital economy in the future. The digital industry is very diverse and differs to a decisive degree from the industries regulated to date, such as banking supervision.[32] In this economic environment, the DMA establishes regulations for undertakings that pursue very varied business models – and indeed do so in complex markets that are subject to constant and rapid change.[33]

40 The new investigative tool of the market investigation helps to understand digital markets better and to efficiently counter threats. As such, it forms an important pillar of the DMA. Consequently, market investigations were rightly assessed as an **effective instrument** even before the DMA came into force.[34] One aspect that the DMA's market investigation has in common with the sector inquiry of the European Commission (Art. 17 Reg. (EC) No 1/2003) and the Federal Cartel Office (§ 32e GWB) as well as, for example, the CMA's market investigation, is that it goes beyond investigating the behaviour of individual undertakings and offers a broad overview of the market and the behaviour of market participants. However, unlike close alignment with the CMA's market investigation tool, which was still being considered for the New Competition Tool, the DMA does not give the European Commission any associated direct powers of intervention.

41 Enforcement practice will show whether market investigations will be an instrument that allows the European Commission to strike a successful balance between **promoting innovation** and ensuring **efficient regulation**. In view of the dynamic change in the digital sector, time and implementation issues may become critical. As the detailed deadlines for the proceedings show, these are **time-consuming proceedings** that will tie up considerable **capacities** on the part of the European Commission.[35] The time factor is, however, particularly crucial when it comes to designating emerging gatekeepers (Art. 17 DMA) and amending the services and obligations covered by the DMA (Art. 19 DMA). In cases in which emerging gatekeepers are to be designated as gatekeepers, the dynamic change and intensifying network effects in the digital industry may, in individual cases, already threaten to tip the market during the period of twelve months required to conduct a market investigation (Art. 17(1) DMA).[36] The DMA does not, however, provide the power to issue interim measures in this case (cf. Art. 24 DMA). The combination of market investigations and legislative or delegated acts to adapt the digital services and practices covered by the DMA is also often assessed as too lengthy a process.[37] In addition to the flexibility of intervention, it will also be important that the European Commission has the knowledge and technical skills to use its investigative powers effi-

[32] Schnitzer, Public hearing on the 'Digital Markets Act' of 27.4.2022, Bundestag Committee Printed Paper 20(9)61, 5.

[33] Schnitzer, Public hearing on the 'Digital Markets Act' of 27.4.2022, Bundestag Committee Printed Paper 20(9)61, 5.

[34] Achleitner NZKart 2022, 359 (366); Zober NZKart 2021, 611 (612); Zimmer/Göhsl ZWeR 2021, 29 (49); Schweitzer ZEuP 2021, 503 (533).

[35] Cf. with regard to sector inquiries: Bischke/Neideck in MüKoWettbR VO (EG) Nr. 1/2003 Art. 17 mn. 1.

[36] Zimmer/Göhsl ZWeR 2021, 29 (45).

[37] Schweitzer ZEuP 2021, 503 (521); Zimmer/Göhsl ZWeR 2021, 29 (39).

ciently – particularly when it comes to the evaluation of data and algorithms that form the basis of digital services.[38]

42 The question as to how significant the market investigation instrument will prove to be therefore also depends on the extent to which the European Commission will or can make use of it and what **limits**, if any, will be set for it by future case law. In any case, it is not unlikely that the European Commission will interpret the power to investigate the market generously.

[38] Schnitzer, Public hearing on the 'Digital Markets Act' of 27.4.2022, Bundestag Committee Printed Paper 20(9)61, 6.

CHAPTER 9
MERGER CONTROL (ART. 14 DMA)

Jens Peter Schmidt

Bibliography: Carugati, 'Merger Review in the Digital Markets Act' (18.8.2022) <http://dx.doi.org/10.2139/ssrn.4203210> (last accessed: 12.7.2023); Richter, 'Prospects of Merger Review in the Digital Age: A Critical Look at the EU, the United States, and Germany', IIC 2023, 223; Schmidt/Steinvorth, 'Fusionskontrolluntersuchungen durch die EU-Kommission ohne Anmeldepflicht – neue Herausforderungen für die M&A-Transaktionspraxis', BB 2021, 1666.

A. Importance of merger control in the digital economy

1 The merger control scrutiny of M&A transactions was, is and will remain a priority of the European Commission's work. The European Commission's enforcement of the EC Merger Control Regulation (ECMR), which has now been ongoing for more than 30 years, is generally considered a successful model, although complaints have been raised increasingly in recent years regarding a **lack of intervention** in the **digital economy.**[1] The repeatedly cited phenomenon of uncontrolled **'killer acquisitions'** has to be mentioned in this context: this relates to takeovers of emerging, highly innovative, (potentially) competing companies by established Internet companies in order to secure the latters' market power, without the possibility of any public merger control scrutiny due to the small (turnover) size of the companies acquired.

2 For example, it is reported that Alphabet/Google, Amazon, Apple, and Meta/Facebook have been able to make over 500 acquisitions in the last two decades,[2] although only a **fraction** of these were notified to, and **analysed** by, the antitrust authorities.[3] According to other sources,[4] by March 2022, out of 841 known acquisitions by Alphabet/Google, Amazon, Apple, Meta/Facebook, and Microsoft, only 20 had been investigated by the European Commission, no acquisitions had been prohibited and conditions had only been imposed in three cases.

[1] 'In the last ten years, the largest operators of digital platforms have strengthened and consolidated their market position through a large number of mergers and acquisitions, without this being prevented by effective application of the standard set of merger control instruments.' (Schnitzer, Public hearing on the 'Digital Markets Act' of 27.4.2022, Bundestag Committee Printed Paper 20(9)61, 4).

[2] US Congressional Subcommittee on Antitrust, Commercial and Administrative Law, 'Investigation of Competition in Digital Markets Report 2020' (2.10.2020) <https://judiciary.house.gov/uploadedfiles/competition_in_digital_markets.pdf?utm_campaign=4493-519> (last accessed: 12.7.2023), p. 406 et seqq. The (incomplete) list includes more than 540 mergers since 2001.

[3] Carugati, 'Merger Review in the Digital Markets Act' (18.8.2022), p. 8 et seqq.

[4] Podszun, Public hearing on the 'Digital Markets Act' of 27.4.2022, Bundestag Committee Printed Paper 20(9)60, 13 fn. 24.

In this respect, it is not surprising that, from the beginning of the legislative process, the question was discussed as to whether the DMA should contain a genuine **special merger control regime** for gatekeepers or whether the ECMR should be **amended** to cover transactions that have so far managed to escape control due to the jurisdictional (turnover) thresholds not being met. 3

B. No DMA merger control, but obligation to inform about intended concentrations (Art. 14 DMA)

The EU ultimately opted for a **middle way** which does not provide for any stand-alone DMA merger control regime and at the same time avoided any amendment of the ECMR, which was deemed politically not achievable. This also means that the DMA **does not serve to tighten up** the substantive merger control test, as demanded by Germany, among others.[5] 4

I. Obligation to inform for gatekeepers

Art. 14(1) sent. 1 DMA obliges gatekeepers to **inform** the **European Commission** of intended concentrations within the meaning of Art. 3 ECMR where the merging entities or the target of the concentration provide core platform services or any other services in the digital sector or enable the collection of data. The obligation to inform applies irrespective of whether the intended concentration is notifiable to the European Commission under the provisions of the ECMR or to any other authority under the national law of the EU Member States. Gatekeepers must inform the European Commission about such intended concentrations **prior to implementation** and following the conclusion of the agreement, announcement of the public bid, or acquisition of a controlling interest (Art. 14(1) sent. 2 DMA). 5

II. Type of information to be provided

Gatekeepers must provide at least the following information (cf. Art. 14(2) DMA): 6

- description of the **undertakings** concerned by the concentration (buyer, target company);
- their Union and worldwide **annual turnovers**;
- their **fields of activity**, including activities directly related to the concentration;
- **transaction value** (estimation);
- summary of the concentration, including its nature and strategic **rationale**;
- list of the **Member States** concerned by the concentration.

In addition, the gatekeeper must provide the Union **annual turnovers**, the numbers of yearly active **business users** and the numbers of monthly active **end users** for any relevant **core platform services** affected by the concentration.

[5] Joint position paper 'Friends of an effective Digital Markets Act' by France, the Netherlands and Germany of 27.5.2021 (Part 1) <https://www.bmwk.de/Redaktion/DE/Downloads/M-O/non-paper-friends-of-an-effective-digital-markets-act.pdf> (last accessed: 12.7.2023). This approach has been criticized as 'insufficient' (Richter IIC 2023, 223 (261 et seq.)).

7 Further details in relation to the format as well as to other procedural issues are set out in the **Implementing Regulation**[6] (cf. Art. 46(1)(h) DMA). When informing the European Commission, gatekeepers must complete a **template**[7] that specifies the minimum information to be provided. Section 1 of the template obliges the gatekeeper to provide a **summary of the concentration** with a non-confidential version that will be included in the list of acquisitions made by gatekeepers which the European Commission will publish annually (cf. Art. 14(4) DMA). In section 2 of the template, contact details must be provided as well as information with respect to ownership structure; **relevant activities** of the gatekeeper and the target/merging company/joint venture company; turnover; the target's/merging company's/joint venture's **core platform services** and other products and services in the digital sector; **product/service overlaps** with the gatekeeper; the **data** whose collection will be enabled by the contemplated transaction and the relationship to the gatekeeper's activities; and other **commercially relevant assets**, including IP rights. Section 3 asks for details of the transaction (structure, timing, strategic and economic rationale, value, merger control notification requirements and status of notifications/investigations). The template further requires **Member States** to be identified in which the companies concerned – other than the gatekeeper – have their headquarters or operational subsidiaries; generate turnover; own assets; have research and development activities; or plan to start commercialising existing or pipeline products. Section 4 requests quantitative information on any **core platform services** provided by the target/merging company/joint venture and the gatekeeper. The European Commission may adapt the template over time to request further information if needed. In essence, the information requirement pursuant to Art. 14 DMA will lead gatekeepers to submit 'short form notifications' – or potentially quiet lengthy submissions – to the European Commission in the future.

8 If **further core platform services** individually reach the **thresholds** set out in Art. 3(2)(b) DMA as a result of the relevant concentration, the gatekeeper concerned must **inform** the European Commission within two months of implementation and provide the information specified in Art. 3(2) DMA (→ Ch. 4 mn. 4).

III. Consequence of the obligation to inform

9 It follows that the DMA does **not provide for any genuine notification requirement**, but only the requirement to inform the European Commission of contemplated transactions. The European Commission is to be able to use the information to verify gatekeeper status effectively and adjust a gatekeeper's list of core platform services. Furthermore, the information is important for monitoring broader contestability trends in the digital sector and can be a useful factor for consideration in the context of the market investigations (rec. 71 DMA). The **real purpose** of the information requirement, however, becomes apparent in the interplay with the European Commission's modified approach to handling **referrals** of **transactions** between Member States and the European Commission,[8] which will be explained below:

[6] Commission Implementing Regulation (EU) 2023/814 of 14 April 2023 on detailed arrangements for the conduct of certain proceedings by the Commission pursuant to Regulation (EU) 2022/1925 of the European Parliament and of the Council (OJ 2023 L 265, 6).

[7] Template relating to the obligation to inform about a concentration pursuant to Article 14 of Regulation (EU) 2022/1925 (Digital Markets Act) <https://digital-markets-act.ec.europa.eu/legislation_en#templates> (last update: 13.7.2023).

[8] Carugati, 'Merger Review in the Digital Markets Act' (18.8.2022), p. 4.

1. Modified approach of the European Commission regarding referrals: Referral Notice

In principle, the **allocation of competences** between the European Commission and competition authorities in the Member States is simple and clear: if a concentration falls under the jurisdiction of the European Commission, applicability of national law and competence of national authorities are excluded pursuant to Art. 21(3) ECMR. This one-stop shop principle is not always adhered to, however. For example, according to Art. 22 ECMR, **Member States** can **refer** a concentration that does not have to be notified to the **European Commission** to the latter if it is likely to affect trade between Member States and threatens to significantly affect competition within the territory of the Member State making the request. 10

On 31.3.2021, new 'Guidance on the application of the referral mechanism set out in Art. 22 of the Merger Control Regulation to certain categories of cases' was published.[9] With this communication, the **European Commission** – also with a view to the digital economy – abandoned its **previous practice** of only accepting referral requests from Member States if the (first) Member State requesting the referral had jurisdiction over the transaction at stake, i.e. if the concentration was **notifiable** under the **national law** of the **referring Member State.**[10] According to point 11 of the Referral Notice, Member States may now also **refer concentrations** to the **European Commission** that were **not** originally **notifiable** in the referring Member State. The Court has already confirmed this very controversial change in the Commission's practice in the first instance (Illumina/Grail)[11] – the appeal before the European Court of Justice is pending. 11

The modified approach turns the **previous predictable** system of merger control in the EU **on its head**, as the European Commission can now systematically review transactions that are not subject to merger control at all – neither in the Member States nor at the EU level.[12] In addition, the **European Commission** intends not just to wait for possible referral requests by Member States, but to actively **'invite' referrals** of such mergers where it sees a need for control[13] – Art. 22(5) sent. 2 ECMR allows the European Commission to act in this way. 12

This is precisely where the provision set out in Art. 14(4) DMA comes into play, pursuant to which the **European Commission** will inform the competent Member State **competition authorities** of the gatekeepers' **transaction plans**, taking into account the legitimate interest of the companies concerned in the protection of their business secrets.[14] Pursuant to Art. 14(5) DMA, national authorities may, in turn, **use** the information received to request a referral to the European Commission pursuant to Art. 22(1) ECMR, if necessary upon request by the European Commission. Interestingly, the **German** Federal Cartel Office will **not** (initially) be making **referral requests** if a contemplated concentration is not notifiable in Germany until the final decision by the **European Court of Justice**[15] clarifies the issue. 13

---

[9] 'Communication from the Commission – Guidance on the application of the referral mechanism set out in Article 22 of the Merger Regulation to certain categories of cases', 31.3.2021 (OJ 2021 C 113, 1; hereinafter: Referral Notice).

[10] Referral Notice para. 8.

[11] EGC 13.7.2022 – case T-227/21, ECLI:EU:T:2022:447 – Illumina v Commission.

[12] For a critical view, see Schmidt/Steinvorth BB 2021, 1666.

[13] Referral Notice para. 11, 26; the European Commission may invite the Member States to make a referral request pursuant to Art. 22(5) ECMR.

[14] Similarly, the European Commission will publish the list of acquisitions of which it has been informed by gatekeepers annually.

[15] According to President Mundt in the press conference held on 30.8.2022 presenting the 2021/2022 Annual Report.

2. Criteria for referral

14 The **Referral Notice** provides some direction for the discretionary decision on whether a referral of non-notifiable concentrations to Brussels is appropriate (the Referral Notice in principle also applies to **referrals** initiated by a notification made pursuant to the **DMA**). The guidance refers to factors related to the acquired company:[16]

- It is a start-up or recent entrant with significant **competitive potential** that has yet to implement its business model (in full);
- it is an important **innovator** or is conducting potentially important research;
- it is an actual or potential **'significant competitive force'** within the meaning of the Commission's Horizontal Merger Guidelines[17] (e.g. because it is particularly innovative or for other reasons is considered a maverick that provides significant competition to incumbents);
- it has **access** to competitively significant **assets** (such as for instance raw materials, infrastructure, data or intellectual property right); and/or
- it provides products or services that are key **inputs**/components for other **industries.**

15 In addition, the European Commission can take into account whether the value of the consideration received by the seller (**transaction value**) is particularly high compared to the current turnover of the target.[18]

16 It can be assumed that the European Commission will be inclined to consider the aforementioned criteria **fulfilled** in cases involving those companies that are to be acquired by gatekeepers.

3. Procedure

17 After being informed of a proposed concentration, the European Commission will examine whether the **referral criteria** are met. It will **inform** the Member State(s) potentially concerned or **ask** the latter to make a **referral request.**

18 The decision to make a referral request ultimately rests with the **competent authority** of the Member States, although it can be assumed that **Member States** will look favourably on a **request** from the European Commission and **act accordingly.**[19] Member States must submit the referral request within 15 working days of being informed of the proposed concentration. Within a further 15 working days, other Member States can join a referral request that has been made. Within another ten working days, the European Commission decides whether it will examine the concentration.[20]

19 The **suspension obligation/prohibition to close** set out in Art. 7 ECMR applies from the time the European Commission has informed the companies involved that a Member State has made a referral request (Art. 22(4) subpara. 1 sent. 2 ECMR). If the European Commission does not agree to the referral request, the suspension obligation will no longer apply, and the parties can implement the concentration.[21]

---

[16] Referral Notice para. 19.

[17] 'Guidelines on the assessment of horizontal mergers under the Council Regulation on the control of concentrations between undertakings', 5.2.2004 (OJ 2004 C 31, 5), para. 37, 38.

[18] Referral Notice para. 19.

[19] As of writing this chapter, the European Commission has applied the new policy in three cases.

[20] Referral Notice para. 28 et seqq.

[21] Referral Notice para. 31; any other restrictions on enforcement, e.g. in third countries, must be taken into account. For further implications for the transaction, see Schmidt/Steinvorth BB 2021, 1666.

IV. Total prohibition on entering into concentrations (Art. 18 DMA)

Pursuant to Art. 18(2) DMA, the European Commission can impose a **total prohibition on entering into concentrations** upon the gatekeeper in the event of **systematic non-compliance** with the DMA obligations. In order to maintain or restore the fairness and contestability affected by systematic non-compliance, the European Commission can impose this prohibition for a limited period of time. This relates to all concentrations as defined by the ECMR (vulgo: merger, acquisition of sole or joint control) with regard to the **core platform services** or the other services provided in the **digital sector** or enabling the **collection of data** which are affected by systematic non-compliance (see also → Ch. 10 mn. 6). 20

CHAPTER 10
EU PENALTIES, INVESTIGATIVE POWERS AND LEGAL PROTECTION

Fabian Hübener/Raphael Reims

Bibliography: Achleitner, 'Digital Markets Act beschlossen: Verhaltenspflichten und Rolle nationaler Wettbewerbsbehörden', NZKart 2022, 359; Akman, 'Regulating Competition in Digital Platform Markets: A Critical Assessment of the Framework and Approach of the EU Digital Markets Act', ELR 2022, 85; Belloso, 'The Proposal for a Digital Markets Act (DMA): A Summary' (2022) <https://papers.ssrn.com/sol3/papers.cfm?abstract_id=3999966> (last accessed: 12.7.2023); Harta, 'Der Digital Markets Act und das Doppelverfolgungsverbot', NZKart 2022, 102; Schöning/von Schreitter, 'Digital Mergers Act? Die Rückwirkungen des DMA auf die Fusionskontrolle in digitalen Märkten', WuW 2022, 582; Schweitzer, 'The Art to Make Gatekeeper Positions Contestable and the Challenge to Know What Is Fair: A Discussion of the Digital Markets Act Proposal', ZEuP 2021, 503; Somek, 'Anwendbarkeit des Doppelbestrafungsverbots in EU-Kartellverfahren', WuW 2021, 545.

1 To enforce the DMA, the European Commission is able to impose a wide variety of penalties and exercise a range of investigative powers that have **far-reaching consequences** for those subject to them. Consequently, precise knowledge of the relevant requirements and the options for legal protection is of crucial importance when it comes to safeguarding their interests.

A. Penalties (Art. 30 et seq. DMA)

2 The **various sanctioning powers** of the European Commission include imposing fines under Art. 30 DMA and imposing periodic penalty payments under Art. 31 DMA. Moreover, it has further behavioural and also structural remedies at its disposal that are set down in Art. 18 DMA, such as the option of prohibiting concentrations in the event of systematic non-compliance with specific DMA standards. While fines are imposed for

past conduct that constitutes an infringement of the DMA, periodic penalty payments and other remedies serve to ensure future compliance with the DMA and decisions based on it. Finally, the European Commission can impose interim measures according to Art. 24 DMA.

The **responsibility** for enforcing the DMA is **concentrated** at the level of the European Commission. As follows from Art. 38(7) DMA, competition authorities in the Member States can also initiate investigations into a DMA infringement on their own initiative. Nevertheless, even in this case only the European Commission is authorised to impose penalties under the DMA as the sole enforcer (end of Art. 38(7) DMA). In parallel, a Member State competition authority is able to impose a penalty under national competition law,[1] for example, in response to abuse of a dominant position within the meaning of Art. 102 TFEU or the corresponding national provisions (e.g. §§ 18 et seqq. GWB).[2] 3

The European Commission can issue **guidelines** on any of the aspects of the DMA Regulation in order to facilitate its effective implementation, but also its enforcement (Art. 47 DMA). No such guidelines have been issued to date. Nevertheless, the European Commission can be expected to draw on its own extensive wealth of experience in competition law, particularly with regard to penalising conduct that constitutes a breach of duty. This is why this section often refers to the decision-making practice under competition law. 4

I. Fines (Art. 30 DMA)

According to Art. 30(1) DMA, the European Commission can impose penalties on substantive DMA infringements and, according to Art. 30(3) DMA, formal DMA infringements by imposing fines. Where substantive infringements are committed, the amount of the fine can be up to 10 % of the gatekeeper's **total worldwide turnover** in the preceding **financial year**, and in the case of repeated infringements even **up to 20 %**.[3] Where formal infringements are committed, the amount can be up to 1 % of the turnover of the company acting in breach of duty, which is to be calculated in the same way. 5

1. Substantive DMA infringements

The imposition of fines under Art. 30(1) DMA first requires a **non-compliance decision** directed against a gatekeeper under Art. 29 DMA. In this decision, the European Commission must find that the gatekeeper **intentionally or negligently** 6

- does not comply with one or more of the obligations laid down in Art. 5, 6 or 7 DMA (Art. 30(1)(a) DMA);
- does not comply with one or more of the measures specified pursuant to Art. 8(2) DMA to ensure compliance with the obligations of gatekeepers under Art. 6 or 7 DMA (Art. 30(1)(b) DMA);

---

[1] On the significance of the ban on double jeopardy *ne bis in idem* → mn. 21 et seqq.

[2] On the relationship between Member State competition authorities and the European Commission under the DMA → Ch. 11 mn. 2 et seqq., cf. also German Monopolies Commission (*Monopolkommission*), 'Biennial Report XXIV, Competition 2022' (5.7.2022) <www.monopolkommission.de/de/gutachten/hauptgutachten/385-xxiv-gesamt.html> (last accessed: 12.7.2023), mn. 503 et seq.; Achleitner NZKart 2022, 359 (364).

[3] For details → mn. 13 et seqq.

- does not comply with one or more of the remedies imposed pursuant to Art. 18(1) DMA to comply with individual DMA requirements following systematic non-compliance with Art. 5, 6 or 7 DMA (Art. 30(1)(c) DMA);
- does not comply with one or more of the interim measures ordered pursuant to Art. 24 DMA (Art. 30(1)(d) DMA); or
- does not comply with one or more of the commitments made legally binding pursuant to Art. 25 (Art. 30(1)(e) DMA).

2. Formal DMA infringements

7 In contrast to infringements under Art. 30(1) DMA, fine notices under Art. 30(3) DMA can **also** be addressed **to undertakings** and associations of undertakings that are **not gatekeepers**. The European Commission can impose a fine on the companies concerned if they **intentionally or negligently**

- fail to provide within the time limit information that is required for assessing their designation as gatekeepers pursuant to Art. 3 DMA or supply incorrect, incomplete or misleading information (Art. 30(3)(a) DMA);
- fail to comply with the obligation to notify the European Commission according to Art. 3(3) DMA that their core platform services meet the thresholds set out in Art. 3(2) DMA (Art. 30(3)(b) DMA);
- fail to notify information or supply incorrect, incomplete or misleading information that is required pursuant to Art. 14 DMA where the merging entities or the target of the concentration provide core platform services or any other services in the digital sector or enable the collection of data (Art. 30(3)(c) DMA);
- fail to submit the description or supply incorrect, incomplete or misleading information that is required pursuant to Art. 15 DMA on any techniques for the profiling of consumers used for its core platform services (Art. 30(3)(d) DMA);
- fail to provide access to data, algorithms or information about testing in response to a request made pursuant to Art. 21(3) DMA (Art. 30(3)(e) DMA);
- fail to supply the information requested within the time limit fixed pursuant to Art. 21(3) DMA or supply incorrect, incomplete or misleading information or explanations that are requested pursuant to Art. 21 DMA or given in an interview pursuant to Art. 22 DMA (Art. 30(3)(f) DMA);
- fail to rectify within a time limit set by the European Commission, incorrect, incomplete or misleading information given by a representative or a member of staff (Art. 30(3)(g) half-sent. 1 DMA);
- fail or refuse to provide complete information on facts relating to the subject-matter and purpose of an inspection, pursuant to Art. 23 DMA (Art. 30(3)(g) half-sent. 2 DMA);
- refuse to submit to an inspection pursuant to Art. 23 DMA (Art. 30(3)(h) DMA);
- fail to comply with the obligations imposed by the European Commission as part of the monitoring of obligations and measures pursuant to Art. 26 DMA (Art. 30(3)(i) DMA);
- fail to introduce a compliance function which is independent from the operational functions of the gatekeeper in accordance with Art. 28 DMA (Art. 30(3)(j) DMA); or
- fail to comply with the conditions for access to the European Commission's file pursuant to Art. 34(4) DMA (Art. 30(3)(k) DMA).

8 If the European Commission's practice on procedural violations in cartel fine proceedings is applied, the formal DMA infringements are also likely to be considered **ag-**

gravating circumstances when assessing the amount of the fine within the meaning of Art. 30(4) DMA for **substantive DMA infringements.**[4]

3. Standard of fault

The company that is to be the addressee of the fine notice must have infringed the DMA intentionally or negligently. If the case law of the ECJ and the **practice** of the European Commission regarding intent in **cartel fine cases** is applied,[5] it is also likely to be sufficient for establishing intent in cases concerning fines under the DMA if the natural person acting on behalf of the gatekeeper was aware that the behaviour in question violated the DMA or if the person could not have been unaware that he or she was violating requirements of the DMA. To establish negligence, it would then be sufficient if the person acting ought to have recognised the infringement. Similarly, conduct in breach of the DMA is likely to be imputed to the company whenever the specific person responsible is authorised to act on behalf of the company and there is a company-related act.[6] 9

4. Limitation

The limitation period for **imposing** fines is **five years** pursuant to Art. 32(1) DMA. 10
Art. 32(2) DMA states that time shall begin to run on the day on which the infringement of the DMA is committed. In cases involving continuing or repeated infringements, however, time shall begin to run on the day on which the infringement ceases.

Art. 32(3) and (4) sent. 1 DMA state that the limitation period is **interrupted** by any 11
action taken by the European Commission for the purpose of a market investigation or proceedings in respect of an infringement. Each interruption starts time running afresh. A prerequisite for interruption is, however, that at least one party involved in the infringement is notified of the action. This means that an interruption is possible, among other things, as a result of requests for information from the European Commission or the initiation of proceedings. In addition, the DMA also mentions written authorisations to conduct inspections 'issued to its officials by the Commission' as a point of reference (Art. 32(3)(b) DMA). Since, based on the wording, interruption depends on one of the parties receiving a notification, the relevant point of reference is likely to be the date of the performance of the inspection on the premises of the party concerned and not the issue of the order regarding the inspection within the authority. When the limitation period restarts, the absolute limitation period must be observed. This occurs when a period equal to twice the limitation period has elapsed, i.e. after ten years (Art. 32(4) sent. 2 DMA). Under Art. 32(5) DMA, the limitation period is suspended for as long as the European Commission's decision on the fine is the subject of proceedings pending before a European Union court. As with cartel fine cases, however, limitation is only likely to be suspended in relation to the party that has appealed against the fine.[7]

The limitation period for **enforcing** fines is **five years** (Art. 33(1) DMA). Pursuant to 12
Art. 33(2) DMA, time begins to run from the day on which the decision on the fine becomes final. The limitation period is only interrupted in the cases listed exhaustively in

---

[4] Cf. for competition law e.g. European Commission, 'Guidelines on the method of setting fines imposed pursuant to Article 23(2)(a) of Regulation No 1/2003', 1.9.2006 (OJ 2006 C 210, 2), para. 28.

[5] Cf. for competition law e.g. ECJ 18.6.2013 – case C-681/11, ECLI:EU:C:2013:404 = BeckRS 2013, 81227 para. 37 – Schenker.

[6] Cf. for competition law e.g. ECJ 16.2.2017 – case C-95/15 P, ECLI:EU:C:2017:125 = BeckRS 2017, 101804 para. 34 – paraffin wax.

[7] Cf. for competition law e.g. ECJ 29.3.2011 – case C-201/09 P, ECLI:EU:C:2009:547 – BeckRS 2011, 80309 para. 142 – ArcelorMittal Luxembourg.

Art. 33(3) DMA and the interruption starts time running afresh. Pursuant to Art. 33(5) DMA, the limitation period is suspended, inter alia, for as long as enforcement of payment is suspended pursuant to a decision of a European Union court or national court.

5. Calculating the amount of a fine

13 When calculating the amount of a fine, the European Commission takes into account the **gravity, duration and recurrence** of an infringement. In cases involving formal DMA infringements, it also takes account of delays caused to the proceedings.

14 The criteria of gravity and duration of an infringement are already in need of clarification as indeterminate legal concepts. In this respect, the European Commission's guidelines for setting cartel fines[8] and the case law of the EU courts in the field of **competition law** should provide a **valuable point of reference** for assessing these criteria. In the law on cartel fines, fines are calculated as a specific percentage of the annual turnover generated by the companies involved in the infringement with the product in question. This means that the turnover generated with the relevant core platform service could serve as a basis for gatekeepers in each case. The European Commission sets an amount of up to 30 % of the relevant turnover, with the exact percentage depending on the gravity of the infringement.

15 In cartel fining law, the **gravity** of an infringement has to be determined on the basis of a comprehensive assessment of the particular circumstances of the case, for which there is no exhaustive list of assessment factors.[9] Factors recognised by case law in cartel cases include, for example, the actual impact of the infringement.[10] In addition, the turnover of products or services and the quantity of products or services affected by the DMA infringement could be taken into account. Furthermore, market shares, turnover and other economic variables of the party subject to the penalty could be used.[11] Finally, one could also consider the deterrent effect of fines.[12]

16 The amount determined on the basis of the turnover is then multiplied in competition law by the number of **years and months** that the company was involved in the infringement. This multiplication rule also appears to be an option for DMA infringements, even though it is important to consider that the obligations incumbent upon gatekeepers under Art. 5 et seqq. DMA are manifold. This means that any assessment of the duration of a DMA infringement must be based on the individual elements of the infringement. For example, in situations involving an infringement of Art. 5(2)(a) DMA by the gatekeeper, the duration of the breach is the period between the beginning and the end of the processing of personal data of end users through the use of third-party services that make use of the gatekeeper's core platform services.

17 The effect of infringements which occurred or started **before the DMA entered into force** has not been treated explicitly. According to the principle of legality in Art. 49 CFR – which applies to criminal offences – no one shall be held guilty on account of an act which did not constitute an offence at the time when it was committed. Infringements

[8] European Commission, 'Guidelines on the method of setting fines imposed pursuant to Article 23(2)(a) of Regulation No 1/2003', 1.9.2006 (OJ 2006 C 210, 2).

[9] Cf. for competition law e.g. ECJ 3.9.2009 – case C-534/07 P, ECLI:EU:C:2009:505 = BeckRS 2009, 70912 para. 54 – Prym and Prym Consumer.

[10] Cf. for competition law e.g. EGC 27.2.2014 – case T-91/11, ECLI:EU:T:2014:92 = BeckRS 2014, 81706 para. 67 – Innolux.

[11] Cf. for competition law e.g. ECJ 7.6.1983 – case 100/80 to 103/80, ECLI:EU:C:1983:158 = BeckRS 2004, 70610 para. 121 – Musique Diffusion française.

[12] Cf. for competition law e.g. ECJ 3.9.2009 – case C-534/07 P, ECLI:EU:C:2009:505 = BeckRS 2009, 70912 para. 54 – Prym and Prym Consumer.

which were finished before the DMA entered into force cannot be considered under the DMA. Application of the DMA for continuous infringements which started before entry into force seems very questionable. Certainly the years before the DMA entered into force should not be considered when determining the duration of the infringement.[13]

A further step would then have to involve considering whether a **repeated offence** might have occurred. It is questionable how the criterion of a repeated offence is to be handled. Various scenarios are conceivable. Apart from the more or less clear scenario in which the gatekeeper infringes the same obligation again with the same platform service, the case already starts to seem less clear if a different obligation is infringed, and even more so if an obligation is infringed with a different platform service. Based on the European Commission's guidelines for setting cartel fines, the fine can be increased by up to 100 % for each infringement established if the infringement continues or if the same infringement or a similar breach is committed again. While this might argue in favour of a broad scope of application for repeated offences, especially in view of the variety and diversity of the DMA obligations and the significant increase in fines in the event of a repeated offence, the scope of application of the provision should actually be interpreted rather narrowly. 18

Pursuant to Art. 30(1) or (2) DMA, however, the fine imposed on gatekeepers must not exceed 10 % – or for repeated offences 20 % – of their total worldwide turnover in the preceding financial year. If a formal DMA infringement has been committed, the fine for the undertaking or association of undertakings must not exceed 1 % of the total worldwide turnover achieved in the preceding financial year, as specified in Art. 30(3) DMA. The **turnover** of the **entire group of companies** is decisive here, as is the case in cartel fining law.[14] This is because, as shown by Art. 2 no. 27 DMA, like in competition law, the term 'undertaking' is to be interpreted broadly, i.e. all connected undertakings 'that form a group through the direct or indirect control of an enterprise or undertaking by another' are also covered. 19

Unlike in cartel law, the DMA does not provide leniency in the case of **cooperation**. However, it should be possible for the Commission to take such cooperation into account when determining the amount of the fine.[15] 20

6. Significance of the ban on double jeopardy – ne bis in idem

In the course of the legislative process, it was discussed whether the ban on double jeopardy (*ne bis in idem*) set out in Art. 50 CFR precludes the cumulative imposition of **fines under the DMA** on the one hand **and competition law** on the other for the same behaviour.[16] Ultimately, in cases involving a repeat offender, for example, a cumulative fine of up to 30 % of the company's total turnover in the financial year preceding the decisions would be possible (cf. Art. 30(2) DMA and Art. 23(2) Reg. (EC) No 1/2003). 21

It is largely undisputed that due to the threatened amount of fine of up to 10 % of the total turnover, fines for competition law infringements have the **criminal nature** required for application of the ban on double jeopardy within the meaning of Art. 50 CFR.[17] Consequently, the same also has to apply to fines according to Art. 30(1) DMA 22

[13] Cf. Huerkamp/Nuys in HK-DMA Art. 30 mn. 76.

[14] Cf. for competition law e.g. ECJ 26.11.2013 – case C-58/12 P, ECLI:EU:C:2013:770 = BeckRS 2013, 82221 para. 52 – Groupe Gascogne.

[15] Cf. Huerkamp/Nuys in HK-DMA Art. 30 mn. 87 et seqq.

[16] The German Federal Cartel Office has also taken up this discussion, cf. Federal Cartel Office Background Paper DMA p. 42.

[17] Cf. e.g. Jarass GRCh Art. 50 mn. 5; Harta NZKart 2022, 102 (103).

with the same fine range (10 %) and – even more so – to fines according to Art. 30(2) DMA for repeat offenders with the increased fine range of 20 %.[18]

23 More controversial, however, was the requirement of what is known as triple identity in cartel cases postulated by ECJ case law. According to this, the ban on double jeopardy only applied if not only (i) the facts and (ii) the companies accused were identical in both proceedings, but also (iii) the protected legal interest had to be identical.[19] The application of this additional criterion relating to identity of legal interest was difficult to reconcile with the wording of Art. 50 CFR, which only specifies the requirement of identity of the facts and the offender, as well as with the requirement of equal interpretation in all areas of law.[20] As a result, the ECJ recently **changed** its **case law** to the effect that at the level of the facts, as required by Art. 50 CFR, only the identity of the facts and the offender are required. If this is the case, an accumulation of penalties restricts the rights of the accused. According to Art. 52(1) CFR, such restrictions must be provided for by law and must also take into account the principle of proportionality, i.e. the restriction must be necessary and must meet objectives of general interest recognised by the Union. The ECJ itself presumably recognises a degree of leeway here, particularly if it emerges during the proportionality review that the objective of the penalty is not identical in the relevant proceedings.[21] If one applies this idea, which was developed by the ECJ in the relationship between competition law and regulatory law, it can be argued that the ban on double jeopardy does not in principle prevent the fines being imposed cumulatively under the DMA and competition law for the same behaviour. This is because, as the DMA itself makes clear, its objective is 'fairness' and 'contestability of markets', whereas competition law protects free competition (see rec. 11 DMA).

24 According to the ECJ, however, double jeopardy must still be taken into account. For example, it is appropriate that proceedings are coordinated and conducted within a proximate time frame; furthermore, the first penalty notice must be taken into account in the second penalty notice to **reduce** the fine.[22]

II. Periodic penalty payments (Art. 31 DMA)

25 Pursuant to Art. 31 DMA, the European Commission can impose on undertakings, including gatekeepers where applicable, and associations of undertakings, periodic penalty payments **not exceeding 5 %** of the average **daily** worldwide **turnover** in the preceding financial year per day. The European Commission can use this penalty to compel the addressees

- to comply with the measures specified by the European Commission in a decision adopted pursuant to Art. 8(2) in conjunction with Art. 20 DMA (Art. 31(1)(a) DMA);

[18] For example with regard to the previous drafts, also Akman ELR 2022, 85 (99); Harta NZKart 2022, 102 (103); Somek WuW 2021, 545 (548 et seqq.).

[19] Cf. e.g. ECJ 7.1.2004 – case C-204/00 P, ECLI:EU:C:2004:6 = BeckRS 2004, 74942 para. 338 – Aalborg Portland.

[20] Cf. e.g. AG Kokott 8.9.2011 – case C-17/10, ECLI:EU:C:2011:552 = BeckRS 2011, 81366 para. 111 et seqq. – Toshiba.

[21] Cf. in particular ECJ 22.3.2022 – case C-117/20, ECLI:EU:C:2022:203 = BeckRS 2022, 5010 para. 34, 41 et seqq. – bpost.

[22] Cf. in particular ECJ 22.3.2022 – case C-117/20, ECLI:EU:C:2022:203 = BeckRS 2022, 5010 para. 58 – bpost; see also Federal Cartel Office Background Paper DMA p. 42; Schweitzer ZEuP 2021, 503 (518).

- to comply with the decision pursuant to Art. 18(1) DMA ordering remedies to comply with individual DMA requirements following systematic non-compliance with Art. 5, 6 or 7 DMA (Art. 31(1)(b) DMA);
- to supply correct and complete information within the time limit required by a request for information made by decision pursuant to Art. 21 DMA (Art. 31(1)(c) DMA);
- to ensure access to data, algorithms and information about testing in response to a request made pursuant to Art. 21(3) DMA and to supply explanations on those as required by a decision pursuant to Art. 21 DMA (Art. 31(1)(d) DMA);
- to submit to an inspection which was ordered by a decision taken pursuant to Art. 23 DMA (Art. 31(1)(e) DMA);
- to comply with a decision ordering interim measures taken pursuant to Art. 24 DMA (Art. 31(1)(f) DMA);
- to comply with commitments made legally binding by a decision pursuant to Art. 25(1) DMA (Art. 31(1)(g) DMA); or
- to comply with a non-compliance decision against a gatekeeper pursuant to Art. 29 DMA (Art. 31(1)(h) DMA).

It follows from the clear wording of Art. 31 DMA and the preventive nature of periodic penalty payments that **no fault** on the part of the addressee of the periodic penalty payment is required for the imposition of such payments (regarding limitation → mn. 10 et seqq.). Apart from the cap of 5 %, Art. 31 DMA does not specify any criteria for assessing the amount of the periodic penalty payment. Nevertheless, the European Commission must at least be guided by the **proportionality principle** set out in Art. 5(1) sent. 2 and (4) TEU. If one applies the principles on penalties for antitrust violations, the European Commission must take into account factors including the significance of the enforced conduct for compliance with the DMA, the intended impact of the periodic penalty payment on the conduct ordered and the degree of fault.[23] If the undertaking or association of undertakings has satisfied the obligation which the periodic penalty payment was intended to enforce, the European Commission can set the definitive amount of the periodic penalty payment at a figure lower than that which would arise under the original decision in accordance with Art. 31(2) DMA. 26

III. Additional remedies (Art. 18 DMA)

In order to enforce the DMA, further remedies are available to the European Commission under Art. 18 DMA in the event of **systematic non-compliance** with individual provisions of the Regulation. This first of all requires a market investigation in which, in principle, according to Art. 18(1) sent. 2 DMA, the gatekeeper concerned is notified of the objections and the intended remedy within six months of initiation of the investigation. In order to enable interested third parties to provide comments effectively, the European Commission must publish a non-confidential summary of the case and the remedies that it is considering imposing or intended commitments to be made binding within this period in accordance with Art. 18(5) and (6) DMA. Finally, the European Commission must complete the market investigation within twelve months of commencing it (Art. 18(1) sent. 2 DMA). These deadlines can, however, be extended pursuant to Art. 18(7) DMA. 27

[23] Cf. for competition law e.g. Hellmann in Wiedemann KartellR-HdB § 46 mn. 140.

28 As stated in Art. 18(1) sent. 3 DMA, the **market investigation** must show that a gatekeeper has systematically infringed one or more of the obligations laid down in Art. 5, 6 or 7 DMA and has maintained, strengthened or extended its gatekeeper position in relation to the requirements set out in Art. 3(1) DMA. Art. 18(3) DMA sets out that a gatekeeper is deemed to have engaged in systematic non-compliance with the obligations laid down in Art. 5, 6 and 7 DMA where the European Commission has issued at least three non-compliance decisions pursuant to Art. 29 DMA against a gatekeeper in relation to any of its core platform services within a period of eight years prior to the opening of a market investigation pursuant to Art. 18 DMA. In this respect, it is of no relevance whether the decisions relate to the same infringement or to the same platform service.[24] It also follows from the wording of Art. 18 DMA that no fault on the part of the gatekeeper is required for the imposition of remedies.

29 If these requirements are met, the European Commission can, pursuant to Art. 18(1) sent. 3 DMA, impose **any behavioural or structural remedy** on the gatekeeper that is proportionate to the infringement at issue and necessary to ensure effective compliance with the requirements of the DMA. The wording does not allow for the conclusion that behavioural remedies – which tend to be less intrusive – take precedence over structural measures.[25] Yet due to the **principle of proportionality** set out in Art. 5(1) sent. 2 and (4) TEU, it has to be assumed that the less intrusive measure must be chosen if it is equally effective in achieving the objective. If one applies the principles applicable to coercive measures in the law on penalties for antitrust violations, the European Commission would also have to take into account the degree of fault when selecting remedies.[26] Finally, Art. 18(2) DMA clarifies that a remedy also includes the prohibition of concentrations with regard to core platform services, other services in the digital domain or the collection of data. However, the European Commission must demonstrate that this intervention is proportionate and necessary to ensure the fairness and contestability of the markets affected by the systematic infringement. In this respect, Art. 18(2) DMA contains a concrete expression of the principle of proportionality. The rationale behind Art. 18(2) DMA is that the competition authorities have identified the acquisition-driven corporate growth of the companies targeted by the DMA as a driver of competition problems in recent years.[27]

30 Art. 18(8) DMA states that the European Commission has to **regularly review** the remedies that it imposes. Within this context, the Commission is also entitled to modify these remedies if, following a new market investigation, it finds that they are not effective.

IV. Interim measures (Art. 24 DMA)

31 Finally, the European Commission can also issue interim measures against gatekeepers under Art. 24 DMA in the context of proceedings opened with a view to possible adoption of a non-compliance decision. This requires a ***prima facie*** finding of an **infringement** of Art. 5, 6 or 7 DMA. Secondly, there needs to be a case of urgency due to the risk of **serious and irreparable damage** for business users or end users.

32 Interim measures must apply **only for a specified** period of time and can be renewed in so far as is necessary and appropriate. Since the requirements set out in Art. 24 DMA

[24] Schöning/von Schreitter WuW 2022, 582 (587).
[25] See also Belloso, 'The Proposal for a Digital Markets Act (DMA): A Summary' (3.1.2022), p. 4.
[26] Cf. for competition law e.g. Hellmann in Wiedemann KartellR-HdB § 46 mn. 140.
[27] Schöning/von Schreitter WuW 2022, 582 (587).

and those for interim measures pursuant to Art. 8 Reg. (EC) No 1/2003 are almost identical, the corresponding decision-making practice under competition law should provide a useful aid to interpretation.

B. Investigative powers (Art. 21 et seqq. DMA)

33 According to Art. 21 et seqq. DMA, the European Commission has a number of investigative powers which it can also exercise **prior to the initiation of proceedings** on the possible issuance of a non-compliance decision pursuant to Art. 20(2) DMA.

34 By way of example, the European Commission may

- pursuant to Art. 21(1) to (4) DMA, by simple request (request for information, RFI) or by decision, require from undertakings and associations of undertakings to provide all necessary information required for the European Commission to carry out its duties unde r the DMA, access to any data and algorithms of undertakings and information about testing, as well as requesting explanations of them;
- pursuant to Art. 21(5) DMA, require of the Member States to provide the European Commission with all necessary information in their possession to carry out the duties assigned to it under the DMA;
- pursuant to Art. 22 DMA, interview any natural or legal person which consents to being interviewed, for the purpose of collecting information relating to the subject-matter of an investigation and record such interviews by any technical means; and
- pursuant to Art. 23 DMA, conduct all necessary inspections of an undertaking or association of undertakings required for the European Commission in order to carry out its duties under the DMA. The officials and other accompanying persons authorised by the Commission to conduct an inspection are empowered, among other things, to enter any premises, land and means of transport of undertakings and associations of undertakings; to examine the books and other records related to the business; to take or obtain in any form copies of or extracts from such books or records; to seal any business premises and books or records for the duration of, and to the extent necessary for, the inspection; and to ask for explanations of facts or documents and to record the answers by any technical means.

35 The European Commission can be expected to draw on its own wealth of experience in competition law when applying its powers to inspect and search In this respect, the **decision-making practice under competition law** is also likely to provide a useful **interpretation aid** in this context.

C. Legal protection

36 The European Commission can take numerous decisions under the DMA that have far-reaching consequences for addressees. The most obvious examples are certainly the DMA penalties in the form of a fine decision, a periodic penalty payment decision or remedies (Art. 29, 30, 31 and 18 DMA), possibly in combination with a non-compliance decision. The addressees' procedural rights to be heard and to access the file (Art. 34 DMA, further elaborated in the Implementing Regulation[28]), although fundamental

[28] Commission Implementing Regulation (EU) 2023/814 of 14 April 2023 on detailed arrangements for the conduct of certain proceedings by the Commission pursuant to Regulation (EU) 2022/1925 of the European Parliament and of the Council (OJ 2023 L 102, 6).

principles of EU law, only provide limited protection.[29] Similarly, however, the gatekeeper designation decision under Art. 3(4) and (8) DMA has far-reaching consequences for the addressee, who must comply with a large number of self-executing obligations after designation. However, an appeal is also conceivable in cases where a gatekeeper's application for a review of gatekeeper status is rejected under Art. 4(1) DMA. The President of the Court, Marc van der Woude, therefore expects **numerous applications for legal protection** after the DMA enters into force and fears that the procedural law of the EGC and the ECJ is not made for quick decisions[30] which would be necessary to meet the DMA's objective of speeding up decisions overall.

I. Parties subject to penalties

37 For those subject to penalties, **the action for annulment** pursuant to Art. 263 TFEU, the interim relief pursuant to Art. 278 and 279 TFEU and, if applicable, appeals pursuant to Art. 256(1), second subparagraph TFEU and Art. 56 et seqq. of the Statute of the Court of Justice are often likely to be an option.

1. Action for annulment

a) Admissibility of the action

38 If an action for annulment is successful as a forfeit action for a modification of rights, the measure is declared void *ex tunc* in full or in part pursuant to Art. 264(1) and (2) TFEU. The case law has specified the admissible **subject matter of the action** to the effect that it must be a legally binding measure with external effect attributable to a body of the European Union.[31] Thus, the action for annulment is an admissible type of action if the annulment of a decision by which the European Commission imposed a DMA penalty, for example a fine, a periodic penalty payment or another remedy, is sought. However, the same also applies to the revocation of a decision designating a party as a gatekeeper or if action is to be taken against the rejection of the gatekeeper's application for a review of gatekeeper status. By contrast, in the absence of any legally binding effect, the initiation of proceedings under Art. 20 DMA, the notification of preliminary findings under Art. 29(3) DMA[32] or an informal letter in the case of novel or unclear questions on the interpretation of the DMA[33] are unlikely to constitute an admissible subject matter of action.

39 An applicant must also have the **right to institute proceedings** within the meaning of Art. 263(2) to (4) TFEU. A distinction is made in this respect between privileged and semi-privileged applicants, which are specific institutions of the European Union; and non-privileged applicants, which are natural persons or legal entities.[34] In the group of natural persons and legal entities, Art. 263(4) TFEU distinguishes between an applicant to whom/which the measure is addressed (first alternative), and an applicant not ad-

---

[29] Cf. Huerkamp/Nuys in HK-DAM Art. 34 mn. 1 et seqq.

[30] Van der Woude in Connor, 'DMA will be a "challenge" for EU courts, General Court president admits' (31.3.2022) <https://globalcompetitionreview.com/article/dma-will-be-challenge-eu-courts-general-court-president-admits> (last accessed: 12.7.2023).

[31] Cf. e.g. ECJ 2.3.1994 – case C-316/91, ECLI:EU:C:1994:76 = BeckRS 2004, 76296 para. 8 – EP v Council; ECJ 28.6.1993 – case C-64/93, ECLI:EU:C:1993:266 = BeckRS 2004, 77654 para. 13 – Donatab.

[32] Regarding the initiation of competition law proceedings and the notification of the relevant objections e.g. ECJ 11.11.1981 – case C-60/81, ECLI:EU:C:1981:264 = BeckRS 2004, 73415 para. 21 – IBM.

[33] Regarding competition law comfort letters of the Commission e.g. also Schütte/Thomas in Wiedemann KartellR-HdB § 49 mn. 195.

[34] Cf. e.g. Dörr in Grabitz/Hilf/Nettesheim AEUV Art. 263 mn. 51 et seqq.

dressed by the measure but where the measure is of direct and individual concern to them (second alternative).

The result is that the right to institute proceedings always applies in the first alternative, meaning that a **party subject to a penalty under the DMA** always has the right to institute proceedings within the meaning of Art. 263(4) alt. 1 TFEU. The same will presumably apply to all consortium companies if the penalty under DMA is directed at a consortium that does not have legal capacity.[35] 40

By contrast, further conditions must be fulfilled for the second alternative. According to case law, a measure is of **direct** concern to an applicant if it produces its legal effects without any further intermediate steps taken by a public authority or if there is no discretion for this intermediate step.[36] Legally binding measures by the European Commission under the DMA are generally likely to be of a direct nature.[37] A measure is of **individual** concern to an applicant, according to what is known as the *Plaumann* formula, if the decision affects them by reason of certain attributes which are peculiar to them or by reason of circumstances in which they are differentiated from all other persons and by virtue of these factors distinguishes them individually just as in the case of the person addressed.[38] If, for example, only a subsidiary of a parent company is the addressee of a penalty under the DMA, the parent company may also have the right to institute proceedings provided it holds all shares in the subsidiary.[39] 41

In addition, an applicant must bring an action for annulment within the **time limit for bringing an action** under Art. 263(6) half-sent. 1 TFEU. The time limit is two months and is extended on account of distance by a single period of 10 days in accordance with Art. 60 of the Rules of Procedure of the General Court. Art. 263(6) half-sent. 2 TFEU stipulates that the start of the time limit is (depending on the situation) – the publication of the measure, or its notification to the applicant, or, in the absence thereof, the day on which it came to the knowledge of the latter. Accordingly, for the party subject to a penalty under the DMA, the start of the time limit is generally determined based on the delivery of the European Commission decision.[40] Pursuant to Art. 58(1)(b) of the Rules of Procedure of the General Court, the time limit ends with the expiry of whichever day in the month after next is the same day on which the time limit for bringing an action, plus ten further days. If that day is a Saturday or Sunday or a public holiday at the seat of the EGC in Luxembourg, the end of the time limit shall be the end of the following working day. The dates of these public holidays are published annually in the Official Journal of the European Union.[41] 42

Finally, the other admissibility requirements must be fulfilled. For example, the European Commission, and not the European Union, is the correct **defendant** if the annulment of a decision by which it has imposed a penalty under the DMA is sought. In addition, general procedural principles dictate that the applicant must have an **interest in le-** 43

[35] Cf. for competition law EGC 19.3.2010 – case T-50/05, ECLI:EU:T:2010:101 = BeckRS 2010, 90345 para. 40 – Evropaïki Dynamiki.

[36] Cf. e.g. ECJ 17.1.1985 – case 11/82, ECLI:EU:C:1985:18 = BeckRS 2004, 71239 para. 7 et seqq. – Piraiki-Patraiki et al.; EGC 18.9.1996 – case T-155/94, ECLI:EU:T:1996:118 = EuZW 1996, 151, juris para. 53 – Climax v Council.

[37] Regarding competition law acts of the European Commission e.g. also Schütte/Thomas in Wiedemann KartellR-HdB § 49 mn. 206.

[38] ECJ 15.7.1963 – case 25/62, ECLI:EU:C:1963:17 = NJW 1963, 2246 – Plaumann.

[39] Cf. for another European law contact e.g. EGC 22.4.1999 – case T-112/97, ECLI:EU:T:1999:83 = BeckRS 1999, 160997 para. 58 – Monsanto.

[40] Regarding competition law acts of the European Commission e.g. also Schütte/Thomas in Wiedemann KartellR-HdB § 49 mn. 21.

[41] For further details, cf. for example Dörr in Grabitz/Hilf/Nettesheim AEUV Art. 263 mn. 118 et seqq.

gal protection at the time the action is brought. Finally, the action must be brought in the **appropriate form** in accordance with Art. 21(1) of the Statute of the Court of Justice and Art. 76 to 78 of the Rules of Procedure of the General Court; in particular, the grounds for the action listed in Art. 263(2) TFEU must be submitted in writing.[42]

b) Merits of the action

44 The action for annulment is well-founded if the applicant can successfully claim one or more of the four grounds for the action **(grounds for annulment) listed in Art. 263(2) TFEU**. Accordingly, an action for annulment relating to a DMA-related penalty can generally only be well-founded if the European Commission was not competent at the time of the adoption of the measure, infringed an essential procedural requirement, abused its discretion or violated other EU law.[43]

45 It is likely that many legal actions relating to the DMA actions will be based on a violation of EU law – namely the DMA. This is because any incorrect interpretation or application of EU law by the Commission is covered by these grounds. The very **far-reaching catalogue of obligations** that **gatekeepers** have to take into account offers particular potential for disputes about correct interpretation in this respect.

46 The EU courts are, however, precluded from substituting their own assessment of the facts or evidence for that of the European Commission in actions for annulment. In the event of legal errors, the European Commission's decision is therefore not rectified as a matter of principle but is simply **declared null and void**.

47 Art. 45 DMA, however, provides for a significant exception. Accordingly, the Court of Justice of the European Union, and thus also the EGC, has the power of **unlimited review** in actions against decisions in which the European Commission has imposed a fine or a periodic penalty payment. This means that EU courts can cancel, reduce or increase the fines and periodic penalty payments and review the fairness and appropriateness of the penalty concerned.[44] This can speed up the proceedings, because it can be assumed that the EU courts will refrain from declaring decisions void in cases involving only selective errors of assessment by the European Commission and will instead uphold the penalty decision with a reduced fine.

48 If the action is well-founded, the EU court will annul the measure. The effect of a penalty under the DMA is thus removed ***ex tunc***.[45] If the European Commission has imposed penalties on several companies for a DMA violation in one decision but only some of these companies have filed an action, the annulment does not affect all other companies. Otherwise, the European Commission could have decided on several separate penalties.[46]

2. Interim relief

49 Interim relief under Art. 278 and 279 TFEU can also become relevant in DMA matters. This is because actions before the Court of Justice do not have any suspensory effect pursuant to Art. 278 sent. 1 TFEU. Despite that, if it considers that circumstances so require, the Court may order that **application** of the contested act be **suspended**, i.e. the

[42] Cf. e.g. Cremer in Calliess/Ruffert AEUV Art. 263 mn. 24 et seqq.

[43] For further details, cf. e.g. Dörr in Grabitz/Hilf/Nettesheim AEUV Art. 263 mn. 118 et seqq.

[44] Cf. for competition law e.g. ECJ 25.2.1986 – case 193/83, ECLI:EU:C:1986:75 = BeckRS 2004, 72156 para. 110 et seqq. – Windsurfing; EGC 9.7.2003 – case T-230/00, ECLI:EU:T:2003:196 = BeckRS 2003, 70346 para. 54 – Daesang and Sewon.

[45] Cf. e.g. Dörr in Grabitz/Hilf/Nettesheim AEUV Art. 263 para. 197.

[46] Cf. for competition law e.g. EGC 10.7.1997 – case T-227/95, ECLI:EU:T:1997:108 = EuZW 1997, 696, juris para. 55 et seqq. – AssiDomän.

DMA-related penalties or other decisions, such as a decision designating a party as a gatekeeper.[47] In addition, the Court of Justice can prescribe **interim measures** pursuant to Art. 279 TFEU.

a) Admissibility of the application

50 The application for interim relief is therefore an **admissible type of application** if the applicant seeks this sort of suspension or prescription. This could be the case, for example, if the European Commission, as in other cases in the past, refrains from imposing a fine during court proceedings if the person subject to the fine provides a bank guarantee. In this respect, an interim injunction could also be applied for in the context of the DMA, requesting a release from the obligation to provide such a guarantee.[48]

51 The application is admissible, inter alia,[49] if (i) the main action is pending pursuant to Art. 156(1) of the Rules of Procedure of the General Court; (ii) the subject matter of the application relates to the main action pursuant to Art. 156(2) of the Rules of Procedure of the General Court; (iii) the form of application within the meaning of Art. 156(4) and (5) of the Rules of Procedure of the General Court is complied with (in particular, a separate pleading is filed); and (iv) the **main action is not evidently inadmissible.**[50]

b) Merits of the application

52 The application is well-founded if the applicant makes a credible case that suspending the execution of a DMA penalty or the issue of an interim injunction is necessary in de facto and legal terms. The action must therefore have a sufficient chance of **success** in the **main proceedings** and the suspension must be **urgent**, i.e. necessary after fully weighing up the interests involved to prevent serious and irreparable damage to the interests of the applicant.[51]

53 Where the application is well-founded, however, the corresponding decision must be of an **interim nature** pursuant to Art. 158(4) of the Rules of Procedure of the General Court and must not pre-empt the decision in the main proceedings. This means that the decision does not neutralise any consequences of the decision in the main proceedings in advance and does not prejudge any issues of law or fact in the decision in the main proceedings.[52]

54 A company is particularly likely to seek interim relief as a result of a decision designating it as a gatekeeper. This is because after being designated as a gatekeeper, a company has to comply with a variety of **self-executing obligations**. Especially in procedures under Art. 3(8) DMA, there are likely to be a number of uncertainties and, as a result, considerable potential for legal defence in practice.

---

[47] The President of the EGC, for example, pursuant to Art. 158(1) of the Rules of Procedure of the General Court.

[48] Cf. for competition law e.g. EGC 21.12.1994 – case T-301/94 R, ECLI:EU:T:1994:316, juris para. 24 et seqq. – Laakmann.

[49] Cf. for more information e.g. Wegener in Calliess/Ruffert AEUV Art. 279 mn. 5 et seqq.

[50] Cf. for competition law e.g. EGC 30.10.2003 – cases T-125/03 R and T-253/03 R, ECLI:EU:T:2003:287 = BeckRS 2003, 14100 para. 56 – Akzo Nobel.

[51] Cf. in another context e.g. ECJ 12.7.1996 – case C-180/96 R, ECLI:EU:C:1996:308 = BeckRS 2004, 74734 para. 44 – United Kingdom.

[52] EGC 29.3.2001 – case T-18/01 R, ECLI:EU:T:2001:110, juris para. 14 – Goldstein.

3. Appeals

55 A party subject to a penalty can file an appeal with the ECJ against a judgment resulting from an action for annulment or against a decision resulting from an application for interim relief within the meaning of Art. 256(1) subpara. 2 TFEU. The **conditions for admissibility** are set out in **Art. 56 et seqq**. of the **Statute of the Court of Justice**. These state that a time limit of two months from service of the contested decision must be observed.[53]

56 The appeal is well-founded if the contested decision incorrectly assesses a legal question under EU law and the operative part of the judgment is also ultimately **incorrect in legal terms**.[54] In the decision-making practice, appeals in DMA cases are in general likely to have fewer, rather than greater, chances of success. This is because appeals cannot merely repeat the pleas in law and arguments already submitted to the EGC without putting forward arguments to establish that the latter erred in law.[55]

II. Third parties

57 For third parties, **reporting** of infringements and **access to the files** are likely to be particularly relevant.

1. Reporting infringements

58 Pursuant to Art. 27(1) DMA, **any** third party, including competitors or end users, can inform the European Commission or a national competition authority about any practice or behaviour by gatekeepers that falls within the scope of the DMA. Pursuant to Art. 27(2) DMA, however, the European Commission and the national competition authorities have full **discretion** as regards the appropriate measures and are under no obligation to follow up on the information received. Where the national competent authority determines, based on the information received, that there may be an issue of non-compliance with the DMA, it has to transfer that information to the European Commission pursuant to Art. 27(3) DMA.

59 Similar to competition law cases, this instrument is likely to play a major role in the initiation of proceedings in DMA cases. For companies of all sizes, the strategic interest in notifying authorities of unwelcome gatekeeper behaviour is obvious. These reports also have the advantage over civil proceedings that the European Commission has special investigative rights and that the European Commission's administrative proceedings are **free of charge**.[56] However, it is advisable for the third party reporting a DMA infringement to have an informal discussion with the European Commission in advance, in order to clarify whether the facts of the case are relevant for the European Commission.[57]

[53] For details e.g. Huber in Streinz AEUV Art. 256 mn. 7 et seqq.

[54] ECJ 16.12.1999 – case C-150/98 P, ECLI:EU:C:1999:616 = BeckRS 2004, 74464 para. 17 – Economic and Social Committee.

[55] ECJ 2.4.2009 – case C-202/07 P, ECLI:EU:C:2009:214 = BeckRS 2011, 80008 para. 69 – France Télécom.

[56] Regarding competition law complaints lodged with the European Commission e.g. also Dieckmann in Wiedemann KartellR-HdB § 47 mn. 1.

[57] Cf. European Commission, 'Report on Competition Policy 2005' <https://ec.europa.eu/competition/publications/annual_report/2005/en.pdf> (last accessed: 12.7.2023), para. 25.

2. Access to files

Under the DMA, third parties that report a violation and other **third parties generally** have **no right** to access the files. If the European Commission nevertheless makes individual documents available to third parties, for example by publishing a non-confidential summary of the facts and the remedies that it is considering imposing, this will unlikely constitute an access to the file but, instead, an investigative process.[58] In any case, however, disclosure of documents must not include documents containing business secrets.[59] 60

The general right of access to documents of the European Commission pursuant to Art. 15 TFEU and Reg. (EC) No 1049/2001 is also not considered a right of access to documents, but instead a right of access of the general public to documents for the purpose of transparency.[60] Under this provision, any EU citizen and any natural or legal person residing or having its registered office in a Member State has a right of access to documents of the EU institutions, bodies, offices and agencies. In order to avoid contradictions with the DMA, the same principles will probably apply as in cartel fine cases. As a result, applications for access to documents of the European Commission in DMA cases are likely to be **regularly rejected** on the basis of exclusion provisions of Art. 4(2) indent 1 and 2 and (3) Reg. (EC) No 1049/2001, because it can be assumed that protection for the commercial interests of the DMA addressees and protection for the legal advice and decision-making process of the European Commission would otherwise be impaired. The applicant can, however, rebut this presumption for individual documents.[61] 61

[58] Cf. e.g. on the non-confidential wording of the statement of objections in competition law cases ECJ 24.6.1986 – case C-53/85, ECLI:EU:C:1986:256 = BeckRS 2004, 73286 para. 27 – AKZO Chemie.

[59] Cf. also Art. 7 and 8 Implementing Regulation; ECJ 17.11.1987 – cases 142 and 156/84, ECLI:EU:C:1987:490 para. 21 – British American Tobacco v Reynolds Industries.

[60] See rec. 1 et seqq. Reg. (EC) No 1049/2001.

[61] Cf. e.g. EGC 5.2.2018 – case T-611/15, ECLI:EU:T:2018:63 = BeckRS 2018, 721 para. 62 et seqq. – Edeka.

CHAPTER 11
ROLE OF NATIONAL AUTHORITIES AND COURTS

Markus Brösamle/Emilia Etz

Bibliography: Achleitner, 'Digital Markets Act beschlossen: Verhaltenspflichten und Rollen nationaler Wettbewerbsbehörden', NZKart 2022, 359; Basedow, 'Das Rad neu erfunden: Zum Vorschlag für einen Digital Markets Act', ZEuP 2021, 217; Gerpott, 'Durchsetzung des DMA-E und dessen Verhältnis zum Kartellrecht', NZKart 2021, 273; Gerpott, 'Wer reguliert zukünftig Betreiber großer Online-Plattformen?', WuW 2021, 481; Grünwald, 'Gekommen um zu bleiben? – § 19a GWB im Lichte des DMA-Entwurfs', NZKart 2021, 496; Haus, 'Digital Markets Act – „duty to deal" für digitale Werbung?', WuW 2021, 478; Kumkar, 'Plattform-Recht revisited: Umgang mit den Marktordnungen digitaler Plattformen de lege lata et ferenda', RDi 2022, 347; Podszun/Bongarzt/Kirk, 'Digital Markets Act – Neue Regeln für Fairness in der Plattformökonomie', NJW 2022, 3249; Podszun/Bongarzt/Langenstein, 'The Digital Markets Act: Moving Away from Competition Law to Regulation for Large Gatekeepers', EuCML 2021, 60; Polley/Konrad, 'Der Digital Markets Act – Brüssels neues Regulierungskonzept für Digitale Märkte', WuW 2021, 198; Research Services of the German Bundestag, 'Sachstand – Die Anwendbarkeit von § 19a GWB im Lichte des europäischen Gesetzgebungsverfahrens zum „Digital Markets Act"', WD 7 – 3000 – 114/21; PE 6 – 3000 – 067/21 (7.1.2022) <https://www.bundestag.de/resource/blob/880748/856d83cb24c61822c508aa47f27e18e7/WD-7-114-21-PE-6-067-21-pdf-data.pdf> (last accessed: 12.7.2023); Schweitzer/Gutmann, 'Unilateral Practices by Digital Platforms: Facts and Myths about the Reach and Effectiveness of Competition Law' (2021) <https://dx.doi.org/10.2139/ssrn.3857751> (last accessed: 12.7.2023); Westermann, 'Der geplante Digital Markets Act: Europäische Regulierung zentraler Plattformdienste außerhalb des Kartellrechts?', ZHR 186 (2022), 325; Zegler, 'The Principle of ne bis in idem in EU Competition Law', WuW 2021, 261; Zimmer/Göhsl, 'Vom New Competition Tool zum Digital Markets Act: Die geplante EU-Regulierung für digitale Gatekeeper', ZWeR 2021, 29; Zober, 'Durchsetzung des DMA-E und dessen Verhältnis zum Kartellrecht', NZKart 2021, 611.

A. Overview

1 The DMA intends to establish a harmonised regulatory framework for gatekeepers (cf. Art. 1(1) DMA and rec. 8 DMA). Simultaneously, the DMA aims to ensure contestability and fairness of digital markets and prevent the fragmentation of the European internal market through divergent national regulatory solutions (cf. rec. 6 and 7 DMA). To these ends, the DMA stipulates a centralised enforcement system through the European Commission (**public enforcement**, cf. also rec. 91 DMA). National authorities have a cooperative and supportive function, i.e. they are to assist the European Commission in

its enforcement measures (→ mn. 3). National courts on the other hand must ensure that they do not take decisions that run counter to a decision adopted by the European Commission under the DMA (they can ask the Commission for information or opinions on questions which arise in this regard). In any case, national courts will play a decisive role in enforcing the DMA within the context of private enforcement (→ Ch. 13 mn. 1).

B. Role of national authorities in relation to the European Commission

In order to ensure uniform conditions with regard to digital markets and gatekeepers, the DMA provides for a **centralised monitoring and implementation** system through the **European Commission** (→ mn. 3 et seqq.). The DMA does not confer independent implementing powers to the national authorities but merely provides for their assistance and support in enforcing the DMA (→ mn. 8 et seqq.). The relationship between the DMA and the application of European and national (in particular competition law) rules by the national authorities, whose objectives are similar (first and foremost 'digital competition law'), must thus be further examined (see rec. 17 et seqq. DMA) 2

I. Centralised enforcement by the European Commission

The European Commission is responsible for the enforcement of the DMA (through new teams in DG Competition and Connect). The national authorities must cooperate and coordinate with the European Commission in this regard (cf. Art. 37, 38 DMA). This means that the European Commission is responsible for designating gatekeepers (Art. 3 DMA), reviewing the conditions for designation (Art. 4 DMA), conducting market investigations (Art. 16 et seqq. DMA) and, last but not least, imposing fines and penalty payments (Art. 29 et seqq. DMA). 3

The DMA sees the **centralisation of powers and responsibilities** with the European Commission as a tool to enable swift and effective application and enforcement (cf. Art. 1(1) and rec. 28, 91 and 92 DMA). The DMA emphasises the necessity for uniform application, enforcement and implementation of the DMA, thus the centralisation shall safeguard the harmonised application and enforcement of the DMA (cf. rec. 99 and conversely rec. 92 DMA). 4

The centralisation is also an expression of the desired and envisaged **full harmonisation** by the DMA (cf. its Art. 1(1)). The DMA stresses that gatekeepers operate throughout the EU (cf. rec. 7 DMA), which is why corresponding EU-wide harmonised rules are necessary in order to eliminate obstacles to the freedom to provide and receive services, including retail services, within the internal market (cf. rec. 8 DMA). Harmonisation is to be supported by preventing the application of national rules which are within the scope of, and pursue the same objectives as the DMA (cf. rec. 9 and 92 DMA). In this way, the European legislator intends to prevent **fragmentation of the internal market** (cf. rec. 7 and 9 DMA). At the same time, harmonisation is said to reduce compliance costs incurred by companies, because a uniform standard applies throughout the EU and no national specificities have to be taken into account (cf. rec. 6 DMA), meaning that there is also a benefit to the economy of the EU through 'proper functioning' of the internal market, and to EU consumers (cf. rec. 8 DMA). 5

6 Since the beginning of the legislative process, the **centralised role** of the European Commission was criticised – namely also by Germany.[1] Lessons learned from the development of EU competition law showed that centralisation can quickly become burdensome for the European Commission. For example, the First Regulation Implementing Art. 85 and 86 of the Treaty (i.e., first EU Competition Regulation, Reg. (EEC) No 17/62) initially stipulated centralised enforcement of EU competition law by the European Commission. From 1965 onwards, however, mechanisms were gradually introduced to take pressure off the European Commission, establishing, for example, the principle of self-assessment by companies and parallel competences of the European Commission, national competition authorities and courts.[2] This resulted in the implementation of a referral system, which also seemed preferable for some Member States within the context of the DMA.[3] There are also concerns that centralisation could lead to enforcement being dependent on the 'political will' of the European Commission.[4]

7 The two **Directorates-General Connect and Competition** are entrusted with the enforcement of the DMA.[5] The European Commission has allegedly created 55 internal and 25 external full-time posts to fulfil its responsibilities under the DMA (100 new posts in total for enforcement of the Digital Services Act (DSA) and the DMA).[6] There are also plans to appoint a Chief Technology Officer. Whether this increase in resources will be sufficient in view of the numerous tasks to be carried out centrally by the European Commission remains doubtful.[7] The risk is that, with insufficient resources, it will be impossible to achieve the swift and effective enforcement envisaged by the DMA (cf. rec. 28 DMA).[8]

II. No independent role for national authorities

8 The DMA does not envisage an independent role for national authorities with regard to application, further development and enforcement of the DMA, although they are to cooperate closely with the Commission on the aforementioned tasks.[9] For example, na-

[1] Joint position paper 'Friends of an effective Digital Markets Act' by France, the Netherlands and Germany of 27.5.2021 (Part 1) and 8.9.2021 (Part 2) <https://www.bmwk.de/Redaktion/DE/Downloads/M-O/non-paper-friends-of-an-effective-digital-markets-act.pdf> (Part 1) and <https://www.bmwk.de/Redaktion/DE/Downloads/XYZ/zweites-gemeinsames-positionspapier-der-friends-of-an-effective-digital-markets-act.pdf> (Part 2) (last accessed: 12.7.2023); Kumkar RDi 2022, 347; Gerpott WuW 2021, 481.

[2] Basedow ZEuP 2021, 217.

[3] Joint position paper 'Friends of an effective Digital Markets Act' by France, the Netherlands and Germany of 8.9.2021 (Part 2) <https://www.bmwk.de/Redaktion/DE/Downloads/XYZ/zweites-gemeinsames-positionspapier-der-friends-of-an-effective-digital-markets-act.pdf> (last accessed: 12.7.2023).

[4] Podszun/Bongarzt/Langenstein EuCML 2021, 60.

[5] Breton, 'Sneak peek: How the Commission will enforce the DSA & DMA' (Blog, 5.7.2022) <https://ec.europa.eu/commission/presscorner/detail/en/STATEMENT_22_4327> (last accessed: 12.7.2023).

[6] Breton, 'Sneak peek: How the Commission will enforce the DSA & DMA' (Blog, 5.7.2022) <https://ec.europa.eu/commission/presscorner/detail/en/STATEMENT_22_4327> (last accessed: 12.7.2023); Gerpott WuW 2021, 481.

[7] See also Gerpott WuW 2021, 481.

[8] Federal Cartel Office Background Paper DMA p. 39; Various organisations, 'Open letter' (2022) <https://content https://content.mlex.com/Attachments/2022-06-27_B97EYT02886KX3PW/beuc-x-2022-068_open_civil_society_letter_-_resources_to_ensure_effective_enforcement_of_the_dma.pdf> (last accessed: 12.7.2023); Mlex, 'EU's Gatekeeper law needs bigger enforcement team to be effective' (2022) <https://mlexmarketinsight.com/news/insight/eu-s-gatekeeper-law-needs-bigger-enforcement-team-to-be-effective-microsoft-chief-says> (last accessed: 12.7.2023); Achleitner NZKart 2022, 359; Podszun/Bongarzt/Langenstein EuCML 2021, 60.

[9] See also German Monopolies Commission, 'Biennial Report' (2022) <https://www.monopolkommission.de/images/HG24/HGXXIV_Gesamt.pdf> (last accessed: 12.7.2023).

tional authorities shall not take any decision which runs counter to a decision adopted by the European Commission under the DMA. To this end, however, all necessary information must be made available to national authorities (including national courts), in order to enable an assessment as to whether a decision risks running counter to a Commission decision (cf. Art. 1(7) and rec. 92 DMA). The European Commission can also consult national authorities on all matters relating to the application of the DMA (for cooperation between national authorities and the European Commission, cf. in particular Art. 37 DMA). This cooperation mechanism is based on the model of Art. 11 of the Regulation on the implementation of the EU rules on competition (Reg. (EC) No 1/2003), which sets out provisions governing cooperation between the Commission and national competition authorities.[10]

The DMA thus merely stipulates a **supporting function** for national authorities. In particular, they are to provide information to the European Commission (cf. rec. 82 and 90 DMA). The European Commission can also ask for **expert support** from national data and consumer protection authorities (cf. rec. 85 DMA) and can consult national authorities on matters concerning the application of the DMA(Art. 37(2) DMA). 9

The DMA nonetheless recognises that for 'coherent, effective and complementary enforcement of available legal instruments applied to gatekeepers', **close cooperation** and coordination between the European Commission and national authorities within the remit of their supporting function is required (cf. Art. 1(7) sent. 2 and rec. 90 DMA). The European Commission and the national authorities are to coordinate their enforcement efforts (cf. rec. 86 DMA), whilst respecting the principle of **sincere cooperation** (principle of Art. 4 TEU, cf. rec. 90 DMA). National authorities are entitled to receive information concerning gatekeepers' conduct (cf. Art. 27(1) DMA), in return they must inform the European Commission if they observe a case of non-compliance with the DMA (Art. 27(3) DMA). 10

Furthermore, it is envisaged that the European Commission can request **assistance** from national authorities **in market investigations** (→ Ch. 8 mn. 31) (Art. 16(5) DMA). This is necessary to relieve the resources of the European Commission and to profit from the expertise of national authorities. In addition, the European Commission can **request support from national authorities during inspections** (→ Ch. 4 mn. 1 et seqq.) (Art. 23 DMA, especially (3)). 11

Cooperation and **coordination** with national **competition** authorities are specified in more detail by the DMA (Art. 38 DMA on cooperation with competition authorities and Art. 37 DMA on general cooperation with national authorities). The DMA provides for a comprehensive exchange of information with national competition authorities (Art. 38(1) DMA) and for obligations of the national competition authorities to inform the European Commission of their intentions to launch an investigation on gatekeepers, to impose obligations on gatekeepers or conduct investigations as to non-compliance with Art. 5, 6 and 7 DMA (Art. 38(2), (3) and (7) DMA). 12

In order to **support the European Commission**, Member States can authorise their competition authorities to launch **investigations** into possible violations of the DMA (cf. Art. 38(2) and (7) and rec. 91 DMA).[11] If the European Commission initiates its own investigations after being informed by a Member State of its intention to conduct an investigation, the Member State must terminate its investigations (cf. Art. 38(7) half-sent. 2 DMA). The European Commission can, however, request the national authorities to assist it in its own investigations (cf. Art. 38(7) half-sent. 2 DMA). 13

[10] Achleitner NZKart 2022, 359 (364).
[11] In Germany this was done by § 32g GWB.

14 This approach is indeed practical, as national competition authorities have accumulated significant expertise through their previous enforcement practice (e.g. the German Federal Cartel Office has investigated digital cases extensively in recent years, cf. for example the proceedings against Facebook). The DMA is also based on the decision-making practice of national competition authorities.[12] The DMA provides for committees for this purpose: For example, it provides for an advisory committee (cf. Art. 50(1) and rec. 101 DMA), whereby Member States decide on the composition of their delegations and can nominate members of the national competition authorities with relevant expertise on a specific issue. The DMA also enables cooperation via the European Competition Network (ECN) (cf. Art. 38(1) DMA), as part of which authorities can exchange information (including confidential information).

15 Initial statements by the national competent authorities suggest that they will cooperate closely in enforcing the DMA. Numerous competition authorities have, for example, explicitly welcomed the **cooperation obligation** and have expressed their willingness to assist.[13] Executive Vice-President of the European Commission and Commissioner for Competition, *Margrethe Vestager*, has also stressed the need for **central enforcement whilst ensuring close cooperation** with national competition authorities and other agencies.[14]

16 Against this backdrop, it is to be expected that the national authorities, especially the competition authorities, will play a notable role when it comes to **effective enforcement** and further development of the DMA, even if the DMA describes their function as purely 'supportive'. They may also contribute their existing expertise, although they have no inherent enforcement powers. Whether the involvement of national authorities will be strong enough to avoid friction between the application of the DMA on the one hand and the application of (national) competition law on the other remains to be seen.[15] It can, however, be assumed that all authorities will be resolute in enforcing the DMA and competition law.

III. Application of national 'digital competition law' by national authorities

17 The DMA makes a distinction between the **application of national rules** that fall within the scope of the DMA (cf. Art. 1(5) and rec. 9 DMA – in this respect Art. 1(5) DMA 'blocks' measures adopted by Member States that are also aimed at contestable and fair markets), and other rules (cf. Art. 1(6) and rec. 10 DMA). As a consequence, Art. 1(6) DMA does not affect the application of 'regular' competition law (prohibition of cartels and abuses of market power). This interaction will be examined further below.

1. Precedence of the DMA over national rules with the aim of contestable and fair markets (Art. 1(5) sent. 1 DMA)

18 The DMA stipulates that Member States/national authorities must not adopt rules or measures or apply regulations vis-à-vis gatekeepers which also pursue the objective of

[12] Federal Cartel Office Background Paper DMA p. 39.

[13] European Competition Network, 'Joint paper' (23.6.2021) <https://www.bundeskartellamt.de/SharedDocs/Publikation/EN/Others/DMA_ECN_Paper.pdf> (last accessed: 12.7.2023).

[14] Margrethe Vestager, 'Data Protection and Competition: enforcement synergies and challenges', speech (2022) <https://ec.europa.eu/commission/presscorner/detail/en/SPEECH_22_3786> (last accessed: 12.7.2023).

[15] Federal Cartel Office Background Paper DMA p. 39.

guaranteeing contestable and fair markets (Art. 1(5) – **'blocking effect' of DMA with regard to the national rules with same objectives – contestable and fair markets – as the DMA**). The DMA prohibits the application of national rules by national authorities that fall within the scope of the DMA and pursue the same objective thereof (cf. Art. 1(5) sent. 1 and rec. 9 DMA). For matters falling outside the scope of the DMA, pursuing a purpose other than contestable and fair markets, Member States are, in principle, free to apply their legislation. This is, however, subject to the supposition that those obligations are compatible with Union law and do not result from the fact that the relevant undertakings have the status of a gatekeeper within the meaning of the DMA (cf. Art. 1(5) sent. 2 DMA). This **'blocking effect'** is intended to ensure full harmonisation (cf. rec. 8 and 31 DMA) and prevent Member States from adopting and enforcing a 'national DMA' (cf. rec. 6 DMA). Similarly, national authorities may not issue regulations which run counter to a decision adopted under the DMA (cf. Art. 1(7) DMA). In this respect, the DMA intends to set a – uniform, i.e. harmonised – standard with regard to contestable and fair markets in the digital sector.

2. Parallel application of competition law rules (Art. 1(6) DMA)

There are separate rules governing the **relationship between the DMA and European and national competition law** (Art. 1(6) DMA). The ban on cartels (Art. 101 TFEU or national regulations such as § 1 GWB) remains fully applicable (Art. 1(6)(a) DMA). Art. 1(6)(b) also stipulates that the ban on abuse of market power (Art. 102 TFEU or national regulations such as § 19 GWB) remains applicable and is not 'blocked' by the DMA if it addresses companies other than gatekeepers (i.e. companies that are not addressees of the DMA) or imposes additional obligations on the gatekeepers – i.e. obligations that go beyond those in Art. 5–7 DMA. 19

The DMA regards itself as both **complementary** and separate to competition law (cf. rec. 11 DMA). For example, the DMA does not rely on Art. 103 TFEU as an **enabling provision** (such as the Regulation on the implementation of the EU rules on competition, Reg. (EC) No 1/2003), but on Art. 114 TFEU (cf. rec. 67 and 73 DMA).[16] Moreover, the DMA serves to fill a regulatory gap 'left' by competition law, as competition law only applies to specific instances of **market power**, i.e. in particular the abuse of a dominant position in a specific market is required and therefore only ***ex post* enforcement** is possible. Accordingly, competition law does not address, or does not effectively address, the **challenges** posed to the effective functioning of the **'digital' internal market** by the conduct of gatekeepers that are not necessarily dominant in competition law terms (cf. rec. 5 DMA; this refers in particular to challenges that arise in connection with digital markets). 20

The DMA and 'standard' European and national **competition law** are therefore applicable in parallel. The DMA justifies this parallel or complementary applicability with the **different objectives** pursued by the two legal mechanisms (cf. Art. 1(1) DMA and rec. 10 and 11 DMA) The DMA aims to ensure contestable and fair markets, while competition law aims to protect undistorted competition in the internal market. 21

This **'complementary' application** of national competition law and the DMA is also favoured by practitioners.[17] The complementary application of national competition law 22

---

[16] For a critical view on the choice of legal basis, see Basedow ZEuP 2021, 217; Polley/Konrad WuW 2021, 198, Zimmer/Göhsl ZWeR 2011, 29.

[17] For example, Mundt (President of the German Federal Cartel Office), 'Statement' (2022) <https://www.bundestag.de/resource/blob/891308/f13edcf322cc218da602e6dc4b58391b/ADrs-20-9-59_Stellungnahme-Mundt-data.pdf> (last accessed: 12.7.2023) – in this respect he refers to Art. 1(5) as opposed to Art. 1(6) DMA, because the latter states that competition law continues to apply.

is explicitly provided for in the DMA and is in line with its objectives. The DMA itself, it is argued, explicitly states that European and national competition law are not 'blocked' by the DMA. This applies in particular to the relevant bans on unilateral conduct by companies, insofar as national competition law imposes obligations that extend beyond the DMA.[18]

23 As a consequence of the complementary application, the question of **parallel sanctioning** of gatekeepers (under the DMA on the one hand and competition law on the other) is raised. The right not to be punished twice within the meaning of Art. 50 CFR does not prevent the cumulative imposition of fines under the DMA and competition law for the same conduct (→ Ch. 10 mn. 21 et seqq.). As described therein, however, an existing sanction can serve to reduce the severity of a further sanction/penalty (→ Ch. 10 mn. 24).

24 The DMA legislator nonetheless identified this issue, as the DMA requires the imposition of sanctions in line with the **proportionality and *ne bis in idem* principle**. For these purposes, national authorities and the European Commission are to coordinate their sanctions and penalties (cf. rec. 86 DMA). In particular, national authorities and the European Commission are to coordinate their enforcement actions and take into account sanction decisions already taken on the basis of the same facts (cf. Art. 37 and rec. 86 DMA). Ultimately, only the ECJ can specify the nature of the relationship between DMA and competition law, and the procedure to be followed by the national authorities and the European Commission as regards fines and penalty payments (cf. rec. 94 DMA).

3. National competition law and DMA – example of classification of § 19a GWB (a German digital competition law rule)

25 A well-documented example of the **complex relationship** between the DMA, competition law and the classification of national rules under Art. 1(5) and (6) DMA arises – for example – in Germany and more specifically in relation to § 19a GWB, a German digital competition law rule that also aims to restrict the market power of larger digital companies. This provision, which was introduced as part of the 10th GWB amendment in 2020 and has been in force since 19.1.2021, relates to companies with 'paramount significance for competition across markets'. The German legislator also had the big tech companies in mind. The obligations of § 19a(2) GWB are very similar and even partly identical to the obligations set out in Art. 5 and 6 DMA.[19] The DMA, however, uses a quantitative approach (thresholds which, if reached, classify a company as a gatekeeper, → Ch. 3 mn. 1 et seqq.), whereas § 19a GWB uses qualitative criteria as part of a twofold procedure: first, the Federal Cartel Office decides whether a company is of paramount significance for competition across markets and then, in a second step, whether there has been a violation of obligations. This allows for a case-by-case classification.[20] Additionally, § 19a GWB requires action to be taken by the Federal Cartel Office i.e. the obligations are not self-executing.

26 When classifying **§ 19a GWB** under Art. 1(5) or (6) DMA, its nature as 'regulatory' or 'competition law is decisive:[21] If § 19a GWB were to be classified as a national competition law provision, then it would be subject to Art. 1(6) DMA. If, on the other hand,

[18] Mundt, 'Statement' (2022) <https://www.bundestag.de/resource/blob/891308/f13edcf322cc218da602e6dc4b58391b/ADrs-20-9-59_Stellungnahme-Mundt-data.pdf> (last accessed: 12.7.2023).

[19] Cf. for a comparison, the table in Gerpott NZKart 2021, 273.

[20] Gerpott NZKart 2021, 273.

[21] Research Services of the German Bundestag, 'Sachstand – Die Anwendbarkeit von § 19a GWB im Lichte des europäischen Gesetzgebungsverfahrens zum „Digital Markets Act"', WD 7 – 3000 – 114/21; PE

§ 19a GWB were recognised as a provision intended to ensure fair and contestable markets, it would fall under the regulatory scope of the DMA and thus the blocking effect of Art. 1(5) DMA.[22] The fact that the obligations under § 19a(2) GWB do not apply de lege, speaks against a classification under Art. 1(5) DMA.[23] In addition, Art. 1(7) DMA prohibits national decisions that conflict with the DMA, meaning that, in principle, no fragmentation of the decision-making practice is to be expected as a result of § 19a GWB. In this respect, it must be emphasised that § 19a GWB provides for more extensive powers of intervention in the digital sector, and can thus be classified as complementing the DMA within the context of Art. 1(6) DMA.[24]

As a national competition rule under Art. 1(6) DMA, **coexistence with the DMA** would be conceivable.[25] Due to the similar addressees of the DMA and § 19a GWB (gatekeepers vs. companies of paramount significance for competition across markets, i.e. the GAFMA companies), and the fact that the obligations resulting from Art. 5, 6 and 7 DMA and the obligations under § 19a(2) GWB are similar, the DMA is nonetheless likely to considerably restrict the application of § 19a GWB with regard to gatekeepers.[26] Since the obligations for gatekeepers in Art. 5, 6 and 7 DMA overlap significantly (cf. § 19a(2) GWB), the primacy of application of European law applies. The self-executing requirements of the DMA (if complied with) thus preclude conduct against which the Federal Cartel Office could act under § 19a GWB. 27

In addition, § 19a GWB continues to apply where the DMA is not applicable, either because the company is not a gatekeeper or because the obligations are not included in Art. 5–7 DMA. This is because the obligations set out in § 19a GWB go beyond the obligations set out in the DMA. This is particularly relevant for § 19a(2) GWB, as this provision stipulates broader obligations than the DMA. For example, self-preferencing (§ 19a(2) no. 1 GWB), the provisions on unlawful obstruction in sales and procurement markets (§ 19a(2) no. 2 GWB), the 'opening up' of markets by fast-growing companies (§ 19a(2) no. 3 GWB) and the regulatory examples with regard to demanding 'inadmissible' advantages (§ 19a(2) no. 7 GWB) are likely to be understood more broadly in linguistic terms, than Art. 5, 6 and 7 DMA.[27] Furthermore, § 19a GWB will also be relevant if a core platform service is not yet listed as a gatekeeper.[28] 28

Finally, § 19a GWB continues to apply in any case if either (i) the obligations of the DMA apply in substantive terms, but the DMA does not apply because the company is not a gatekeeper, or if (ii) the company is a gatekeeper but the conduct is not 'DMA relevant' (i.e. is not conduct in the sense of the obligations set out in Art. 5–7 DMA). 29

---

6 – 3000 – 067/21 (7.1.2022) <https://www.bundestag.de/resource/blob/880748/856d83cb24c61822c508aa47f27e18e7/WD-7-114-21-PE-6-067-21-pdf-data.pdf> (last accessed. 12.7.2023), p. 9 et seqq.

[22] Cf. Westermann ZHR 186 (2022), 325; for details, also Grünwald NZKart 2021, 496 and Zimmer/Göhsl ZWeR 2021, 29; cf. also Polley/Konrad WuW 2021, 198 (29); Wolf in MüKoWettbR GWB § 19a mn. 97 – Wolf emphasises that the DMA, as a Regulation based on Art. 114 TFEU, has more characteristics of fair trading law, because it is intended to set a general framework for fair business practices of gatekeepers meaning that it can be assumed that national law – despite possible overlaps – is not generally superseded.

[23] Federal Cartel Office Background Paper DMA p. 43.

[24] Mundt, Public hearing on the 'Digital Markets Act' of 27.4.2022, Bundestag Committee Printed Paper 20(9)59, 5.

[25] Grünwald NZKart 2021, 496.

[26] German Monopolies Commission, 'Biennial Report' (2022) <https://www.monopolkommission.de/images/HG24/HGXXIV_Gesamt.pdf> (last accessed: 12.7.2023), p. 238.

[27] German Monopolies Commission, 'Biennial Report' (2022) <https://www.monopolkommission.de/images/HG24/HGXXIV_Gesamt.pdf> (last accessed: 12.7.2023), p. 239.

[28] Mundt, Public hearing on the 'Digital Markets Act' of 27.4.2022, Bundestag Committee Printed Paper 20(9)59, 5.

4. Implementation measures in Germany (11th GWB Amendment Act)

30 National legislators are likely to adopt measures to support the effective application of the DMA. For example, the German legislator adopted the 11th GWB amendment (Competition Enforcement Act) in order to ensure effective enforcement of the DMA in Germany and to contribute to effective enforcement of the DMA by the European Commission by granting the Federal Cartel Office investigative competencies foreseen under the DMA (§ 32g GWB).[29] The amendment gives the Federal Cartel Office the powers it needs to assist the European Commission in enforcing the DMA, including rules on private enforcement (→ Ch. 13 mn. 1 et seqq.).

C. National courts

31 In addition to the implementation of the DMA by the European Commission in cooperation with national (competition) authorities, **national courts** are also involved in the application and enforcement of the DMA. The DMA defines various functions for the national courts. These relate, on the one hand, to cooperation with the European Commission (→ mn. 32 et seqq.). On the other hand, the national courts are decisively responsible for private enforcement – i.e. the private enforcement of third parties' rights (→ mn. 36 et seqq.).

I. Cooperation between the European Commission and national courts (Art. 39 DMA)

32 Cooperation between the European Commission and national courts (Art. 2 no. 33 DMA) focuses on the **exchange of information** (cf. Art. 39 DMA). For example, national courts may ask the European Commission to transmit to them information in its possession or present its opinion on questions concerning the application of the DMA (Art. 39(1) DMA). At the same time, the Member States shall forward written judgements to the Commission deciding on the application of the DMA (Art. 39(2) DMA).[30]

33 The European Commission can also submit written observations or – with the permission of the court in question – oral **observations** where coherent application of the DMA so requires (Art. 39(3) DMA).[31] The European Commission can request the courts to transmit or ensure the transmission of any documents necessary for the assessment of the case (Art. 39(4) DMA).[32] Due to **judicial independence**, however, the courts are not bound by these observations. This also follows from Art. 1(7) DMA, which imposes a prohibition only for decisions by the European Commission but not for observations.[33]

34 The DMA thus creates different mechanisms for the information exchange, which are primarily intended to ensure a **harmonised application and enforcement** of the DMA. The possibility for national courts to request information or observations from the European Commission, as well as the transmission obligations on the part of national

---

[29] The powers are not without controversy: cf. statement of the competition law association Studienvereinigung Kartellrecht e.V. on the amendments proposed with the 11th GWB amendment (Competition Enforcement Act) <https://www.studienvereinigung.de/sites/default/files/2022-11/20221028_Stellungnahme_Wettbewerbsdurchsetzungsgesetz.PDF> (last accessed: 12.7.2023).

[30] See the identical provision set out in Art. 15(2) Reg. (EC) No 1/2003 for competition law.

[31] See the identical provision set out in Art. 15(3) Reg. (EC) No 1/2003 for competition law.

[32] See the identical provision set out in Art. 15(3) Reg. (EC) No 1/2003 for competition law.

[33] Zober NZKart 2021, 611.

courts, aim to deter fragmentation resulting from diverging court decisions (cf. rec. 92 DMA).

National courts shall also not take decisions running counter to a decision adopted by the European Commission under the DMA (Art. 39(5) DMA). In the event of a conflict, the court in question should therefore also consider the possibility to suspend the proceedings. This regulatory mechanism is in line with the central principle of ensuring the **uniformity of EU law** (Art. 267 TFEU). National courts therefore still have the option of referring a case to the European Court of Justice for a preliminary ruling. 35

II. National courts and enforcement of third-party claims (private enforcement)

In addition, unfair practices by gatekeepers leading to non-compliance with the relevant Union or national law (cf. rec. 42 DMA) can be addressed in litigation proceedings before national courts. 36

It is expected that private enforcement – i.e. the enforcement of the obligations for gatekeepers by private actors, such as companies or even private end users – will lead to national courts playing a critical role in the application and enforcement of the DMA (for comprehensive information, → Ch. 13 mn. 1 et seqq.). Within this context, the view of the Monopolies Commission in Germany is worth mentioning. It goes as far as to call for the DMA to be supplemented by national regulations in order to facilitate enforcement of claims for injunctive relief or damages.[34] For example, a presumption of damage and interest rates on damages could be introduced.[35] 37

Gatekeepers must furthermore not directly or indirectly prevent or restrict business users or end users from raising any issue of non-compliance with the relevant Union or national law by the gatekeeper with a national court (cf. Art. 5(6) DMA). To this end, any practice that would in any way inhibit or hinder business users or end users in raising their concerns or in seeking damages should be prohibited (cf. rec. 42 DMA). To support this, a Union-based alternative **dispute resolution mechanism** is to be established. This mechanism is, however, intended to be without prejudice to the right of users to seek recourse before judicial authorities in accordance with Union and national law (cf. rec. 62 DMA). 38

III. Assistance

National courts can also play a role in inspections. For example, if judicial authorisation is required for assistance in the context of inspections under Art. 23(8) DMA (cf. Art. 23(9) and (10) DMA), the European Commission must apply for authorisation before the judicial authorities. For example, before granting authorisation, the national court verifies whether the European Commission's decision is authentic and that the coercive measures envisaged are neither arbitrary nor excessive. However, the DMA also clarifies that the court may not call into question the necessity of the inspection nor demand that it be provided with the information in the file of the European Commission. 39

[34] German Monopolies Commission, 'Biennial Report' (2022) <https://www.monopolkommission.de/images/HG24/HGXXIV_Gesamt.pdf> (last accessed: 12.7.2023)

[35] German Monopolies Commission, 'Biennial Report' (2022) <https://www.monopolkommission.de/images/HG24/HGXXIV_Gesamt.pdf> (last accessed: 12.7.2023).

IV. Evaluation

40 In conclusion, the role of national courts in the **application and enforcement** of the DMA should not be underestimated. Although the DMA sets out comprehensive provisions on cooperation and collaboration between courts and the European Commission and does not explicitly refer to private enforcement, this is set out in rec. 42 DMA and is a guiding principle of European law (→ Ch. 13 mn. 2). The courts will not least serve as interpreters of the DMA, given that not all provisions of the DMA are unambiguously worded.[36]

[36] For example, Mundt, President of the Federal Cartel Office: Mlex, '"Self enforcing" DMA provisions will trigger litigation' (2022) <https://mlexmarketinsight.com/news/insight/self-enforcing-dma-provisions-will-trigger-litigation-mundt-says> (last accessed: 12.7.2023).

CHAPTER 12
THIRD-PARTY RIGHTS BEFORE THE EUROPEAN COMMISSION AND NATIONAL AUTHORITIES

Jens Peter Schmidt

A. Importance of third parties for effective enforcement

Third parties contribute significantly to the **outcome** and **success** of public enforcement of European state aid, merger control and competition law. Competition law **complaints** are explicitly recognised in Art. 7(2) Reg. (EC) No 1/2003[1]; further provisions can be found in Reg. (EC) No 773/2004[2] (Regulation relating to the conduct of proceedings on Art. 101 and 102 TFEU). In addition, the European Commission's 'Complaint' Notice[3] offers further guidance. 1

Particularly in abuse of dominance cases pursuant to Art. 102 TFEU, it is often **customers**, **suppliers** and **competitors** who bring to the **attention** of the European Commission (potentially) abusive business practices; they contribute significantly to the fact finding and thereby **prompt** administrative action. 2

The DMA does **not** provide **any right** for third parties to lodge a **formal complaint**. This may be surprising in light of the fact that business users and end users are supposed to benefit directly from the obligations imposed on gatekeepers under the DMA. **Business users** in particular will have the **greatest commercial interest** in ensuring that gatekeepers comply with the obligations and prohibitions in full. Furthermore, it is precisely the business users who, due to their commercial proximity to the gatekeepers and their technical understanding of the core platform services, can help **remedy** the glaring **information asymmetry** between gatekeepers on the one hand and the European Commission's services on the other. 3

However, negative repercussions for the administrative case handling (e.g. access to file, confidentiality) have led the legislator to deny third parties a formal right to complain. At the same time, the legislator is not insensitive to the benefits that third 4

[1] Council Regulation (EC) No 1/2003 of 16 December 2002 on the implementation of the rules on competition laid down in Articles 81 and 82 of the Treaty (OJ 2003 L 1, 1).

[2] Commission Regulation (EC) No 773/2004 of 7 April 2004 relating to the conduct of proceedings by the Commission pursuant to Articles 81 and 82 of the EC Treaty (OJ 2004 L 123, 4).

[3] Commission Notice of 27 April 2004 on the handling of complaints by the Commission under Articles 81 and 82 of the EC Treaty (2004/C 101/05).

parties bring to effective public enforcement and, hence, has created a number of **opportunities for third parties** to **become involved** in compliance, monitoring and reporting obligations of gatekeepers (→ Ch. 7 mn. 11 et seq.). In addition, **informal channels** will also be open to third parties vis-à-vis the European Commission and national competition authorities to address non-compliance with the DMA obligations.

B. Information on practices or behaviour of gatekeepers (Art. 27 DMA)

5 Art. 27(1) DMA gives third parties by far the **most important right**, namely the right **to bring** practices or behaviour addressed by the DMA – in praxi: practices or behaviour deemed to be unlawful/non-compliant – to the **attention** of competent **national authorities** or directly to the attention of the **European Commission**. In other words, third parties essentially have the right to submit quasi-complaints with authorities regarding gatekeepers' business conduct without, however, becoming party to a formal procedure against that gatekeeper (→ mn. 3 et seq.).

I. Third parties

6 The right to information is available to third parties, including **business users, competitors** or **end users** of the core platform services listed in the designation decision (cf. Art. 3(9) DMA), as well as their representatives. The term 'third party' is not legally defined in the DMA. However, it already follows from syntax and the word 'including' in Art. 27(1) DMA that it is not limited to business users, competitors or end users. **Business associations** and **consumer associations** should also be included, as they can effectively communicate common areas of concerns to the regulators.

7 A **broad interpretation** of the term **'third party'** is justified given that effective enforcement of the DMA will largely depend on whether the national authorities and ultimately the European Commission, which has sole decision-making authority, will be in a position, in terms of resources and technology, to factually verify, legally assess and effectively enforce compliance with the DMA obligations in an administratively efficient manner. The involvement of third parties that are able to assist the authorities in the identification, assessment and prosecution of compliance deficits with their **expertise, technical knowledge**, and the provision of **data** and **information** that are **essential** for the purposes of the review, therefore is more than appropriate.

8 By way of reference, in **competition law procedures**, a **'legitimate interest'** is necessary in lodging a complaint. Such legitimate interest is **interpreted** quite **generously** by the European Commission (cf. Art. 7(2) Reg. (EC) No 1/2003, Art. 5(1) sent. 1 Reg. (EC) No. 773/2004). Hence, alongside customers and competitors, business[4] and consumer associations can also lodge a complaint.[5] The European Commission only considers an interest not to be legitimate if persons or organisations wish to come forward on general interest considerations without showing that they or their members are liable to be directly and adversely affected by the infringement (pro bono publico).[6]

[4] EGC 24.1.1995 – case T-114/92, ECLI:EU:T:1995:11 para. 28 – BEMIM v Commission.

[5] EGC 18.5.1994 – T-37/92, ECLI:EU:T:1994:54 para. 36 – BEUC v Commission.

[6] Commission Notice of 27 April 2004 on the handling of complaints by the Commission under Articles 81 and 82 of the EC Treaty (2004/C 101/05), para. 38.

In the context of the right to inform the European Commission or national authorities pursuant to Art. 27 DMA, a **legitimate interest** in the information is **not necessary**. The right to information on gatekeepers' practices and behaviour confers **fewer procedural rights** on third parties than on the complainant in competition law proceedings. For example, in DMA proceedings, third parties have no right to access documents on which the provisional assessment of the European Commission is based in competition law proceedings (cf. Art. 8 Reg. (EC) No 773/2004) – a right that requires a high degree of administration by the European Commission. Nor do third parties have the right to be involved in the proceedings initiated by the European Commission after the assessment of the complaint. The lesser procedural rights third parties benefit from therefore correspond with a **lower** level of **concern** third parties must show to inform the authorities. In any case, based on a **generous interpretation** also appropriate in the context of the DMA, third parties will regularly be able to show that their interests are directly affected. 9

II. Content of the information

Pursuant to Art. 27(1) of the DMA, third parties can only inform national authorities or the European Commission of **practices** or **behaviour** that fall within the scope of the **DMA**. These include first of all the **obligations** and **prohibitions** set out in Art. 5 and 6 DMA, as well as the **compliance**, **reporting** and **monitoring duties**, because they are essential to compliance and its comprehensibility by third parties (cf. only Art. 11(2) sent. 3 DMA – public provision of the non-confidential annual report). 10

III. Procedure

Information about gatekeepers' practices or behaviour is not bound by **any time limit** or **requirement regarding a specific form**. Unlike in competition procedural law, where the complaint must be lodged by using 'Form C', the DMA does not provide for a specific form. Nevertheless, it would seem sensible to submit a **substantiated description** of the practices or behaviour to the national authorities and/or the European Commission. 11

IV. Information provided to a national authority or the European Commission

According to Art. 27(1) DMA, third parties can inform the **national authority** competent to enforce national competition law (antitrust, abuse of dominance, merger control, see Art. 1(6) DMA) or directly the **European Commission**. The competent authority in France for these areas is the *Autorité de la concurrence*; in Germany it is the *Bundeskartellamt* (Federal Cartel Office) (cf. now § 32g GWB); in Ireland the *Competition and Consumer Protection Commission* (CCPC); in Italy the *Autorita' Garante della Concorrenza e del Mercato* (AGCM); in the Netherlands it is the *Autoriteit Consument & Markt* (ACM); in Portugal the *Autoridade da Concorrência* (AdC); and in Spain the *Comisión Nacional de Mercados y la Competencia* (CNMC). The fact that only the European Commission has the power to issue decisions according to the DMA could, on the one hand, argue in favour of third parties informing the European Commission alone. On the other hand, national authorities with greater **proximity** to specific business practices and potentially **available resources** may be a more attractive point of contact 12 for third parties to initiate possible investigations. It remains to be seen, however, to what extent the EU Member States' authorities have the appetite to investigate a (potential) DMA infringement which they ultimately cannot decide upon (→ mn. 13).

V. Consequence of the information

13 After being informed, the national authorities responsible for the enforcement of national competition law and the European Commission can decide on **appropriate measures** at their own discretion. The national authorities and the European Commission are under **no obligation to follow-up** on the information received (Art. 27(2) DMA). However, should the **national authority** be of the opinion that the information allows the conclusion that the case may involve non-compliance with the DMA, it shall **forward** this information to the **European Commission**, because the latter is exclusively authorised to make decisions vis-à-vis gatekeepers (→ Ch. 11 mn. 3 et seqq.).

C. Comments on compliance measures by gatekeepers (Art. 8 DMA)

14 Pursuant to Art. 8(1) DMA, gatekeepers must ensure and demonstrate compliance with the obligations laid down in Art. 5, 6 and 7 DMA (→ Ch. 7 mn. 10). In doing so, gatekeepers may request the European Commission to engage in a process (**'regulatory dialogue'**, → Ch. 7 mn. 12) to determine whether the **measures** that they intend to implement or have implemented are effective in achieving the objective (Art. 8(3) DMA). This request must be accompanied by a **non-confidential reasoned submission** from the gatekeeper explaining the measures. Where such regulatory dialogue occurs, the reasoned submissions will be an **important source** for **third parties** to comment on, which in turn will greatly assist the European Commission in understanding and assessing the appropriateness of the measures (→ Ch. 7 mn. 11).

15 When communicating its preliminary findings to the gatekeeper or as soon as possible thereafter, the European Commission will publish a **non-confidential summary** of the **case** and the **measures** that it is considering taking or those it considers the gatekeeper concerned should take. Interested **third parties** may then submit **comments** within a reasonable period set by the Commission (cf. Art. 8(6) DMA). The European Commission will very much need and welcome the **substantiated feedback** from the **market** in order to evaluate whether the proposed measures are indeed **appropriate** and **sufficient** to ensure **compliance** (→ Ch. 7 mn. 11 et seq.).

16 Even if this is not explicitly provided for in the DMA, the European Commission is likely to be open to **accompanying discussions** with third parties, which should be prepared on the basis of a **briefing paper**, similar to proceedings in merger control, competition or state aid.

D. Comments in the context of a market investigation into systematic non-compliance (Art. 18 DMA)

17 According to Art. 18(1) DMA, the Commission can conduct a **market investigation** to examine whether a gatekeeper systematically fails to comply with its **obligations** (→ Ch. 8 mn. 14 et seqq.). The European Commission will notify the gatekeeper of its preliminary findings, in particular whether it preliminarily considers that the case in-

volves systematic non-compliance and which remedy or remedies it preliminarily considers necessary and proportionate.

At the same time as communicating its preliminary findings to the gatekeeper or as soon as possible thereafter, the European Commission will publish a **non-confidential summary** of the **case** and the **remedies** that it is considering imposing. Interested **third parties** can provide **comments** on this summary in accordance with Art. 18(5) DMA within a reasonable timeframe determined by the European Commission. Insofar as the European Commission intends to declare **commitments** offered by the gatekeeper to be binding (→ Ch. 8 mn. 18), the European Commission will also publish a **non-confidential summary** of the **case** and the main content of the **commitments**, on which **third parties** can also submit their **comments** within a reasonable timeframe (Art. 18(6) DMA). 18

As explained for the case set out in Art. 8 DMA (→ mn. 16), the European Commission is also likely to be open to **accompanying discussions** with third parties in the context of the market investigation. 19

E. Consultation in the context of a market investigation into new services and new practices (Art. 19 DMA)

Pursuant to Art. 19(1) DMA, the European Commission may conduct a **market investigation** for the purpose of examining whether **further core platform services** should be included in the scope of the DMA or for the purpose of detecting practices that limit the contestability of core platform services or that are unfair and are not effectively addressed by the DMA (→ Ch. 8 mn. 20 et seqq.). 20

When a market investigation is conducted, third parties may be consulted by the European Commission (cf. Art. 19(2) DMA), including business users and end users of services within the digital sector that are being investigated and business users and end users that are subject to practices under investigation. Within the context of the consultation, **third parties** will have the opportunity to submit **comments** as well as to hold accompanying discussions with the European Commission. 21

F. Consultation in the event of a non-compliance decision (Art. 29 DMA)

Pursuant to Art. 29 DMA, the European Commission can issue a **non-compliance decision** where it finds that a gatekeeper is not complying with the obligations under Art. 5, 6 and 7 DMA or measures specified by the European Commission (→ Ch. 10 mn. 6). In accordance with Art. 29(4) DMA, the European Commission can **consult third parties** where it intends to adopt a non-compliance decision. Within the context of the consultation, third parties will have the opportunity to submit **comments** as well as to hold accompanying discussions with the European Commission. 22

CHAPTER 13
THE DMA AS THE SUBJECT MATTER OF PRIVATE ENFORCEMENT

Bibliography: Achleitner, 'Digital Markets Act beschlossen: Verhaltenspflichten und Rolle nationaler Wettbewerbsbehörden', NZKart 2022, 359; Achleitner, 'Selbstbegünstigung als Konzept des Marktmissbrauchs unter Art. 102 AEUV. Das Grundsatzurteil des EuG zu Google Shopping als Initialzündung für einen Wandel in der Digitalwirtschaft?', EuR 2022, 253; Albrecht, 'Digital Markets Act kommt – Regulierung von Plattformen und Auswirkungen auf Unternehmen', GWR 2022, 181; Basedow, 'Das Rad neu erfunden: Zum Vorschlag für einen Digital Markets Act', ZEuP 2021, 217; Costa e Silva/Trigo dos Reis, 'O financiamento por terceiro das despesas conexas com a acção popular de private enforcement. O Caso português', Ius Dictum 2022, 62; Costa e Silva/Trigo dos Reis, Private Enforcement e Tutela Coletiva, Coimbra 2022; De Angel Yágüez, La responsabilidad civil (Derecho), 2nd edn, Bilbao 1988; De Streel/Larouche, 'The European Digital Markets Act: A Revolution Grounded on Traditions', JECLAP 2021, 542; Ferreres Comella/Ayo Ferrándiz, 'Spain' in Scott Davidson (ed), The Global Damages Review, 5th edn, London 2022 <https://www.uria.com/documentos/colaboraciones/3341/documento/Spain-ldtr.pdf?id=13091_en&forceDownload=true> (last accessed: 12.7.2023); Grewe/Stegemann, 'EU-Verbandsklagerichtlinie', ZD 2021, 183; Haus/Rudel, 'Neue Missbrauchsaufsicht für digitale Ökosysteme', RDi 2022, 125; Herbers, 'Der Digital Markets Act (DMA) kommt – neue Dos and Don'ts für Gatekeeper in der Digitalwirtschaft', RDi 2022, 252; Herbers/München, 'Digital Markets Act – Auswirkungen auf den Zahlungsverkehr', RdZ 1.2023, 4; Karbaum/Schulz, 'Antitrust Litigation 2.0' – Private Enforcement beim DMA?, NZKart 2022, 107; Klumpe, '„Think twice" – Die private Rechtsdurchsetzung des DMA nach dem Referentenentwurf zum Wettbewerbsdurchsetzungsgesetz', in Kirk/Offergeld/Rohner (eds), Kartellrecht in der Zeitenwende – Auf dem Weg zur 11. und 12. GWB-Novelle, Baden-Baden 2023, p. 131; Koenig/Mezey, 'Zu guter Letzt ... schießt die Regulierung digitaler Märkte über das Ziel hinaus?', N&R 2022, 192; Komninos, 'The Digital Markets Act and Private Enforcement: Proposals for an Optimal System of Enforcement', in Charbit/Gachot (ed), Liber Amicorum Eleanor M. Fox, 2021, p. 425; Koolen, 'The Refusal to Allow Interoperability Between Android Auto and Third-Party Apps – A Deep Dive into Enel X Italia v. Google', IIC 2022, 758; Körber, 'Lessons from the Hare and the Tortoise: Legally imposed self-regulation, proportionality and the right to defence under the DMA – Part 2', NZKart 2021, 436; Kumkar, 'Der Digital Markets Act nach dem Trilog-Verfahren', RDi 2022, 347; Lundqvist, 'The Proposed Digital Markets Act and Access to Data: A Revolution, or Not?', IIC 2021, 239; Lamadrid de Pablo/Bayón, 'Why The Proposed DMA Might be Illegal Under Article 114 TFEU and How to Fix It', JECLAP 2021, 576; Marsden/Podszun, 'Restoring Balance to Digital Competition – Sensible Rules, Effective Enforcement, Study for KAS' (2020) <https://www.kas.de/de/einzeltitel/-/content/restoring-balance-to-digital-competition> (last accessed: 12.7.2023); Matos/Torres-Sarmiento, 'FRAND for Dominant Digital Platforms: Enhancing the Way Essential Inputs are Accessed, Transferred and Shared', GRUR-Int 2022, 516; Otero, 'Da dimensão constitucional dos acordos de financiamento ("litigation funding agreements") de ações populares indemnizatórias: um problema de abuso de direitos fundamentais', Revista da Ordem dos Advogados 2022, 701; Paal/Kieß, 'Digitale Plattformen im DAS-E, DMA-E und § 19a GWB', ZfDR 2022, 1; Podszun, 'The Digital Markets Act: What's in it for Consumers?', EuCML 2022, 1; Podszun/Bongartz/Kirk, 'Digital Markets Act – Neue Regeln für Fairness in der Plattformökonomie', NJW 2022, 3249; Polley/Konrad, 'Der Digital Markets Act – Brüssels neues Regulierungskonzept für Digitale Märkte', WuW 2021, 198; Sack, 'Die Kognitionsbefugnis nach Art. 7 Nr. 2 EuGVVO und das internationale Lauterkeitsrecht', WRP 2018, 897; Schläfke/Lühmann/Stegemann, 'Vorschlag des BMJ zur Umsetzung der EU-Verbandsklagenrichtlinie', PHi 2022, 138; Teixeira de Sousa, A Legitimidade Popular na Tutela dos Interesses Difusos, Lisboa 2003; Westermann, 'Der geplante Digital Markets Act: Europäische Regulierung zentraler Plattformdienste außerhalb des Kartellrechts?', ZHR 186 (2022), 325; Zimmer/Göhsl, 'Vom New Competition Tool zum Digital Markets Act: Die geplante EU-Regulierung für digitale Gatekeeper', ZWeR 2021, 29; Zober, 'Durchsetzung des DMA-E und dessen Verhältnis zum Kartellrecht', NZKart 2021, 611.

A. Private enforcement – a key implementation mechanism of the DMA *(Henner Schläfke/Immo Schuler)*

1 The main objective of the DMA is to make the gatekeeper market fair and contestable (Art. 1(1) DMA). Claims are already brought before civil courts today regarding fair ac-

cess or, alternatively, damages, albeit usually based on Art. 102 TFEU or statutory provisions already in place in the respective Member State (for example Art. 1240 of the French Civil Code, Art. 6:162 of the Dutch Civil Code, or Art. 1902 of the Spanish Civil Code).[1] From an international perspective, we can see that an active litigation industry is turning against the major platform operators.[2] It is to be expected that **private enforcement** – i.e. the enforcement, by private parties such as companies or even private end users, of the legal obligations incumbent on gatekeepers as set out in the DMA – will **play a very significant role in the future.** Even after a gatekeeper has been designated, claims prior to a decision by the European Commission would – to a certain extent – be considered standalone claims. But once the European Commission has issued a decision based on DMA provisions, **individual and collective follow-on claims for access or damages** will be accessible with national courts obliged to cooperate or even bound by the respective decision.

While there is no explicit reference to private enforcement in the DMA, it is a **cornerstone of European law**: Where individual rights are also established in European law, the vigilance of individuals interested in safeguarding their rights – and individual law enforcement – represents an additional level of effective control.[3] Further, the DMA presupposes private enforcement in its regulations: Art. 39 DMA stipulates an **obligation for national courts to cooperate with the European Commission** showing that private enforcement in national courts was envisioned. Also, the possibility of **collective redress by consumer associations** and the application of Dir. (EU) 2020/1828 on representative actions for the protection of the collective interests of consumers (RAD), was explicitly included in Art. 42 DMA. 2

Some jurisdictions are planning to introduce **national law provisions specifically governing private enforcement** of the DMA at this point. Germany has introduced statutory rules governing private enforcement with its 11th GWB amendment, which are nearly identical to those governing antitrust damages based on the implementation 3

[1] Cf. e.g. in Germany based on § 19 GWB a lawsuit involving Idealo versus Google because of alleged preferential treatment of Google's own price comparison service, see LTO, 'Idealo klagt gegen Google' (15.4.2019) <https://www.lto.de/recht/kanzleien-unternehmen/k/freshfields-bruckhaus-deringer-hausfeld-idealo-klage-google-preisvergleich/> (last accessed: 12.7.2023). In the area of public enforcement, see also the warning issued to Deutsche Bahn by the German Federal Cartel Office due to possible obstacles to competition for digital mobility services: German Federal Cartel Office, 'Fairer Wettbewerb um digitale Mobilitätsdienstleistungen – Bundeskartellamt mahnt Deutsche Bahn wegen möglicher Behinderung von Mobilitätsplattformen ab' (20.4.2022) <https://www.bundeskartellamt.de/SharedDocs/Meldung/DE/Pressemitteilungen/2022/20_04_2022_Bahn.html> (last accessed: 12.7.2023).

[2] See for example the collective actions against Apple in the Netherlands (Peterson, 'Apple facing new $5.5 billion App Store antitrust lawsuit in the Netherlands' (AppleInsider, 29.3.2022) <https://appleinsider.com/articles/22/03/29/apple-facing-new-55-billion-app-store-antitrust-lawsuit-in-the-netherlands> (last accessed: 12.7.2023)) or Portugal (Becker, 'iPhone-Leistungsdrosselung: Neue Klage wirft Apple geplante Obsoleszenz vor' (heise online, 1.3.2021) <https://www.heise.de/news/iPhone-Leistungsdrosselung-Neue-Klage-wirft-Apple-geplante-Obsoleszenz-vor-5068727.html> (last accessed: 12.7.2023)). In the United Kingdom, class actions have been brought before the Competition Appeal Tribunal against Apple (case no. 1403/7/7/21 – Dt Rachael Kent v Apple Inc. and Others), Google (case no. 1408/7/7/21 – Elisabeth Helen Call v Alphabet Inc. et al.) and Meta (case no. 1433/7/7/22 – Dr Liza Lovdahl Gormsen v Meta Platforms Inc. et al.).

[3] For key information, see ECJ 5.2.1963 – case 26/62, ECLI:EU:C:1963:1 – Van Gend & Loos. See also draft bill amending the Competition Act and other laws, introduced to Parliament by the German Government on 16.5.2023 (BT-Drs. 20/6824) <https://www.bmwk.de/Redaktion/DE/Pressemitteilungen/2023/04/20230405-bundeskabinett-beschliesst-verschaerfung-des-gesetzes-gegen-wettbewerbsbeschraenkungen.html> (hereafter: BT-Drs. 20/6824; last accessed: 12.7.2023), p. 21: 'zweite Säule neben der behördlichen Durchsetzung' (second pillar besides official enforcement).

of the Damages Directive[4] (→ mn. 110 et seqq.). Other jurisdictions seem to rely on pre-existing provisions in regard to the question of judicial enforcement of the DMA at this point. The latter is for example the case in France, the Netherlands and Spain, where future claimants will have to resort to existing rules in their respective Civil Code to enforce secondary claims based on DMA violations by gatekeepers.

4 This Chapter explains the basic structures of the enforcement mechanism of the DMA, which is unwritten in European law, and the intended implementation in several key EU Member States.[5] The first step will involve presenting the basis for private enforcement of the DMA (→ mn. 5 et seqq.). Next, details on private enforcement of the DMA by business users (→ mn. 13 et seqq.) will be explained. A brief look at the question of international jurisdiction will then follow (→ mn. 55 et seqq.). Subsequently, the focus of this Chapter then lays on the implementation of private enforcement of the DMA in the EU Member States France (→ mn. 59 et seqq.), Germany (→ mn. 108 et seqq.), Ireland (→ mn. 154 et seqq.), Italy (→ mn. 182 et seqq.), the Netherlands (→ mn. 210 et seqq.), Portugal (→ mn. 248 et seqq.), and Spain (→ mn. 284 et seqq.).

B. Basis for private enforcement of the DMA
(Henner Schläfke/Immo Schuler)

I. Direct applicability as the basis of private enforcement

5 The DMA is initially aimed at gatekeepers and imposes obligations on them that serve to ensure the proper functioning of the internal market.[6] In order to be able to make these obligations the subject of private enforcement, they must be **directly applicable**. General applicability of the provisions set out in the DMA is already required under Art. 288(2) TFEU as a matter of principle.[7] As a Regulation, the DMA has direct effect in the Member States, just like any other law.

6 In order to also be able to create rights for individuals via direct applicability, the legal norm concerned has to be **specific enough** in the case in question.[8] The decisive criterion in this context is whether further measures by European Union institutions or Member States are required to implement the provision concerned, or whether the norm can be regarded as **self-executing**.[9] This specificity of content must ultimately lead to the

[4] Directive 2014/104/EU of the European Parliament and of the Council of 26 November 2014 on certain rules governing actions for damages under national law for infringements of the competition law provisions of the Member States and of the European Union (OJ 2014 L 349, 1).

[5] For information on the mechanisms of enforcement by the European Commission see, for example, Basedow ZEuP 2021, 217 (222–224); Polley/Konrad WuW 2021, 198 (205); → Ch. 10 mn. 1 et seqq.

[6] Cf. Art. 1(1) DMA; → Ch. 2 mn. 1 et seqq.

[7] Cf. for general information Wagner in MüKoBGB BGB § 823 mn. 539.

[8] See ECJ 5.2.1963 – case 26/62, ECLI:EU:C:1963:1 = Rep. 1963, 7 para. 25 – Van Gend & Loos; see also Komninos in Charbit/Gachot, p. 425 (428) with further substantiation; Schroeder in Streinz AEUV Art. 288 mn. 45; Ruffert in Calliess/Ruffert AEUV Art. 288 mn. 21.

[9] See ECJ 16.6.1966 – case 57/65, ECLI:EU:C:1966:34 = Rep. 1966, 239 (266) – Lütticke v Hauptzollamt Saarlouis; Schroeder in Streinz AEUV Art. 288 mn. 45; Komninos in Charbit/Gachot, p. 425 (428).

conclusion that rights or obligations can also be created precisely for individuals – i.e. business users or end users[10].[11]

1. Specificity of the individual provisions

a) Obligations under Art. 5 DMA

In particular, the **obligations set out** in **Art. 5 DMA** are to be regarded as largely **self-executing** as defined above (→ mn. 6). This Article refers to special obligations for gatekeepers, even specifying the beneficiaries (business users or end users) directly. This clearly reveals the party against which the claim is directed and the rightful claimant, as well as the content of the claim.[12] 7

Even if reference is initially made to the European Commission's designation decision, this is unlikely to change the clarity of the obligations (see, for example, Art. 5(8) DMA). This is because **classification as a gatekeeper is always a prerequisite for the applicability** of Art. 5 et seqq. DMA. Insofar as reference is made to the associated decision, this does not open up any scope for implementation by the Member States or the European Commission that would stand in the way of direct applicability.[13] Rather, it merely provides a more detailed link to the decision, which is always necessary. 8

b) Obligations under Art. 6 DMA

The precise scope for implementation does not pose a problem for direct horizontal applicability of the requirements set out in Art. 6 DMA. Further, the heading of the section setting out these obligations says that they are 'susceptible of being further specified [under Art. 8]' does not impede with the requirements for **direct horizontal applicability** either. This is because the obligations are already, for the most part, spelled out specifically in Art. 6 DMA, with corresponding guidance for action.[14] The beneficiaries are also specified in Art. 6 DMA. 9

In addition, the actual obligation under Art. 6 DMA is not fleshed out in greater detail by the European Commission. Rather, only the implementation measures are examined to determine their compatibility with these obligations.[15] After all, as a glance at Art. 8(2), (7) and also (8) DMA shows, the reference to 'further specification' of the provisions contained in Art. 6 DMA refers to a check on the implementation measures tak- 10

[10] Art. 2 point (21) DMA defines a business user as any natural or legal person acting in a commercial or professional capacity using core platform services provided by gatekeepers for the purpose of or in the course of providing goods or services to end users. End users are defined in Article 2(22) DMA as natural or legal persons using core platform services 'other than as a business user' – i.e. for the initiation and performance of contracts for goods or services. This means that end users are first and foremost, but not only, consumers, cf. also rec. 14 DMA. The focus here is primarily on consumers in the narrower sense of the term. Art. 5(9) and (10) as well as Art. 6(7) sent. 1 and (8), (11) DMA each provide for special rights for publishers and advertisers, providers of search engines or other service providers or hardware providers. These are not discussed in depth here. Ultimately, however, the principles described apply accordingly.

[11] Cf. ECJ 20.9.2001 – case C-453/99, ECLI:EU:C:2001:465 = Rep. 2001, I-06297 para. 23 – Courage v Crehan, on the predecessor norms set out in Art. 101 and 102 TFEU.

[12] See also Westermann ZHR 186 (2022), 325 (329).

[13] Westermann ZHR 186 (2022), 325 (330). Cf. also Podszun EuCML 2022, 1, who emphasises that the obligations of the DMA are effective *ex ante*, i.e. as a matter of principle, and do not require activation by the authorities.

[14] Zimmer/Göhsl ZWeR 2021, 29 (43); Podszun, however, takes a less clear position in EuCML 2022, 1 (4).

[15] See also rec. 65 DMA: 'It may [...] be appropriate for the Commission [...] to further specify some of the measures that the gatekeeper concerned should adopt in order to effectively comply with obligations that are susceptible of being further specified or, in the event of circumvention, with all obligations.'

en by the gatekeepers.[16] If necessary, the European Commission can impose appropriate implementation measures in the event of deviations. The intent and purpose of this regulatory concept is to enable a **dialogue between the European Commission and gatekeepers** in order to ensure compliance with the requirements set out in Art. 6 DMA.[17]

c) *Obligations under Art. 7 DMA*

11 Finally, Art. 7 DMA, which was not inserted until later on in the legislative process and which provides for an **interoperability obligation** for interpersonal (number-independent) communication services, could also be understood as being intended to create specific entitlements – for example for end users of such services.[18] Thus, the obligation to enable interoperability, but also the requirements for its specific design, for example with regard to features (Art. 7(2)(a) DMA) and data security (Art. 7(3) DMA), can be understood as horizontally applicable rights. The 11th GWB amendment seems to assume this: Insofar as it sets out provisions on private enforcement of the DMA, Art. 7 DMA is also covered (see § 33(1) 11th GWB Amendment Act). This obligation should make the DMA most visible to end users. The European lawmakers believe that in a few years, it will be as natural to use different messenger services together as it is today with e-mail traffic between different providers.

12 Admittedly, the question arises as to what extent specific legal consequences can be derived from an abstract entitlement to interoperability, as this will generally be technically viable in not just one specific manner. In this respect, it seems **questionable whether** the **entitlement to interoperability** contained in Art. 7 DMA **can be privately enforced** in its own right. For this reason, it is excluded from the comments below.

2. Rights of business users under the DMA

13 In detail, Art. 5 and 6 DMA give rise to the following rights for business users, which can be split into rights of access and rights of use (→ mn. 14 et seqq.), prohibitions of use and exploitation (→ mn. 20 et seqq.), as well as requirements governing the establishment of legal relationships (→ mn. 23 et seqq.).

a) *Rights of access and use*

14 The first group of specific rights consists of rights of access and use that business users are entitled to *vis-à-vis* the gatekeeper concerned. If these rights are sufficiently specific in the individual case, they are amenable to private enforcement and can also give rise to enforceable claims (→ mn. 48 et seqq.).

15 Business users have the **right**, *vis-à-vis* gatekeepers, **to communicate with end users** under Art. 5(4) DMA. They can communicate with them free of charge to promote offers, even under different conditions. This applies to end users acquired via the gatekeeper's core platform services or through other channels, regardless of whether the business users use the platform services to communicate. This right can be enforced through private enforcement. For example, conflicting terms of use or technical barriers implemented by gatekeepers can be the subject of claims for injunctive relief.

16 The right under Art. 6(4) subpara. 1 DMA, according to which gatekeepers must allow and technically enable the **installation and effective use of third-party software**

[16] Komninos in Charbit/Gachot, p. 425 (430).
[17] See rec. 65 DMA; Zimmer/Göhsl ZWeR 2021, 29 (42 et seq.).
[18] For details on Art. 7 DMA, see Herbers RDi 2022, 252 (257 et seq.).

applications or software application stores, is also amenable to private enforcement. No special differentiation is made here between business users and end users, meaning that both groups can derive individual rights from the provision. Where subpara. 2 and 3 provide for exceptions for technical security, this does not pose any obstacle, as such restrictions are not unusual (cf. e.g. § 58a of the German Payment Services Oversight Act (*Zahlungsdiensteaufsichtsgesetz*, ZAG).

Business users also have a **right** under Art. 6(7) DMA to **interoperability** of their services with the hardware or software features, including the operating system, of the gatekeeper's platform services. They also have a right to access these systems.[19] The European legislators envisaged access to NFC technology (near field communication), secure elements and processors, and authentication mechanisms (including the necessary software).[20] It is questionable, however, whether the specific access entitlement is privately enforceable, as the degree of access is determined by how the gatekeeper also grants access to its own corresponding services. In this respect, the vague technical nature of this requirement[21] could stand in the way of practical enforcement.[22] 17

Art. 6(10) DMA gives business users extensive **rights of access to data generated or disclosed** in the context of their services.[23] This applies particularly to personal data provided or generated in connection with the use of the platform services in the context of relationships between business users and end users. Access must be free of charge, effective, high-quality, continuous and in real time. According to sent. 2, personal data is only provided if it originates from a relationship with the business user in question and the end user has consented to this.[24] Private enforcement can also be used to enforce claim for access, because the right of business users in this regard is sufficiently outlined by the requirements set out in Art. 6(10) DMA. 18

A, for private enforcement, sufficiently specific **right of access** also follows from Art. 6(11) DMA. Under this provision, providers of online search engines must grant access to certain data on **fair terms**. While it is true that Art. 6(11) DMA (and also the remaining obligations of the gatekeeper regulated in Art. 6 DMA) are provisions that need to be further elaborated, this can also be done by the courts.[25] 19

b) Prohibitions of use and exploitation

A second group of sufficiently specific individual rights is made up of **prohibitions of use and exploitation**. In this respect, civil law claims in the context of private enforcement are usually aimed at injunctive relief or damages. 20

Pursuant to Art. 6(2) subpara. 1 DMA, gatekeepers are **prohibited from using**, in competition with business users, any **data** that the gatekeeper has received from the business users or that business users have generated when using platform services. This only applies insofar as this data is not publicly available, and also refers explicitly to data provided or generated by end users. Subpara. 2 clarifies that data which is not publicly 21

[19] A recent example that may have to be judged on this basis in the future is the lack of interoperability of Google Auto with third-party apps, which was sanctioned by the Italian market regulator. See Koolen IIC 2022, 758.

[20] See rec. 56 DMA.

[21] Cf. Achleitner NZKart 2022, 359 (361, 362) for criticism of the inclusion of this provision in the legislative process.

[22] On Art. 7 DMA → mn. 11 et seq.

[23] For general information on this aspect, see Lundqvist IIC 2021, 239; Achleitner NZKart 2022, 359 (361).

[24] In this context, see also Art. 13(5) DMA.

[25] Wolf-Posch in HK-DMA DMA Art. 6 mn. 276; Podszun/Bongartz/Kirk NJW 2022, 3249 (3253) with further references.

available also includes data which can be derived from the commercial activities of business users or their end users, e.g. via click or search data.

22 According to Art. 6(5) DMA, gatekeepers must **not treat** their **own products and services more favourably in ranking and indexing** than those of third parties. Gatekeepers must apply the conditions for such rankings transparently, fairly and in a non-discriminatory manner. Although the term 'third party' is not defined in the provision, the provision is likely to apply primarily to business users. In this respect, the DMA addresses the problem of **self-preferencing**, which has long been discussed under competition law and pursued by the authorities.[26] There are links to Reg. (EU) 2019/1150, which sets out specific transparency obligations for online intermediation services in Art. 5.[27] Under rec. 12 DMA, the regulation continues to apply without prejudice.

c) Requirements governing the establishment of legal relationships

23 A third group of rights consists of requirements governing the establishment of legal relationships with regard to civil law provisions. In the context of private enforcement, abstention from certain conduct can be sought, and if necessary also the annulment of some contractual clauses; furthermore, an indicative effect can be sought in the context of a review of general terms and conditions. Admittedly, **individual requirements governing the establishment of legal relationships require considerable specification**, which only the European Commission can provide, as it alone is empowered to set out further details (cf. Art. 12(1) and 46(1)(b) DMA).

24 On the other hand, Art. 5(3) DMA contains a clear requirement, according to which gatekeepers may not contractually assure themselves that business users restrain from offering their goods or services to third parties or through **their own online sales channels at prices or conditions that are different** from those offered through the services of the gatekeeper.[28] This can be enforced directly in private enforcement proceedings.

25 An equally specific obligation is provided in Art. 5(6) DMA, which obliges gatekeepers not to obstruct or impede **complaints about non-compliance with relevant European Union or national law requirements** lodged with relevant public authorities.[29] The same applies insofar as gatekeepers **may not** (also) **require** business users to **use** certain **applications of the gatekeeper in the context of payments** if this is in the context of services that business users provide to end users using platform services (**Art. 5(7) DMA**). The gatekeepers' obligation under **Art. 5(8) DMA not to require** business or end users to **register with a platform service** in order to use another platform service of the gatekeeper, can also be enforced directly via private enforcement.

26 One requirement that is more open to interpretation is the requirement set out in **Art. 6(12) DMA**, according to which gatekeepers are obliged to apply **fair, reasonable and non-discriminatory general conditions of access** for business users to the software application stores, online search engines and online social networking services listed in a

[26] From a competition law perspective, see in particular ECJ 10.11.2021 – case T-612/17, ECLI:EU:T:2021:763 – Google and Alphabet v Commission (Google Shopping). Google has appealed against the judgment. Achleitner EuR 2022, 253 (268) points out that the ruling of the ECJ could nevertheless have an impact on the interpretation of the DMA. See also Reumann/Weber NZKart 2022, 314.

[27] Regulation (EU) 2019/1150 of the European Parliament and of the Council of 20 June 2019 on promoting fairness and transparency for business users of online intermediation services (OJ 2019 L 186, 57).

[28] Achleitner NZKart 2022, 359 (362). Cf. for example 'narrow best price clauses' BGH 18.5.2021 – KVR 54/20, BeckRS 2021, 21209 – Booking.com. The scenario covered by that case is now (also) likely to be covered by Art. 5(3) DMA.

[29] See also Art. 13(6) DMA in relation to Art. 5(6) DMA.

decision pursuant to Art. 3(9) DMA.[30] This is, however, set out in greater detail in the sense that general conditions of access must be published. The European Commission is responsible for checking whether the general conditions of access comply with the provision, Art. 6(12) subpara. 3 DMA. Ultimately, it should therefore also be possible to enforce privately the requirement to use general conditions of access. To the extent that these conditions of access are intended to include an alternative dispute settlement mechanism, this reveals another element of private enforcement.

Insofar as **Art. 6(13) DMA** generally stipulates that the gatekeeper shall **not impose 'disproportionate' conditions for the termination of the use of a platform service**, this is also a principle that can be enforced in the context of civil disputes. 27

3. Rights of end users under the DMA

As far as end users are concerned, Art. 5 and 6 DMA give rise to the following rights, which can once again be split into rights of access and rights of use (→ mn. 29), prohibitions of use and exploitation (→ mn. 30 et seq.) as well as requirements governing the establishment of legal relationships (→ mn. 32 et seqq.). 28

a) Rights of access and use

End users have a **right** under **Art. 5(5) DMA** to **access** and use **content, subscriptions, features or other items** via the platform services if they use software applications from a business user for this access. In particular, this should also apply if the end users have acquired such items from the relevant business user without using the core platform services of the gatekeeper. In view of the multitude of possible interactions, which will also have to be coordinated technically, it is currently unclear whether this will result in a specific, privately enforceable right. However, the DMA at least includes the right of end users **not** to have gatekeepers **actively restrict options for use**. The right to **use third-party software and third-party software stores** set out in **Art. 6(4) subpara. 1 DMA** also applies to end users. Finally, end users have a right *vis-à-vis* the platform service under **Art. 6(9) DMA** to **free portability of data** that end users have provided to the platform service or generated in its context. Free tools are also to be made available in order to facilitate the effective exercise of this right. This includes continuous and real-time access to such data. The portability of the data collected, including with regard to different technical implementation options, is essentially specific enough to be the subject to private enforcement. 29

b) Prohibitions of use and exploitation

The requirements for the use of end user **data** are particularly well-developed.[31] Art. 5(2) subpara. 1(a) to (d) DMA state that gatekeepers 30

- shall **not** process, **for the purpose of providing online advertising services**, personal data of end users where such data was collected while using services that third parties offer using platform services of the gatekeeper (a);

[30] The term 'FRAND' ('fair, reasonable and non-discriminatory') is sometimes used for these conditions, see for example Achleitner NZKart 2022, 359 (362) and generally for competition law Matos/Torres-Sarmiento GRUR-Int 2022, 516.

[31] Achleitner NZKart 2022, 359 (362); Herbers RDi 2022, 252 (256). For a critical view, see Koenig/Mezey N&R 2022, 192.

- shall **not combine** personal data of end users from the relevant platform services **with personal data** from any further platform services or from any other services provided by the gatekeeper or with personal data from third-party services (b);
- shall **not** cross-**use** personal data of end users from a platform service **in other services**, including other platform services of the gatekeeper, and vice versa (c);
- shall not **sign in** end users to **other services of the gatekeeper** in order to combine personal data (d).

31 These requirements do not apply if end users have been given a choice and have **consented** to the relevant processing of the data by the gatekeeper (Art. 5(2) subpara. 2 DMA).[32] If consent is refused or withdrawn, the gatekeeper shall not repeat its request for consent for the same data processing purpose more than once within a period of one year (Art. 5(2) subpara. 3 DMA). Overall, these requirements are clearly worded and impose clear obligations on gatekeepers that end users can enforce privately.

c) Requirements governing the establishment of legal relationships

32 As with business users, the **requirements governing the establishment of legal relationships** with end users require some degree of specification. The provisions contained in Art. 5(6), (7) and (8) DMA as well as in Art. 6(13) DMA (→ mn. 27) also apply, mutatis mutandis, to end users. In addition, Art. 6(3) subpara. 1 DMA requires gatekeepers to allow and technically enable end users to easily **un-install any software application** on the operating system. In this context, un-installation may be restricted for technically necessary applications, provided that it is not technically possible to replace them with offers from third parties. The private enforceability of this requirement, which is highly dependent on the technical details, is questionable. However, it once again seems possible that the core of the obligation – the provision of an un-installation option – could again be subject to private enforcement.

33 Art. 6(3) subpara. 2 DMA also states that it must be possible for end users to **change default settings on operating systems** and similar basic applications (such as the web browser) easily if these direct end users to certain products or services provided by the gatekeeper. This includes, for example, prompting end users when they use a search engine for the first time to choose to which search engine they would like to be directed to automatically in the future. As far as the specific structure of this obligation is concerned, private enforcement seems rather difficult to implement. However, Art. 6(3) subpara. 2 DMA also contains a specific fundamental obligation to provide for such corresponding setting options in the first place.

34 This also applies to Art. 6(6) DMA. This provision specifies that it is not permitted to restrict end users, technically or otherwise, in their ability to switch between and subscribe to, different software applications if they are accessed using the platform services of the gatekeeper. This includes the **choice of Internet access services**.

II. No strong arguments against private enforcement of the DMA

35 Although it is sometimes argued that the DMA is not, or only to a very limited extent, amenable to direct private enforcement, the reasons cited to support this argument are ultimately not valid.

[32] Explicit reference is made here to Art. 4 and 7 GDPR. Art. 5(2) subpara. 4 DMA also clarifies that the applicability of Art. 6(1)(c), (d) and (e) GDPR is not affected.

1. Lack of regulation as an argument against private enforcement

Some voices see the **lack of any positive regulation on private enforcement in the DMA** as sufficient reason to doubt the possibility of private enforcement of the obligations in principle.[33] In this respect, in view of the related competition law and the explicit provisions on private enforcement supporting Art. 101 et seqq. TFEU in this area,[34] the argument is that the absence of such supporting regulations for the DMA means that private enforcement is, in fact, out of the question with regard to the latter.[35] Conversely, it is argued that the comprehensive regulation of *public* enforcement in the DMA indicates that *private* enforcement, which is not explicitly covered, is precisely not intended to be a part of the Regulation's enforcement mechanism.[36] 36

Both approaches are contradicted by clear statements made during the legislative process.[37] At least in terms of legislative history, there is therefore no reason to interpret the legislative restraint in the elaboration of private enforcement in the context of the DMA as an implicit 'exclusion' of corresponding options – and thus as a deviation from fundamental principles of effective European law enforcement. In addition, rec. 42 DMA now emphasises the **role of national courts**. They are obviously only called upon to make decisions in the context of private enforcement. Similarly, Art. 39 DMA, which was only inserted later and sets out provisions on **cooperation between the European Commission and national courts**, makes it clear that private enforcement is possible.[38] There is no other explanation for the option of cooperation, as the European Commission itself is charged with enforcing the DMA. This is all the more true as the provision is partly modelled on the wording of Art. 15 and 16 Reg. (EC) No 1/2003 on the implementation of the rules on competition, which allows for private enforcement.[39] At least in Germany, the draft bill on the 11th GWB amendment assumes that Art. 39 DMA requires – at least implicitly – that the DMA is also to be amenable to private enforcement.[40] Furthermore, in the field of competition law, the ECJ initially led the way with its decision in the Courage case[41]. This makes it clear that private enforcement does not depend on explicit authorisation by the European Union legislature. 37

[33] See Komninos in Charbit/Gachot, p. 425 (431). For another cautious view, see also Basedow ZEuP 2021, 217 (223, 225–226) and Podszun EuCML 2022, 1 (5). Vehemently rejecting the idea is Körber NZKart 2021, 436 (442): it would be a 'serious mistake' to enable or promote private enforcement.

[34] Cf. only Directive 2014/104/EU of the European Parliament and of the Council of 26 November 2014 on certain rules governing actions for damages under national law for infringements of the competition law provisions of the Member States and of the European Union (OJ 2014 L 349, 1) (hereinafter: Damages Directive) and Council Regulation (EC) No 1/2003 of 16 December 2002 on the implementation of the rules on competition laid down in Articles 81 and 82 of the Treaty (OJ 2003 L 1, 1).

[35] This is at least how it sounds in Basedow ZEuP 2021, 217 (223). Art. 101 et seqq. TFEU are specified in particular by Dir. 2014/104/EU and Reg. (EC) No 1/2003, with the Directive mainly defining the area of private enforcement in more detail.

[36] See Komninos in Charbit/Gachot, p. 425 (431).

[37] See for example BMWK, Joint paper 'Friends of an effective Digital Markets Act' (27.5.2021) <https://www.bmwk.de/Redaktion/DE/Downloads/M-O/non-paper-friends-of-an-effective-digital-markets-act.pdf> (last accessed: 12.7.2023); German Federal Cartel Office, Joint paper 'How national competition agencies can strengthen the DMA' (23.6.2021) <https://www.bundeskartellamt.de/SharedDocs/Publikation/EN/Others/DMA_ECN_Paper.pdf> (last accessed: 12.7.2023); European Commission, 'Q&A: Digital Markets Act: Ensuring fair and open digital markets' (2.5.2023) <https://ec.europa.eu/commission/presscorner/detail/en/QANDA_20_2349> (last accessed: 12.7.2023); Komninos in Charbit/Gachot, p. 425 (427 et seq.) with further substantiation.

[38] Kumkar RDi 2022, 347 (353); Klumpe in Kirk/Offergeld/Rohner, p. 131 (134).

[39] Cf. also Zober NZKart 2021, 611 (614), still regarding a corresponding proposal in the parliamentary draft at that point.

[40] BT-Drs. 20/6824, 21.

[41] ECJ 20.9.2001 – case C-453/99, ECLI:EU:C:2001:465 – Courage.

38 The remaining uncertainties as to whether the DMA can be privately enforced may make further amendments to the DMA or additional legal acts of the EU appear a desirable option. However, this legal policy argument is not sufficient to dispute the **private enforceability of the DMA**.

2. No risk of fragmentation

39 The most widespread argument against private enforcement of the DMA – the risk of fragmented DMA enforcement – cannot be upheld either.[42] In this respect, reference is often made to the experience gleaned in competition law, where private enforcement was only permitted as part of a cautious development in the proverbial slipstream of the progressive and unified practice of the European Commission and ECJ, or was made more attractive by further legal acts.[43] A similar approach, it is argued, would also make sense for the DMA.[44] One suggestion is to limit private enforcement to follow-on claims, but not to allow standalone claims against gatekeepers unless there is sufficient precedent on the interpretation of the DMA.[45] Recourse to Art. 114 TFEU as a legal basis and the general quest to standardise the legal framework for gatekeepers are also used as arguments against private enforcement in this context.[46]

40 Although the argument of fragmentation has some weight in principle, it cannot, at a legal level, remove the basis for the private enforcement options described above. This is because the DMA itself addresses the issue of fragmentation and solves it by giving **primacy to the application of European law and the decisions of the European Commission**. Art. 1(5) DMA states that, in order to avoid fragmentation of the internal market, Member States may not, in principle, impose any further obligations on gatekeepers. Rec. 9 DMA points out that national rules that are within the scope of the DMA may not be applied. However, Art. 38(7) DMA allows national authorities which have the relevant powers under the law of their Member State to carry out preliminary investigations and to report their findings to the European Commission. In particular, this is intended to cover situations where the national competition authority also considers that there has been an infringement of competition law and can therefore apply the DMA and competition law in parallel.[47]

41 Art. 39 DMA also refutes the arguments that concerns about fragmentation stand in the way of private enforcement of the DMA, as it is intended to ensure uniform application and enforcement through **cooperation between the European Commission and national courts** (for more information → Ch. 11 para. 32). Finally, Art. 47 DMA gives the European Commission the option of adopting guidelines on the DMA in order to facilitate its effective implementation and enforcement.

42 Therefore, given the **genesis of the DMA**, which also incorporated increasing echoes of private enforcement during the various drafting stages, it cannot be assumed that the risk of fragmentation would stand in the way of private enforcement of the DMA. In-

[42] Cf. Komninos in Charbit/Gachot, p. 425 (435 et seqq.); Karbaum/Schulz NZKart 2022, 107 (111 et seqq.); Zober NZKart 2021, 611 (614).

[43] Cf. for example Komninos in Charbit/Gachot, p. 425 (436); Zimmer/Göhsl ZWeR 2021, 29 (52).

[44] Zimmer/Göhsl ZWeR 2021, 29 (52); for an extremely critical view, see also Körber NZKart 2021, 436 (442).

[45] Cf. for example Komninos in Charbit/Gachot, p. 425 (438).

[46] Cf. Zimmer/Göhsl ZWeR 2021, 29 (51).

[47] Herbers/München RdZ 2023, 4 (6).

stead, this risk can be countered on the basis of the DMA by involving the European Commission and, if necessary, the ECJ via Art. 267 TFEU.[48]

Pursuant to Art. 39 DMA, national courts may not give a decision that is contrary to a decision adopted by the European Commission under the DMA. The risk of legal fragmentation, which is addressed in Art. 39 DMA, can be prevented by various means. The predominant solution is a stay of proceedings, which can be requested under Dutch law, would be considered by Irish courts to prevent conflicts and is allowed by Art. 378 et seq. of the French Code of Civil Procedure as well as by § 148(1) of the German Code of Civil Procedure. In Germany, the 11th GWB amendment further weakens the risk of fragmentation in the enforcement of the DMA by extending the existing **duty of the courts to cooperate with the European Commission** under § 90a GWB to **DMA-related proceedings in the future**.[49] In addition, according to § 33b 11th GWB Amendment Act, the German courts are bound by the Commission's decisions on the DMA, so that a uniform interpretation of the DMA is also ensured in this respect.[50] Against this backdrop, fragmentation is less likely to happen. 43

C. Civil law claims under the DMA *(Henner Schläfke/Immo Schuler)*

Private enforcement primarily plays a role when the rights arising from the DMA are breached. If one of the prohibitions of exploitation is breached, **claims for injunctive relief and damages** may **arise**. 44

With regard to the access rights of business users, it is also possible to take action to provide the necessary **access options or tolerate corresponding measures** by business users. Ultimately, this means that the question as to whether business users have a corresponding basis for claims has to be analysed on a case-by-case basis.[51] Rights for business users that can be enforced already arise from the DMA itself (→ mn. 48 et seqq.). Secondary claims, such as claims for damages, however, do not arise directly from European Union law (→ mn. 52 et seqq.). In this respect, recourse must be made to national bases for claims. The analysis of significant jurisdictions in this book will show that all jurisdictions offer the resort to claims for tort both for business users and end users. 45

Additionally, injunctive relief based on provisions governing restrictive business practices or unfair competition practices (e.g. the *pratiques restrictives de concurrence* in France, the German UWG) is available in most jurisdictions, although in some jurisdictions claims are limited to business users only. 46

Further, courts might consider the DMA in the context of the interpretation of contracts. While the extent might vary, some jurisdictions as Italy even allow courts to modify contracts to accommodate the DMA by way of Art. 1374 ICC. 47

I. Enforceable rights under the DMA

The DMA explicitly grants various rights to business users and end users. Different types of rights or – from the gatekeepers' perspective – obligations can be identified here. Specifically, the DMA requires gatekeepers to provide **access and use options** for 48

[48] See also rec. 92 DMA, which points out that the harmonisation mechanisms contained in Art. 39 DMA are not to the detriment of Art. 267 TFEU.

[49] See BT-Drs. 20/6824, 45.

[50] See BT-Drs. 20/6824, 38.

[51] Cf. also Achleitner NZKart 2022, 359 (363).

business users. On the other hand, there are specific **prohibitions**, for example with regard to the use of data. Finally, various provisions also address the **structuring of contractual relationships** between gatekeepers and business users.

49 These rights and obligations may in themselves already be suitable for the purposes of granting enforceable individual rights.[52] The DMA is binding in its entirety as a Regulation within the meaning of Art. 288(2) TFEU. This means that regulations 'have direct effect and are, as such, capable of creating individual rights which national courts must protect'.[53] It is, therefore, not necessary for the provisions of a regulation to have been implemented into national law before they can be invoked before a national court. In view of the **direct horizontal applicability** of the individual provisions contained in Art. 5, 6 and 7 DMA, as described above, it follows that these have a direct impact on the legal relations between private parties.[54] There is no need for any government to pass an act of implementation in this regard.

50 Rather, the **provisions of the Regulation itself** can be used **as a basis for claims**.[55] In this respect, the rights of access and use are particularly suitable for the assertion of claims by means of an action for performance. For example, if a claim is asserted for access to certain data, a business user can rely on Art. 6(10) DMA as the inherent basis for a claim in addition to any contractual entitlements.

51 In addition to business users, the DMA primarily serves the interests of end users of platform services (cf. rec. 7 DMA). For direct claims by end users arising from the DMA, such as claims for damages or injunctive relief, **the same options as described above in regard to business users are available**.

II. Secondary claims under European Union law

52 On the other hand, it is **more difficult to derive secondary claims** – i.e. principally claims for damages – directly **from European Union law**. In competition law, the ECJ has assumed for Art. 101 and 102 TFEU that the provisions contained therein also include an entitlement to assert a claim for the individual damage incurred after infringements. This, it argues, is necessary for the requirements to have an effective impact.[56] The question as to 'whether' there is a claim for damages was thus assigned to European Union law.[57]

53 At the same time, however, the Court points out that 'in the absence of EU rules governing the matter, it is for the domestic legal system of each Member State to lay down the detailed rules governing the exercise of the right to claim compensation for the harm resulting from an agreement or practice prohibited under Art. 101 TFEU [...], provided that the **principles of equivalence and effectiveness** are observed'.[58] The **basis for the**

---

[52] For example Albrecht GWR 2022, 181 (182).

[53] ECJ 13.12.1971 – case 43/71, ECLI:EU:C:1971:122 para. 9 – Politi S.A.S., Robecco sul Naviglio v Ministry of Finance of the Italian Republic.

[54] See, in general, Geismann in von der Groeben/Schwarze/Hatje AEUV Art. 288 mn. 33; Nettesheim in Grabitz/Hilf/Nettesheim AEUV Art. 288 mn. 98; W. Schroeder in Streinz AEUV Art. 288 mn. 41.

[55] Lundqvist IIC 2021, 239 (240). Cf. on direct recourse to Union law as a basis for a claim, e.g. ECJ 17.9.2002 – case C-253/00, ECLI:EU:C:2002:497 = Rep. 2002, I-07289 para. 30–32 – Muñoz and Superior Fruiticola. The GDPR also contains directly applicable bases for claims, see for example the OLG Schleswig 3.6.2022 – 17 U 5/22 para. 47, NZI 2022, 714.

[56] ECJ 20.9.2001 – case C-453/99, ECLI:EU:C:2001:465 = Rep. 2001, I-6297 para. 26 – Courage; ECJ 6.10.2021 – case C-882/19, ECLI:EU:C:2021:800 = NJW 2021, 3583 para. 33 – Sumal SL v Mercedes Benz Trucks España SL.

[57] Stockenhuber in Grabitz/Hilf/Nettesheim AEUV Art. 101 mn. 260.

[58] ECJ 14.3.2019 – case C-724/17, ECLI:EU:C:2019:204 = EuZW 2019, 374 para. 27 – Skanska.

claim is therefore generally **national law**, not Art. 101 and 102 TFEU themselves.[59] Consequently, the question as to 'how' to deal with damages is left to national law, subject to the requirements of European Union law. As far as competition law is concerned, the European Union legislature has taken this as an opportunity to issue detailed provisions in **Dir. 2014/104/EU**. The wording of Art. 3(1) Dir. 2014/104/EU, according to which Member States 'shall ensure that any natural or legal person who has suffered harm caused by an infringement of competition law is able to claim and to obtain full compensation for that harm', indicates that the basis of the claim for damages is not European Union law but rather the law of the Member State.[60]

Against this backdrop, it seems doubtful whether the DMA will allow not just inherent rights but also claims derived from such rights. The fact that corresponding regulations are not explicitly provided for, argues against this.[61] It is true that the ECJ's reasoning on the necessity of a claim for damages in competition law can also be applied to the related provisions of the DMA.[62] This means at best, however, that **national law must provide for the necessary regulations and align them with the concept of effectiveness and equivalence**. National law, however, remains the legal basis for such claims. 54

D. International jurisdiction *(Henner Schläfke/Immo Schuler)*

The regulatory subject matter of the DMA suggests that there will be regular cross-border litigation regarding its implementation. In particular, the question of international jurisdiction has to be clarified. In the present case, we can only take a brief look at the conditions subject to which courts have international jurisdiction for private enforcement of the DMA. 55

In this context, the Recast Brussels I Regulation[63] is particularly relevant, at least insofar as the potential gatekeeper also has a registered office in the territory of the EU (Art. 6(1) in conjunction with Art. 63 Recast Brussels I Regulation). The jurisdiction based on the place where the harmful event took place pursuant to Art. 7 no. 2 Recast Brussels I Regulation is likely to be particularly relevant.[64] Under this provision, international jurisdiction is based on both the place where the harmful act was committed and the place where it had its effects.[65] It should be obvious that questions regarding **dispersed damages** and **forum shopping** arise in this context.[66] The problem is similar to that of dispersed torts, which also play a role in competition law. In these scenarios, the injured party can in any case liquidate the full damage at the centre of its main interest.[67] If a business user seeks preventive legal protection, the same applies in principle.[68] 56

[59] Stockenhuber in Grabitz/Hilf/Nettesheim AEUV Art. 101 mn. 252.

[60] Cf. as a whole also Stockenhuber in Grabitz/Hilf/Nettesheim AEUV Art. 101 mn. 261; Weiß in Calliess/Ruffert AEUV Art. 101 mn. 150.

[61] Zober NZKart 2021, 611 (614).

[62] With recourse also to ECJ 17.9.2002 – case C-253/00, ECLI:EU:C:2002:497 – Muñoz and Superior Fruiticola; Komninos in Charbit/Gachot, p. 425 (432).

[63] Regulation (EU) No 1215/2012 of the European Parliament and of the Council of 12 December 2012 on jurisdiction and the recognition and enforcement of judgments in civil and commercial matters (recast) (OJ 2012 L 351, 1).

[64] This also applies to claims under the UWG, see Fritzsche in MüKoUWG UWG § 9 mn. 114a.

[65] Gottwald in MüKoZPO EuGVVO Art. 7 mn. 55, so-called 'ubiquity theory'.

[66] See also on fair trading law, Sack WRP 2018, 897.

[67] Gottwald in MüKoZPO EuGVVO Art. 7 mn. 61.

[68] Cf. Art. 7 no. 2 Recast Brussels I Regulation, at the end: '[...] where the harmful event occurred or may occur'. See also Gottwald in MüKoZPO EuGVVO Art. 7 mn. 52.

57 Against this background, the international (and thus also local) jurisdiction for the private enforcement of the DMA will generally be determined based on the **registered office of the business user concerned**, as this is usually the center of the latter's main interest.[69]

58 End users can also enforce their rights in the civil courts. Regarding the question of international jurisdiction, it is important to note that there are special jurisdictions for consumers under the Recast Brussels I Regulation (Art. 17 and 18 Brussels I Regulation). Accordingly, in contractual disputes, consumers can opt to **bring proceedings** before the **courts of their domicile** (see Art. 18(1) Recast Brussels I Regulation). In addition, Art. 7 no. 2 Recast Brussels I Regulation also remains relevant for tortious claims.

E. Private enforcement in France *(Franck Audran/Elsa Mandel)*

59 This section explains the fundamental structures of the private enforcement of the DMA in France. To date, French law **does not contain specific provisions** implementing the DMA. However, French law provides for a **set of specific rules which, similarly to the DMA, are designed to protect business users and consumers**. The section will consider how the DMA could impact such rules (→ mn. 60 et seqq.) and subsequently focus on the legal basis for damages claims, i.e. the provisions of ordinary civil law (→ mn. 76 et seqq.). Finally, an overview of the procedural specifies will be given (→ mn. 99 et seqq.).

I. National provisions implementing the DMA

1. Protection of business users: sanction of so-called 'restrictive practices'

60 In addition to the **prohibition of anti-competitive behaviour** under Art. 101 and 102 TFEU and L.420 – 1 and L.420 – 2 French Commercial Code, other business practices that are considered to 'restrict competition' are specifically prohibited by French law (*pratiques restrictives de concurrence* – **PRC**s).[70]

61 These specific rules have the same general purpose as the DMA, i.e. protecting business users from being abused by stronger partners. In particular, the law on PRCs notably prohibits behaviours which create an **'imbalance' between commercial partners**, such as: obtaining benefits from another party without adequate compensation (*avantage sans contrepartie*); subjecting or attempting to subject the other party to a significant imbalance (*déséquilibre significatif*) or abruptly terminating an established business relationship (*rupture brutale de relation commerciale établie*).

a) Significant imbalance

62 **Significant imbalance** may be qualified where (i) one party subjects or attempts to subject the other party (ii) to terms or conditions which create a significant imbalance in the relationship.

63 This notion can be compared to Art. 12(5)(b) DMA, which uses very similar language and provides that 'practice […] shall be considered to […] be unfair where: […] there is an imbalance between the rights and obligations of business users and the gate-

[69] Cf. Stadler in Musielak/Voit EuGVVO Art. 7 mn. 20b. On the criticism of the ECJ's 'centre of main interest' theory, Sack WRP 2018, 897 mn. 29.

[70] These behaviours are listed in Article L.442 – 1 et seq. French Commercial Code.

keeper obtains an advantage from business users that is disproportionate to the service provided by the gatekeeper to the business users.'

As the wording and conditions of this Article are similar to the prohibition of PRCs, this could encourage French courts to resort to PRCs to indirectly enforce obligations contained in the DMA, without its actual implementation into national law. **64**

In fact, French courts have already sanctioned unbalanced behaviours of undertakings that could qualify as gatekeepers (such as Amazon or Booking), using the legal basis of the prohibition of PRCs. The Commercial Court of Paris sanctioned Amazon for subjecting its partners to significantly unbalanced terms, taking into account Amazon's **market position** and the **unavoidable nature of its services.**[71] In another decision, the Commercial Court of Paris took into account Booking's predominant position and **'unbalanced economic power'** to sanction it for subjecting its business partners to unbalanced conditions.[72] **65**

In the future, it may also be the case that an infringement of the DMA could be considered by courts as a PRC in itself, which could trigger the gatekeeper's liability (e.g. violation of the prohibition of non-switching clauses;[73] the obligation to apply fair, reasonable and non-discriminatory general conditions of access to software application stores, online search engine or social networks (Art. 8(12) DMA) or the obligation to restrain from providing disproportionate termination terms (Art. 8(13) DMA). **66**

A clarification on the articulation between the DMA and PRCs could thus be useful. The legislator could consider **introducing violations of the DMA into the list of PRCs**, similarly to what it did with the P2B Regulation,[74] for which a new paragraph was added to Art. L.442 – 1 French Commercial Code, according to which an undertaking can be held liable for breaching the obligations contained in the P2B Regulation.[75] In this case, such provision could serve as a basis for private enforcement actions. **67**

In the absence of such a modification, the DMA could still be used as a **framework for sanctioning 'significant imbalance'** by creating some kind of (rebuttable) presumption of imbalance where a gatekeeper is involved. Such reasoning would be coherent with the reasoning of French courts, which tend to assume that there is a 'subjection' where an undertaking has significant economic power.[76] **68**

---

[71] Commercial Court of Paris, 2.9.2019, no. 2017050625.

[72] Commercial Court of Paris, 29.11.2016, no. 2014027403: 'That the French Competition Authority has confirmed the predominant position of Booking on the market for the reservation of overnight stays – "Booking's market share is greater than 30 %"; that given the unbalanced economic power existing in the sector, the condition of submission of Article L.442 6 | 2° [now Article L. 442 1] of the Commercial Code is therefore met.'.

[73] Art. 5(3) DMA: 'The gatekeeper shall not prevent business users from offering the same products or services to end users through third-party online intermediation services or through their own direct online sales at prices or conditions that are different from those offered through the online intermediation service of the gatekeeper.'.

[74] Regulation (EU) 2019/1150 of the European Parliament and of the Council of 20 June 2019 on promoting fairness and transparency for business users of online intermediation services (OJ 2019 L 186, 57).

[75] 'Any person offering an online intermediation service within the meaning of Regulation (EU) 2019/1150 and who fails to comply with the obligations expressly laid down in the same Regulation shall incur liability and be required to compensate for the damage caused.'

[76] See for instance Cour de Cassation, 4.10.2016, no. 14–28.013. Also see Paris Commercial Court's appreciation in the Amazon case (Commercial Court of Paris, 2.9.2019, no. 2017050625): 'the submission is revealed in particular by the existence of an economically unbalanced power relationship between the parties.'

b) Abrupt termination of an established commercial relationship

69 Under French law, the termination of a commercial relationship can trigger the terminating party's liability where such party **'abruptly' terminates its commercial relationship without** providing reasonable **prior notice** to its partner. To determine the duration of what constitutes a 'reasonable' notice period, courts usually take into account several factors, including: the duration of the relationship, the nature of the products or services, or the existence of a dependency of one party on the other.

70 The question of whether the termination is 'abrupt' may thus depend on an unbalance/dependency between the parties. Therefore, again, the DMA may influence the courts' decisions and facilitate the claimant's **burden of proof** where the party terminating the relationship has been qualified as a gatekeeper by the Commission.

c) Enforcement of PRCs

71 An undertaking committing PRCs may be held liable for the damage caused to its business partner and be ordered to compensate such prejudice (Article L.442 – 1 French Commercial Code). Claims may be introduced either by the business user itself or by French authorities to protect effective competition on the market (Article L.442–4 French Commercial Code). These authorities may request the immediate termination of the practices. Additionally, the Public Ministry or the Ministry for Economy may request the imposition of an administrative fine of up to five million EUR (Article L.442–4 I. French Commercial Code, section 3).

2. Protection of end users: the prohibition of unfair commercial practices

72 French law prohibits commercial practices considered **unfair towards consumers**[77] (*pratiques commerciales déloyales*; Article L.121 – 1 French Consumer Code (public order provision)). A commercial practice is **'unfair'** if it is contrary to the requirements of **professional diligence** and significantly alters the **economic behaviour** of an average consumer. Such practices can lead to a civil or administrative fine of up to two million EUR (Article L.132 – 1 A French Consumer Code).

73 Similarly, some obligations of the DMA aim at protecting the consumers' freedom of choice, such as the prohibition of self-preferencing practices (Art. 8(5) DMA) or the obligation to allow the un-instalment of software (Art. 8(3) DMA). Other obligations are aimed at ensuring fair competition between undertakings and ultimately preserving the consumers' freedom of choice, such as the obligation to apply fair, reasonable and non-discriminatory terms of access for business users to software applications, online search services or social networks (Art. 8(12) DMA).

74 In line with previous comments regarding PRCs, interactions between the DMA and unfair commercial practices should be addressed to facilitate enforcement. For example, one may consider the introduction of a specific provision under which any breach of the DMA would be considered an unfair commercial practice.

3. Conclusion

75 Although the introduction of the DMA does not – to this day – change the applicable provisions on PRCs and unfair commercial practices, it can be anticipated that under-

[77] The notion of consumer is defined in the introductory Article of the Code, as 'any natural person acting for purposes which do not fall within the scope of his / her commercial, industrial, craft, liberal or agricultural activity'.

takings qualified as gatekeepers by the Commission will increasingly be subject to such claims.

II. Basis for claims

76 There are no specific provisions for the enforcement of the DMA. In this regard, the framework applicable to **damages claims** for violations of **competition law is of no help**. This is because the provisions of the French Commercial Code implementing the **Damages Directive**[78] clearly **limit its scope to claims based on infringement of competition law**, namely infringements of Art. 101 and 102 TFEU and L.420 – 1 (anti-competitive agreements), L.420 – 2 (abuse of dominance) and L.420 – 5 (abuse of economic dependency) French Commercial Code.[79] Therefore, any damages claim for a violation of the DMA will be based on the general rules of **French civil liability**. This continues to be the case for most of the recent damages claims based on competition law breaches to this day, since the provisions implementing the Damages Directive do not always apply.

77 It can be anticipated that claimants seeking damages for infringement of the DMA will face similar issues encountered by claimants requesting compensation for competition law infringements who cannot yet rely on the Damages Directive.

78 Under French law, civil liability claims are based on one single legal provision of the French Civil Code, i.e. **Art. 1240** ('Any act of man, which causes damage to another, obliges the person by whose fault it was done to repair it') and a long-standing and abundant **case law**.

79 Under the general civil liability regime of Art. 1240 French Civil Code, a claimant seeking compensation from a gatekeeper who has breached the DMA will have to demonstrate: (i) a fault, (ii) a prejudice and (iii) a causal link between the fault and the prejudice suffered.

1. Fault

80 In case of **'follow-on'** proceedings, one of the first question to arise will be whether a **sanction decision of the Commission** for non-compliance with the DMA automatically qualifies as a **'civil fault'** within the meaning of Art. 1240 French Civil Code.

81 By analogy with damages claims for violations of competition law, French courts could consider that a mere **infringement of the DMA will automatically constitute a civil fault** within the meaning of Art. 1240 French Civil Code, although case law in this regard is not completely frozen.[80] This issue is anticipated to cause some debate in case of litigation.

82 The claimant could further argue that a violation of the DMA constitutes an **'unfair competition' fault**, which would also give rise to civil liability on the basis of Art. 1240 French Civil Code. Indeed, French case law provides that it is an offence of unfair com-

[78] Directive 2014/104/EU of the European Parliament and of the Council of 26 November 2014 on certain rules governing actions for damages under national law for infringements of the competition law provisions of the Member States and of the European Union (OJ 2014 L 349, 1).

[79] See Article L.481 – 1 French Commercial Code: 'Any natural or legal person forming an undertaking or a body referred to in Article L.464 – 2 shall be liable for the damage it has caused as a result of the commission of an anticompetitive practice defined in Articles L. 420–1, L. 420–2, L. 420–2–1, L. 420–2–2 and L. 420–5 and Articles 101 and 102 of the Treaty on the Functioning of the European Union.'.

[80] As an example, in a decision of 2020, the Court of Appeal of Paris indicated that 'the violation of the law resulting of this anti-competitive practice necessarily constitutes a civil fault. Thus, the fault committed by X, likely to incur civil liability on the basis of Article 1240, is established' (Court of Appeal of Paris, 17.6.2020, no. 17/23041).

petition for a professional to disregard the regulations applicable to him because, by avoiding the constraints imposed by such regulations, he gives himself an unfair competitive advantage.[81]

83 By way of example, the Court of Appeal of Paris found that the marketing of dairy products under the name 'Feta', while the products did not comply with the European Regulations **on such geographical indications, constituted** a civil fault of unfair competition, because the sale of such products, at a lower price distorted competition, as a result of which the claimant was entitled to seek compensation.[82] In a similar manner, claimants could argue that non-compliance with the DMA enables the gatekeeper to avoid the constraints imposed to it by the Regulation, thus giving itself an unfair competitive advantage and allowing claimants to seek compensations.

84 It should be noted that compensation claims on the ground of unfair competition, which are based on Art. 1240 French Civil Code, do not necessarily need to be initiated by competitors of the defendant. Thus, in theory, a user of the gatekeeper's service – who is not a competitor – could still have a successful claim on the basis of 'unfair competition'. Reciprocally, this means that third-party claimants, which do not have any relationship with the gatekeeper, may seek damages under Art. 1240 French Civil Code.

85 As far as **standalone claims** are concerned, although the question that whether the undertaking qualifies as a gatekeeper, will be answered by the Commission, French courts may be asked to decide whether or not said gatekeeper has breached the DMA, and whether or not such breach may have caused a prejudice triggering compensation.

86 In theory, French courts will indeed be competent to decide whether or not the behaviour of a gatekeeper infringes the DMA. It would not be the first time that French judges would be asked to rule on the application of a European regulation, which are of direct application. In the same manner, French courts have, in some cases (albeit not that frequently), ordered compensation of prejudice caused by an anti-competitive practice, even though no competition authority had ruled on the existence of such anti-competitive practice.[83]

87 In fact, violations of the DMA, at least to a certain extent, may be easier to prove than certain competition law infringements, for which an extensive knowledge of the market may be necessary. This is all the more true since the DMA provides for very specific infringements, which may be easier to qualify than anti-competitive practices.

88 In the case of standalone claims, where the Commission is investigating against the gatekeeper (or where a decision of the Commission is under appeal), defendants may (and would be well advised to do so) request a **stay of proceedings** (*sursis à statuer*) on the basis of Art. 378 et seq. French Code of Civil Procedure. Courts will have discretionary power to decide to grant such stay of proceedings and may even order it on their own volition.[84] A stay of proceedings will be justified by the principle of 'proper administration of justice'. Notably, courts usually order stays of proceedings in order to avoid a contradiction of decisions between two different courts. Here, there may be some debate on how the Commission's decision may affect the court's decision, in particular whether the infringement investigated by the Commission is the same infringement assessed by the court.

---

[81] Cour de Cassation, 17.3.2021, no. 19–10.414.

[82] Court of Appeal of Paris, 22.10.2020, no. 09/11691.

[83] See for instance Court of Appeal of Paris, 19.10.2018, no. 16/07213 – Bubble diving c/ La Spirotechnique industrielle et commerciale.

[84] Cour de Cassation, 12.4.2018, no.17 – 16.945.

Standalone claims will most likely be more suited for co-contractors of the gatekeepers, who may be able to provide evidence of the gatekeeper's behaviour more easily than third-parties or competitors. 89

2. Prejudice and causal link

Punitive damages are not awarded in France: the sole purpose of Art. 1240 French Civil Code is to repair the **loss suffered by a claimant**. In order to trigger compensation, such loss must be **'direct and certain'**. 90

The **burden of proof** for the existence and amount of the alleged loss lies entirely on the plaintiff, in application of **Art. 1315 French Civil Code**, according to which 'A person who claims the performance of an obligation must prove it'. 91

The multiplication of damages claims for violations of competition law, which often involve independent or judicial economic expertise, has shown the difficulties in assessing the amount of the prejudice. Is it likely that the same type of issue will arise in damages claims relating to infringements of the DMA. In fact, it may be even more so, because the link between the gatekeeper's behaviour and the loss suffered by the claimant may be even more difficult to define than in cases of private enforcement following, for example, a cartel decision. Indeed, in the latter cases, the theoretical link between the infringement and the loss suffered is easier to grasp: the anti-competitive practices are usually considered to have had an effect on the prices paid by the infringer's customers. 92

The notion of a **'causal link'** is not defined by any provision of the French Civil Code, but the necessity for the claimant to effectively demonstrate such a causal relationship between the fault and the prejudice is constantly underlined by French courts. 93

The Court of Appeal of Paris did admit that such causal link can be particularly difficult to demonstrate, since a specific loss may be attributable to the unfair behaviour of a competitor as well as to normal competition or economic conditions. This is why, in some specific cases, French courts have introduced a **rebuttable presumption** that the defendant's behaviour has caused some level of harm. This is the case, for instance, in matters of unfair competition, where some courts have ruled that 'damage is necessarily inferred from an act of unfair competition'[85] even if this prejudice is only moral. 94

A similar presumption was recently applied in the world of competition law, against an undertaking that had failed to comply with the remedies agreed upon in the context of a merger authorisation. In its decision, the Court of Appeal considered that: 95

Non-compliance with commitments to which the Authority has made a concentration subject, to ensure the competitive operation of the market concerned by such a merger, necessarily creates a commercial disturbance for the undertakings operating on the market in question, constituting damage, even if only moral.[86] 96

In other words, any infringement likely to distort competition may be presumed to have caused a prejudice, even if it is only a symbolic one. Such presumption could also apply to infringements of the DMA. 97

Finally, Art. 1240 French Civil Code allows courts to **order the cessation of the infringing behaviours**. 98

---

[85] Cour de Cassation, 28.9.2010, no. 09-69.272. See also Cour de Cassation, 11.1.2017, no. 15-18669.
[86] Cour de Cassation, 16.11.2022, no. 21-19.728.

III. Noteworthy procedural specifics

1. Evidence

99 One issue that claimants will face is how to prove the DMA infringement and its consequences. In both follow-on and standalone cases, undertakings which consider to be victims of a DMA infringement may use **'summary proceedings'** on the basis of **Art. 145 French Code of Civil Procedure** in order to obtain the forced production of certain documents, either from the Commission's file (in the case of a follow-on claim) or from the gatekeeper's records, in order to prove the infringement and, possibly, its consequences on the plaintiff.

100 Art. 145 French Code of Civil Procedure allows plaintiffs to ask a judge to order 'any legally admissible measures of inquiry', such as having a bailiff go into the other party's premises to collect relevant evidence. In follow-on proceedings, this provision could be used to obtain elements from the Commission's file that are not in the public version of the Commission's decision and that could help to understand the extent of the infringement and assess the possible amount of the prejudice better.

101 In order to be granted such measures, the plaintiff invoking Art. 145 must demonstrate that there is **a legitimate reason** to preserve or establish, before any trial, the proof of facts on which the resolution of a dispute may depend. In a nutshell, the plaintiff will have to demonstrate that (i) the elements requested will be useful to prove the existence and assess the amount of its prejudice and (ii) the measures requested are not disproportionate.

102 In the field of anti-trust private enforcement, there have already been several examples of courts ruling on claims based on Art. 145 French Code of Civil Procedure. In a judgment of 18.5.2022 concerning the so-called 'trucks cartel',[87] the Court of Appeal of Paris upheld the decision of the French Supreme Court (*Cour de Cassation*) and refused to grant the plaintiff's request on the ground that he had not shown that he acquired trucks covered by the cartel, and had therefore not demonstrated a 'legitimate reason' within the meaning of Art. 145 French Code of Civil Procedure. The court added that even if the plaintiff had established a legitimate reason, the requested documents would still be useless for the evaluation of its prejudice, because the documents concerned the imputation and existence of a cartel without providing any information on its effects. In another case relating to the same cartel,[88] the court also rejected most of the claimant's request for access to the Commission's file either on the grounds that the documents were not useful for assessing the claimant's damage, or that disclosure would be disproportionate and/or would violate the rule protecting leniency applicants.

103 Similar issues may be encountered by claimants under the DMA, where the Commission's decision does not provide sufficient detail on the extent of the violation or where claimants have difficulties in calculating their loss.

2. Statute of limitation

104 The general rule of **Art. 2224 French Civil Code** should apply: damages claims will be 'time-barred after five years from the day when the holder of the right [the claimant] knew or should have known the facts enabling him to exercise its claim'.

105 Here, it can be anticipated that a discussion on the starting point of the statute of limitation will arise. In cases of follow-on claims, this could be the date on which the

[87] Court of Appeal of Paris, 18.5.2022, no. 20/13878.
[88] Court of Appeal of Paris, 20.4.2022, no. 21/06313.

Commission published its decision, its press release, or even before this date. The same discussion can be held with regard to standalone claims.

3. Competence

106 As indicated in this section, it is likely that DMA damages claims will initially be based on the basic civil liability regime of Art. 1240 French Civil Code. Regarding the question of **competence** claimants should refer to the rules laid down in the **Recast Brussels I Regulation.**[89] Accordingly, they will have to decide between the courts of the defendant's residence (Art. 4(1) Recast Brussels I Regulation) or such located where the harmful event occurred or may occur (Art. 7(2) Recast Brussels I Regulation).

107 In case a claim is brought on the ground of PRCs, **Art. D.442 – 3 French Commercial Code** provides a list of exclusively competent courts. In case of appeal, the Court of Appeal of Paris will have sole jurisdiction.

F. Private enforcement in Germany *(Henner Schläfke/Immo Schuler)*

108 This section focuses on the potential legal basis for claims relating to an infringement of the DMA under German law. First in relation to business users (→ mn. 109 et seqq.) and then in relation to end users (→ mn. 130 et seqq.). In the end, it describes noteworthy procedural specifics of the German law system (→ mn. 133 et seqq.).

I. Basis for claims of business users under national law

109 The German legislator has **extended the provisions of the GWB** that apply to the private enforcement of competition law infringements to include **infringements of the DMA** with the **11th GWB Amendment Act ('Wettbewerbsdurchsetzungsgesetz').**[90] Insofar as claims based on §§ 823(2) and 1004 BGB as well as §§ 3 and 3a in connection with §§ 8 et seqq. UWG could also be considered,[91] they would be displaced, at least in practice, by these statutory provisions. Further gateways for the legal evaluation required by the DMA in the context of contractual relationships – to the extent that a provision of the DMA is a prohibition statute – consequently also include § 134 BGB and – in particular if a provision of the DMA postulates a requirement governing the establishment of legal relationship or performance obligations – a review on general terms and conditions, in particular pursuant to § 307(2) no. 1 BGB.

1. Claims under the GWB as amended by the 11th GWB Amendment Act

110 The **bill on the 11th GWB amendment** assumes that the obligations for gatekeepers set out in Art. 5 to 7 DMA give rise to corresponding rights.[92] Accordingly, the amended § 33(1) GWB states that infringements of the obligations set out in Art. 5 to 7 DMA may give rise to claims without making any further differentiation. In this respect, it remains unclear whether the courts will still have to examine, on a case-by-case basis, whether

---

[89] Regulation (EU) No 1215/2012 of the European Parliament and of the Council of 12 December 2012 on jurisdiction and the recognition and enforcement of judgments in civil and commercial matters (recast) (OJ 2012 L 351, 1).

[90] See BT-Drs. 20/6824, 20.

[91] On the possible bases for claims outside the scope of the GWB, see also Karbaum/Schulz NZKart 2022, 107 (110).

[92] See BT-Drs. 20/6824, 2.

the obligations contained in the DMA confer rights on the individual. This is not always clear, as will be demonstrated below.

111 Claims under the GWB for infringements of the DMA will only arise after the 11th GWB amendment comes into force. While the DMA and competition law have some similarities, it is important to note that, despite their close relationship, the **DMA** does not, in fact, have its roots in Art. 103 TFEU, but rather is **based on Art. 114 TFEU**. Accordingly, competition law provisions stand alongside the system of the DMA (Art. 1(6) DMA, see also rec. 11 DMA; for more details → Ch. 2 mn. 43 et seqq.). This systematic difference and the underlying considerations relating to legal competence prohibit recourse to the provisions of competition law.[93] This differentiation is relevant as even based on the amended GWB, differences between the legal regimen covering damages claims based on infringements of Art. 101 and 102 TFEU and infringements of the DMA exist. Also, presumptions and rules of experience developed by courts in the context of competition law infringements do not necessarily apply. Insofar as the bases for claims contained in §§ 33 et seqq. GWB only referred to Art. 101 and 102 TFEU, they were not available for the enforcement of the DMA, neither with regard to a direct nor an analogue application.[94]

112 This changed with the 11th GWB Amendment Act. It transfers the system developed for the **private enforcement of competition law** and the enforcement of cartel damage claims to **violations of the DMA**. The same civil law claims now apply for violations of competition law and the DMA. The amendment act explicitly recognises parallels between competition law and the DMA.[95] In this context, much of the private enforcement relief available under cartel damages law as a result of the implementation of the Damages Directive is also to be applied to the enforcement of the DMA.[96]

113 Pursuant to § 33(1) GWB, affected users are entitled to assert **claims for abatement or removal and for injunctive relief** against the gatekeeper in the event of infringements of Art. 5 to 7 DMA. If the gatekeeper commits the violation intentionally or negligently, the affected parties also have **claims for damages** under § 33a(1) GWB.[97] The other requirements for the claim remain identical, since the wording of the norm simply equates infringements of Art. 5 to 7 DMA with infringements of competition law. It remains to be seen whether § 33 GWB will also be used in the DMA as a no-fault claim for damages in form of a removal claim, as is the case under competition law.[98]

114 According to § 33b GWB, users will also be able to rely on the **binding effect of decisions of the European Commission**, which already applies to infringements of competition law, in order to enforce their claims. Follow-on actions are thus also likely to play a major role in DMA enforcement. Pursuant to § 89b(5) GWB, publication of the Commission's decision by the gatekeeper can be enforced by way of interim relief. Of course, a prior decision by the European Commission is not a prerequisite, meaning that a standalone action is also possible, although it is up to the user to prove the infringement of Art. 5 to 7 DMA.

115 Just like cartel damages, damages resulting from infringements of the DMA are **subject to interest at five percentage points above the relevant base rate** as of the time

[93] See also Basedow ZEuP 2021, 217 (223); Karbaum/Schulz NZKart 2022, 107 (110); Zober NZKart 2021, 611 (614); Zimmer/Göhsl ZWeR 2021, 29 (34); Albrecht GWR 2022, 181 (183); Kumkar RDi 2022, 347 (353).

[94] Klumpe in Kirk/Offergeld/Rohner, p. 131 (137).

[95] Cf. BT-Drs. 20/6824, 50.

[96] BT-Drs. 20/6824, 2.

[97] BT-Drs. 20/6824, 50.

[98] Klumpe in Kirk/Offergeld/Rohner, p. 131 (139).

they occur under § 33a(4) GWB in conjunction with § 288 BGB. Obviously, such a claim for statutory interest due to an infringement of the DMA can only arise after the 11th GWB Amendment Act was enacted and not before a gatekeeper has been designated, as this is a prerequisite of rights under the DMA. Before, identical interest could only be claimed based on a competition law infringement. Insofar as the infringement of the DMA concerns a remuneration claim of business users, an interest rate that is nine percentage points above the relevant base rate may also be relevant pursuant to § 288(2) BGB.

Finally, the **limitation rules set out in § 33h GWB** are also to be applicable to private enforcement of the DMA.[99] This means that, depending on when knowledge arose, claims would only become statute-barred five calendar years after termination of the infringement of the DMA and knowledge or grossly negligent lack of knowledge and, regardless of when knowledge arose, at the earliest ten years after termination of the infringement of the DMA. Also worth mentioning is the suspension of the statute of limitations during administrative proceedings, which is likely to be of similar practical importance in the area of DMA violations as it is in the area of cartel damages.[100] 116

Despite these extensive parallels between the claim standards, there may be **overlaps between competition law and the DMA** with regard to the issues arising in judicial disputes. In individual cases, a gatekeeper's conduct may constitute both an abuse of a dominant position and an infringement of the DMA. The bill on the 11th GWB amendment recognises these parallels, which is why it **assigns** disputes for both regulatory areas **to the same courts** (§§ 87 and 89 GWB).[101] 117

2. Other bases for claims

With the 11th GWB Amendment Act extensive provisions on private enforcement of the DMA were included in the GWB. Thus, a preceding discussion as to which existing provisions could give rise to civil law claims under German law has likely come to an end. This is because in the field of cartel damages the prevailing opinion assumes that claims under **§ 823(2) BGB or the UWG**, for example, are **superseded by the bases for claims** for abatement or removal, injunctive relief and damages under tort law **contained in the GWB.**[102] In principle, it seems obvious to apply the same approach to infringements of the DMA – and the bill on the 11th GWB amendment does not indicate that there should be any parallels with other bases for claims either. 118

Nevertheless, there might be a residual application insofar as these more general provisions grant a basis for claim not specifically addressed by the GWB. However, in view of the relief to be provided to users affected by DMA infringements in the GWB, it can be assumed that other claims will not play any significant role in practice. As the debate shines light on the perception of the DMA in Germany, we briefly outline where bases of claim could be seen prior to the entry into force of the 11th GWB Amendment Act. 119

---

[99] BT-Drs. 20/6824, 43.

[100] Klumpe in Kirk/Offergeld/Rohner, p. 131 (141).

[101] BT-Drs. 20/6824, 50 et seq. Cf. also Haus/Rudel RDi 2022, 125 (131 et seq.); Paal/Kieß ZfDR 2022, 1 (18); for the area of competition law cf. for example BGH 7.2.2006 – KZR 33/04, GRUR 2006, 773 para. 14 – Abonnentenwerbung; Kersting in LMRKM GWB Vor § 33 mn. 16; Bechtold/Bosch in Bechtold/Bosch GWB § 33 mn. 43.

[102] See, for example, BGH 7.2.2006 – KZR 33/04, GRUR 2006, 773 para. 14 – Abonnentenwerbung; Kersting in LMRKM GWB Vor § 33 mn. 16; Bechtold/Bosch in Bechtold/Bosch GWB § 33 mn. 43.

a) Damages according to § 823(2) BGB in connection with norms set out in the DMA

120 § 823(2) BGB can constitute a basis for a claim in tort in conjunction with norms set out in the DMA. The prerequisite for this is that the **norms set out in the DMA** are of an **individual protective nature**, i.e. that the protection of individual interests is intended and, therefore, lies within the remit of the norm.[103] This is the case for the rights constituted under Art. 5 to 7 DMA,[104] particularly in cases involving potential statutes that are intended to protect another person under European Union law. In this regard, the principle of effectiveness (effet utile) and the principle of equivalence may suggest an individual protective nature.[105]

121 The DMA's starting point is primarily to ensure contestable and fair digital markets (see Art. 1(1) DMA). Insofar, the general public, which has an interest in precisely these markets, is the primary audience to be protected. This is, however, not sufficient to call into question the individual protective nature of the DMA as a whole.[106] As the above analysis of Art. 5 to 7 DMA shows, these purposes are mainly promoted by various obligations that gatekeepers have *vis-à-vis* third parties, i.e. business users or end users. Consequently, the very structure of the gatekeepers' obligations, which explicitly names the beneficiaries, reveals that the DMA is of an **individual protective nature**.[107] This individual protective nature permeates the DMA. The recitals contain numerous considerations that are geared to the specific interests of business users.[108] The general requirements of European Union law on the effectiveness and equivalence of national interpretations also imply such understanding.[109] This is also consistent with the considerations of the German legislator expressed in the bill on the 11th GWB amendment that led to the application of §§ 33 et seq. GWB for infringements of Art. 5 to 7 DMA parallel to infringements of Art. 101, 102 TFEU.

b) Claims for injunctive relief under § 1004 BGB

122 If **claims for injunctive relief and abatement or removal** are to be asserted, recourse can also be made to **§ 1004 BGB** (in addition to the rights inherently enshrined in the DMA). Although its wording is limited to impairments of property, it is generally accepted that the provision also applies, in particular, to violations of statutes that are intended to protect another person within the meaning of § 823(2) BGB.[110]

123 With regard to the provisions set out in **Art. 5 to 7 DMA**, due to their nature as statutes that are intended to protect another person, infringements of these provisions may also result in claims for injunctive relief or claims for abatement or removal pursuant to § 1004 BGB.[111] This is likely to apply, in particular, to those obligations that relate to specific prohibitions of use and exploitation for gatekeepers. Claims for injunctive relief may also be relevant with regard to the requirements, contained in the DMA, gov-

---

[103] This is the wording widely used by the BGH, see for example BGH 23.7.2019 – VI ZR 307/18, VersR 2019, 1378 para. 12. See also Wagner in MüKoBGB BGB § 823 mn. 562; Förster in BeckOK BGB § 823 mn. 276.

[104] Wolf-Posch in HK-DMA DMA Art. 6 mn. 199.

[105] See Wagner in MüKoBGB BGB § 823 mn. 540.

[106] Zober NZKart 2021, 611 (614); Karbaum/Schulz NZKart 2022, 107 (110).

[107] Accordingly, the absence of specific beneficiaries is considered an indication arguing against an individual protective nature, see for instance BGH 13.3.2018 – VI ZR 143/17, NJW 2018, 1671 para. 22 and 27.

[108] See, for example, rec. 7, 31, 33, 39, 40, 42, 43 etc. DMA. Albrecht GWR 2022, 181 (183) also concurs.

[109] Cf. Wagner in MüKoBGB BGB § 823 mn. 541 et seq.

[110] Fritzsche in BeckOK BGB § 1004 mn. 53 et seq.; Raff in MüKoBGB BGB § 1004 mn. 41; Thole in Staudinger BGB § 1004 mn. 7.

[111] Albrecht GWR 2022, 181 (183).

erning the establishment of legal relationships for the use of platform services if gatekeepers design their terms of use in a manner that is contrary to this.

Temporary legal protection is likely to be of particular interest in this respect: Depending on the scenario, it may be permissible, even before an infringement has occured, to oblige the tortfeasor to cease and desist if there is a risk of an initial infringement.[112] Particularly in the case of ongoing changes to the (legal as well as technical) architecture of platform services, business users can therefore safeguard their rights as a precautionary measure if corresponding infringements become apparent. While the basis of such a claim now likely would be § 33a GWB, the legal principles applied are basically the same. **124**

c) Claims under the UWG

Without the 11th GWB amendment, the UWG would allow business users to enforce provisions under the DMA as infringements of the latter can be regarded as **unfair conduct by gatekeepers within the meaning of § 3a UWG**. Even after the 11th GWB amendment the UWG might grant collective claims that are not covered by the GWB for infringements of the DMA. The prerequisite for any claim based on § 3a UWG is the violation of statutory provisions that also regulate market conduct in the interest of market participants.[113] The infringement must also be capable of significantly impairing the interests of consumers, other market participants or competitors. **125**

The first condition can be clearly affirmed in view of what has already been set out above. The DMA is a law within the meaning of the UWG.[114] Moreover, the DMA regulates the market for platform services not just for the sake of the market; its provisions also aim to **protect the interests of other participants in this market**, in particular business users.[115] The many references to fair and non-discriminatory behaviour by gatekeepers highlight this finding.[116] In the area of the DMA, it is also more than conceivable that infringements – depending on the individual case – constitute a considerable impairment of the market protected by the DMA, especially since infringements by a gatekeeper will affect a large number of users in each case. **126**

An infringement under § 3a UWG committed by means of a commercial practice (§ 2(1) no. 2 UWG) simultaneously constitutes an **unfair commercial practice within the meaning of § 3(1) UWG**.[117] Subsequently, the provisions set out in §§ 8 and 9 UWG provide a basis for claims, provided that further requirements are met. Accordingly, competitors and associations in particular are entitled to demand injunctive relief and the elimination of the infringement (§ 8(1) sent. 1, (3) UWG).[118] Individual business users may also claim damages if they are to be regarded as competitors of the gatekeepers (cf. § 9(1) UWG). Consequently, only competitors of the gatekeepers can be considered as creditors of these claims for damages. According to the legal definition used in § 2(1) no. 4 UWG, this includes 'any person who has a concrete competitive relationship with one or more entrepreneurs supplying or demanding goods or services'. A 'concrete competitive relationship' is assumed if the parties seek to sell similar goods and services **127**

[112] See for example Förster in BeckOK BGB § 823 mn. 51.
[113] Ohly in Ohly/Sosnitza UWG § 3a mn. 9, 21 also speaks of the necessary protection of third parties.
[114] Albrecht GWR 2022, 181 (182).
[115] Albrecht GWR 2022, 181 (182).
[116] Cf. also Karbaum/Schulz NZKart 2022, 107 (110).
[117] Schaffert in MüKoUWG UWG § 3a mn. 563.
[118] Regarding the enforcement of these claims via representative actions, → mn. 134 et seqq.

to the same group of end consumers.[119] Furthermore, the relevant conduct of the potential tortfeasor must be capable of hindering, or interfering with, the competitor's sales.[120]

128 There are various norms in the DMA that assume that **gatekeepers and business users** meet **as competitors** in this sense.[121] For example, the interoperability obligation in Art. 6(7) sent. 2 DMA is linked to services provided by both the gatekeeper and the business user. Art. 6(5) DMA, on the other hand, provides for a prohibition of self-preferencing for gatekeepers when compiling rankings. Accordingly, in the event of infringements of such norms, business users can enforce their rights with the help of the UWG.

129 For specific **associations** listed in § 8(3) no. 2 to 4 UWG, there is also the option to **sue for the surrender of profit** due to an intentional infringement of § 3 UWG (§ 10(1) UWG). § 34a GWB – which sets out provisions governing the disgorgement of benefits by associations due to an infringement of competition law – is only linked to an infringement of competition law even after the 11th GWB amendment. In the event of infringements of the obligations under the UWG, more far-reaching representative action for the surrender of profits could also follow directly from the UWG. This is especially relevant as recent changes to § 10 UWG expressly allow for a percentage fee for litigation funders.

II. Basis for claims of end users under national law

130 Once again, **essentially the same overall conditions** apply to end users as to **business users**. The amendments to the GWB also benefit them. This applies in particular to consumers, who may also be 'persons affected' within the meaning of §§ 33, 33a GWB.[122] The 11th GWB Amendment does not provide for any changes in this respect.

131 Prior to the entry into force of the 11th GWB Amendment Act, end users could assert claims under §§ 823 (2) and 1004 BGB.[123] Consumers in particular were covered by the **DMA's individual protection** even before the most recent amendments to the GWB. On the one hand, this is because they can derive concrete rights directly from various norms. On the other hand, the DMA emphasises in many places that the protection of consumer interests is one of its objectives (see, for example, rec. 1 and Art. 8(1) DMA).

132 As far as the UWG is concerned, it is primarily the claim under § 9(2) in conjunction with § 3(2) UWG that applies to consumers. The purpose of this claim for damages, however, is specifically aimed at the **consumer's freedom of choice**.[124] General adverse effects on the market pursuant to § 3a UWG are not sufficient in this respect. The end user rights in the DMA can also be used in this regard. Not infrequently, they are ultimately intended to safeguard the freedom of choice of end users (see, for example, Art. 6(3) subpara. 2 DMA). Nevertheless, the range of potentially relevant circumstances in which consumers can enforce the DMA through the UWG is smaller than for business users. Other end users are left with the abovementioned (→ mn. 51) claims for injunctive relief or damages, insofar as these users are to be regarded as competitors of the gatekeepers.

[119] Köhler/Feddersen in Köhler/Bornkamm/Feddersen UWG § 8 mn. 3.27 with further substantiation.
[120] Ottofülling in MüKoUWG UWG § 8 mn. 412.
[121] Cf. also Albrecht GWR 2022, 181 (183).
[122] Lübbig in MüKoWettbR GWB § 33 mn. 11.
[123] For a critical view of what was originally more indirect protection for end users: Podszun EuCML 2022, 1 (3). As demonstrated, however, many rights also apply directly to end users in the current version.
[124] See the explanatory memorandum, BT-Drs. 19/27873, 40.

III. Noteworthy procedural specifics

1. Concentration of jurisdiction under the 11th GWB Amendment Act

Pursuant to §§ 87, 89 GWB legal disputes concerning infringements of the DMA will be bundled **at the regional courts also responsible for competition law proceedings**. This is to be welcomed. The links between the two subject matters hold the promise of synergy effects.[125] Due to the foreseeable number of cases, it can be assumed that the limitation of jurisdiction will in due course lead to a significant specialisation of the courts and to a certain consolidation of case law with regard to the interpretation of Art. 5 to 7 DMA.[126] A swift development of case law in Germany by qualified courts – as seen in the field of cartel claims in the past years – would also strengthen Germany's status as a relevant forum. The concentration on a limited number of courts is also, however, likely to be positive from the perspective of the courts. The draft bill of the 11th GWB Amendment Act rightly points out that in the complex and technical area covered by the DMA it makes sense to pool expertise.[127] 133

2. Collective private enforcement: the role of representative action

In addition to the individual enforcement of claims, representative actions are likely to provide an important impetus for the enforcement of the DMA. Here, a distinction has to be made between representative actions in favour of business users (→ mn. 135 et seqq.) and representative actions in favour of end users (→ mn. 140 et seqq.). 134

a) Representative actions in favour of business users

The DMA does not provide business users with any independent means of enforcing their interests through representative action. Although the possibility of collective redress by consumer associations was explicitly included in Art. 42 DMA in the course of the legislative process (→ mn. 142), similar explicit provisions for business associations, on the other hand, were included. 135

Rec. 12 DMA clarifies that the DMA applies without prejudice to the rules resulting from Dir. 2005/29/EC (UCP Directive).[128] The same applies to Reg. (EU) 2019/1150 (fairness and transparency). With regard to the **UCP Directive**, this means that business users can take representative action against infringements of the DMA, in particular if the law derived from the UCP Directive provides for this option. It is important to note that the UCP Directive itself does not contain any mandatory provisions on collective enforcement options, but leaves these to the discretion of the Member States in Art. 11(1) subpara. 2 UCP Directive, also for 'competitors'.[129] 136

Future options, in this regard, will depend on how the relationship between the 11th GWB Amendment Act and the **UWG** is defined. In principle, the UWG provides for representative actions. Based on what has already been said about the UWG, it is therefore also possible to collectively enforce the interests of business users through corre- 137

[125] BT-Drs. 20/6824, 50.

[126] Klumpe in Kirk/Offergeld/Rohner, p. 131 (142); Herbers/München RdZ 2023, 4 (6).

[127] BT-Drs. 20/6824, 50.

[128] Directive 2005/29/EC of the European Parliament and of the Council of 11 May 2005 concerning unfair business-to-consumer commercial practices in the internal market and amending Council Directive 84/450/EEC, Directives 97/7/EC, 98/27/EC and 2002/65/EC of the European Parliament and of the Council and Regulation (EC) No 2006/2004 of the European Parliament and of the Council ('Unfair Commercial Practices Directive') (OJ 2005 L 149, 22).

[129] Micklitz/Namysłowska in MüKoUWG UGP-RL Art. 11 mn. 6.

sponding associations (see § 8(1) sent. 1, (3), § 8b UWG, → mn. 129). Pursuant to § 8(3) no. 2 UWG, enforcement requires that entrepreneurs who supply goods or services of the same or similar type on the same market are organised in the relevant associations. This means that members of the association concerned must ultimately be composed of competitors as defined by the UWG.[130] Furthermore, the infringement must affect the interests of the members of the association.

138 **Art. 14 Reg. (EU) 2019/1150** also provides for the option of representative action for business users. This is also emphasised in § 8a UWG. According to this provision, associations with a legitimate interest in representing business users are entitled to have non-compliance with the requirements set out in the Regulation terminated or prohibited by court order. This option makes it possible, at least indirectly, to collectively enforce the requirements set out in Art. 6(5) DMA. This is because, in individual cases, these may overlap with the transparency requirements set out in Art. 5 Reg. (EU) 2019/1150 (→ mn. 22). Collective enforcement of Reg. (EU) 2019/1150 thus offers the option of indirectly supporting the requirements of the DMA in this sub-area.

139 However, the fact that under the 11th GWB Amendment Act, § 33(4) no. 1 GWB now also entitles **associations for the promotion of commercial or independent professional interests** to collectively enforce claims for injunctive relief under § 33(1) GWB is likely to become much more relevant. A need for 'detours' via the UWG or Art. 14 Reg. (EU) 2019/1150 should with that become unnecessary. By contrast, German law lacks a procedural instrument for the collective enforcement of claims for damages by companies of any size. But smaller companies are able to join representative actions brought by qualified entities once an Act Implementing the Collective Redress Directive has come into force.

b) Representative action in favour of end users

140 The DMA contains a clearer positioning with regard to representative actions in the interest of **consumers**, which the Regulation covers in their capacity as end users. It is true that the Commission's original draft did not explicitly provide for this. As a result of changes in the legislative process, the DMA now explicitly refers to the **Representative Actions Directive** (Dir. (EU) 2020/1828[131]) in several places. Thus, claims based on the DMA can be enforced in all European countries as part of the European representative actions that are mandatory since June 2023 – also on a cross-border basis.

141 The implementation of Dir. (EU) 2020/1828 is to be achieved in Germany by the **Representative Actions Directive Implementation Act**, which has been passed by the Bundestag on 5.7.2023.[132] In essence, this act creates a new Consumer Rights Enforcement Act governing means of collective redress. It now provides for qualified entities to bring actions for establishment of liability and also performance – action for redress (Abhilfeklage) – in cases involving materially similar claims. Consumers and small businesses can participate in those actions by **opting in**. The relevant Higher Regional Court will first have to establish the claim on the merits by an interlocutory judgment on

---

[130] Büscher in Fezer/Büscher/Obergfell UWG § 8 mn. 253.

[131] Directive (EU) 2020/1828 of the European Parliament and of the Council of 25 November 2020 on representative actions for the protection of the collective interests of consumers and repealing Directive 2009/22/EC (OJ 2020 L 409, 1).

[132] Cf. Schläfke/Lühmann/Stegemann PHi 2022, 138 et seqq. and Schläfke/Lühmann NJW 2023 (forthcoming) for more information on the structure of the new action for redress under the Consumer Rights Enforcement Act (*Verbraucherrechtedurchsetzungsgesetz*, VDuG) provided for in an earlier version of the draft bill on the Act Implementing the Collective Redress Directive (*Verbandsklagerichtlinienumsetzungsgesetz*).

redress. If a claim has merits, the court will set out in its judgment the way to calculate individual damages and on which conditions they can be sought by individuals. In a next step, the court seeks to achieve a settlement. If such a settlement is unsuccessful the court estimates the total damage incurred, which it awards as a collective total amount in a final judgment on redress to be paid into an implementation fund administered by a court-appointed administrator. The examination of the individual claims and the distribution of the collective total amount are subsequently carried out by a court-appointed administrator.[133]

Rec. 104 DMA clarifies that consumers also should be able to enforce their rights in relation to gatekeepers by means of representative actions. For this purpose, Art. 52 DMA supplements Annex I to Dir. (EU) 2020/1828 by including the DMA.[134] Art. 42 DMA also expressly states that Dir. (EU) 2020/1828 applies to **representative actions brought against gatekeepers** that breach their obligations under the DMA and, in doing so, harm or may harm the collective interests of consumers. 142

An additional, indirect option of enforcing the obligations under the DMA by means of representative actions also arises from Art. 8(1) DMA. According to this provision, gatekeepers must ensure that the measures they take to fulfil their obligations under the DMA also comply with otherwise applicable law. Reg. (EU) 2016/679 (GDPR)[135] and Dir. 2002/58/EC (ePrivacy Directive)[136] as well as general requirements for consumer protection, cybersecurity and product safety are explicitly mentioned. The two legal acts mentioned are also subject to Annex I of Dir. (EU) 2020/1828, meaning that a review and enforcement of compliance with these regulations in the context of the European representative action at least **indirectly** enables a **review of gatekeepers' conduct** in the context of the DMA. The areas of regulation generally referred to in Art. 8(1) DMA may also overlap with a large number of the provisions listed in Annex I of Dir. (EU) 2020/1828. This could result in convergence to the extent that representative action is based on the measures taken by gatekeepers under the DMA. 143

3. Evidence

In the course of the 11th GWB amendment, some of the evidentiary provisions applicable to private cartel actions have been extended to the DMA where necessary. With regard to DMA infringements, users will be able to rely on the **binding effect of decisions of the European Commission** in order to enforce their claims (§ 33b GWB). Although this is not a prerequisite for legal action following a DMA infringement, this will be helpful for the effective enforcement of private claims, as it is otherwise up to the user to prove the existence of an infringement. 144

According to § 33a(3)GWB, the **standard set out in § 287 of the German Code of Civil Procedure (*Zivilprozessordnung*, ZPO)** applies to the **assessment of the damage** – both in terms of amount and its occurrence.[137] This provision gives the court considerable leeway, stating that 'the court shall rule on this issue at its discretion and conviction, 145

---

[133] For details, see Schläfke/Lühmann/Stegemann PHi 2022, 138 et seqq. and Schläfke/Lühmann NJW 2023 (forthcoming).

[134] Regarding the original draft, see also the proposal with the same wording in Podszun EuCML 2022, 1 (5).

[135] Regulation (EU) 2016/679 of the European Parliament and of the Council of 27 April 2016 on the protection of natural persons with regard to the processing of personal data and on the free movement of such data, and repealing Directive 95/46/EC (General Data Protection Regulation) (OJ 2016 L 119, 1).

[136] Directive 2002/58/EC of the European Parliament and of the Council of 12 July 2002 concerning the processing of personal data and the protection of privacy in the electronic communications sector (Directive on privacy and electronic communications) (OJ 2002 L 201, 37).

[137] BGH 28.1.2020 – KZR 24/17, BGHZ 224, 281 para. 25 – Schienenkartell II.

based on its evaluation of all circumstances'. However, even with the reduced standard of proof under § 287 ZPO, it is not sufficient to merely refer to principles of experience, as these do not have any abstractly qualifiable influence on the result of the overall assessment.[138]

146 §§ 287(1) ZPO further states that 'the court may decide at its discretion whether or not – and if so, in which scope – any taking of evidence should be ordered as applied for, or whether or not any experts should be involved to prepare a report'.

147 The German Supreme Court denied the applicability of ***prima facie* evidence** in the context of cartel claims.[139] Thus, with regard to DMA claims, it can be concluded that the value of expert reports is higher the more the expert opinion is based on concrete circumstances of the case at hand.

148 Furthermore, expert evidence does not constitute immediate proof for the occurrence or absence of a damage. This is because the expert, like the court, can only derive his assessment from connecting facts. Such a report is, therefore, a merely hypothetical finding rather than an actual statement of fact. In the overall assessment to be made, expert opinions are to be considered. However, they cannot replace the overall assessment by the court, nor does the submission of party expert opinions prejudice the assessment in one direction or the other.[140]

149 An essential difference to cartel damages law would be that the affected parties could **not rely on the presumption of damage** in **§ 33a(2) GWB**. Of course, this presumption does not apply in the legacy cases that currently dominate the case law on cartel damages. In those cases courts find that there are rules of experience – supported by economic theory and evidence – that if undertakings enter into price or quota cartels despite the considerable risks involved, there is a factual presumption that the prices achieved within the framework of a cartel are on an average higher than those that would have been achieved in the absence of the restrictive agreement.[141] It remains to be seen if courts find similar theorems in a more developed market based on economic theory.

150 However, the applicability of **§ 33g GWB** and the substantive right of **access to evidence** contained therein is intended to provide relief. Users could then demand the information and evidence necessary to enforce and quantify their claim from the gatekeeper and third parties (§ 33g(1) GWB). Gatekeepers would have a corresponding claim to the information and surrender of evidence necessary to defend against the claim (§ 33g(2) GWB).

151 Insofar as the procedural provisions of §§ 89a et seqq. GWB do not already apply by virtue of their link to §§ 33a and 33g GWB, their applicability is to be clarified and specific information added. In this context, § 89b(5) GWB should be highlighted, as it is likely to prove particularly effective in enforcing the DMA.[142]

IV. Conclusion

152 With the **11th GWB amendment** a **model for implementation of private enforcement of the DMA** is already available in Germany. This involves applying familiar and tried-and-tested effective private law enforcement mechanisms from competition law to the DMA, including many relief options introduced by the Damages Directive for

---

[138] BGH 28.1.2020 – KZR 24/17, BGHZ 224, 281 para. 51 – Schienenkartell II.
[139] BGH 28.1.2020 – KZR 24/17, BGHZ 224, 281 para. 31 – Schienenkartell II.
[140] BGH 28.1.2020 – KZR 24/17, BGHZ 224, 281 para. 48 – Schienenkartell II.
[141] BGH 11.12.2018 – KZR 26/17, NZKart 2019, 101 para. 55 – Schienenkartell I.
[142] Klumpe in Kirk/Offergeld/Rohner, p. 131 (141).

the assertion of claims for damages. As chambers of the regional courts responsible for competition law are to supervise the enforcement of the DMA as well, a coherent approach considering both the DMA and competition law in the individual proceeding is to be expected.

In connection with the **implementation of Dir. (EU) 2020/1828** in Germany and its new action for redress that includes enforcement of the DMA but also competition law, this means that qualified entities from Germany and abroad can enforce claims asserted by consumers and small businesses against gatekeepers by way of an action for redress in bundled form. 153

G. Private enforcement in Ireland *(Rob Corbet/Richard Willis)*

In the following, the basic structures used to enforce the DMA in Ireland will be explained. First, this section will give a brief overview about the question of implementation of the DMA in Ireland (→ mn. 155 et seqq.). Afterwards, it will provide details on the private enforcement of the DMA by business and end users (→ mn. 160 et seqq.). Finally, procedural points, such as forum, jurisdiction and representative actions, will be discussed (→ mn. 167 et seqq.). 154

I. National provisions implementing the DMA

1. Legislation

There is **no implementing legislation** in Ireland, nor is there any definitive sign that such legislation will be forthcoming. According to the Summer 2023 Legislative Programmes published by the Oireachtas (the Irish Parliament) on 19.4.2023, there is no draft legislation or intention to give further effect to the DMA under national law. It is worth noting that the Summer Programme includes the introduction of the Digital Services Bill, which aims to implement **Reg. (EU) 2022/2065 on a Single Market for Digital Services (DSA)**. It is possible that a bill may be introduced in the Autumn Programme to implement the DSA's counterpart, the DMA. 155

2. Wider debate and commentary on implementation

The DMA has received consistent support in the Oireachtas. In July 2021, the then Minister of State at the Department of Enterprise, Trade and Employment, *Robert Troy*, stated to the Dáil (the lower house of the Irish Parliament) that 'Ireland agrees with the problem definition as defined in the Digital Markets Act and fully supports the high-level objectives outlined therein'. The former Minister also stated, in the same forum in November 2021, that 'Ireland has supported these objectives since the DMA proposal was published and it will continue to do so throughout the rest of the negotiations […]'. 156

The **Competition and Consumer Protection Commission (CCPC)** is the competent authority for Ireland under the DMA. It is an independent statutory body that enforces competition and consumer protection law in Ireland. In January 2021 the CCPC published a submission to the Irish Department of Enterprise, Trade and Employment on the proposal for the DMA. This submission, which generally called for clarification as to the CCPC's role in relation to the European Commission, welcomed the proposal and lauded its objectives. 157

In a recent Joint Committee on Enterprise, Trade and Employment Debate, Ms *Una Fitzpatrick*, the director of Technology Ireland (a business organisation representing 158

Ireland's tech sector), stated, '[h]ow we implement the Digital Services Act, and the Digital Markets Act will set the eyes of Europe, if not the world, on Ireland'. This is suggestive of the views shared by those persons in Ireland who will be designated as gatekeepers under the DMA.

159 The centrality of Ireland to the private enforcement of the DMA has been recognised at a European level. MEP Ms *Gwendoline Delbos-Corfield*, in attendance at a Joint Committee on Justice Debate, stated that Ireland is in an ambiguous situation in terms of the large numbers of big tech companies based here. She observed that:

> [I]t is also interesting for the European Parliament to enter into a discussion or conversation with the Irish political world about what competences should remain at Member State level, what Ireland feels is sometimes too much of a burden and how we can work on it. With the Digital Services Act and the Digital Markets Act, some competences have gone to the European level.[143]

II. Basis for claims

1. Types of actions

160 The Q&A[144] published by the European Commission states that direct actions for damages can be enforced in national courts for those harmed by non-complying gatekeepers. There is a dearth of commentary on any possible approach to persons taking private actions in Ireland under the DMA. However, it is clear that the DMA has **direct effect** and creates certain **enforceable obligations** which can be used by private parties within the EU. In particular, the **obligations under Art. 5 and 6 DMA** are intentionally precise and unconditional to ensure that there is the possibility of enforcement on a national level through Art. 288 TFEU.

161 It is likely that private enforcement of the DMA in Ireland will arise through **tort claims** in respect of alleged breach of statutory duty under the DMA. Business claimants will likely seek damages to compensate for economic loss and harm sustained as a result of the default of a gatekeeper. A gatekeeper will be held liable for the full extent of the economic loss that the claimant would not otherwise have suffered but for the default of the gatekeeper. This principle is balanced against the duty of a claimant to take reasonable steps to mitigate its loss, and where this duty is breached, any award will be reduced accordingly. In addition, in theory at least, business claimants may also seek **injunctive relief**, in lieu of, or in addition to, damages, which will require a gatekeeper to carry out specified actions (e.g. comply with its obligations under the DMA) or indeed to cease actions that may fall foul of the DMA.

162 In addition, consumer claimants will also likely engage the provisions of the **Representative Actions for the Protection of the Collective Interests of Consumers Act 2023**. This legislation is the subject of further commentary below (→ mn. 176 et seqq.).

[143] Houses of the Oireachtas, Joint Committee on Justice Debate: Thursday 22 September 2023. General Data Protection Regulation Enforcement: Discussion <https://www.oireachtas.ie/en/debates/debate/joint_committee_on_justice/2022-09-22/3/> (last accessed: 12.7.2023).

[144] European Commission, 'Q&A: Digital Markets Act: Ensuring Fair and open digital markets' (31.10.2022) <https://ec.europa.eu/commission/presscorner/detail/en/QANDA_20_2349> (last accessed: 12.7.2023).

2. Potential conflict of laws

The private enforcement of the DMA has the potential to cast the decisions of Irish courts in conflict with interpretations of the European Commission in factually analogous cases. However, Irish courts are conscious of their **duty of sincere cooperation under Art. 4(3) TEU**. It is worth noting that **Art. 39(5) DMA** provides: 163

> National courts shall not give a decision which runs counter to a decision adopted by the Commission under this Regulation. They shall also avoid giving decisions which would conflict with a decision contemplated by the Commission in proceedings it has initiated under this Regulation. To that effect, the national court may assess whether it is necessary to stay its proceedings. This is without prejudice to the possibility for national courts to request a preliminary ruling under Article 267 TFEU.

Irish courts have shown themselves willing to comply with their **requirement to stay proceedings** where their contemplated judgment might conflict with an existing or future decision of the CJEU. By way of example, in the recent Circuit Court judgment in Cunniam v Parcel Connect Limited and Ors. [2023] IECC 1, the court stayed proceedings to allow for a determination by the CJEU as to the recoverability of damages under the GDPR for non-material loss arising from a data breach. This deference is typical of Irish courts in circumstances where the GDPR is a relatively new piece of legislation which is still maturing. It is reasonable to expect Irish courts to act with similar deference to the Commission as the central authority. 164

In light of Art. 39(5) DMA, it is likely that Irish courts will stay proceedings, where appropriate, to allow the Commission to create a helpful precedent. Where there is no immediate prospect of a useful precedent emanating from the Commission, the court may instead make a referral under Art. 267 TFEU. 165

In a similar vein, there may be complications in the private enforcement of obligations arising under the DMA due to the possibility of **suspension or exemption of a gatekeeper's obligations under Art. 9 and 10 DMA**. Where the decision of the Commission to suspend obligations comes in advance of or during any domestic litigation, this could affect the possibility of the right being conferred to individuals being removed in that specific instance. Moreover, there is the risk of Commission decisions contradicting judgments already made at a national level. 166

III. Noteworthy procedural specifics

1. Forum

The Irish courts system exists in a **'common law' jurisdiction** and is broadly divided into two branches: the civil side and the criminal side, each with its own specialised courts. Actions under the DMA will fall on the civil side. 167

In civil cases, the plaintiff sues the defendant for the wrong caused. The compensation sought for damage caused is usually monetary in nature. The different courts can hear cases for compensation for different amounts. The District Court hears claims up to 15,000 EUR. The Circuit Court hears claims above 15,000 EUR and up to 75,000 EUR (60,000 EUR for personal injury actions). The High Court hears claims above 75,000 EUR. The appropriate venue for a claim under the DMA is therefore determined by the size of the claim, but in most cases the High Court would be the appropriate venue. 168

169 The Commercial Court is a division of the High Court which deals with significant commercial cases. To appear before the Commercial Court, the value of a claim must have a commercial dimension and generally must have a value of not less than one million EUR.

170 Proceedings in the **Commercial Court** are conducted on a case managed and expedited basis, relative to proceedings in the High Court generally. The Commercial Court has a number of specialist lists, including a list dedicated to competition cases. It is possible that **claims under the DMA could be addressed under the competition list**. It is perhaps equally likely that these cases might fall under the **intellectual property and technology list**. Alternatively, particularly in light of the number of gatekeepers which will be based in Ireland, we may see the **establishment of a new list** dedicated specifically to these private enforcement actions **or a judge with specialist expertise** been given command of the management and hearing of the actions.

171 This specialisation is an attractive aspect of the Irish courts system. Judges are all former legal practitioners who frequently have practical experience working in the areas of law which appear before their courts. The Irish courts are expected to be an efficient forum for the resolution of disputes arising under a provision of the DMA.

2. Jurisdiction

172 As discussed above, awards of damages in Ireland aim principally to put a claimant in the position that it would have occupied but for the unlawful act or omission of the defendant. In addition to an award of damages, a successful claimant is generally entitled to obtain a contribution from the defendant towards its reasonable costs in the action. In these circumstances, Ireland is an attractive jurisdiction for a potential claimant under the DMA. This is particularly the case where claims are brought by large corporate parties who are not practically or operationally limited in their choice of venue for litigation.

173 When seeking to ground a claim before the Irish courts, a claimant must have regard to Reg. (EU) 1215/2012 of the European Parliament and of the Council on jurisdiction and the recognition and enforcement of judgments in civil and commercial matters (recast) (OJ 2012 L 351, 1) (**Recast Brussels I Regulation**). Under Art. 4(1) of the Recast Brussels I Regulation, persons domiciled in Ireland are to be sued in Ireland. It is likely that the large number of future gatekeepers who are based in Ireland will find it impossible to resist a claim on the basis that an Irish court does not have jurisdiction.

174 It should be noted, however, that any jurisdictional challenge is assessed on its own facts, and all claims are subject to the normal rules of challenge under the Recast Brussels I Regulation. Moreover, most commercial agreements contain **exclusive jurisdiction clauses**, which will prevail, subject to certain exceptions, pursuant to **Art. 25 Recast Brussels I Regulation**.

3. Representative actions

175 **Art. 42 DMA** refers to Representative Actions Directive, providing that 'Directive (EU) 2020/1828 shall apply to the representative actions brought against infringements by gatekeepers of provisions of this Regulation that harm or may harm the collective interests of consumers'.

176 The Commission has announced that it will be commencing its infringement procedure and issuing a formal notice to Ireland (among other Member States) for failing to transpose the Directive by the 25.12.2022 deadline. The Directive was ultimately transposed in Ireland under the **Representative Actions for the Protection of the**

Collective Interests of Consumers Act 2023 which was signed into law on 4.7.2023. Once the Act is commenced, representative actions against gatekeepers may be litigated by qualified entities in Ireland.

A form of representative action is already permitted in Ireland by **Order 15, Rule 9 of the Rules of the Superior Courts**. Where numerous persons have the same interest in a cause or matter, one or more of them may sue or be sued on behalf of all interested parties. The 'representative' party in these circumstances must be duly authorised to act on behalf of each 'represented' party. These claims are rare in Irish courts, partly because separate claims are still needed to resolve individual damages claims and to address specific issues arising for particular parties. 177

IV. Conclusion

The Irish position in respect of the DMA has not been widely discussed to date. 178 Although the government and other interested stakeholders have been supportive of the DMA, there is as yet **no sign of forthcoming implementing legislation**.

In other areas, Irish courts have proven themselves faithful to their duty of sincere 179 cooperation, and are willing to stay proceedings, where appropriate, to avoid their judgments contradicting the position of the CJEU. It is likely that they will be similarly deferential to the authority of the Commission in the context of the DMA.

The Irish courts offer **attractive remedies for a claimant under the DMA**. It is 180 likely that any such actions will be brought in the Commercial Court, a division of the High Court which provides for an expedited case management and hearings. These attractive features, combined with the fact that many of the largest gatekeepers are based in Ireland, mean that Ireland is expected to be a locus for private enforcement under the DMA. It remains to be seen whether a dedicated court list will be established to deal with these claims, or if they will fall within the embrace of another specialist list.

The regime for representative action in Ireland has been severely underdeveloped. 181 However, since the recent enactment of the Representative Actions for the Protection of the Collective Interests of Consumers Act 2023, qualified entities will be entitled to take actions against gatekeepers.

H. Private enforcement in Italy

(Francesco Maria Salerno/Edoardo Ricci)

This section will deal with questions related to the private enforcement of the DMA 182 in Italy. The focus will lay on the potential legal basis for claims relating to an infringement of the DMA under Italian law (→ mn. 183 et seqq.) as well as noteworthy procedural specifics of the Italian law system (→ mn. 203 et seqq.). Therein, the question of representative action in favour of end users (→ mn. 203 et seqq.), jurisdiction (→ mn. 205 et seqq.) and interim measures will be raised (→ mn. 208 et seq.).

I. Basis for claims

Unlike, for example Germany, Italy has not yet adapted its national law to the DMA 183 in any way. However, to the extent that the provisions of the DMA can be considered self-executing, the gatekeeper's competitors, for example, seem to be able to take tort actions (extracontractual) to compensate themselves in case of infringement (→ mn. 184

et seqq.). In addition, business and end users will be able to defend their rights by taking contractual action against the gatekeepers (→ mn. 186 et seqq.).

1. Actions in torts (extracontractual liability)

184 Failure by gatekeepers to fulfil their obligations under the DMA could give rise to a **claim for damages**. For instance, Art. 6(3) DMA obliges the gatekeeper to enable the user to reconfigure its home screen. While granting a right to the user, this provision also preserves the position of a third-party competitor. The gatekeeper's failure to comply with this obligation may damage the third-party competitors insofar as it may cause a foreclosure effect. In this scenario, the competitor could invoke **Art. 2043 of the Italian Civil Code** (**ICC**), which provides that 'any intentional or negligent act, which causes unjust damage to others, obliges the author of the act to compensate the damage'.

185 The competitor wishing to bring an action for damages would have to prove the damage suffered, the **causal link** with the conduct and the psychological element of the agent. In particular, with regard to the causal link, the rule of **'more likely than not'** is generally applied in civil law.[145] This standard entails the *condicio sine qua non* test and efficient causation, so as to assess whether the conduct was necessary in causing the damage and whether there was no subsequent event per se capable of causing the damage. The limitation period for non-contractual damages is five years.

2. Actions for contractual liability

186 European law has often been used to rebalance unequal positions between contracting parties by imposing **limitations on contractual freedom**. The DMA can be seen as part of this trend, one of its purposes being to ensure greater fairness and contestability in those markets where gatekeepers have amassed a position of entrenched dominance to the detriment of businesses and end users.

187 Thus, the DMA can be seen as an instrument that directly impacts the contractual arrangements governing the use of the gatekeepers' **core platform services** (**CPS**) by business and end users. The rules laid down by the DMA must be regarded as **mandatory** (within the meaning of Art. 41 of the Italian Constitution and Art. 1322 ICC) and, therefore, restrictive of freedom of negotiation in the sense that the parties are obliged to comply with these rules and cannot waive their rights and obligations under the DMA.

188 In particular, the mandatory nature of these provisions stems from the need to protect users who, compared to the position of gatekeepers, are in a contractually weak position when it comes to the use of CPSs indispensable for many users.

189 Prior to the DMA, gatekeepers were investigated in Italy for practices that closely resembled the obligations under the DMA under **unfair commercial practices law**.[146] The similarity between the objectives pursued by unfair commercial practices law and the DMA suggests that the actions that can be pursued at the domestic level may also be similar.

190 Due to the indispensable nature of CPSs, users have a limited interest in pursuing **nullification**. Instead, it is more likely that users will seek to keep the contract, but force the gatekeepers to perform in a way that is consistent with the rights under the DMA. With regard to the case law on unfair commercial practices, it is well-settled in Italy that the judge has a certain degree of latitude in **modifying the contract** in the pursue of

[145] Judgment of the Supreme Court no. 47 of 3.1.2017.

[146] See in this sense cases PS11147, PS10601 and PS11112, all concerning the collection of consent and use of data by Google, Facebook and WhatsApp respectively.

substantial justice and social solidarity, in line with Art. 2 of the Italian Constitution.[147] This objective has been pursued in various ways.

For instance, the Supreme Court has endorsed the use of the general **good faith clause** to assess the adequacy of the cause of the contract with respect to the interests of the parties and the legal balance of the contract.[148] 191

Moreover, based on **Art. 1374 ICC**, the judge may **supplement a contract** with regulatory sources that have the same force and effect as the law.[149] For the judge to use this power, it is necessary that the will expressed by the parties is considered incomplete or unclear.[150] Moreover, according to an interpretation of Art. 1375 ICC, good faith in the performance of the contract implies that the debtor must comply not only with the provisions of the contract but also with all the protective obligations arising from the other provisions of the law and, in particular, the Constitution. 192

There are **limits to the judge's ability to uphold a contract** against the will of the parties. In particular, the Court of Justice has taken a restrictive view of such possibilities, stating that a national rule which grants the court the power to supplement the contract by revising the content of the unfair term is not compatible with Dir. 3/13/EEC.[151] Recently, this position has gone so far as to state that the conflict with the Directive cannot be resolved by a national judge through means of interpretation.[152] However, where the nullity of the clause leads to the nullity of the entire contract, the Court seems to have taken a less severe approach, stating that 'the substitution of an unfair term for a supplementary provision of national law is consistent with the objective of Art. 6(1) of Directive 93/13'.[153] 193

In light of the foregoing, the DMA imposes contractual constraints and failure to respect the DMA may result in a 'correction' of the contract in a way similar to what happens in cases of breach of the law of unfair commercial practices. 194

For a number of reasons stated below, the DMA may justify an **even higher degree of protection for consumers**: 195

First of all, the fact that the European legislator opted for a regulation rather than a directive to regulate digital markets is symptomatic of the desire to ensure greater uniformity at the European level and to be able to rely on sufficiently precise provisions that can be applied without the need for further specification by the legislator or the Commission. 196

---

[147] On this point, the Constitutional Court took position on the margins of intervention available to the judge with respect to a clause that reflects a regulation of the opposing interests that is unfair and seriously unbalanced to the detriment of one party, by referring to 'the power of the judge to act ex officio stating the (total or partial) voidness, pursuant to Article 1418 of the Civil Code, of the clause itself, for conflict with the provision of Article 2 of the Constitution [...] which enters directly into the contract, in conjunction with the principle of good faith' (Order no. 77 of 26.3.2014).

[148] Judgment of the Supreme Court no. 4224 of 17.2.2017.

[149] Judgment of the Court of Rome of 4.7.2009.

[150] Judgment of the Supreme Court no. 6747 of 21.3.2014.

[151] See ECJ 14.6.2012 – case C-618/10, ECLI:EU:C:2012:349 – Banco Español de Crédito.

[152] See ECJ 18.11.2021 – case C-212/20, ECLI:EU:C:2021:934 para. 68, 70 – A. S.A. On this point, the Court has stated that 'if the national court finds that an unfair term in a contract concluded between a seller or supplier and a consumer is void, Article 6(1) of Directive 93/13 must be interpreted as precluding a rule of national law which allows the national court to modify that contract by revising the content of that term (judgment of 29 April 2021, Bank BPH, C-19/20, EU:C:2021:341, paragraph 67 and the case-law cited)' and that 'the interpretative exercise contemplated by the referring court on the basis of Article 65 of the Civil Code would ultimately amount to revising the content of the indexation clause at issue in the main proceedings, as it would result in the understanding of that clause being altered by the introduction into it of the reference to the "market value" of the foreign currency'.

[153] See ECJ 30.4.2014 – case C-26/13, ECLI:EU:C:2014:282 – KáslerandKáslerné Rábai.

197 Secondly, the absence of an implementing provision at the national level governing possible private enforcement actions necessarily requires recourse to the general categories of the Italian legal system. Despite that, the provisions of the ICC must be interpreted in such a way as to ensure that the objectives of the DMA are properly achieved, in accordance with the principle of effectiveness of EU law.

198 There are several ways in which the DMA may become part of the content of a contract between a gatekeeper and its users. First, the provisions of the DMA should guide the **interpretation** of the terms of a contract. Pursuant to Art. 1367 ICC, a contract must be interpreted in such a way that in case of doubt, preference is given to the interpretation that ensures that the contract produces effects rather than not. Therefore, according to the principle of preservation, the contract must be interpreted in conformity with the law since a conflict with the law would render it ineffective. The rule laid down in Art. 1367 ICC applies only in cases where the contract cannot be interpreted, provided that the preservation of the contract cannot entail an interpretation substituting the will of the parties.[154]

199 A further rule relevant to the interpretation of contracts is Art. 1374 ICC, which, as noted above, provides that the parties are bound not only by contractual obligations but also by those arising from all regulatory sources that have the same force and effect as the law.

200 In all cases where an agreement is interpreted or supplemented in the light of the DMA, the provisions of the DMA become part of the contractual content. Accordingly, pursuant to Art. 1453 of the ICC, in the event that the gatekeeper fails to fulfil its obligations under the contract because it does not guarantee users the rights enshrined in the DMA, the other party may, at its option, demand the **enforcement or termination of the contract**, without prejudice to compensation for damages. Such action shall be time-barred in ten years from the moment of breach of the contract.

201 If the content of the contract is in irremediable conflict with the provisions of the DMA, the interested party may request that the contract be declared **null and void**. In this case, reference should be made to Art. 1418(1) ICC that operates as a general clause sanctioning with nullity the violation of a mandatory provision. An action for nullity of a contract is not time-barred and may be brought by any person having an interest therein as well as *ex officio* by the court. The reason why nullity can be detected *ex officio* is that it is placed to protect general interests (in this case, the fairness and contestability of the digital markets).[155]

202 In the event that only a single clause of the contract is in conflict with the DMA, pursuant to Art. 1419 ICC, the nullity will not affect the entire contract but that **single clause**, provided that it was not decisive for the parties' choice to conclude the contract. If it turns out that the unfair term in conflict with the DMA was essential to the parties, the consequence would be the invalidation of the **entire contract**. As noted, however, nullity is a last resort, given that the preservation of the contract with a gatekeeper is in many cases indispensable for the everyday needs of end users.

[154] Order of the Supreme Court no. 19493 of 23.8.2018.
[155] See on this point the Judgment of the Supreme Court no. 14828 of 4.9.2012.

II. Noteworthy procedural specifics

1. Representative action in favour of end users

Class actions were introduced in Italy in 2005 and amended for the first time by Law No. 31 of 12.4.2019 with the introduction of Title VIII-bis to Book IV of the Code of Civil Procedure. This legislation has been completed with the legislative decree no. 28/2023 implementing **Dir. 2020/1828/EU** and introducing the so-called representative action for the protection of the collective interests of consumers into the Italian legal system. 203

According to the newly enacted Art. 140-quarter of the Italian Consumer Code, the consumer and user associations included in the list referred to in Art. 137 of the Italian Consumer Code and the national public bodies referred to in Art. 3(6) Reg. (EU) 2017/2394, as well as the entities qualified in another Member State and included in the appropriate list published by the European Commission, are entitled to bring such an action. Art. 140-septies of the Italian Consumer Code provides that actions may be brought without the need for a specific mandate by the consumers concerned in order to obtain injunctive or compensatory relief. These rules may be applicable to actions that users might bring against gatekeepers for their breach of DMA obligations. 204

2. Jurisdiction

Where the plaintiff is a consumer, the rules of the Italian Consumer Code provide that the court of the **place of residence or domicile of the consumer** has jurisdiction (Art. 33(u) and 66-bis Italian Consumer Code). For **representative actions**, Art. 140-septies(4) of the Italian Consumer Code establishes the mandatory jurisdiction of the specialised chambers of the courts located in the **place where the defendant is established**. 205

If an action is brought based on the general rules, and assuming that the matter exceeds 10,000 EUR, the competent court will be the one where the **defendant has its registered office** or where the **obligation arose or is to be performed**. 206

In matters relating to **tort**, the action must be brought before the court of the place **where the damage occurs**. In general, this is the place of business for the injured party. 207

3. Interim measures

Interim measures are common under Italian law, also taking into account the time it takes to reach a judgment. They are therefore a very effective way to secure the plaintiff's legal position, especially in matters relating to torts. 208

As far as representative actions are concerned, Art. 140-octies Italian Consumer Code provides for the possibility to apply for an injunction aimed at obtaining the **cessation or prohibition of the repetition of the conduct**. 209

I. Private enforcement in the Netherlands

(Rick Cornelissen/Lumine van Uden)

This section will provide an overview of the relevant framework of private enforcement of the DMA in the Netherlands. It will focus on the national provisions transposing the DMA into Dutch law (→ mn. 211 et seqq.) and the potential legal basis for claims relating to an infringement of the DMA under Dutch law (→ mn. 214 et seqq.). 210

After that, it will describe noteworthy material and procedural specifics of the Dutch law system (→ mn. 223 et seqq.).

I. National provisions implementing the DMA

211 As pursuant to Art. 288 TFEU, the DMA is binding in its entirety and directly applicable in all Member States (→ mn. 4 et seqq. and → mn. 49), it is not necessary for the provisions of a regulation to have been implemented into national law before they can be invoked before a national court.

212 The Dutch legislature has not prepared a legislative proposal to fully transpose the provisions of the DMA into Dutch law, nor has it yet proposed amendments to extend the provisions governing the private enforcement of competition law infringements to also include infringements of the DMA.[156] The Dutch legislature has, however, prepared a legislative proposal to implement the DMA to such an extent that the Dutch Competition Authority (ACM) will be granted powers to monitor compliance with the DMA, initiate investigations and exchange information with the European Commission.[157] As far as consumer representative actions are concerned, the Dutch legislature has now implemented **Dir. (EU) 2020/1828 on representative actions for the protection of the collective interests of consumers (RAD)**, which is explicitly referred to in **Art. 42 DMA**. According to Art. 42 DMA, the RAD 'shall apply to the representative actions brought against infringements by gatekeepers of provisions of the DMA that harm or may harm the collective interests of consumers'.

213 Pursuant to Art. 24 RAD, Member States had to adopt and publish the laws implementing the RAD into national law by 25.12.2022. The Dutch legislature transposed the RAD into Dutch law by law of 2.11.2022.[158] As Dutch law already provided for an extensive collective actions regime (the **Act on Damages Claims in a Collective Action** (*Wet afwikkeling massaschade in collectieve actie*, **WAMCA**)) that served, at least in part, as an inspiration for the RAD, only a few amendments and additions to the WAMCA and the Dutch Code of Civil Procedure (**DCCP**) were necessary to implement the RAD into Dutch law. The law implementing the RAD entered into force on 25.6.2023 and applies to collective actions that are brought on or after that date. The different types of mass claims under Dutch law, including the possibilities pursuant to the WAMCA and law implementing the RAD, will be discussed below (→ mn. 228 et seqq.).

II. Basis for claims

214 The DMA provides in **Art. 5, 6 and 7** for rights of access and rights of use, prohibitions of use and exploitation, and requirements governing the establishment of legal relationships *vis-à-vis* both business users and end users within the meaning of the DMA (→ mn. 7 et seqq.). Insofar as rights for business users and end users *vis-à-vis* the designated gatekeeper cannot already be enforced pursuant to the DMA itself, several legal

[156] It was only recently that the Dutch legislature extended the provisions governing the private enforcement of EU competition law infringements to competition law infringements of Dutch competition law, Bulletin of Acts and Decrees (*Staatsblad*) 2022, 159.

[157] Legislative proposal Implementation Act Digital Markets Act (*Uitvoeringswet digitalemarktenverordening*) – document for public consultation, see: <https://www.internetconsultatie.nl/uitvoeringswetdma/b1> (last accessed: 12.7.2023) (in Dutch).

[158] Implementation Act Representative Actions Directive (*Implementatiewet richtlijn representatieve vorderingen*), Bulletin of Acts and Decrees (*Staatsblad*) 2022, 459.

grounds under Dutch law can form the basis for claims for damages (→ mn. 215 et seqq.), claims for condemnatory relief (→ mn. 218 et seqq.) and claims for a declaratory judgment (→ mn. 221 et seqq.).

1. Claims for damages

Under Dutch law, **claims for damages** can be based on the general tort provision laid down in **Art. 6:162 Dutch Civil Code (DCC)**. Art. 6:162(1) DCC reads as follows: 'A person who commits an unlawful act against another person that can be attributed to him, is obliged to compensate the damage suffered by the other person as a result thereof.' This provision requires four cumulative criteria to be fulfilled: (i) an unlawful act, (ii) the unlawful act can be attributed to the tortfeasor, (iii) damage, and (iv) a causal link between the unlawfulness and the damage. In addition, Art. 6:163 DCC contains the requirement of relativity, meaning that the norm that is violated by the tortfeasor serves to protect the injured party. 215

Under Dutch law, **an infringement of a directly applicable provision of EU law is considered an unlawful act**.[159] As the obligations under **Art. 5 and 6 DMA**[160] seem to meet the requirements for **direct horizontal applicability** (→ mn. 5 et seqq.), an infringement of these provisions by the gatekeeper would constitute an unlawful act under Dutch law. If the European Commission were to establish an infringement of Art. 5 and/or 6 DMA[161] by a gatekeeper, that gatekeeper's unlawful act would be a given in civil proceedings before a Dutch court (a **follow-on action**). However, even if the European Commission were not to establish an infringement of the DMA, it would still be possible for a business user or end user to initiate a tort action against the gatekeeper, albeit that it would then be up to the business user or end user to state and substantiate and – when contested – evidence the unlawful act consisting of an infringement of the DMA (a **standalone action**). During the legislative process of the DMA, it was argued that the EU legislature should not allow for private enforcement through standalone actions, to avoid situations where a national court renders a judgment relating to an infringement of the DMA while the European Commission does not find an infringement, or worse, where the European Commission takes a decision that conflicts with the national judgment.[162] The EU legislature did not, however, include any restrictions in this regard in the final version of the DMA, and there is, therefore, nothing that stands in the way of private enforcement through standalone actions (→ mn. 39 et seqq.). If desirable to avoid conflicting decisions, however, the Dutch court could stay the proceedings during an investigation by the European Commission (→ mn. 233 et seqq.). 216

An alternative legal basis for a claim for damages due to an infringement of the DMA under Dutch law is **unjust enrichment** as laid down in **Art. 6:212 DCC**.[163] Pursuant to that article, 'a person who has been unjustifiably enriched at the expense of another person, has the obligation towards that other person to compensate the damage up to the amount of his enrichment, as far as this is reasonable.' This provision requires four cumulative criteria to be fulfilled: (i) the enrichment of one person, (ii) the impoverishment of another person, (iii) a link between the enrichment and the impoverishment, and (iv) the unjustified nature of the enrichment. The compensation that can be derived 217

[159] Explanatory Notes Meijers, Parliamentary History, Book 6, p. 615 (Art. 6:162 DCC).
[160] And potentially Art. 7 DMA or a part thereof (→ mn. 11 et seqq.).
[161] And potentially Art. 7 DMA or a part thereof (→ mn. 11 et seqq.).
[162] Komninos in Charbit/Gachot, p. 425 (436).
[163] Alternatively, and subject to the content of the agreement between the gatekeeper and the business user, a business user could potentially also claim damages following a breach of contract pursuant to Art. 6:74 DCC.

from Art. 6:212 DCC is limited to the amount of enrichment and cannot be more than the amount of the impoverishment. When considering a claim for compensation based on Art. 6:212 DCC, the Dutch court should consider all circumstances of the case to assess whether the compensation is reasonable.[164]

2. Claims for condemnatory relief

218 In addition to claims for damages, Dutch law permits business users and end users to enforce their rights under the DMA by applying for a court order or requesting an injunction. The basis for this is found in **Art. 3:296 DCC** and reads as follows: 'Unless otherwise follows from the law, from the nature of the obligation or from a legal act, he who is obliged to give, do or refrain from doing something towards another shall be ordered to do so by the court, at the request of the entitled party.' The obligation to which Art. 3:296 DCC refers also covers tort. That means that if it can be established that the gatekeeper acted unlawfully *vis-à-vis* a business user or end user, this business or end user can request the Dutch court to order the gatekeeper to refrain from certain conduct (a prohibition) or to actively do something (an order). The business or end user seeking the injunction or court order should have **sufficient interest** in that injunction or court order,[165] but there is no requirement to the effect that the business user or end user has suffered harm or will suffer harm due to the conduct.

219 An example of a prohibition in the context of the DMA would be that, if a gatekeeper treats its own products more favourably than the products of a business user in ranking (Art. 6(5) DMA), the business user may request the court to order the gatekeeper to cease this conduct pursuant to Art. 3:296 DCC. An example of an order in the context of the DMA would be that the gatekeeper is ordered to allow and technically enable the installation of third-party software applications or software application stores (Art. 6(4) DMA). Both prohibitions and court orders are often subject to a penalty payment for each breach thereof.

220 Under Dutch law, a claim for condemnatory relief can be instituted both in proceedings on the merits and in **preliminary relief proceedings** (*kort geding*). In proceedings on the merits, the court is obliged to impose the condemnatory relief if the requirements of Art. 3:296 DCC have been met. In preliminary relief proceedings, the court may refrain from ordering the condemnatory relief even if all conditions of Art. 3:296 DCC have been fulfilled. The court could do so if it finds that the interests of the injured party have been met in another way.[166]

3. Claims for a declaratory judgment

221 Pursuant to **Art. 3:302 DCC**, a party can claim a **declaration regarding a legal relationship** this party is directly involved in. For a claim for a declaratory judgment to be admissible, four cumulative requirements must be met. There must be (i) a legal relationship and (ii) a claim by a person (or entity) directly involved in the legal relationship; whereby (iii) the judgment must serve to establish in a binding manner the existence or details of the content of that legal relationship (which implies that it must be possible to attach some legal consequence to a declaratory judgment); and (iv) the party claiming the declaratory judgment must have a sufficient interest.[167]

---

[164] Supreme Court 30.10.2015, ECLI:NL:HR:2015:3195.

[165] Art. 3:303 DCC: 'Without a sufficient interest, no one has a legal claim.'

[166] Supreme Court 15.12.1995, ECLI:NL:HR:1995:ZC1919 – Procter & Gamble Benelux NV.

[167] Art. 3:303 DCC: 'Without a sufficient interest, no one has a legal claim.'

Under Dutch law, it is not unusual for claims for damages to be preceded by a claim for a declaratory judgment establishing that the defendant acted unlawfully and is correspondingly liable. Under Dutch law, a sole declaratory judgment is often followed by follow-up proceedings to **establish the amount of damages**. It can, however, also be used as a **starting point for a (collective) settlement** or in **litigation in another jurisdiction** as, if recognised by a foreign court, it establishes the legal relationship between the parties involved at a certain point in time. 222

III. Noteworthy procedural specifics

1. Representation: mandates, assignment of claims and class actions

In addition to bringing a claim individually, there are three different ways in which special purpose vehicles or claim vehicles (foundations or associations) can bring **mass claims** under Dutch law. First, they can litigate on behalf of a group of several injured parties based on a power of attorney or mandate. Second, they can bring a bundle of individual claims that have been assigned and transferred to them (assignment model), usually by different injured parties (assignors), and third, they can litigate in their own name and bring a class action for the benefit of a group of (legal or natural) injured persons whose interests the claim vehicle seeks to protect, based on the WAMCA or its predecessor, the 'WCA'). As the assignment model is often used in competition damages actions, and both this model and the class action seem particularly relevant in relation to private enforcement of the DMA, they will thus be discussed in more detail below. 223

a) Assignment of claims

In competition damages actions, **claim vehicles** generally use the **assignment model**, with powers of attorney and/or mandates as a fallback. Although the assignment model makes it possible to bundle claims, the claims remain individual, meaning that claim vehicles still have the obligation to furnish facts and substantiate the claims for each individual underlying party (→ mn. 235).[168] 224

As regards the validity of assignments, the Amsterdam Court of Appeal has ruled that it is up to claim vehicles to substantiate the position that the assignments can be relied upon against the debtor (i.e. the defendant). A claim vehicle will have in principle fulfilled its **burden of proof** regarding the validity of assignments if it (i) has notified the debtor and (ii) has provided for each assignor (a) an extract of the assignment deed and (b) title to the assignment (i.e. the assignment agreement).[169] Similarly, the Amsterdam District Court ruled in a recent judgment regarding the validity of assignments that if (i) the documentation brought into the proceedings contains, for each alleged assignor, (a) the assignment agreement (title), and (b) the deed of assignment, and (ii) it is clear that these were signed/provided by the assignor, it is thereby sufficiently established that the claim vehicles are entitled to the claims. It is subsequently up to the defendants to put forward concrete indications showing that nevertheless, no legally valid assignment took place.[170] 225

[168] Arnhem-Leeuwarden Court of Appeal 5.2.2019, ECLI:NL:GHARL:2019:1060 – Elevators and Escalators; Amsterdam District Court 15.5.2019, ECLI:NL:RBAMS:2019:3574 – Trucks; Rotterdam District Court 23.10.2019, ECLI:NL:RBROT:2019:8230 – Elevators and Escalators.

[169] Amsterdam Court of Appeal 10.3.2020, ECLI:NL:GHAMS:2020:713 – Air Freight.

[170] Amsterdam District Court 27.7.2022, ECLI:NL:RBAMS:2022:4466 – Trucks.

226 In the same judgment, the Amsterdam District Court ruled that the safeguards laid down in the **WAMCA** in relation to the standing of claim vehicles and the admissibility of the claims do not apply to claim vehicles that act by means of assignments. The defendants argued that the mass claims brought by the claim vehicles based on the assignment model did not deviate in essence from a class action, as a result of which the safeguards should also apply to the claim vehicles and to their bundles of assigned claims. According to the Amsterdam District Court, however, the WAMCA does not stipulate that collective actions can only be brought based on **Art. 3:305a et seq. DCC** (**class action**). The Court considered it relevant that the case at hand almost exclusively involved professional parties, including the assignors, whereas the safeguards laid down in the WAMCA are mainly meant to protect **non-professional injured parties**, who are often consumers.[171]

227 Based on the above, it therefore seems possible in principle for claim vehicles to bundle the claims that business users may have against gatekeepers under the DMA through the assignment of claims. The same applies to end users' claims, albeit that higher standards for claim vehicles – and perhaps even the statutory requirements regarding standing and admissibility for bringing a class action under the WAMCA – might apply if a specific case mainly involves consumers.

b) Class actions

228 With the entry into force of the WAMCA on 1.1.2020, the scope of potential redress mechanisms was extended to **collective actions for monetary damages**. The WAMCA applies to collective actions brought on or after 1.1.2020 relating to events that took place on or after 15.11.2016. As the events allegedly giving rise to damage in the pending competition damages proceedings generally took place before that date, only a few competition damages claims have been brought under the WAMCA so far. Nor have many claims been brought under the WAMCA's predecessor (the WCA), as that 'old regime' does not provide for monetary damages. The WAMCA may be used more often as regards collective actions relating to claims from both business users and end users following an infringement of the DMA, as these infringements will relate to events that took place after 15.11.2016. Moreover, the law implementing the **RAD** will apply to collective actions that are brought on or after 25.6.2023, as a result of which the WAMCA will have an immediate effect in relation to DMA infringement claims that fall **within the scope** of the RAD.

229 The WAMCA sets strict requirements for the standing and **admissibility of a claim vehicle**, dealing with governance and third-party funding but also, for example, with the interests of the (injured) persons that are represented in the action. These interests must be sufficiently similar and they must be sufficiently safeguarded by the claim vehicle. Also, the collective claim must have a **sufficiently close relationship** with the Netherlands. In addition to the WAMCA, the **'Claim Code 2019'** provides a code of conduct for foundations and associations that bring representative collective actions or negotiate collective settlement agreements. The Code and its 2011 predecessor have been recognised by the legislature as a body of **soft law** that provides guidelines for the courts on how to assess the standing of representative entities.

230 The WAMCA provides for **specific procedural rules**. If multiple claim vehicles bring separate collective actions relating to the same event(s) under the WAMCA, the court will appoint one claim vehicle as the exclusive representative, and the separate actions will be consolidated and treated as one case, but all other claim vehicles will remain parties to the proceedings provided they have standing (Art. 1018e(1) DCCP). The court

[171] Amsterdam District Court 27.7.2022, ECLI:NL:RBAMS:2022:4466 – Trucks.

also defines the group of (legal or natural) persons that will be bound by the outcome of the proceedings (the narrowly defined group). Members of this group that are domiciled or resident in the Netherlands are bound to the outcome of the collective action unless they **opt out** either after the exclusive representative has been appointed or after a class settlement has been approved by the court (Art. 1018f(1) DCCP). Members of the group that are not domiciled or resident in the Netherlands can **opt in** after the exclusive representative has been appointed, unless the court orders that an opt-out system applies. Those who opted in can decide to opt out after court approval of a settlement agreement. There is no possibility to opt in after the settlement has been approved (Art. 1018f(5) DCCP).

231 The following diagram shows the standard WAMCA proceedings:

WAMCA class actions – since 1.1.2020

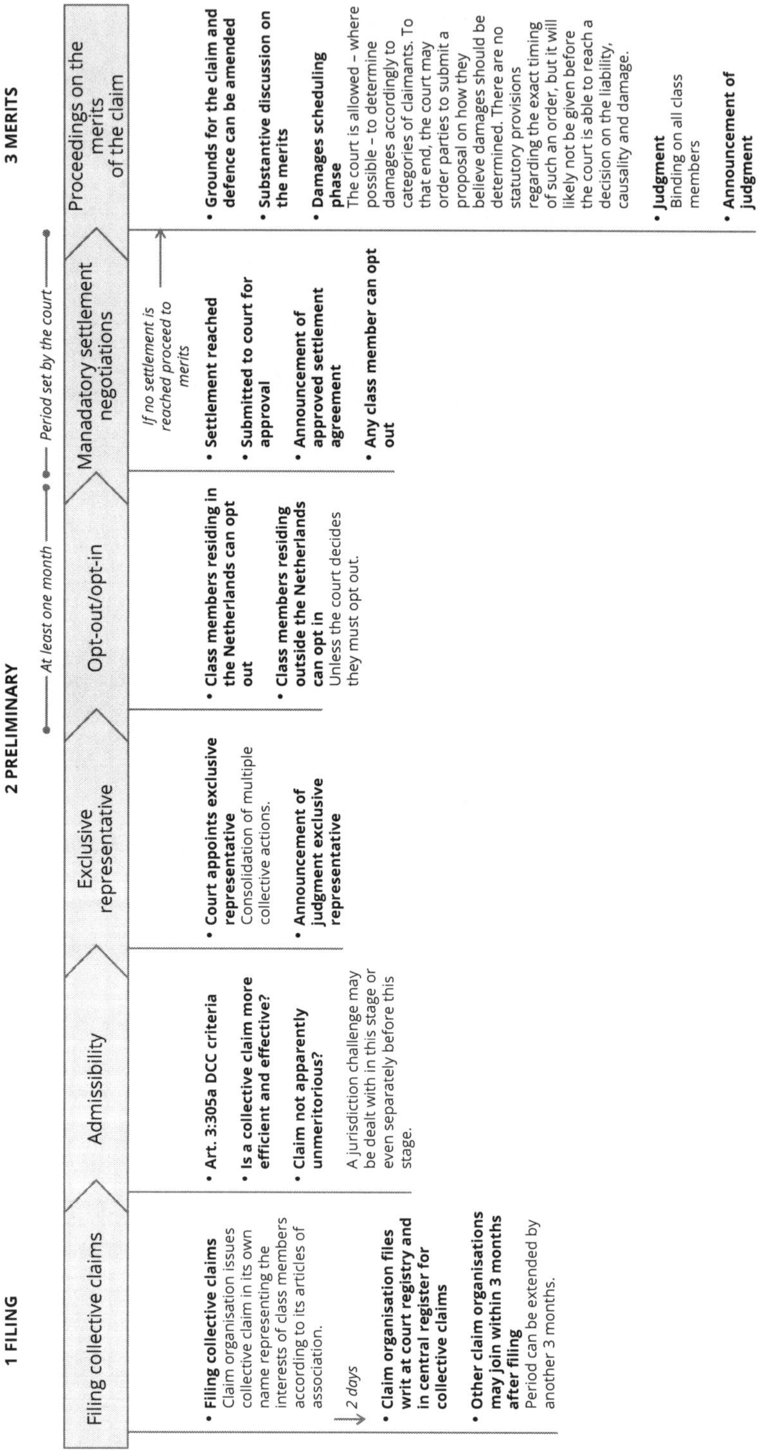

Most requirements under the RAD are already included in the Dutch class regime by virtue of the entry into force of the WAMCA. Only a limited number of amendments and additions to the WAMCA and the DCCP were necessary to transpose the RAD into Dutch law. The provisions that have been added to the WAMCA following the implementation of the RAD are only relevant for infringements of the DMA by gatekeepers that harm or may harm the collective interests of consumers (i.e. the provisions only apply to end users within the meaning of the DMA that are also consumers).[172] One of the main amendments relates to additional requirements for litigation funding, stipulating, for example, that a litigation funder is not allowed to fund a class action against a competitor (Art. 3:305a(f)(new) DCC). Another main amendment relates to the scope of the **narrowly defined group** that may be bound by the outcome of the collective action. The amendments following the RAD ensure that the outcome of the collective action will not apply to members of the narrowly defined group whose interests are represented in similar proceedings against the same defendant in another EU or EEA Member State. If members of the narrowly defined group who are not living in the Netherlands want to opt in, they are required to inform the court's registry that their interests are not represented in a similar collective action in another EU or EEA Member State (Art. 1018f(6) (new) DCCP). In addition, the law implementing the RAD prohibits an opt-out regime for claims brought under the RAD for consumers living outside the Netherlands. 232

2. Stay of proceedings

Pursuant to **Art. 39 DMA**, national courts must not give a decision that is contrary to a decision adopted by the European Commission under the DMA. National courts must also avoid giving decisions which would conflict with a decision contemplated by the European Commission in proceedings it has initiated under the DMA. 233

It is possible under Dutch law to request a **stay of proceedings**. This may also be relevant if a gatekeeper has initiated appeal proceedings before the EU Courts against a European Commission decision finding an infringement under the DMA. In a private enforcement case following a European Commission decision establishing an infringement of EU competition law, the Amsterdam Court of Appeal held that where one party relies on a European Commission decision in support of its claims, it is up to the other party who challenges the validity of that decision and wishes the case to be stayed to (i) demonstrate that it filed a timely action for annulment of that European Commission decision, (ii) explain that it reasonably opposes the European Commission's decision in the proceedings before the EU court, and (iii) raise the defences which it intends to raise in the proceedings. This should enable the national court to assess whether and to what extent the assessment of those defences depends on the validity of the European Commission's decision and hence the outcome of the proceedings before the EU courts. The court can then decide whether and to what extent the case should be stayed.[173] It should be noted that even if the above-mentioned requirements are met, the court may still decide to continue the proceedings by dealing with issues and defences that do not depend on the outcome of the EU proceedings. 234

[172] According to Art. 3(1) RAD, 'consumer' means any natural person who acts for purposes which are outside that person's trade, business, craft or profession.

[173] Amsterdam Court of Appeal 24.9.2013, ECLI:NL:GHAMS:2013:3013 – Air Freight.

3. Obligation to furnish facts and evidence

a) Obligation to furnish facts

235 Under Dutch procedural law, the writ of summons should, among other things, contain the claim and the grounds thereof (Art. 111(2)(d) DCCP). The claimant has the **obligation to state and substantiate the facts** necessary to grant the claim in the writ of summons (Art. 149 and Art. 150 DCCP). The facts that the claimant must bring forward should be complete and truthful (Art. 21 DCCP). Under Dutch law, evidence may, in principle, be given by any means (Art. 152(1) DCCP). The court is free to evaluate the evidence before it, except where the law provides otherwise (Art. 152(2) DCCP).

236 As described in → mn. 224 et seqq., claim vehicles that act based on the assignment of claims and bring a bundle of claims have the obligation to furnish facts for each individual assignor that has (allegedly) assigned claims to the claim vehicle.[174]

b) Disclosure

237 Dutch procedural law **does not** provide for the possibility of **discovery procedures** comparable to those in Anglo-Saxon legal systems. Nevertheless, a legal basis for filing an application for a disclosure order can be found in **Art. 843a DCCP**. Such court order can be requested in separate preliminary relief proceedings or during the proceedings on the merits. For a court order for disclosure to be granted, four cumulative conditions should be fulfilled. First, the applicant must demonstrate that it has a **legitimate interest** in the disclosure, i.e. the documents in question should be relevant for the applicant's legal position. This comes down, in principle, to a balancing of interests: whether a party enjoys an unreasonable advantage or whether its opposing party suffers an unreasonable disadvantage because a particular document is not available as evidence in the proceedings.[175] Second, the application should relate to **specific documents**. It must be sufficiently clear to which documents the application relates. Fishing expeditions should be avoided. Third, the application must relate to documents concerning the **legal relationship** to which the applicant or the applicant's predecessors are parties. The legal relationship arising in tort is also covered in this respect. Fourth, disclosure can only be sought for documents **at the disposal** of the party against whom the order is requested. This means that the documents must be in this party's possession or that this party can access the documents relatively easily. Following a judgment of the Supreme Court, it is also possible to request the disclosure of documents that are held by a third party.[176]

238 The above-mentioned conditions restrict the possibilities for disclosure. In addition, a party against whom the disclosure of certain documents is sought is not obliged to comply if there are compelling reasons **opposing that disclosure** (Art. 843a(4) DCCP), for example in relation to confidential information or medical data. In competition litigation cases, there is an additional exception for leniency statements and submissions to the European Commission in the context of a settlement (Art. 846 DCCP).

239 In addition to a request for disclosure on the initiative of one of the parties, the court may also order the parties or one of them to clarify certain statements or produce certain documents relating to the case, at any stage of the proceedings, pursuant to **Art. 22 DCCP**. Although this article does not grant a party an independent right of action, a party that has an interest in the disclosure of a particular document by the opposing party may request the court to exercise its power under this provision.

---

[174] Amsterdam District Court 15.5.2019, ECLI:NL:RBAMS:2019:3574 – Trucks.

[175] Explanatory Memorandum, Parliamentary History revised Dutch Code of Civil Procedure, p. 553.

[176] Supreme Court 10.7.2015, ECLI:NL:HR:2015:1834.

c) Use of witnesses

Dutch procedural law provides for the possibility to substantiate a claim by written and oral **witness statements**. A person lawfully summoned to give evidence is obliged to do so, unless this person is a spouse, a former spouse or a blood relative to a party or is a professional that is required to observe confidentiality obligations (Art. 165 DCCP). If a party summoned to give evidence as a witness does not appear at the hearing, fails to answer the questions put to it or refuses to sign its statement, the court may draw the inference it deems fit (Art. 164(3) DCCP). Contrary to Anglo-Saxon legal systems, Dutch law **does not** provide for the **right of cross examination**. Witnesses are examined by a judge and the examination of witnesses takes place at a hearing (Art. 166(3) DCCP). The parties and their counsel may put questions to the witnesses as well, subject to the judge's power to prevent a particular question from being answered (Art. 179(2) DCCP). Under Dutch procedural law, it is possible to request the examination of witnesses before a case is pending and during pending proceedings (Art. 186 DCCP). 240

d) Use of experts

Under Dutch procedural law, parties may use **expert evidence** to prove their statements, for example regarding the interpretation of foreign law (if applicable) or the calculation of the damages. Courts can also appoint an independent expert. 241

4. Statute of limitation

Under Dutch law, there are two different **limitation periods** applicable in relation to a general tort action or an action for unjust enrichment: (i) a relative limitation period of five years, and (ii) an absolute limitation period of 20 years (Art. 3:310(1) DCC). The relative limitation period starts to run from the day following that on which the injured party became aware of the damage and the person liable for the damage. Specifically for **competition damages** claims,[177] there is also a requirement for the infringement of EU or Dutch competition law to have ceased (Art. 6:193s DCC). According to the established case law of the Supreme Court, the requirement for the injured party to be aware of both the damage and the person liable for it must be construed to mean **actual awareness**.[178] The requirement of 'subjective knowledge' entails that it is up to the defendant to state and to substantiate the assertion that the injured party was actually aware of the damage and the person liable for it. Whether the limitation period has started to run is subject to all circumstances of the case.[179] The absolute limitation period starts to run from the day following that on which the event causing the damage occurred. There is no requirement for the injured person to have any knowledge of the claim. The limitation periods under Dutch law **can be interrupted** by a simple letter to the liable party, in which the injured party unequivocally reserves his rights (Art. 3:317 DCC). 242

[177] That fall within the temporal scope of the act implementing the Damages Directive.

[178] Supreme Court 6.4.2001, ECLI:NL:HR:2001:AB0900 – Vellekoop/Wilton Fijenoord; Supreme Court 24.1.2003, ECLI:NL:HR:2003:AF0694 – BASF/Rensink; Supreme Court 31.3.2017, ECLI:NL:HR:2017:552 – Mispelhoef/Staat; Supreme Court 4.5.2018, ECLI:NL:HR:2018:677 – TMG/Staat. See also Supreme Court 20.4.2001, ECLI:NL:HR:2001:AB1208 – Wong/Mr X.

[179] Supreme Court 9.7.2010, ECLI:NL:HR:2010:BM1688; Supreme Court 14.11.2014, ECLI:NL:HR:2014:3240; Supreme Court 31.3.2017 ECLI:NL:HR:2017:552 – Mispelhoef/Staat.

5. Damage, damage calculation and statutory interest

243 Insofar as an injured party initiates a claim for damages in tort (for example for an infringement of the DMA), this party can claim losses incurred and lost profit suffered because of the unlawful act, as well as reasonable costs to prevent or reduce the damage suffered. The court will award compensation for damage only to the extent that such damage is related to the event on which the defendant's liability is based (Art. 6:96 DCC). In other words, the court must ensure that the injured party is put in a position it would have been but for the event that gave rise to the gatekeeper's liability. The court determines the damage in a manner most appropriate for the nature of the damage (Art. 6:97 DCC). This is generally an actual **damage calculation**, in which all relevant circumstances of the case are considered. If the actual damage cannot be calculated, the court can estimate it (Art. 6:97 DCC).

244 If a class action is brought based on the **WAMCA**, the rules regarding the calculation of damage are generally the same as those that apply to other type of proceedings. That means that the court must in principle assess the actual damage. However, as this may be impossible in practical terms, **Art. 1018i(2) DCCP** provides for the possibility to determine the damage for different categories of persons (damage scheduling). In determining these categories of affected persons, the court can consider, as far as possible, the different circumstances relevant to different groups of affected persons.[180] This may also mean in practice that the damage assessment takes place at a more abstract level. The court can order the exclusive representative and the defendant to submit a proposal to that end.

245 In addition to a claim for damages governed by Dutch law, an injured party can claim compound **statutory interest** annually (Art. 6:119 DCC). If a party is obliged to pay damages in tort, the statutory interest on damages claimed is calculated from the day the loss is suffered until the damages have been paid.

6. Legal costs

246 Under Dutch law, the general rule is that the party that is unsuccessful in the proceedings pays the costs of the successful party (Art. 237(1) DCCP). It is **unusual** for the courts to order the unsuccessful party to pay the actual **lawyers' fees**, with a few exceptions, for example in case of abuse of process. The lawyers' fees that are awarded are limited fixed fees determined in accordance with the court-approved scale of costs *(liquidatietarief).*[181] The amount awarded will depend on the type and amount of work performed by the lawyer(s), as well as on the financial interest of the case. The amount awarded usually only covers a fraction of the actual lawyers' fees. In addition to the lawyers' fees, an adverse costs order can comprise the court fee, which is a limited fixed amount depending on the type and the amount of the claim, and extrajudicial costs, such as the actual costs of witness and/or expert reports (in full or in part).

247 For claims based on the **WAMCA**, the court can deviate from the usual limited cost order: (i) if the court finds after summary enquiry that the claim was without merit, the claim organisation can be ordered to pay up to a maximum of five times the usual fixed amount; or (ii) if the damages claim[182] is awarded, the defendant can be ordered to pay all reasonable and proportionate legal costs and other costs that the claim organisation has incurred (Art. 1018l DCCP).

---

[180] See also Parliamentary Documents II 2017–2018, 34 608, no. 6, p. 16.

[181] See in general: <www.rechtspraak.nl/Voor-advocaten-en-juristen/Reglementen-procedures-en-formulieren/Civiel/paginas/liquidatietarief.aspx> (last accessed: 12.7.2023).

[182] This is not applicable for claims for condemnatory relief.

J. Private enforcement in Portugal
(Gonçalo Machado Borges/Sofia Vaz Sampaio/Leonor Martins Machado)

In this section the fundamental structures of the private enforcement of the DMA in Portugal will be outlined. At the beginning, the question of the basis of claims of business users (→ mn. 257 et seqq.) and end users will be explored (→ mn. 267 et seqq.). Then, procedural specifics will be discussed (→ mn. 281 et seqq.). 248

I. Basis for claims by business users under national law

1. General considerations

Following the implementation of **Dir. 2014/104/EU** (the Damages Directive) into Portuguese law, the right to submit claims for damages resulting from infringements of competition law (Art. 101 and 102 TFEU and the Portuguese Competition Act, approved by Law no. 19/2012, of 8.5.2012) is regulated by Law no. 23/2018, of 5.6.2018 – Portuguese Private Enforcement Law). 249

To date, however, no attempt has been made or is anticipated to be made, to extend the scope of this regime and any of its specific rules (access to evidence, presumed damages, evidentiary value of infringement decisions etc.) to cover also, in addition to claims resulting from competition law infringements, claims based on breaches by gatekeepers of obligations imposed by the DMA. This is the more correct approach given the structural differences between competition rules and the DMA, which, although inspired by the outcome of a significant number of abuse of dominance cases under Art. 102 TFEU, is an *ex ante* statute imposing **prescriptive, detailed, obligations** (notably those contained in Art. 5, 6 and 7 DMA) on large tech companies rather than an enunciation of general principles to be applied and consolidated on a case-by-case basis. The DMA presents itself as an instrument of economic regulation, based on **Art. 114 TFEU**, designed to complement competition law – not to implement it.[183] 250

The first general observation, therefore, is that in Portugal there are currently **no legal grounds** for private enforcement of the DMA to be confused with, or assimilated to, the specific (substantive and procedural) regime for private enforcement of the competition rules. 251

As the Commission has repeatedly stated,[184] the DMA does not seek to achieve specific outcomes but is a **process-oriented regulation**, i.e. its overriding objective is to lower barriers to entry into markets for the more important digital services which are currently dominated by a designated gatekeeper. Therefore, rather than achieving a particular market structure for the supply of core platform services, the DMA seeks a more intermediate goal: that of enabling or facilitating market entry or growth by new entrants or by smaller providers of core platform services. 252

The concepts of contestability and fairness are both designed with the immediate goal of assisting competing tech firms and business users although, naturally, end users are also expected to benefit indirectly from the DMA. As stated in rec. 32 DMA, 'contestability should relate to the ability of undertakings to effectively overcome barriers to entry and expansion and challenge the gatekeeper on the merits of their products and services'. 253

---

[183] De Streel/Larouche JECLAP 2021, 542 (553).

[184] For example, very recently by Thomas Kramler, Head of Unit for E-commerce and data economy at DG COMP, at the GCR TMT Conference held in London, on 9.3.2023.

254 As for fairness, this concept should relate to an imbalance between the rights and obligations of business users where the gatekeeper obtains a disproportionate advantage. **Market participants**, including business users of core platform services and alternative providers of services provided together with, or in support of, such core platform services, should have the ability to adequately **capture the benefits** resulting from their innovative or other efforts (rec. 33 DMA).

255 The second general comment is, therefore, that the DMA introduces rights that are primarily of direct benefit to **business users** and/or competing providers of core platform services. Although **end users** are expected to indirectly benefit from the enforcement of the DMA, questions of procedural standing and possibly passing-on, depending on the specifics of each case, may be reasonably raised by defendants faced with future claims by end users (→ mn. 272 et seqq.).

256 One final point to clarify is that, at least for the time being, Portuguese law does not provide for any **specialised courts** to hear claims arising from potential non-compliance with the DMA. As such, and with the possible exception of claims based on unfair competition (→ mn. 266), the Portuguese common civil courts will be **competent** to adjudicate on claims based on the DMA, whether these are brought by business users, competing service providers or end users.

2. Claims under the tort liability rules of the Portuguese Civil Code

257 Assuming that the provisions stipulating prohibitions and proactive obligations for gatekeepers in **Art. 5, 6 and 7 DMA** are sufficiently **precise** and **unconditional** to create rights for individuals, and thus can be considered to have **direct effect**, they may be relied upon by these individuals in claims brought against gatekeepers before national courts.

258 According to **Art. 2(2) of the Portuguese Civil Code** (Código Civil, **CCiv**):

> To every right, except where the law provides otherwise, corresponds the adequate legal action to obtain its recognition by the courts, to prevent or remedy its violation and to obtain its compulsory performance, as well as the procedures required to safeguard the effectiveness of the relevant legal action.[185]

259 This comprehensive provision of the Portuguese rules of civil procedure is intended to ensure **access to the courts** for the exercise or remediation of any legal or contractual rights, by the most adequate procedural means, which includes legal actions (for performance or compensation of damages) and interim injunctions[186] in situations where the delay associated to adjudicating a legal action might be detrimental to the full effectiveness of the claimant's right.

a) *Actions for compensation of damages*

260 Presumably, a significant proportion of future claims against gatekeepers will be brought in the context of actions for **damages** based on **Art. 483(1) of the Portuguese Civil Code**. This provision stipulates the basic requirements for **tort liability** under Portuguese law and provides for the liability of anyone who '[…] with intent or negligence,

---

[185] Our translation (unofficial).

[186] Interim injunctions (or *providências cautelares*) are always dependent on a subsequent legal action with an equivalent object and claim and, therefore, provide only temporary relief (although this may last for a significant period of time depending on how long it takes for the court to issue a final decision).

unlawfully violates another person's right or any legal provision designed to protect the interests of others'.[187]

261 Liability for damages resulting from a gatekeeper's non-compliance will depend on the existence of a **subjective element** (intent or negligence), which distinguishes this legal basis from other situations where the law provides for strict liability. In addition, business users seeking compensation for alleged damages will have to show the infringement occurred, prove the ensuing damages and demonstrate the existence of a causal link between the one and the other (without the benefit of presumptions of harm). Pursuant to Art. 556(2) CCiv monetary compensation for damages incurred must be set in accordance with the difference between the claimant's financial situation at the latest date on which the court can be apprised of and the (hypothetical) financial situation the claimant would have been in without the damages caused.

b) Injunctive relief

262 In addition to actions for compensation of damages, claimants can resort to **injunctive actions** seeking definitive measures to cease or prohibit a practice or even provisional measure, notably to a general injunction aimed at preventing **serious and potentially irreparable harm** to their rights based on the DMA. This type of general interim injunctive relief is provided for in **Art. 362(1) CCiv**. It aims to provide urgent relief to a rights holder that presents *prima facie* evidence of the right relied on and successfully demonstrates to the court that the delay in awaiting a decision in a declaratory legal action would cause almost irreversible detrimental damage.

263 Interim injunctions of this nature are almost always **conservatory** in nature, although, exceptionally, courts have granted anticipatory relief (in the sense that the injunction anticipates the outcome of the subsequent legal action). These injunctions are not available for purposes associated with securing monetary compensation (for damages) unless the risk against which the claimant seeks protection is related to the defendant's potential insolvency or inability to pay damages awarded. Even when claimants are successful, injunctions provide interim relief only if confirmed by a final decision in the subsequent legal action which the claimant must also file.

3. Other bases for claims

264 Possibly for some of the obligations laid out in Art. 5, 6 and 7 DMA (the ban on self-preferencing contained in Art. 6(5) DMA for instance), alternative providers of digital services seeking to compete with a gatekeeper may be able to rely on the legal **prohibition of unfair competition**. This is contained, rather unusually, in the **Portuguese Industrial Property Code** (Código da Propriedade Industrial, **CPI**), of which **Art. 311(1)** proscribes any 'act of competition that is contrary to the norms or honest customs of any field of economic activity'.[188] The same provision contains a non-exhaustive list of examples of which heading a) may be the most relevant, since it prohibits any 'acts liable to create confusion as to the company, its establishment, or the products and services of a competitor, whatever the means used'.[189]

265 Unfair competition is not only an administrative offence (misdemeanour) punishable by a fine but also provides for interim relief in the form of **inhibitory measures** designed to prevent imminent infringement or of cease-and-desist orders designed to stop an existing infringement.

[187] Our translation (unofficial).
[188] Our translation (unofficial).
[189] Our translation (unofficial).

266 Although there has been some controversy as to whether the Intellectual Property Court should have exclusive **jurisdiction** to adjudicate on unfair competition cases, the court itself has limited the scope of its jurisdiction to unfair competition practices involving infringements of intellectual property rights only. For other types of unfair competition, claims should be brought before the common civil court with territorial competence.

II. Basis for claims by end users under national law

1. General considerations

267 In general, the framework described above for business users applies equally to individual end users, notably consumers of digital services, and the comments above apply to this section also. There is one notable difference, that of collective redress mechanisms, or representative actions, which are available only to end users (though business associations should not be necessarily excluded → mn. 277) and therefore warrant a more extended consideration below.

2. Collective private enforcement: the role of representative action

268 In addition to individual claims, representative actions are also an available mechanism to enforce the DMA, notably for end users.

a) Representative actions

269 The **Dir. (EU) 2020/1828** – expressly mentioned in Art. 42 DMA and therefore applicable to representative actions brought against gatekeepers that breach their obligations under the DMA and, in doing so, harm or may harm the collective interests of consumers – has not yet been implemented in Portugal. However, there is a collective action mechanism system in place since 1995 which applies to all areas and sectors of the law. As such, the Directive's main goal (that all Member States have at least one mechanism) has been accomplished in Portugal for quite some time. While the implementation of Dir. (EU) 2020/1828 will certainly bring changes, in particular regarding cross-border actions and qualified entities, a radical overhaul of the current regime is not expected.

270 The general procedure and framework for bringing representative actions are set out in the Law on the participation in administrative proceedings and collective action (**Law No. 83/95 of 31.8.1995** – Collective Action Act).

271 The aim is to prevent infringements of, notably, public health, environment, quality of life, goods and services, consumer protection, cultural heritage and public interests. Apart from this general procedure and framework for bringing representative actions, there are other provisions that explicitly prescribe the right to representative actions. These include the Consumer Protection Act, in connection with consumer claims and the powers of the consumer associations to file a class action (**Law No. 24/96 of 31.7.1996**), which should be relevant in the context of representative actions brought by consumers to enforce the DMA, and the Private Enforcement Law regarding compensation for infringements of competition law (**Law No. 23/2018 of 5.6.2018**), which, though containing relevant dispositions in terms of legal standing, presumptions, or burden of proof, is not applicable to the enforcement of DMA obligations[190].

---

[190] Law of Environment Policy, providing the possibility of filing class actions on environmental matters (Law No. 19/2014 of 14.4.2014); Law of Cultural Heritage, providing the scope and the parties entitled to bring class actions on cultural heritage matters (Law No. 107/2001 of 8.9.2001); Consumer Protection Act,

According to the Collective Action Act, a collective action may be brought by any citizen, in the exercise of his or her civil and political rights, and legal associations or foundations, regardless of their own direct interest in the proceedings. 272

With regard to the legal requirements provided for **legal associations**, it is undisputed that the association or foundation must have legal personality, that the relevant interest to be protected must be covered by the corporate purpose as set out in its articles of association, and that the association or foundation cannot carry out an activity that could, in any way, be considered to be in competition with an activity carried out by a corporate entity or a liberal professional. The application of additional legal requirements regarding consumer associations, pursuant to the Consumer Protection Act (notably a minimum number of associates), has been under discussion[191]. 273

Dir. (EU) 2020/1828 requires **qualified entities** to be designated in each Member State, at least for the purpose of cross-border actions, and to comply with legal requirements established therein.[192] Portugal is, therefore, expected to designate qualified entities for cross-border actions that meet such legal requirements (some of them being already applicable under the current regime). It is to be seen, however, which legal requirements will have to be met by the relevant entities for the purpose of bringing domestic actions. In any case, because the implementation of Dir. (EU) 2020/1828 cannot reduce the existing levels of consumer protection, Portuguese law should, in principle, continue to grant legal standing to all citizens and other legal entities, at least for the purpose of bringing domestic actions. 274

Art. 42 DMA expressly allows representative actions against infringements by gatekeepers that harm or may harm the collective interests of **consumers**, but there is no similar provision for business users or business associations. As stated above, under the Collective Action Act representative actions may be initiated by any citizen or association or foundation, but not by companies or professionals. Similarly, under Dir. (EU) 2020/1828, representative actions may only be brought on behalf of consumers defined as 'any natural person who acts for purposes which are outside that person's trade, business, craft or profession', meaning that no changes will have to be made to Portuguese law in this respect. It is, therefore, clear that under the current regime, **business users cannot bring representative actions against gatekeepers**. 275

The clarification in rec. 12 of the Regulation that the DMA applies without prejudice to the rules deriving from **Dir. 2005/29/EC** (UCP Directive) is irrelevant in this respect. This is because Art. 16 of Decree-Law no 57/2008, which transposed the UCP Directive, establishes that any person, including competitors, may bring injunctive proceedings, concerning unfair business-to-consumer commercial practices in the internal market, said article then refers to the Consumer Protection Act, which in turn, concerning the legal standing to bring injunctive actions, refers to the Collective Action Act, which, as previously mentioned, states that representative actions can only be brought by citizens and associations or foundations. 276

---

in connection with consumer claims and the powers of the consumer associations to file a class action (Law No. 24/96 of 31.7.1996); Portuguese Securities Code, regarding the class actions seeking to protect interests of non-qualified investors in financial instruments (Art. 31, Decree-Law No. 486/99 of 13.11.1999); Private Enforcement Law regarding compensation for infringements of competition law (Law No. 23/2018 of 5.6.2018).

[191] Teixeira de Sousa; Costa e Silva/Trigo dos Reis, p. 57 et seq.

[192] Law No. 25/2004 of 8.7.2004, which transposed Dir. 98/27/EC on injunctions for the protection of consumers' interests, already foresees a similar solution though with different legal requirements and a narrower scope and, in that context, there are already four qualified entities.

277 Whilst it is true that, currently, business users cannot bring representative actions against gatekeepers, there is no provision regarding their representation in general, so **business associations** should not be necessarily excluded.[193]

278 Portugal has an **opt-out system**, meaning that when a representative action is brought, after being summoned to the proceedings, the members of the class, as identified by the claimant, may exercise their right to be or not to be represented in the proceedings (intervening and accepting the proceedings as they stand, declaring whether or not they accept the claimant's representation, or remaining silent, in which case their silence will be deemed as an acceptance of the representation). In this respect, it is worth noting that while there is no certification phase in Portuguese representative actions – as in the US or the UK – the court may dismiss the proceedings at an early stage if it considers that the claims are manifestly unlikely to proceed.

279 In terms of the available **remedies**, the current regime already covers both injunctive measures, including provisional or definitive measures to stop an infringement, and redress measures. Furthermore, all types of damages (except for punitive damages) can be awarded, including general and special damages and compensation for loss of profit. To obtain compensation for damages, the plaintiff has to prove the defendant's fault or negligence (except in exceptional cases of strict liability that may only occur when expressly stated in the law) in performing the unlawful conduct, the extent of the injury and the link between the two (except when rebuttable or unreputable presumptions apply if expressly applicable to the case at hands).

b) Third-party funding

280 The possibility – mentioned in Art. 10 Dir. (EU) 2020/1828, which lays down assurances that each Member State must provide, where a representative action for redress measures is funded by a third party, insofar as allowed in accordance with national law – is not regulated in Portugal. This issue has raised several constitutional and legal issues within representative actions.[194]

III. Noteworthy procedural specifics

281 The Recast Brussels I Regulation applies to the question of whether Portuguese courts have **jurisdiction** to hear and decide on cases brought under the DMA, whenever there is an international legal relationship giving rise to a conflict of laws and the matter is of a civil or commercial nature, provided that the scope of the Regulation is fully complied with.

282 Portuguese courts may, in particular, be competent to hear and decide on cases where the gatekeeper has a registered office in the European Union (based on Art. 6(1) and 63 Recast Brussels I Regulation), taking particularly into account the place where the harmful event might have taken place (pursuant to Art. 7(2) Recast Brussels I Regulation) and the State in which the consumer (if a consumer is involved) has its domicile (under Art. 18(1) Recast Brussels I Regulation).

283 Hence, whenever the previously mentioned Regulation determines that Portuguese courts are competent, the matter of the **applicable law** will arise. In civil and commer-

[193] In this respect it should be noted that the Private Enforcement Law, which is not applicable to the DMA, expressly confers the right of popular action to associations of companies injured by the infringement of competition law.

[194] Otero ROA 2022, 701; Costa e Silva/Trigo dos Reis Ius Dictum 2022, 62; Costa e Silva/Trigo dos Reis, p. 96 et seq.

cial contractual obligations, a Portuguese court will determine the law applicable based on **Reg. (EC) No 593/2008** of the European Parliament and of the Council of 17.6.2008 on the law applicable to contractual obligations (Rome I); when it comes to extracontractual obligations, it is **Reg. (EC) No 864/2007** of the European Parliament and of the Council of 11.7.2007 on the law applicable to non-contractual obligations (Rome II) that determines the applicable law. However, under Art. 1(2) DMA, the applicability of the DMA does not depend on the applicable law to the specific obligations at stake.

K. Private enforcement in Spain
(Pablo Figueroa/Jorge Masía/Ana Parés)

This section will explain the fundamental structures of the private enforcement of the DMA in Spain. First, it will provide details on private enforcement of the DMA by business users and consumers (→ mn. 285 et seqq.). Second, it will explore procedural points (→ mn. 300 et seqq.). Therein, it will focus on options for representative action (→ mn. 303 et seqq.), also known as a 'collective action' (arguably similar to US-style 'class actions'). 284

I. Basis for claims

There is **no legislative provision** that adapts the Spanish legal system to the DMA.[195] Private enforcement of the DMA in Spain could take place through the following separate routes, all of which are untested at this stage: 285

1. First approach: non-contractual claims

The first way to enforce the DMA provisions would be through **torts** (*responsabilidad extracontractual*, in Spanish, non-contractual claims, in English),[196] which the claimant (end user) could bring to the civil courts based on **Art. 1902** of the Spanish Civil Code (*Código Civil*, **CC**).[197] 286

These claims could be based on a previous decision from any competition authority via a **follow-on action**. A **standalone action** in these cases can be very complex to demonstrate due to the lack of nexus via a contract or a competing relationship in the same market. 287

In general terms, the current common regime for private enforcement of DMA infringements in Spain is the civil action for non-contractual liability brought before the civil courts. Claimants may bring private claims under the DMA. These claims may originate via the civil courts under **Art. 1902 CC**, which regulates tortious damage arising from non-contractual obligations (until the Spanish legislature transposes the regulation into national law): 'Whoever by act or omission causes damage to another, through fault or negligence, is obliged to repair the damage caused.' 288

Similarly to French law (→ mn. 59 et seqq.) on which it is modelled, a claimant seeking compensation under Art. 1902 CC from a gatekeeper who has breached the DMA 289

[195] There is also no legislative provision to adapt the recently approved Implementing Regulation (EU) 2023/814 of 14.4.2023. Although the Regulation (EU) 2023/814 has been passed to enforce some DMA proceeding rules, there has not been a modification of the current private enforcement proceedings in Spain (explained hereafter) as a result.

[196] Hereafter we will prefer the expression non-contractual liability over torts but they could be used interchangeably.

[197] Royal Decree of 24.7.1889, publishing the Civil Code.

will have to demonstrate: (i) fault, (ii) prejudice/harm, and (iii) a causal link between the fault and the prejudice/harm suffered.[198]

290 As no existing Spanish law has adapted the DMA, Art. 1902 CC applies with a **limitation period** of one year within which to initiate a claim.

291 Proof of the existence and the amount of actual damages resulting from somebody else's acts or behaviour is an essential requirement for any compensatory claim brought before the Spanish courts. Thus, Spanish tort law is based on the principle that no legal action for compensation can be brought in the absence of actual damage.

292 Therefore, the **standard of proof** for (i) the existence of the claimed damages, (ii) their exact calculation, and (iii) their causal relationship with the wrongdoing or act that caused the damages is high.[199] The claimant is expected to provide the court with documentary evidence that supports the existence of direct damages and expert witness evidence on the calculation of their monetary value and on the existence and calculation of loss of profit. **Punitive damages** are not available under Spanish law, but only compensatory damages (aimed at restoring the aggrieved party to the financial position it was in before the act that caused the damages).

293 An example of such a claim based on Art. 1902 CC could be non-compliance with Art. 5(5) DMA on restrictions on use, since the gatekeeper shall allow end users to access and use, through its core platform services, content, subscriptions, features or other items, by using the software application of a business user, including where those end users acquired such items from the relevant business user without using the core platform services of the gatekeeper.

2. Second approach: unfair trade

294 The second approach would be the private enforcement of the DMA through **unfair trade** (*competencia desleal*). Gatekeepers who breach the DMA and thereby gain a competitive advantage in the market, which they exploit *vis-à-vis* business users or other gatekeepers, potentially engage in unfair conduct under **Art. 15 of the Spanish Unfair Trade Act.**[200] A claim for damages arising from such unfair conduct must be brought before the commercial courts under the umbrella of the Spanish Unfair Trade Act.

295 In this respect, the non-compliance with the obligation of Art. 6(2) DMA may be invoked:

> The gatekeeper shall not use, in competition with business users, any data that is not publicly available that is generated or provided by those business users in the context of their use of the relevant core platform services or the services provided together with, or in support of, the relevant core platform services, including data generated or provided by the customers of those business users.

3. Third approach: claims arising from contractual relationships

296 The third approach would be **claims arising from contractual relationships**. A breach of the DMA by a gatekeeper under a contractual relationship with a business user will be subject to civil litigation and private enforcement. A contractual liability action may be brought to assess the loss and damage suffered by the business user. In this regard, business users may sometimes have a contractual relationship with the

---

[198] Spanish Supreme Court Ruling, Civil Chamber, of 29.10.2008, Rec. 942/2003 (ECLI:ES:TS:2008:5541). See further, for the classic work on Spanish torts law, De Ángel Yagüez, p. 573–576.

[199] We follow here the explanation of Ferreres Comella/Ayo Ferrándiz, p. 120.

[200] Act 3/1991 of 10.1.1991 on Unfair Trade.

gatekeeper, and claims arising from said relationships and DMA infringements may be part of the private enforcement.

This could be the case, for example, where a gatekeeper breaches its obligation under **297**
Art. 5(9) DMA to provide free daily information to each advertiser to which it supplies online advertising services.

In addition, it must be taken into account that many commercial contracts under **298**
Spanish law contain an obligation to fully comply with all applicable laws. Therefore, in such cases, compliance with the DMA becomes a full privately enforceable contractual obligation.

It must be highlighted that the DMA is not considered as competition legislation, **299**
and Spain has not amended its competition law, nor its procedural law to take into account damages claims arising from the DMA. Therefore, the common system for private enforcement, except for special cases to be judged on a case-by-case basis, will normally be non-contractual claims for damages established in the CC.

II. Noteworthy procedural specifics

1. Interim measures under Spanish law

The essential prerequisites for the adoption of **interim measures** are closely linked to **300**
the material right that is to be secured by the issuance of such measures. **Art. 728** of the Spanish Civil Procedural Act (*Ley de Enjuiciamiento Civil*, **LEC**)[201] lists the principles that an application for precautionary measures must conform with to be accepted by the court: (i) danger of procedural delay, (ii) appearance of good law and (iii) security.

The preventive measures to be adopted are ***numerus apertus*** ('open to the free deter- **301**
mination of the judge') as provided in Art. 727 LEC. However, in addition to the list of the possible measures, it is also possible to adopt other measures expressly provided for by law for the protection of certain rights or which are deemed necessary to ensure the effectiveness of the judicial protection which may be granted in the judgment delivered in the proceedings.

As a corollary of the above, depending on the case, interim measures may be adopted **302**
in the main proceedings of a private enforcement action under the DMA in Spain. Provisional or interim measures may also be requested in other Member States if the main DMA private enforcement proceedings take place in Spain.

2. Collective actions under Spanish law

Spanish law provides that **collective actions** apply to consumer claims or class actions **303**
rather than contractual business agreements or merchants.

Dir. (EU) 2019/216 of the European Parliament and of the Council of 27.11.2019 **304**
regarding the better enforcement and modernisation of Union consumer protection rules is not yet transposed into Spanish law. Infringements in Spain may also lead to civil-commercial legal actions through consumer representation or class actions, as provided for in **Dir. (EU) 2020/1828** of the European Parliament and of the Council of 25.11.2020 on representative actions for the protection of the collective interests of consumers, which is yet to be transposed as well.

According to **Art. 52 DMA**, Dir. (EU) 2020/1828 applies to acts of gatekeepers that **305**
infringe the provisions of the DMA. This is done to add a reference to representative actions against breaches of the DMA.

---

[201] Act 1/2000 of 7.1.2000.

306 On 9.1.2023, the Ministry of Justice published the Draft Bill on representative actions for the protection of the collective interests of consumers (the **'Draft Bill'**). The purpose of the Preliminary Draft is to advance with the process of transposing the **Dir. (EU) 2020/1828** in Spain. The transposition deadline expired on 25.12.2022. The new procedural system ensures that entities entitled to bring actions for injunctive and redress measures on behalf of consumers and users whose rights have been affected by an infringement have standing to sue.

307 An action for **injunctive relief** may seek the cessation of conduct that is harmful to the interests of the affected consumers or users, as well as the prohibition of such conduct in the future. Actions for **injunctions** may also be brought where the harmful conduct has ceased at the time of bringing the injunctive action, but there are sufficient indications that it may be repeated in the future.

308 The action for **redress measures** may seek compensation for the loss and damage caused to consumers or users harmed as a result of the infringing conduct. This remedy may consist, *inter alia*, in the payment of compensation, replacement of goods, reimbursement of the price paid or termination of the contracts in which the prohibited conduct has materialised.

309 Both actions can be brought together, although it is possible for the court to agree to suspend the action for redress measures pending the resolution of the action for injunctive relief if there is good reason to do so (for example, if the combined proceedings generate excessive complexity or delay in the proceedings). In addition, proceedings in which representative actions are brought may be both domestic (where the representative action is brought by a qualified entity in Spain, before a Spanish court) and cross-border (where the representative action is brought by a qualified entity in another Member State of the European Union, in accordance with the provisions of the Directive, before a Spanish court). In any case, consumers are not able to participate in the proceedings, except to determine the subjective **scope of the proceedings** where appropriate.[202]

310 Finally, with regard to the forum for collective non-contractual actions, the LEC establishes that the courts of first instance of the place where the damage occurs shall have **jurisdiction** (Art. 45 and 50–53 LEC). However, if the gatekeeper against whom the action is brought is located abroad, the legal basis changes, as EU and Spanish rules on international jurisdiction must be taken into account. The **Recast Brussels I Regulation** provides for a general forum based on the defendant's domicile if the gatekeeper is established in the European territory. However, it also provides for a special forum for tort matters. This allows jurisdiction to be redirected to the court of the place where the damage occurred. If the gatekeeper is established outside the EU, then **Spanish Organic Law 6/1985** of 1.7.1985 of the Judiciary offers the parallel provisions to the Recast Brussels I Regulation (Art. 22 ter. 1 and 22 quinquies (b), respectively).

[202] For additional information on the Draft Bill, see García Marrero/Rodríguez Cárcamo/García/Frigola/Masía/de Paz/de Arcos Tejerizo/Rodríguez/Cabrera, 'Pérez-Llorca Legal briefing: The Draft Bill on representative actions for the protection of the collective interests of consumers is published' (16.1.2023) <https://www.perezllorca.com/en/news/legal-briefing/se-publica-el-anteproyecto-de-ley-de-acciones-de-representacion-para-la-proteccion-de-los-intereses-colectivos-de-los-consumidores-2/> (last accessed: 12.7.2023).

III. Conclusion

Although the introduction of the DMA does not – to this day – change the applicable provisions on Spanish procedural law, it can be anticipated that undertakings qualified as gatekeepers by the Commission will increasingly be subject to different forms of claims. This will likely have a decisive impact on Spanish procedural rules. 311

L. Conclusion and outlook *(Henner Schläfke)*

The DMA will, in the future, give users of platform services the possibility to control the market power of gatekeepers in a targeted manner. They will be able to take **individual and collective legal action** for this purpose. Perhaps due to the swift legislative process, private enforcement was not covered by clearer and more detailed provisions.[203] This should not, however, lead to the conclusion that private enforcement does not play any role in the context of the DMA. The opinions of the institutions involved in the legislative process suggest something different in this respect. In addition, familiar mechanisms can also be used in the context of the DMA in order to ensure private enforcement of the requirements set out therein in terms of legal dogma. The DMA may represent a new approach within the competition law system – but the EU law foundations of private enforcement, which are not limited to competition law but also encompass the GDPR and emissions, remain valid. 312

Most of the jurisdictions covered in this Chapter have **not transposed the provisions of the DMA into national law**, nor have they extended the existing provisions on private enforcement of competition law to also include infringements of the DMA. The direct effect of the DMA as a European regulation suffices to have effect on claims, contracts, and the practice of courts. Secondary claims will usually be pursued by resorting to existing provisions governing the law of tort or the review of contractual terms, often located in the respective Civil Codes or laws governing proper conduct of business. 313

Claims for **damages** regularly are to be addressed through tort actions. For such a claim to be successful, the existence of a fault, damage and the causal like between the fault and the damage must be proven. Depending on the jurisdiction, there may be additional requirements. An infringement of a directly applicable provision of EU law (such as it is the case for Art. 5, 6 and 7 DMA) is considered a fault in the context of such claims. Damages claims may be proceeded by a declaratory judgment establishing that the defendant acted unlawfully and is correspondingly liable. It is apparent that a follow-on claim based on a decision by the European Commission finding that a gatekeeper has infringed a provision of the DMA will be a significantly clearer case than proving an infringement in a standalone action based solely on the European Commission's designation decision. In the latter situation, the question arises whether individual provisions of the DMA create sufficiently clear and specific rights to be enforceable without a prior decision by the European Commission. In addition, the national court's obligation to co-operate with the European Commission and the European Commission's exclusive competence to enforce the DMA make it quite likely that many private enforcement proceedings will be stayed for the duration of European Commission proceedings. 314

In Germany, a unique approach is taken by the 11th GWB amendment, which sets out provisions extending the GWB regulations applicable to the private enforcement of 315

---

[203] Herbers RDi 2022, 252 (252) also emphasises the intensive but comparatively short legislative process.

competition law infringements to infringements of the DMA. In practice, at least, the GWB provisions as set out by the amendment would displace other considerable civil claims under German law. The German approach is noteworthy as it – with the singular exception that no presumption of damages is enacted – fully applies the German transposition of the Damages Directive and thus applies the standard used for private enforcement of Art. 101 and 102 TFEU to the DMA and Commission decisions based thereon.

316 In contrast to the DMA's effect on material law, the unified procedural option of **private enforcement by way of representative action** stands out clearly. In this respect, the DMA gives business associations no clear rights to represent the interests of their members. The DMA does, however, offer considerable potential through its close links to Dir. (EU) 2020/1828 by way of Art. 52 DMA: This puts consumer associations in a strong position to enforce the provisions of the DMA across the board and to assert consumer claims for damages as part of representative action. This possibility of collective enforcement of the DMA arises from the **implementation of Dir. (EU) 2020/1828** across Europe. The implementation differs between jurisdictions with opt-out claims in the Netherlands, Portugal and possibly Spain and opt-in regimes in France, Germany and Ireland. However, the international dimension of digital markets might be mirrored in such litigation, as qualified entities will be able to bring claims for redress cross-border and end users from multiple countries will be able to join.

317 All in all, the DMA offers an opportunity to complement the comparatively more stagnant field of competition law with its specific requirements for platform operators.[204] The *ex ante* approach taken by the DMA enables users to enforce their rights more quickly in the long term.

[204] Regarding the duration of proceedings, for example, cf. ECJ 10.11.2021 – case T-612/17, ECLI:EU:T:2021:763 – Google and Alphabet v Commission (Google Shopping). See Achleitner EuR 2022, 253 (255).

Annex: Digital Markets Act

REGULATION (EU) 2022/1925 OF THE EUROPEAN PARLIAMENT AND OF THE COUNCIL

of 14 September 2022

on contestable and fair markets in the digital sector and amending Directives (EU) 2019/1937 and (EU) 2020/1828 (Digital Markets Act)

(Text with EEA relevance)

THE EUROPEAN PARLIAMENT AND THE COUNCIL OF THE EUROPEAN UNION,

Having regard to the Treaty on the Functioning of the European Union, and in particular Article 114 thereof,

Having regard to the proposal from the European Commission,

After transmission of the draft legislative act to the national parliaments,

Having regard to the opinion of the European Economic and Social Committee[1],

Having regard to the opinion of the Committee of the Regions[2],

Acting in accordance with the ordinary legislative procedure[3],

Whereas:

(1) Digital services in general and online platforms in particular play an increasingly important role in the economy, in particular in the internal market, by enabling businesses to reach users throughout the Union, by facilitating cross-border trade and by opening entirely new business opportunities to a large number of companies in the Union to the benefit of consumers in the Union.

(2) At the same time, among those digital services, core platform services feature a number of characteristics that can be exploited by the undertakings providing them. An example of such characteristics of core platform services is extreme scale economies, which often result from nearly zero marginal costs to add business users or end users. Other such characteristics of core platform services are very strong network effects, an ability to connect many business users with many end users through the multisidedness of these services, a significant degree of dependence of both business users and end users, lock-in effects, a lack of multi-homing for the same purpose by end users, vertical integration, and data driven-advantages. All these characteristics, combined with unfair practices by undertakings providing the core platform services, can have the effect of substantially undermining the contestability of the core platform services, as well as impacting the fairness of the commercial relationship between undertakings providing such services and their business users and end users. In practice, this leads to rapid and potentially far-reaching decreases in business users' and end users' choice, and therefore can confer on the provider of those services the position of a so-called gatekeeper. At the same time, it should be recognised that

[1] OJ C 286, 16.7.2021, p. 64.

[2] OJ C 440, 29.10.2021, p. 67.

[3] Position of the European Parliament of 5 July 2022 (not yet published in the Official Journal) and decision of the Council of 18 July 2022.

services which act in a non-commercial purpose capacity such as collaborative projects should not be considered as core platform services for the purpose of this Regulation.

(3) A small number of large undertakings providing core platform services have emerged with considerable economic power that could qualify them to be designated as gatekeepers pursuant to this Regulation. Typically, they feature an ability to connect many business users with many end users through their services, which, in turn, enables them to leverage their advantages, such as their access to large amounts of data, from one area of activity to another. Some of those undertakings exercise control over whole platform ecosystems in the digital economy and are structurally extremely difficult to challenge or contest by existing or new market operators, irrespective of how innovative and efficient those market operators may be. Contestability is reduced in particular due to the existence of very high barriers to entry or exit, including high investment costs, which cannot, or not easily, be recuperated in case of exit, and the absence of, or reduced access to, some key inputs in the digital economy, such as data. As a result, the likelihood increases that the underlying markets do not function well, or will soon fail to function well.

(4) The combination of those features of gatekeeper is likely to lead, in many cases, to serious imbalances in bargaining power and, consequently, to unfair practices and conditions for business users, as well as for end users of core platform services provided by gatekeepers, to the detriment of prices, quality, fair competition, choice and innovation in the digital sector.

(5) It follows that the market processes are often incapable of ensuring fair economic outcomes with regard to core platform services. Although Articles 101 and 102 of the Treaty on the Functioning of the European Union (TFEU) apply to the conduct of gatekeepers, the scope of those provisions is limited to certain instances of market power, for example dominance on specific markets and of anti-competitive behaviour, and enforcement occurs *ex post* and requires an extensive investigation of often very complex facts on a case by case basis. Moreover, existing Union law does not address, or does not address effectively, the challenges to the effective functioning of the internal market posed by the conduct of gatekeepers that are not necessarily dominant in competition-law terms.

(6) Gatekeepers have a significant impact on the internal market, providing gateways for a large number of business users to reach end users everywhere in the Union and on different markets. The adverse impact of unfair practices on the internal market and the particularly weak contestability of core platform services, including the negative societal and economic implications of such unfair practices, have led national legislators and sectoral regulators to act. A number of regulatory solutions have already been adopted at national level or proposed to address unfair practices and the contestability of digital services or at least with regard to some of them. This has created divergent regulatory solutions which results in the fragmentation of the internal market, thus raising the risk of increased compliance costs due to different sets of national regulatory requirements.

(7) Therefore, the purpose of this Regulation is to contribute to the proper functioning of the internal market by laying down rules to ensure contestability and fairness for the markets in the digital sector in general, and for business users and

end users of core platform services provided by gatekeepers in particular. Business users and end users of core platform services provided by gatekeepers should be afforded appropriate regulatory safeguards throughout the Union against the unfair practices of gatekeepers, in order to facilitate cross-border business within the Union and thereby improve the proper functioning of the internal market, and to eliminate existing or likely emerging fragmentation in the specific areas covered by this Regulation. Moreover, while gatekeepers tend to adopt global or at least pan-European business models and algorithmic structures, they can adopt, and in some cases have adopted, different business conditions and practices in different Member States, which is liable to create disparities between the competitive conditions for the users of core platform services provided by gatekeepers, to the detriment of integration of the internal market.

(8) By approximating diverging national laws, it is possible to eliminate obstacles to the freedom to provide and receive services, including retail services, within the internal market. A targeted set of harmonised legal obligations should therefore be established at Union level to ensure contestable and fair digital markets featuring the presence of gatekeepers within the internal market to the benefit of the Union's economy as a whole and ultimately of the Union's consumers.

(9) Fragmentation of the internal market can only effectively be averted if Member States are prevented from applying national rules which are within the scope of and pursue the same objectives as this Regulation. That does not preclude the possibility of applying to gatekeepers within the meaning of this Regulation other national rules which pursue other legitimate public interest objectives as set out in the TFEU or which pursue overriding reasons of public interest as recognised by the case law of the Court of Justice of the European Union ('the Court of Justice').

(10) At the same time, since this Regulation aims to complement the enforcement of competition law, it should apply without prejudice to Articles 101 and 102 TFEU, to the corresponding national competition rules and to other national competition rules regarding unilateral conduct that are based on an individualised assessment of market positions and behaviour, including its actual or potential effects and the precise scope of the prohibited behaviour, and which provide for the possibility of undertakings to make efficiency and objective justification arguments for the behaviour in question, and to national rules concerning merger control. However, the application of those rules should not affect the obligations imposed on gatekeepers under this Regulation and their uniform and effective application in the internal market.

(11) Articles 101 and 102 TFEU and the corresponding national competition rules concerning anticompetitive multilateral and unilateral conduct as well as merger control have as their objective the protection of undistorted competition on the market. This Regulation pursues an objective that is complementary to, but different from that of protecting undistorted competition on any given market, as defined in competition-law terms, which is to ensure that markets where gatekeepers are present are and remain contestable and fair, independently from the actual, potential or presumed effects of the conduct of a given gatekeeper covered by this Regulation on competition on a given market. This Regulation therefore aims to protect a different legal interest from that protected by those rules and it should apply without prejudice to their application.

(12) This Regulation should also apply without prejudice to the rules resulting from other acts of Union law regulating certain aspects of the provision of services covered by this Regulation, in particular Regulations (EU) 2016/679[4] and (EU) 2019/1150[5] of the European Parliament and of the Council and a Regulation on a single market for digital services, and Directives 2002/58/EC[6], 2005/29/EC[7], 2010/13/EU[8], (EU) 2015/2366[9], (EU) 2019/790[10] and (EU) 2019/882[11] of the European Parliament and of the Council, and Council Directive 93/13/EEC[12], as well as national rules aimed at enforcing or implementing those Union legal acts.

(13) Weak contestability and unfair practices in the digital sector are more frequent and pronounced for certain digital services than for others. This is the case in particular for widespread and commonly used digital services that mostly directly intermediate between business users and end users and where features such as extreme scale economies, very strong network effects, an ability to connect many business users with many end users through the multisidedness of these services, lock-in effects, a lack of multi-homing or vertical integration are the most prevalent. Often, there is only one or very few large undertakings providing those digital services. Those undertakings have emerged most frequently as gatekeepers for business users and end users, with far-reaching impacts. In particular, they have gained the ability to easily set commercial conditions and terms in a unilateral and detrimental manner for their business users and end users. Accordingly, it is necessary to focus only on those digital services that are most broadly used by business users and end users and where concerns about weak contestability and unfair practices by gatekeepers are more apparent and pressing from an internal market perspective.

[4] Regulation (EU) 2016/679 of the European Parliament and of the Council of 27 April 2016 on the protection of natural persons with regard to the processing of personal data and on the free movement of such data, and repealing Directive 95/46/EC (General Data Protection Regulation) (OJ L 119, 4.5.2016, p. 1).

[5] Regulation (EU) 2019/1150 of the European Parliament and of the Council of 20 June 2019 on promoting fairness and transparency for business users of online intermediation services (OJ L 186, 11.7.2019, p. 57).

[6] Directive 2002/58/EC of the European Parliament and of the Council of 12 July 2002 concerning the processing of personal data and the protection of privacy in the electronic communications sector (OJ L 201, 31.7.2002, p. 37).

[7] Directive 2005/29/EC of the European Parliament and of the Council of 11 May 2005 concerning unfair business-to-consumer commercial practices in the internal market and amending Council Directive 84/450/EEC, Directives 97/7/EC, 98/27/EC and 2002/65/EC of the European Parliament and of the Council and Regulation (EC) No 2006/2004 of the European Parliament and of the Council ('Unfair Commercial Practices Directive') (OJ L 149, 11.6.2005, p. 22).

[8] Directive 2010/13/EU of the European Parliament and of the Council of 10 March 2010 on the coordination of certain provisions laid down by law, regulation or administrative action in Member States concerning the provision of audiovisual media services (Audiovisual Media Services Directive) (OJ L 95, 15.4.2010, p. 1).

[9] Directive (EU) 2015/2366 of the European Parliament and of the Council of 25 November 2015 on payment services in the internal market, amending Directives 2002/65/EC, 2009/110/EC and 2013/36/EU and Regulation (EU) No 1093/2010, and repealing Directive 2007/64/EC (OJ L 337, 23.12.2015, p. 35).

[10] Directive (EU) 2019/790 of the European Parliament and of the Council of 17 April 2019 on copyright and related rights in the Digital Single Market and amending Directives 96/9/EC and 2001/29/EC (OJ L 130, 17.5.2019, p. 92).

[11] Directive (EU) 2019/882 of the European Parliament and of the Council of 17 April 2019 on the accessibility requirements for products and services (OJ L 151, 7.6.2019, p. 70).

[12] Council Directive 93/13/EEC of 5 April 1993 on unfair terms in consumer contracts (OJ L 95, 21.4.1993, p. 29).

(14) In particular, online intermediation services, online search engines, operating systems, online social networking, video sharing platform services, number-independent interpersonal communication services, cloud computing services, virtual assistants, web browsers and online advertising services, including advertising intermediation services, all have the capacity to affect a large number of end users and businesses, which entails a risk of unfair business practices. Therefore, they should be included in the definition of core platform services and fall into the scope of this Regulation. Online intermediation services can also be active in the field of financial services, and they can intermediate or be used to provide such services as listed non-exhaustively in Annex II to Directive (EU) 2015/1535 of the European Parliament and of the Council[13]. For the purposes of this Regulation, the definition of core platform services should be technology neutral and should be understood to encompass those provided on or through various means or devices, such as connected TV or embedded digital services in vehicles. In certain circumstances, the notion of end users should encompass users that are traditionally considered business users, but in a given situation do not use the core platform services to provide goods or services to other end users, such as for example businesses relying on cloud computing services for their own purposes.

(15) The fact that a digital service qualifies as a core platform service does not in itself give rise to sufficiently serious concerns of contestability or unfair practices. It is only when a core platform service constitutes an important gateway and is operated by an undertaking with a significant impact in the internal market and an entrenched and durable position, or by an undertaking that will foreseeably enjoy such a position in the near future, that such concerns arise. Accordingly, the targeted set of harmonised rules in this Regulation should apply only to undertakings designated on the basis of those three objective criteria, and they should only apply to those of their core platform services that individually constitute an important gateway for business users to reach end users. The fact that it is possible that an undertaking providing core platform services not only intermediates between business users and end users, but also between end users and end users, for example in the case of number-independent interpersonal communications services, should not preclude the conclusion that such an undertaking is or could be an important gateway for business users to reach end users.

(16) In order to ensure the effective application of this Regulation to undertakings providing core platform services which are most likely to satisfy those objective requirements, and where unfair practices weakening contestability are most prevalent and have the most impact, the Commission should be able to directly designate as gatekeepers those undertakings providing core platform services which meet certain quantitative thresholds. Such undertakings should in any event be subject to a fast designation process which should start once this Regulation becomes applicable.

(17) The fact that an undertaking has a very significant turnover in the Union and provides a core platform service in at least three Member States constitutes compelling indication that that undertaking has a significant impact on the internal market. This is equally true where an undertaking providing a core platform ser-

[13] Directive (EU) 2015/1535 of the European Parliament and of the Council of 9 September 2015 laying down a procedure for the provision of information in the field of technical regulations and of rules on Information Society services (OJ L 241, 17.9.2015, p. 1).

vice in at least three Member States has a very significant market capitalisation or equivalent fair market value. Therefore, an undertaking providing a core platform service should be presumed to have a significant impact on the internal market where it provides a core platform service in at least three Member States and where either its group turnover realised in the Union is equal to or exceeds a specific, high threshold, or the market capitalisation of the group is equal to or exceeds a certain high absolute value. For undertakings providing core platform services that belong to undertakings that are not publicly listed, the equivalent fair market value should be used as the reference. It should be possible for the Commission to use its power to adopt delegated acts to develop an objective methodology to calculate that value.

A high group turnover realised in the Union in conjunction with the threshold number of users in the Union of core platform services reflects a relatively strong ability to monetise those users. A high market capitalisation relative to the same threshold number of users in the Union reflects a relatively significant potential to monetise those users in the near future. This monetisation potential in turn reflects, in principle, the gateway position of the undertakings concerned. Both indicators, in addition, reflect the financial capacity of the undertakings concerned, including their ability to leverage their access to financial markets to reinforce their position. This can, for example, happen where this superior access is used to acquire other undertakings, an ability which has in turn been shown to have potential negative effects on innovation. Market capitalisation can also reflect the expected future position and effect on the internal market of the undertakings concerned, despite a potentially relatively low current turnover. The market capitalisation value should be based on a level that reflects the average market capitalisation of the largest publicly listed undertakings in the Union over an appropriate period.

(18) Whereas a market capitalisation at or above the threshold in the last financial year should give rise to a presumption that an undertaking providing core platform services has a significant impact on the internal market, a sustained market capitalisation of the undertaking providing core platform services at or above the threshold over three or more years should be considered as further strengthening that presumption.

(19) By contrast, there could be a number of factors concerning market capitalisation that would require an in-depth assessment in determining whether an undertaking providing core platform services should be deemed to have a significant impact on the internal market. This could be the case where the market capitalisation of the undertaking providing core platform services in preceding financial years was significantly lower than the threshold and the volatility of its market capitalisation over the observed period was disproportionate to overall equity market volatility or its market capitalisation trajectory relative to market trends was inconsistent with a rapid and unidirectional growth.

(20) Having a very high number of business users that depend on a core platform service to reach a very high number of monthly active end users enables the undertaking providing that service to influence the operations of a substantial part of business users to its advantage and indicate, in principle, that that undertaking is an important gateway. The respective relevant levels for those numbers should be set representing a substantive percentage of the entire population of

the Union when it comes to end users and of the entire population of businesses using core platform services to determine the threshold for business users. Active end users and business users should be identified and calculated in such a way as to adequately represent the role and reach of the specific core platform service in question. In order to provide legal certainty for gatekeepers, the elements to determine the number of active end users and business users per core platform service should be set out in an Annex to this Regulation. Such elements can be affected by technological and other developments. The Commission should therefore be empowered to adopt delegated acts to amend this Regulation by updating the methodology and the list of indicators used to determine the number of active end users and active business users.

(21) An entrenched and durable position in its operations or the foreseeability of enjoying such a position in the future occurs notably where the contestability of the position of the undertaking providing the core platform service is limited. This is likely to be the case where that undertaking has provided a core platform service in at least three Member States to a very high number of business users and end users over a period of at least 3 years.

(22) Such thresholds can be affected by market and technical developments. The Commission should therefore be empowered to adopt delegated acts to specify the methodology for determining whether the quantitative thresholds are met, and to regularly adjust it to market and technological developments where necessary. Such delegated acts should not amend the quantitative thresholds set out in this Regulation.

(23) An undertaking providing core platform services should be able, in exceptional circumstances, to rebut the presumption that the undertaking has a significant impact on the internal market by demonstrating that, although it meets the quantitative thresholds set out in this Regulation, it does not fulfil the requirements for designation as a gatekeeper. The burden of adducing evidence that the presumption deriving from the fulfilment of the quantitative thresholds should not apply should be borne by that undertaking. In its assessment of the evidence and arguments produced, the Commission should take into account only those elements which directly relate to the quantitative criteria, namely the impact of the undertaking providing core platform services on the internal market beyond revenue or market cap, such as its size in absolute terms, and the number of Member States in which it is present; by how much the actual business user and end user numbers exceed the thresholds and the importance of the undertaking's core platform service considering the overall scale of activities of the respective core platform service; and the number of years for which the thresholds have been met.

Any justification on economic grounds seeking to enter into market definition or to demonstrate efficiencies deriving from a specific type of behaviour by the undertaking providing core platform services should be discarded, as it is not relevant to the designation as a gatekeeper. If the arguments submitted are not sufficiently substantiated because they do not manifestly put into question the presumption, it should be possible for the Commission to reject the arguments within the timeframe of 45 working days provided for the designation. The Commission should be able to take a decision by relying on information available on the quantitative thresholds where the undertaking providing core platform services obstructs the investigation by failing to comply with the investigative measures taken by the Commission.

(24) Provision should also be made for the assessment of the gatekeeper role of undertakings providing core platform services which do not satisfy all of the quantitative thresholds, in light of the overall objective requirements that they have a significant impact on the internal market, act as an important gateway for business users to reach end users and benefit from an entrenched and durable position in their operations or it is foreseeable that they will do so in the near future. When the undertaking providing core platform services is a medium-sized, small or micro enterprise, the assessment should carefully take into account whether such an undertaking would be able to substantially undermine the contestability of the core platform services, since this Regulation primarily targets large undertakings with considerable economic power rather than medium-sized, small or micro enterprises.

(25) Such an assessment can only be done in light of a market investigation, while taking into account the quantitative thresholds. In its assessment the Commission should pursue the objectives of preserving and fostering innovation and the quality of digital products and services, the degree to which prices are fair and competitive, and the degree to which quality or choice for business users and for end users is or remains high. Elements can be taken into account that are specific to the undertakings providing core platform services concerned, such as extreme scale or scope economies, very strong network effects, data-driven advantages, an ability to connect many business users with many end users through the multisidedness of those services, lock-in effects, lack of multi-homing, conglomerate corporate structure or vertical integration. In addition, a very high market capitalisation, a very high ratio of equity value over profit or a very high turnover derived from end users of a single core platform service can be used as indicators of the leveraging potential of such undertakings and of the tipping of the market in their favour. Together with market capitalisation, high relative growth rates are examples of dynamic parameters that are particularly relevant to identifying such undertakings providing core platform services for which it is foreseeable that they will become entrenched and durable. The Commission should be able to take a decision by drawing adverse inferences from facts available where the undertaking providing core platform services significantly obstructs the investigation by failing to comply with the investigative measures taken by the Commission.

(26) A particular subset of rules should apply to those undertakings providing core platform services for which it is foreseeable that they will enjoy an entrenched and durable position in the near future. The same specific features of core platform services make them prone to tipping: once an undertaking providing the core platform service has obtained a certain advantage over rivals or potential challengers in terms of scale or intermediation power, its position could become unassailable and the situation could evolve to the point that it is likely to become entrenched and durable in the near future. Undertakings can try to induce this tipping and emerge as gatekeeper by using some of the unfair conditions and practices regulated under this Regulation. In such a situation, it appears appropriate to intervene before the market tips irreversibly.

(27) However, such early intervention should be limited to imposing only those obligations that are necessary and appropriate to ensure that the services in question

remain contestable and enable the qualified risk of unfair conditions and practices to be avoided. Obligations that prevent the undertaking providing core platform services concerned from enjoying an entrenched and durable position in its operations, such as those preventing leveraging, and those that facilitate switching and multi-homing are more directly geared towards this purpose. To ensure proportionality, the Commission should moreover apply from that subset of obligations only those that are necessary and proportionate to achieve the objectives of this Regulation and should regularly review whether such obligations should be maintained, suppressed or adapted.

(28) Applying only those obligations that are necessary and proportionate to achieve the objectives of this Regulation should allow the Commission to intervene in time and effectively, while fully respecting the proportionality of the measures considered. It should also reassure actual or potential market participants about the contestability and fairness of the services concerned.

(29) Gatekeepers should comply with the obligations laid down in this Regulation in respect of each of the core platform services listed in the relevant designation decision. The obligations should apply taking into account the conglomerate position of gatekeepers, where applicable. Furthermore, it should be possible for the Commission to impose implementing measures on the gatekeeper by decision. Those implementing measures should be designed in an effective manner, having regard to the features of core platform services and the possible circumvention risks, and in compliance with the principle of proportionality and the fundamental rights of the undertakings concerned, as well as those of third parties.

(30) The very rapidly changing and complex technological nature of core platform services requires a regular review of the status of gatekeepers, including those that it is foreseen will enjoy an entrenched and durable position in their operations in the near future. To provide all of the market participants, including the gatekeepers, with the required certainty as to the applicable legal obligations, a time limit for such regular reviews is necessary. It is also important to conduct such reviews on a regular basis and at least every 3 years. Furthermore, it is important to clarify that not every change in the facts on the basis of which an undertaking providing core platform services was designated as a gatekeeper should require amendment of the designation decision. Amendment will only be necessary if the change in the facts also leads to a change in the assessment. Whether or not that is the case should be based on a case-by-case assessment of the facts and circumstances.

(31) To safeguard the contestability and fairness of core platform services provided by gatekeepers, it is necessary to provide in a clear and unambiguous manner for a set of harmonised rules with regard to those services. Such rules are needed to address the risk of harmful effects of practices by gatekeepers, to the benefit of the business environment in the services concerned, of users and ultimately of society as a whole. The obligations correspond to those practices that are considered as undermining contestability or as being unfair, or both, when taking into account the features of the digital sector and which have a particularly negative direct impact on business users and end users. It should be possible for the obligations laid down by this Regulation to specifically take into account the nature of the core platform services provided. The obligations in this Regulation should not only ensure contestability and fairness with respect to core platform services listed in the designation decision, but also with respect to other digital products and

services into which gatekeepers leverage their gateway position, which are often provided together with, or in support of, the core platform services.

(32) For the purpose of this Regulation, contestability should relate to the ability of undertakings to effectively overcome barriers to entry and expansion and challenge the gatekeeper on the merits of their products and services. The features of core platform services in the digital sector, such as network effects, strong economies of scale, and benefits from data have limited the contestability of those services and the related ecosystems. Such a weak contestability reduces the incentives to innovate and improve products and services for the gatekeeper, its business users, its challengers and customers and thus negatively affects the innovation potential of the wider online platform economy. Contestability of the services in the digital sector can also be limited if there is more than one gatekeeper for a core platform service. This Regulation should therefore ban certain practices by gatekeepers that are liable to increase barriers to entry or expansion, and impose certain obligations on gatekeepers that tend to lower those barriers. The obligations should also address situations where the position of the gatekeeper may be entrenched to such an extent that inter-platform competition is not effective in the short term, meaning that intra-platform competition needs to be created or increased.

(33) For the purpose of this Regulation, unfairness should relate to an imbalance between the rights and obligations of business users where the gatekeeper obtains a disproportionate advantage. Market participants, including business users of core platform services and alternative providers of services provided together with, or in support of, such core platform services, should have the ability to adequately capture the benefits resulting from their innovative or other efforts. Due to their gateway position and superior bargaining power, it is possible that gatekeepers engage in behaviour that does not allow others to capture fully the benefits of their own contributions, and unilaterally set unbalanced conditions for the use of their core platform services or services provided together with, or in support of, their core platform services. Such imbalance is not excluded by the fact that the gatekeeper offers a particular service free of charge to a specific group of users, and may also consist in excluding or discriminating against business users, in particular if the latter compete with the services provided by the gatekeeper. This Regulation should therefore impose obligations on gatekeepers addressing such behaviour.

(34) Contestability and fairness are intertwined. The lack of, or weak, contestability for a certain service can enable a gatekeeper to engage in unfair practices. Similarly, unfair practices by a gatekeeper can reduce the possibility of business users or others to contest the gatekeeper's position. A particular obligation in this Regulation may, therefore, address both elements.

(35) The obligations laid down in this Regulation are therefore necessary to address identified public policy concerns, there being no alternative and less restrictive measures that would effectively achieve the same result, having regard to the need to safeguard public order, protect privacy and fight fraudulent and deceptive commercial practices.

(36) Gatekeepers often directly collect personal data of end users for the purpose of providing online advertising services when end users use third-party websites

and software applications. Third parties also provide gatekeepers with personal data of their end users in order to make use of certain services provided by the gatekeepers in the context of their core platform services, such as custom audiences. The processing, for the purpose of providing online advertising services, of personal data from third parties using core platform services gives gatekeepers potential advantages in terms of accumulation of data, thereby raising barriers to entry. This is because gatekeepers process personal data from a significantly larger number of third parties than other undertakings. Similar advantages result from the conduct of (i) combining end user personal data collected from a core platform service with data collected from other services; (ii) cross-using personal data from a core platform service in other services provided separately by the gatekeeper, notably services which are not provided together with, or in support of, the relevant core platform service, and vice versa; or (iii) signing-in end users to different services of gatekeepers in order to combine personal data. To ensure that gatekeepers do not unfairly undermine the contestability of core platform services, gatekeepers should enable end users to freely choose to opt-in to such data processing and sign-in practices by offering a less personalised but equivalent alternative, and without making the use of the core platform service or certain functionalities thereof conditional upon the end user's consent. This should be without prejudice to the gatekeeper processing personal data or signing in end users to a service, relying on the legal basis under Article 6(1), points (c), (d) and (e), of Regulation (EU) 2016/679, but not on Article 6(1), points (b) and (f) of that Regulation.

(37) The less personalised alternative should not be different or of degraded quality compared to the service provided to the end users who provide consent, unless a degradation of quality is a direct consequence of the gatekeeper not being able to process such personal data or signing in end users to a service. Not giving consent should not be more difficult than giving consent. When the gatekeeper requests consent, it should proactively present a user-friendly solution to the end user to provide, modify or withdraw consent in an explicit, clear and straightforward manner. In particular, consent should be given by a clear affirmative action or statement establishing a freely given, specific, informed and unambiguous indication of agreement by the end user, as defined in Regulation (EU) 2016/679. At the time of giving consent, and only where applicable, the end user should be informed that not giving consent can lead to a less personalised offer, but that otherwise the core platform service will remain unchanged and that no functionalities will be suppressed. Exceptionally, if consent cannot be given directly to the gatekeeper's core platform service, end users should be able to give consent through each third-party service that makes use of that core platform service, to allow the gatekeeper to process personal data for the purposes of providing online advertising services.

Lastly, it should be as easy to withdraw consent as to give it. Gatekeepers should not design, organise or operate their online interfaces in a way that deceives, manipulates or otherwise materially distorts or impairs the ability of end users to freely give consent. In particular, gatekeepers should not be allowed to prompt end users more than once a year to give consent for the same processing purpose in respect of which they initially did not give consent or withdrew their consent. This Regulation is without prejudice to Regulation (EU) 2016/679, including its enforcement framework, which remains fully applicable with respect to any claims by data subjects relating to an infringement of their rights under that Regulation.

(38) Children merit specific protection with regard to their personal data, in particular as regards the use of their personal data for the purposes of commercial communication or creating user profiles. The protection of children online is an important objective of the Union and should be reflected in the relevant Union law. In this context, due regard should be given to a Regulation on a single market for digital services. Nothing in this Regulation exempts gatekeepers from the obligation to protect children laid down in applicable Union law.

(39) In certain cases, for instance through the imposition of contractual terms and conditions, gatekeepers can restrict the ability of business users of their online intermediation services to offer products or services to end users under more favourable conditions, including price, through other online intermediation services or through direct online sales channels. Where such restrictions relate to third-party online intermediation services, they limit inter-platform contestability, which in turn limits choice of alternative online intermediation services for end users. Where such restrictions relate to direct online sales channels, they unfairly limit the freedom of business users to use such channels. To ensure that business users of online intermediation services of gatekeepers can freely choose alternative online intermediation services or direct online sales channels and differentiate the conditions under which they offer their products or services to end users, it should not be accepted that gatekeepers limit business users from choosing to differentiate commercial conditions, including price. Such a restriction should apply to any measure with equivalent effect, such as increased commission rates or de-listing of the offers of business users.

(40) To prevent further reinforcing their dependence on the core platform services of gatekeepers, and in order to promote multi-homing, the business users of those gatekeepers should be free to promote and choose the distribution channel that they consider most appropriate for the purpose of interacting with any end users that those business users have already acquired through core platform services provided by the gatekeeper or through other channels. This should apply to the promotion of offers, including through a software application of the business user, and any form of communication and conclusion of contracts between business users and end users. An acquired end user is an end user who has already entered into a commercial relationship with the business user and, where applicable, the gatekeeper has been directly or indirectly remunerated by the business user for facilitating the initial acquisition of the end user by the business user. Such commercial relationships can be on either a paid or a free basis, such as free trials or free service tiers, and can have been entered into either on the core platform service of the gatekeeper or through any other channel. Conversely, end users should also be free to choose offers of such business users and to enter into contracts with them either through core platform services of the gatekeeper, if applicable, or from a direct distribution channel of the business user or another indirect channel that such business user uses.

(41) The ability of end users to acquire content, subscriptions, features or other items outside the core platform services of the gatekeeper should not be undermined or restricted. In particular, a situation should be avoided whereby gatekeepers restrict end users from access to, and use of, such services via a software applica-

tion running on their core platform service. For example, subscribers to online content purchased outside a software application, software application store or virtual assistant should not be prevented from accessing such online content on a software application on the core platform service of the gatekeeper simply because it was purchased outside such software application, software application store or virtual assistant.

(42) To safeguard a fair commercial environment and protect the contestability of the digital sector it is important to safeguard the right of business users and end users, including whistleblowers, to raise concerns about unfair practices by gatekeepers raising any issue of non-compliance with the relevant Union or national law with any relevant administrative or other public authorities, including national courts. For example, it is possible that business users or end users will want to complain about different types of unfair practices, such as discriminatory access conditions, unjustified closing of business user accounts or unclear grounds for product de-listings. Any practice that would in any way inhibit or hinder those users in raising their concerns or in seeking available redress, for instance by means of confidentiality clauses in agreements or other written terms, should therefore be prohibited. This prohibition should be without prejudice to the right of business users and gatekeepers to lay down in their agreements the terms of use including the use of lawful complaints-handling mechanisms, including any use of alternative dispute resolution mechanisms or of the jurisdiction of specific courts in compliance with respective Union and national law. This should also be without prejudice to the role gatekeepers play in the fight against illegal content online.

(43) Certain services provided together with, or in support of, relevant core platform services of the gatekeeper, such as identification services, web browser engines, payment services or technical services that support the provision of payment services, such as payment systems for in-app purchases, are crucial for business users to conduct their business and allow them to optimise services. In particular, each browser is built on a web browser engine, which is responsible for key browser functionality such as speed, reliability and web compatibility. When gatekeepers operate and impose web browser engines, they are in a position to determine the functionality and standards that will apply not only to their own web browsers, but also to competing web browsers and, in turn, to web software applications. Gatekeepers should therefore not use their position to require their dependent business users to use any of the services provided together with, or in support of, core platform services by the gatekeeper itself as part of the provision of services or products by those business users. In order to avoid a situation in which gatekeepers indirectly impose on business users their own services provided together with, or in support of, core platform services, gatekeepers should also be prohibited from requiring end users to use such services, when that requirement would be imposed in the context of the service provided to end users by the business user using the core platform service of the gatekeeper. That prohibition aims to protect the freedom of the business user to choose alternative services to the ones of the gatekeeper, but should not be construed as obliging the business user to offer such alternatives to its end users.

(44) The conduct of requiring business users or end users to subscribe to, or register with, any other core platform services of gatekeepers listed in the designation

decision or which meet the thresholds of active end users and business users set out in this Regulation, as a condition for using, accessing, signing up for or registering with a core platform service gives the gatekeepers a means of capturing and locking-in new business users and end users for their core platform services by ensuring that business users cannot access one core platform service without also at least registering or creating an account for the purposes of receiving a second core platform service. That conduct also gives gatekeepers a potential advantage in terms of accumulation of data. As such, this conduct is liable to raise barriers to entry and should be prohibited.

(45) The conditions under which gatekeepers provide online advertising services to business users, including both advertisers and publishers, are often non-transparent and opaque. This opacity is partly linked to the practices of a few platforms, but is also due to the sheer complexity of modern day programmatic advertising. That sector is considered to have become less transparent after the introduction of new privacy legislation. This often leads to a lack of information and knowledge for advertisers and publishers about the conditions of the online advertising services they purchase and undermines their ability to switch between undertakings providing online advertising services. Furthermore, the costs of online advertising services under these conditions are likely to be higher than they would be in a fairer, more transparent and contestable platform environment. Those higher costs are likely to be reflected in the prices that end users pay for many daily products and services relying on the use of online advertising services. Transparency obligations should therefore require gatekeepers to provide advertisers and publishers to whom they supply online advertising services, when requested, with free of charge information that allows both sides to understand the price paid for each of the different online advertising services provided as part of the relevant advertising value chain.

This information should be provided, upon request, to an advertiser at the level of an individual advertisement in relation to the price and fees charged to that advertiser and, subject to an agreement by the publisher owning the inventory where the advertisement is displayed, the remuneration received by that consenting publisher. The provision of this information on a daily basis will allow advertisers to receive information that has a sufficient level of granularity necessary to compare the costs of using the online advertising services of gatekeepers with the costs of using online advertising services of alternative undertakings. Where some publishers do not provide their consent to the sharing of the relevant information with the advertiser, the gatekeeper should provide the advertiser with the information about the daily average remuneration received by those publishers for the relevant advertisements. The same obligation and principles of sharing the relevant information concerning the provision of online advertising services should apply in respect of requests by publishers. Since gatekeepers can use different pricing models for the provision of online advertising services to advertisers and publishers, for instance a price per impression, per view or any other criterion, gatekeepers should also provide the method with which each of the prices and remunerations are calculated.

(46) In certain circumstances, a gatekeeper has a dual role as an undertaking providing core platform services, whereby it provides a core platform service, and possibly other services provided together with, or in support of, that core platform service to its business users, while also competing or intending to compete with those

same business users in the provision of the same or similar services or products to the same end users. In those circumstances, a gatekeeper can take advantage of its dual role to use data, generated or provided by its business users in the context of activities by those business users when using the core platform services or the services provided together with, or in support of, those core platform services, for the purpose of its own services or products. The data of the business user can also include any data generated by or provided during the activities of its end users. This can be the case, for instance, where a gatekeeper provides an online marketplace or a software application store to business users, and at the same time provides services as an undertaking providing online retail services or software applications. To prevent gatekeepers from unfairly benefitting from their dual role, it is necessary to ensure that they do not use any aggregated or non-aggregated data, which could include anonymised and personal data that is not publicly available to provide similar services to those of their business users. That obligation should apply to the gatekeeper as a whole, including but not limited to its business unit that competes with the business users of a core platform service.

(47) Business users can also purchase online advertising services from an undertaking providing core platform services for the purpose of providing goods and services to end users. In this case, it can happen that the data are not generated on the core platform service, but are provided to the core platform service by the business user or are generated based on its operations through the core platform service concerned. In certain instances, that core platform service providing advertising can have a dual role as both an undertaking providing online advertising services and an undertaking providing services competing with business users. Accordingly, the obligation prohibiting a dual role gatekeeper from using data of business users should apply also with respect to the data that a core platform service has received from businesses for the purpose of providing online advertising services related to that core platform service.

(48) In relation to cloud computing services, the obligation not to use the data of business users should extend to data provided or generated by business users of the gatekeeper in the context of their use of the cloud computing service of the gatekeeper, or through its software application store that allows end users of cloud computing services access to software applications. That obligation should not affect the right of the gatekeeper to use aggregated data for providing other services provided together with, or in support of, its core platform service, such as data analytics services, subject to compliance with Regulation (EU) 2016/679 and Directive 2002/58/EC, as well as with the relevant obligations in this Regulation concerning such services.

(49) A gatekeeper can use different means to favour its own or third-party services or products on its operating system, virtual assistant or web browser, to the detriment of the same or similar services that end users could obtain through other third parties. This can for instance happen where certain software applications or services are pre-installed by a gatekeeper. To enable end user choice, gatekeepers should not prevent end users from un-installing any software applications on their operating system. It should be possible for the gatekeeper to restrict such un-installation only when such software applications are essential to the functioning of the operating system or the device. Gatekeepers should also allow end users

to easily change the default settings on the operating system, virtual assistant and web browser when those default settings favour their own software applications and services. This includes prompting a choice screen, at the moment of the users' first use of an online search engine, virtual assistant or web browser of the gatekeeper listed in the designation decision, allowing end users to select an alternative default service when the operating system of the gatekeeper directs end users to those online search engine, virtual assistant or web browser and when the virtual assistant or the web browser of the gatekeeper direct the user to the online search engine listed in the designation decision.

(50) The rules that a gatekeeper sets for the distribution of software applications can, in certain circumstances, restrict the ability of end users to install and effectively use third-party software applications or software application stores on hardware or operating systems of that gatekeeper and restrict the ability of end users to access such software applications or software application stores outside the core platform services of that gatekeeper. Such restrictions can limit the ability of developers of software applications to use alternative distribution channels and the ability of end users to choose between different software applications from different distribution channels and should be prohibited as unfair and liable to weaken the contestability of core platform services. To ensure contestability, the gatekeeper should furthermore allow the third-party software applications or software application stores to prompt the end user to decide whether that service should become the default and enable that change to be carried out easily.

In order to ensure that third-party software applications or software application stores do not endanger the integrity of the hardware or operating system provided by the gatekeeper, it should be possible for the gatekeeper concerned to implement proportionate technical or contractual measures to achieve that goal if the gatekeeper demonstrates that such measures are necessary and justified and that there are no less-restrictive means to safeguard the integrity of the hardware or operating system. The integrity of the hardware or the operating system should include any design options that need to be implemented and maintained in order for the hardware or the operating system to be protected against unauthorised access, by ensuring that security controls specified for the hardware or the operating system concerned cannot be compromised. Furthermore, in order to ensure that third-party software applications or software application stores do not undermine end users' security, it should be possible for the gatekeeper to implement strictly necessary and proportionate measures and settings, other than default settings, enabling end users to effectively protect security in relation to third-party software applications or software application stores if the gatekeeper demonstrates that such measures and settings are strictly necessary and justified and that there are no less-restrictive means to achieve that goal. The gatekeeper should be prevented from implementing such measures as a default setting or as pre-installation.

(51) Gatekeepers are often vertically integrated and offer certain products or services to end users through their own core platform services, or through a business user over which they exercise control which frequently leads to conflicts of interest. This can include the situation whereby a gatekeeper provides its own online intermediation services through an online search engine. When offering those products or services on the core platform service, gatekeepers can reserve a better position, in terms of ranking, and related indexing and crawling, for their own

offering than that of the products or services of third parties also operating on that core platform service. This can occur for instance with products or services, including other core platform services, which are ranked in the results communicated by online search engines, or which are partly or entirely embedded in online search engines results, groups of results specialised in a certain topic, displayed along with the results of an online search engine, which are considered or used by certain end users as a service distinct or additional to the online search engine.

Other instances are those of software applications which are distributed through software application stores, or videos distributed through a video-sharing platform, or products or services that are given prominence and display in the newsfeed of an online social networking service, or products or services ranked in search results or displayed on an online marketplace, or products or services offered through a virtual assistant. Such reserving of a better position of gatekeeper's own offering can take place even before ranking following a query, such as during crawling and indexing. For example, already during crawling, as a discovery process by which new and updated content is being found, as well as indexing, which entails storing and organising of the content found during the crawling process, the gatekeeper can favour its own content over that of third parties. In those circumstances, the gatekeeper is in a dual-role position as intermediary for third-party undertakings and as undertaking directly providing products or services. Consequently, such gatekeepers have the ability to undermine directly the contestability for those products or services on those core platform services, to the detriment of business users which are not controlled by the gatekeeper.

(52) In such situations, the gatekeeper should not engage in any form of differentiated or preferential treatment in ranking on the core platform service, and related indexing and crawling, whether through legal, commercial or technical means, in favour of products or services it offers itself or through a business user which it controls. To ensure that this obligation is effective, the conditions that apply to such ranking should also be generally fair and transparent. Ranking should in this context cover all forms of relative prominence, including display, rating, linking or voice results and should also include instances where a core platform service presents or communicates only one result to the end user. To ensure that this obligation is effective and cannot be circumvented, it should also apply to any measure that has an equivalent effect to the differentiated or preferential treatment in ranking. The guidelines adopted pursuant to Article 5 of Regulation (EU) 2019/1150 should also facilitate the implementation and enforcement of this obligation.

(53) Gatekeepers should not restrict or prevent the free choice of end users by technically or otherwise preventing switching between or subscription to different software applications and services. This would allow more undertakings to offer their services, thereby ultimately providing greater choice to the end users. Gatekeepers should ensure a free choice irrespective of whether they are the manufacturer of any hardware by means of which such software applications or services are accessed and should not raise artificial technical or other barriers so as to make switching impossible or ineffective. The mere offering of a given product or service to consumers, including by means of pre-installation, as well as the improvement of the offering to end users, such as price reductions or increased quality, should not be construed as constituting a prohibited barrier to switching.

(54) Gatekeepers can hamper the ability of end users to access online content and services, including software applications. Therefore, rules should be established to ensure that the rights of end users to access an open internet are not compromised by the conduct of gatekeepers. Gatekeepers can also technically limit the ability of end users to effectively switch between different undertakings providing internet access service, in particular through their control over hardware or operating systems. This distorts the level playing field for internet access services and ultimately harms end users. It should therefore be ensured that gatekeepers do not unduly restrict end users in choosing the undertaking providing their internet access service.

(55) A gatekeeper can provide services or hardware, such as wearable devices, that access hardware or software features of a device accessed or controlled via an operating system or virtual assistant in order to offer specific functionalities to end users. In that case, competing service or hardware providers, such as providers of wearable devices, require equally effective interoperability with, and access for the purposes of interoperability to, the same hardware or software features to be able to provide a competitive offering to end users.

(56) Gatekeepers can also have a dual role as developers of operating systems and device manufacturers, including any technical functionality that such a device may have. For example, a gatekeeper that is a manufacturer of a device can restrict access to some of the functionalities in that device, such as near-field-communication technology, secure elements and processors, authentication mechanisms and the software used to operate those technologies, which can be required for the effective provision of a service provided together with, or in support of, the core platform service by the gatekeeper as well as by any potential third-party undertaking providing such service.

(57) If dual roles are used in a manner that prevents alternative service and hardware providers from having access under equal conditions to the same operating system, hardware or software features that are available or used by the gatekeeper in the provision of its own complementary or supporting services or hardware, this could significantly undermine innovation by such alternative providers, as well as choice for end users. The gatekeepers should, therefore, be required to ensure, free of charge, effective interoperability with, and access for the purposes of interoperability to, the same operating system, hardware or software features that are available or used in the provision of its own complementary and supporting services and hardware. Such access can equally be required by software applications related to the relevant services provided together with, or in support of, the core platform service in order to effectively develop and provide functionalities interoperable with those provided by gatekeepers. The aim of the obligations is to allow competing third parties to interconnect through interfaces or similar solutions to the respective features as effectively as the gatekeeper's own services or hardware.

(58) The conditions under which gatekeepers provide online advertising services to business users, including both advertisers and publishers, are often non-transparent and opaque. This often leads to a lack of information for advertisers and publishers about the effect of a given advertisement. To further enhance fairness, transparency and contestability of online advertising services listed in the designation decision, as well as those that are fully integrated with other core

platform services of the same undertaking, gatekeepers should provide advertisers and publishers, and third parties authorised by advertisers and publishers, when requested, with free of charge access to the gatekeepers' performance measuring tools and the data, including aggregated and non-aggregated data, necessary for advertisers, authorised third parties such as advertising agencies acting on behalf of a company placing advertising, as well as for publishers to carry out their own independent verification of the provision of the relevant online advertising services.

(59) Gatekeepers benefit from access to vast amounts of data that they collect while providing the core platform services, as well as other digital services. To ensure that gatekeepers do not undermine the contestability of core platform services, or the innovation potential of the dynamic digital sector, by restricting switching or multi-homing, end users, as well as third parties authorised by an end user, should be granted effective and immediate access to the data they provided or that was generated through their activity on the relevant core platform services of the gatekeeper. The data should be received in a format that can be immediately and effectively accessed and used by the end user or the relevant third party authorised by the end user to which the data is ported. Gatekeepers should also ensure, by means of appropriate and high quality technical measures, such as application programming interfaces, that end users or third parties authorised by end users can freely port the data continuously and in real time. This should apply also to any other data at different levels of aggregation necessary to effectively enable such portability. For the avoidance of doubt, the obligation on the gatekeeper to ensure effective portability of data under this Regulation complements the right to data portability under the Regulation (EU) 2016/679. Facilitating switching or multi-homing should lead, in turn, to an increased choice for end users and acts as an incentive for gatekeepers and business users to innovate.

(60) Business users that use core platform services provided by gatekeepers, and end users of such business users provide and generate a vast amount of data. In order to ensure that business users have access to the relevant data thus generated, the gatekeeper should, upon their request, provide effective access, free of charge, to such data. Such access should also be given to third parties contracted by the business user, who are acting as processors of this data for the business user. The access should include access to data provided or generated by the same business users and the same end users of those business users in the context of other services provided by the same gatekeeper, including services provided together with or in support of core platform services, where this is inextricably linked to the relevant request. To this end, a gatekeeper should not use any contractual or other restrictions to prevent business users from accessing relevant data and should enable business users to obtain consent of their end users for such data access and retrieval, where such consent is required under Regulation (EU) 2016/679 and Directive 2002/58/EC. Gatekeepers should also ensure the continuous and real time access to such data by means of appropriate technical measures, for example by putting in place high quality application programming interfaces or integrated tools for small volume business users.

(61) The value of online search engines to their respective business users and end users increases as the total number of such users increases. Undertakings providing online search engines collect and store aggregated datasets containing informa-

tion about what users searched for, and how they interacted with, the results with which they were provided. Undertakings providing online search engines collect these data from searches undertaken on their own online search engine and, where applicable, searches undertaken on the platforms of their downstream commercial partners. Access by gatekeepers to such ranking, query, click and view data constitutes an important barrier to entry and expansion, which undermines the contestability of online search engines. Gatekeepers should therefore be required to provide access, on fair, reasonable and non-discriminatory terms, to those ranking, query, click and view data in relation to free and paid search generated by consumers on online search engines to other undertakings providing such services, so that those third-party undertakings can optimise their services and contest the relevant core platform services. Such access should also be given to third parties contracted by a provider of an online search engine, who are acting as processors of this data for that online search engine. When providing access to its search data, a gatekeeper should ensure the protection of the personal data of end users, including against possible re-identification risks, by appropriate means, such as anonymisation of such personal data, without substantially degrading the quality or usefulness of the data. The relevant data is anonymised if personal data is irreversibly altered in such a way that information does not relate to an identified or identifiable natural person or where personal data is rendered anonymous in such a manner that the data subject is not or is no longer identifiable.

(62) For software application stores, online search engines and online social networking services listed in the designation decision, gatekeepers should publish and apply general conditions of access that should be fair, reasonable and non-discriminatory. Those general conditions should provide for a Union based alternative dispute settlement mechanism that is easily accessible, impartial, independent and free of charge for the business user, without prejudice to the business user's own cost and proportionate measures aimed at preventing the abuse of the dispute settlement mechanism by business users. The dispute settlement mechanism should be without prejudice to the right of business users to seek redress before judicial authorities in accordance with Union and national law. In particular, gatekeepers which provide access to software application stores are an important gateway for business users that seek to reach end users. In view of the imbalance in bargaining power between those gatekeepers and business users of their software application stores, those gatekeepers should not be allowed to impose general conditions, including pricing conditions, that would be unfair or lead to unjustified differentiation.

Pricing or other general access conditions should be considered unfair if they lead to an imbalance of rights and obligations imposed on business users or confer an advantage on the gatekeeper which is disproportionate to the service provided by the gatekeeper to business users or lead to a disadvantage for business users in providing the same or similar services as the gatekeeper. The following benchmarks can serve as a yardstick to determine the fairness of general access conditions: prices charged or conditions imposed for the same or similar services by other providers of software application stores; prices charged or conditions imposed by the provider of the software application store for different related or similar services or to different types of end users; prices charged or conditions imposed by the provider of the software application store for the same service in different geographic regions; prices charged or conditions imposed by the provider of the software application store for the same service the gatekeeper provides to itself. This obligation should not establish an access right and it should be without prejudice to the ability of providers of software application stores, online search engines and online social networking services to take the required responsibility in the fight against illegal and unwanted content as set out in a Regulation on a single market for digital services.

(63) Gatekeepers can hamper the ability of business users and end users to unsubscribe from a core platform service that they have previously subscribed to. Therefore, rules should be established to avoid a situation in which gatekeepers undermine the rights of business users and end users to freely choose which core platform service they use. To safeguard free choice of business users and end users, a gatekeeper should not be allowed to make it unnecessarily difficult or complicated for business users or end users to unsubscribe from a core platform service. Closing an account or un-subscribing should not be made be more complicated than opening an account or subscribing to the same service. Gatekeepers should not demand additional fees when terminating contracts with their end users or business users. Gatekeepers should ensure that the conditions for terminating contracts are always proportionate and can be exercised without undue difficulty by end users, such as, for example, in relation to the reasons for termination, the notice period, or the form of such termination. This is without prejudice to national legislation applicable in accordance with the Union law laying down rights and obligations concerning conditions of termination of provision of core platform services by end users.

(64) The lack of interoperability allows gatekeepers that provide number-independent interpersonal communications services to benefit from strong network effects, which contributes to the weakening of contestability. Furthermore, regardless of whether end users 'multi-home', gatekeepers often provide number-independent interpersonal communications services as part of their platform ecosystem, and this further exacerbates entry barriers for alternative providers of such services and increases costs for end users to switch. Without prejudice to Directive (EU) 2018/1972 of the European Parliament and of the Council[14] and, in particular, the conditions and procedures laid down in Article 61 thereof, gatekeepers should therefore ensure, free of charge and upon request, interoperability with certain basic functionalities of their number-independent interpersonal communications services that they provide to their own end users, to third-party providers of such services.

Gatekeepers should ensure interoperability for third-party providers of number-independent interpersonal communications services that offer or intend to offer their number-independent interpersonal communications services to end users and business users in the Union. To facilitate the practical implementation of such interoperability, the gatekeeper concerned should be required to publish a reference offer laying down the technical details and general terms and conditions of interoperability with its number-independent interpersonal communications services. It should be possible for the Commission, if applicable, to consult the Body of European Regulators for Electronic Communications, in order to determine whether the technical details and the general terms and conditions

[14] Directive (EU) 2018/1972 of the European Parliament and of the Council of 11 December 2018 establishing the European Electronic Communications Code (OJ L 321, 17.12.2018, p. 36).

published in the reference offer that the gatekeeper intends to implement or has implemented ensures compliance with this obligation.

In all cases, the gatekeeper and the requesting provider should ensure that interoperability does not undermine a high level of security and data protection in line with their obligations laid down in this Regulation and applicable Union law, in particular Regulation (EU) 2016/679 and Directive 2002/58/EC. The obligation related to interoperability should be without prejudice to the information and choices to be made available to end users of the number-independent interpersonal communication services of the gatekeeper and the requesting provider under this Regulation and other Union law, in particular Regulation (EU) 2016/679.

(65) To ensure the effectiveness of the obligations laid down by this Regulation, while also making certain that those obligations are limited to what is necessary to ensure contestability and tackling the harmful effects of the unfair practices by gatekeepers, it is important to clearly define and circumscribe them so as to allow the gatekeeper to fully comply with them, whilst fully complying with applicable law, and in particular Regulation (EU) 2016/679 and Directive 2002/58/EC and legislation on consumer protection, cyber security, product safety and accessibility requirements, including Directive (EU) 2019/882 and Directive (EU) 2016/2102 of the European Parliament and of the Council[15]. The gatekeepers should ensure the compliance with this Regulation by design. Therefore, the necessary measures should be integrated as much as possible into the technological design used by the gatekeepers.

It may in certain cases be appropriate for the Commission, following a dialogue with the gatekeeper concerned and after enabling third parties to make comments, to further specify some of the measures that the gatekeeper concerned should adopt in order to effectively comply with obligations that are susceptible of being further specified or, in the event of circumvention, with all obligations. In particular, such further specification should be possible where the implementation of an obligation susceptible to being further specified can be affected by variations of services within a single category of core platform services. For this purpose, it should be possible for the gatekeeper to request the Commission to engage in a process whereby the Commission can further specify some of the measures that the gatekeeper concerned should adopt in order to effectively comply with those obligations.

The Commission should have discretion as to whether and when such further specification should be provided, while respecting the principles of equal treatment, proportionality, and good administration. In this respect, the Commission should provide the main reasons underlying its assessment, including any enforcement priorities. This process should not be used to undermine the effectiveness of this Regulation. Furthermore, this process is without prejudice to the powers of the Commission to adopt a decision establishing non-compliance with any of the obligations laid down in this Regulation by a gatekeeper, including the possibility to impose fines or periodic penalty payments. The Commission should be able to reopen proceedings, including where the specified measures turn out not to be effective. A reopening due to an ineffective specification adopted by decision should enable the Commission to amend the specification prospectively.

[15] Directive (EU) 2016/2102 of the European Parliament and of the Council of 26 October 2016 on the accessibility of the websites and mobile applications of public sector bodies (OJ L 327, 2.12.2016, p. 1).

The Commission should also be able to set a reasonable time period within which the proceedings can be reopened if the specified measures turn out not to be effective.

(66) As an additional element to ensure proportionality, gatekeepers should be given an opportunity to request the suspension, to the extent necessary, of a specific obligation in exceptional circumstances that lie beyond the control of the gatekeeper, such as an unforeseen external shock that has temporarily eliminated a significant part of end user demand for the relevant core platform service, where compliance with a specific obligation is shown by the gatekeeper to endanger the economic viability of the Union operations of the gatekeeper concerned. The Commission should identify the exceptional circumstances justifying the suspension and review it on a regular basis in order to assess whether the conditions for granting it are still viable.

(67) In exceptional circumstances, justified on the limited grounds of public health or public security laid down in Union law and interpreted by the Court of Justice, the Commission should be able to decide that a specific obligation does not apply to a specific core platform service. If harm is caused to such public interests that could indicate that the cost to society as a whole of enforcing a certain obligation is, in a specific exceptional case, too high and thus disproportionate. Where appropriate, the Commission should be able to facilitate compliance by assessing whether a limited and duly justified suspension or exemption is justified. This should ensure the proportionality of the obligations in this Regulation without undermining the intended *ex ante* effects on fairness and contestability. Where such an exemption is granted, the Commission should review its decision every year.

(68) Within the timeframe for complying with their obligations under this Regulation, gatekeepers should inform the Commission, through mandatory reporting, about the measures they intend to implement or have implemented in order to ensure effective compliance with those obligations, including those measures concerning compliance with Regulation (EU) 2016/679, to the extent they are relevant for compliance with the obligations provided under this Regulation, which should allow the Commission to fulfil its duties under this Regulation. In addition, a clear and comprehensible non-confidential summary of such information should be made publicly available while taking into account the legitimate interest of gatekeepers in the protection of their business secrets and other confidential information. This non-confidential publication should enable third parties to assess whether the gatekeepers comply with the obligations laid down in this Regulation. Such reporting should be without prejudice to any enforcement action by the Commission at any time following the reporting. The Commission should publish online a link to the non-confidential summary of the report, as well as all other public information based on information obligations under this Regulation, in order to ensure accessibility of such information in a usable and comprehensive manner, in particular for small and medium enterprises (SMEs).

(69) The obligations of gatekeepers should only be updated after a thorough investigation into the nature and impact of specific practices that may be newly identified, following an in-depth investigation, as unfair or limiting contestability in the same manner as the unfair practices laid down in this Regulation while potentially escaping the scope of the current set of obligations. The Commission

should be able to launch an investigation with a view to determining whether the existing obligations need to be updated, either on its own initiative or following a justified request of at least three Member States. When presenting such justified requests, it should be possible for Member States to include information on newly introduced offers of products, services, software or features which raise concerns of contestability or fairness, whether implemented in the context of existing core platform services or otherwise. Where, following a market investigation, the Commission deems it necessary to modify essential elements of this Regulation, such as the inclusion of new obligations that depart from the same contestability or fairness issues addressed by this Regulation, the Commission should advance a proposal to amend this Regulation.

(70) Given the substantial economic power of gatekeepers, it is important that the obligations are applied effectively and are not circumvented. To that end, the rules in question should apply to any practice by a gatekeeper, irrespective of its form and irrespective of whether it is of a contractual, commercial, technical or any other nature, insofar as the practice corresponds to the type of practice that is the subject of one of the obligations laid down by this Regulation. Gatekeepers should not engage in behaviour that would undermine the effectiveness of the prohibitions and obligations laid down in this Regulation. Such behaviour includes the design used by the gatekeeper, the presentation of end-user choices in a non-neutral manner, or using the structure, function or manner of operation of a user interface or a part thereof to subvert or impair user autonomy, decision-making, or choice. Furthermore, the gatekeeper should not be allowed to engage in any behaviour undermining interoperability as required under this Regulation, such as for example by using unjustified technical protection measures, discriminatory terms of service, unlawfully claiming a copyright on application programming interfaces or providing misleading information. Gatekeepers should not be allowed to circumvent their designation by artificially segmenting, dividing, subdividing, fragmenting or splitting their core platform services to circumvent the quantitative thresholds laid down in this Regulation.

(71) To ensure the effectiveness of the review of gatekeeper status, as well as the possibility to adjust the list of core platform services provided by a gatekeeper, the gatekeepers should inform the Commission of all of their intended acquisitions, prior to their implementation, of other undertakings providing core platform services or any other services provided within the digital sector or other services that enable the collection of data. Such information should not only serve the review process regarding the status of individual gatekeepers, but will also provide information that is crucial to monitoring broader contestability trends in the digital sector and can therefore be a useful factor for consideration in the context of the market investigations provided for by this Regulation. Furthermore, the Commission should inform Member States of such information, given the possibility of using the information for national merger control purposes and as, under certain circumstances, it is possible for the national competent authority to refer those acquisitions to the Commission for the purposes of merger control. The Commission should also publish annually a list of acquisitions of which it has been informed by the gatekeeper. To ensure the necessary transparency and usefulness of such information for different purposes provided for by this Regulation, gatekeepers should provide at least information about the undertakings concerned by the concentration, their Union and worldwide annual turnover,

their field of activity, including activities directly related to the concentration, the transaction value or an estimation thereof, a summary of the concentration, including its nature and rationale, as well as a list of the Member States concerned by the operation.

(72) The data protection and privacy interests of end users are relevant to any assessment of potential negative effects of the observed practice of gatekeepers to collect and accumulate large amounts of data from end users. Ensuring an adequate level of transparency of profiling practices employed by gatekeepers, including, but not limited to, profiling within the meaning of Article 4, point (4), of Regulation (EU) 2016/679, facilitates contestability of core platform services. Transparency puts external pressure on gatekeepers not to make deep consumer profiling the industry standard, given that potential entrants or start-ups cannot access data to the same extent and depth, and at a similar scale. Enhanced transparency should allow other undertakings providing core platform services to differentiate themselves better through the use of superior privacy guarantees.

To ensure a minimum level of effectiveness of this transparency obligation, gatekeepers should at least provide an independently audited description of the basis upon which profiling is performed, including whether personal data and data derived from user activity in line with Regulation (EU) 2016/679 is relied on, the processing applied, the purpose for which the profile is prepared and eventually used, the duration of the profiling, the impact of such profiling on the gatekeeper's services, and the steps taken to effectively enable end users to be aware of the relevant use of such profiling, as well as steps to seek their consent or provide them with the possibility of denying or withdrawing consent. The Commission should transfer the audited description to the European Data Protection Board to inform the enforcement of Union data protection rules. The Commission should be empowered to develop the methodology and procedure for the audited description, in consultation with the European Data Protection Supervisor, the European Data Protection Board, civil society and experts, in line with Regulations (EU) No 182/2011[16] and (EU) 2018/1725[17] of the European Parliament and of the Council.

(73) In order to ensure the full and lasting achievement of the objectives of this Regulation, the Commission should be able to assess whether an undertaking providing core platform services should be designated as a gatekeeper without meeting the quantitative thresholds laid down in this Regulation; whether systematic non-compliance by a gatekeeper warrants imposing additional remedies; whether more services within the digital sector should be added to the list of core platform services; and whether additional practices that are similarly unfair and limiting the contestability of digital markets need to be investigated. Such assessment should be based on market investigations to be carried out in an appropriate timeframe, by using clear procedures and deadlines, in order to

[16] Regulation (EU) No 182/2011 of the European Parliament and of the Council of 16 February 2011 laying down the rules and general principles concerning mechanisms for control by the Member States of the Commission's exercise of implementing powers (OJ L 55, 28.2.2011, p. 13).

[17] Regulation (EU) 2018/1725 of the European Parliament and of the Council of 23 October 2018 on the protection of natural persons with regard to the processing of personal data by the Union institutions, bodies, offices and agencies and on the free movement of such data, and repealing Regulation (EC) No 45/2001 and Decision No 1247/2002/EC (OJ L 295, 21.11.2018, p. 39).

support the *ex ante* effect of this Regulation on contestability and fairness in the digital sector, and to provide the requisite degree of legal certainty.

(74) The Commission should be able to find, following a market investigation, that an undertaking providing a core platform service fulfils all of the overarching qualitative criteria for being identified as a gatekeeper. That undertaking should then, in principle, comply with all of the relevant obligations laid down by this Regulation. However, for gatekeepers that have been designated by the Commission because it is foreseeable that they will enjoy an entrenched and durable position in the near future, the Commission should only impose those obligations that are necessary and appropriate to prevent that the gatekeeper concerned achieves an entrenched and durable position in its operations. With respect to such emerging gatekeepers, the Commission should take into account that this status is in principle of a temporary nature, and it should therefore be decided at a given moment whether such an undertaking providing core platform services should be subjected to the full set of gatekeeper obligations because it has acquired an entrenched and durable position, or the conditions for designation are ultimately not met and therefore all previously imposed obligations should be waived.

(75) The Commission should investigate and assess whether additional behavioural, or, where appropriate, structural remedies are justified, in order to ensure that the gatekeeper cannot frustrate the objectives of this Regulation by systematic non-compliance with one or several of the obligations laid down in this Regulation. This is the case where the Commission has issued against a gatekeeper at least three non-compliance decisions within the period of 8 years, which can concern different core platform services and different obligations laid down in this Regulation, and if the gatekeeper has maintained, extended or further strengthened its impact in the internal market, the economic dependency of its business users and end users on the gatekeeper's core platform services or the entrenchment of its position. A gatekeeper should be deemed to have maintained, extended or strengthened its gatekeeper position where, despite the enforcement actions taken by the Commission, that gatekeeper still holds or has further consolidated or entrenched its importance as a gateway for business users to reach end users.

The Commission should in such cases have the power to impose any remedy, whether behavioural or structural, having due regard to the principle of proportionality. In this context, the Commission should have the power to prohibit, to the extent that such remedy is proportionate and necessary in order to maintain or restore fairness and contestability as affected by the systematic non-compliance, during a limited time-period, the gatekeeper from entering into a concentration regarding those core platform services or the other services provided in the digital sector or services enabling the collection of data that are affected by the systematic non-compliance. In order to enable effective involvement of third parties and the possibility to test remedies before its application, the Commission should publish a detailed non-confidential summary of the case and the measures to be taken. The Commission should be able to reopen proceedings, including where the specified remedies turn out not to be effective. A reopening due to ineffective remedies adopted by decision should enable the Commission to amend the remedies prospectively. The Commission should also be able to set a reasonable time period within which it should be possible to reopen the proceedings if the remedies prove not to be effective.

(76) Where, in the course of an investigation into systematic non-compliance, a gatekeeper offers commitments to the Commission, the latter should be able to adopt a decision making these commitments binding on the gatekeeper concerned, where it finds that the commitments ensure effective compliance with the obligations set out in this Regulation. That decision should also find that there are no longer grounds for action by the Commission as regards the systematic non-compliance under investigation. In assessing whether the commitments offered by the gatekeeper are sufficient to ensure effective compliance with the obligations under this Regulation, the Commission should be allowed to take into account tests undertaken by the gatekeeper to demonstrate the effectiveness of the offered commitments in practice. The Commission should verify that the commitments decision is fully respected and reaches its objectives, and should be entitled to reopen the decision if it finds that the commitments are not effective.

(77) The services in the digital sector and the types of practices relating to these services can change quickly and to a significant extent. To ensure that this Regulation remains up to date and constitutes an effective and holistic regulatory response to the problems posed by gatekeepers, it is important to provide for a regular review of the lists of core platform services, as well as of the obligations provided for in this Regulation. This is particularly important to ensure that a practice that is likely to limit the contestability of core platform services or is unfair is identified. While it is important to conduct a review on a regular basis, given the dynamically changing nature of the digital sector, in order to ensure legal certainty as to the regulatory conditions, any reviews should be conducted within a reasonable and appropriate timeframe. Market investigations should also ensure that the Commission has a solid evidentiary basis on which it can assess whether it should propose to amend this Regulation in order to review, expand, or further detail, the lists of core platform services. They should equally ensure that the Commission has a solid evidentiary basis on which it can assess whether it should propose to amend the obligations laid down in this Regulation or whether it should adopt a delegated act updating such obligations.

(78) With regard to conduct by gatekeepers that is not covered by the obligations set out in this Regulation, the Commission should have the possibility to open a market investigation into new services and new practices for the purposes of identifying whether the obligations set out in this Regulation are to be supplemented by means of a delegated act falling within the scope of the empowerment set out for such delegated acts in this Regulation, or by presenting a proposal to amend this Regulation. This is without prejudice to the possibility for the Commission to, in appropriate cases, open proceedings under Article 101 or 102 TFEU. Such proceedings should be conducted in accordance with Council Regulation (EC) No 1/2003[18]. In cases of urgency due to the risk of serious and irreparable damage to competition, the Commission should consider adopting interim measures in accordance with Article 8 of Regulation (EC) No 1/2003.

(79) In the event that gatekeepers engage in a practice that is unfair or that limits the contestability of the core platform services that are already designated under this Regulation but without such practices being explicitly covered by the obligations laid down by this Regulation, the Commission should be able to update this

[18] Council Regulation (EC) No 1/2003 of 16 December 2002 on the implementation of the rules on competition laid down in Articles 81 and 82 of the Treaty (OJ L 1, 4.1.2003, p. 1).

Regulation through delegated acts. Such updates by way of delegated act should be subject to the same investigatory standard and therefore should be preceded by a market investigation. The Commission should also apply a predefined standard in identifying such types of practices. This legal standard should ensure that the type of obligations that gatekeepers could at any time face under this Regulation are sufficiently predictable.

(80) In order to ensure effective implementation and compliance with this Regulation, the Commission should have strong investigative and enforcement powers, to allow it to investigate, enforce and monitor the rules laid down in this Regulation, while at the same time ensuring the respect for the fundamental right to be heard and to have access to the file in the context of the enforcement proceedings. The Commission should dispose of these investigative powers also for the purpose of carrying out market investigations, including for the purpose of updating and reviewing this Regulation.

(81) The Commission should be empowered to request information necessary for the purpose of this Regulation. In particular, the Commission should have access to any relevant documents, data, database, algorithm and information necessary to open and conduct investigations and to monitor the compliance with the obligations laid down in this Regulation, irrespective of who possesses such information, and regardless of their form or format, their storage medium, or the place where they are stored.

(82) The Commission should be able to directly request that undertakings or associations of undertakings provide any relevant evidence, data and information. In addition, the Commission should be able to request any relevant information from competent authorities within the Member State, or from any natural person or legal person for the purpose of this Regulation. When complying with a decision of the Commission, undertakings are obliged to answer factual questions and to provide documents.

(83) The Commission should also be empowered to conduct inspections of any undertaking or association of undertakings and to interview any persons who could be in possession of useful information and to record the statements made.

(84) Interim measures can be an important tool to ensure that, while an investigation is ongoing, the infringement being investigated does not lead to serious and irreparable damage for business users or end users of gatekeepers. This tool is important to avoid developments that could be very difficult to reverse by a decision taken by the Commission at the end of the proceedings. The Commission should therefore have the power to order interim measures in the context of proceedings opened in view of the possible adoption of a non-compliance decision. This power should apply in cases where the Commission has made a *prima facie* finding of infringement of obligations by gatekeepers and where there is a risk of serious and irreparable damage for business users or end users of gatekeepers. Interim measures should only apply for a specified period, either one ending with the conclusion of the proceedings by the Commission, or for a fixed period which can be renewed insofar as it is necessary and appropriate.

(85) The Commission should be able to take the necessary actions to monitor the effective implementation of and compliance with the obligations laid down in this Regulation. Such actions should include the ability of the Commission to

appoint independent external experts and auditors to assist the Commission in this process, including, where applicable, from competent authorities of the Member States, such as data or consumer protection authorities. When appointing auditors, the Commission should ensure sufficient rotation.

(86) Compliance with the obligations imposed by this Regulation should be enforceable by means of fines and periodic penalty payments. To that end, appropriate levels of fines and periodic penalty payments should also be laid down for non-compliance with the obligations and breach of the procedural rules subject to appropriate limitation periods, in accordance with the principles of proportionality and *ne bis in idem*. The Commission and the relevant national authorities should coordinate their enforcement efforts in order to ensure that those principles are respected. In particular, the Commission should take into account any fines and penalties imposed on the same legal person for the same facts through a final decision in proceedings relating to an infringement of other Union or national rules, so as to ensure that the overall fines and penalties imposed correspond to the seriousness of the infringements committed.

(87) In order to ensure effective recovery of fines imposed on associations of undertakings for infringements that they have committed, it is necessary to lay down the conditions on which it should be possible for the Commission to require payment of the fine from the members of that association of undertakings where it is not solvent.

(88) In the context of proceedings carried out under this Regulation, the undertaking concerned should be accorded the right to be heard by the Commission and the decisions taken should be widely publicised. While ensuring the rights to good administration, the right of access to the file and the right to be heard, it is essential to protect confidential information. Furthermore, while respecting the confidentiality of the information, the Commission should ensure that any information on which the decision is based is disclosed to an extent that allows the addressee of the decision to understand the facts and considerations that led to the decision. It is also necessary to ensure that the Commission only uses information collected pursuant to this Regulation for the purposes of this Regulation, except where specifically envisaged otherwise. Finally, it should be possible, under certain conditions, for certain business records, such as communication between lawyers and their clients, to be considered confidential if the relevant conditions are met.

(89) When preparing non-confidential summaries for publication in order to effectively enable interested third parties to provide comments, the Commission should give due regard to the legitimate interest of undertakings in the protection of their business secrets and other confidential information.

(90) The coherent, effective and complementary enforcement of available legal instruments applied to gatekeepers requires cooperation and coordination between the Commission and national authorities within the remit of their competences. The Commission and national authorities should cooperate and coordinate their actions necessary for the enforcement of the available legal instruments applied to gatekeepers within the meaning of this Regulation and respect the principle of sincere cooperation laid down in Article 4 of the Treaty on European Union (TEU). It should be possible for the support from national authorities to the

Commission to include providing the Commission with all necessary information in their possession or assisting the Commission, at its request, with the exercise of its powers so that the Commission is better able to carry out its duties under this Regulation.

(91) The Commission is the sole authority empowered to enforce this Regulation. In order to support the Commission, it should be possible for Member States to empower their national competent authorities enforcing competition rules to conduct investigations into possible non-compliance by gatekeepers with certain obligations under this Regulation. This could in particular be relevant for cases where it cannot be determined from the outset whether a gatekeeper's behaviour is capable of infringing this Regulation, the competition rules which the national competent authority is empowered to enforce, or both. The national competent authority enforcing competition rules should report on its findings on possible non-compliance by gatekeepers with certain obligations under this Regulation to the Commission in view of the Commission opening proceedings to investigate any non-compliance as the sole enforcer of the provisions laid down by this Regulation.

The Commission should have full discretion to decide whether to open such proceedings. In order to avoid overlapping investigations under this Regulation, the national competent authority concerned should inform the Commission before taking its first investigative measure into a possible non-compliance by gatekeepers with certain obligations under this Regulation. The national competent authorities should also closely cooperate and coordinate with the Commission when enforcing national competition rules against gatekeepers, including with regard to the setting of fines. To that end, they should inform the Commission when initiating proceedings based on national competition rules against gatekeepers, as well as prior to imposing obligations on gatekeepers in such proceedings. In order to avoid duplication, it should be possible for information of the draft decision pursuant to Article 11 of Regulation (EC) No 1/2003, where applicable, to serve as notification under this Regulation.

(92) In order to safeguard the harmonised application and enforcement of this Regulation, it is important to ensure that national authorities, including national courts, have all necessary information to ensure that their decisions do not run counter to a decision adopted by the Commission under this Regulation. National courts should be allowed to ask the Commission to send them information or opinions on questions concerning the application of this Regulation. At the same time, the Commission should be able to submit oral or written observations to national courts. This is without prejudice to the ability of national courts to request a preliminary ruling under Article 267 TFEU.

(93) In order to ensure coherence and effective complementarity in the implementation of this Regulation and of other sectoral regulations applicable to gatekeepers, the Commission should benefit from the expertise of a dedicated high-level group. It should be possible for that high-level group to also assist the Commission by means of advice, expertise and recommendations, when relevant, in general matters relating to the implementation or enforcement of this Regulation. The high-level group should be composed of the relevant European bodies and networks, and its composition should ensure a high level of expertise and a geographical balance. The members of the high-level group should regularly report

to the bodies and networks they represent regarding the tasks performed in the context of the group, and consult them in that regard.

(94) Since the decisions taken by the Commission under this Regulation are subject to review by the Court of Justice in accordance with the TFEU, in accordance with Article 261 TFEU, the Court of Justice should have unlimited jurisdiction in respect of fines and penalty payments.

(95) It should be possible for the Commission to develop guidelines to provide further guidance on different aspects of this Regulation or to assist undertakings providing core platform services in the implementation of the obligations under this Regulation. It should be possible for such guidance to be based in particular on the experience that the Commission obtains through the monitoring of compliance with this Regulation. The issuing of any guidelines under this Regulation is a prerogative and at the sole discretion of the Commission and should not be considered to be a constitutive element in ensuring that the undertakings or associations of undertakings concerned comply with the obligations under this Regulation.

(96) The implementation of some of the gatekeepers' obligations, such as those related to data access, data portability or interoperability could be facilitated by the use of technical standards. In this respect, it should be possible for the Commission, where appropriate and necessary, to request European standardisation bodies to develop them.

(97) In order to ensure contestable and fair markets in the digital sector across the Union where gatekeepers are present, the power to adopt acts in accordance with Article 290 TFEU should be delegated to the Commission in respect of amending the methodology for determining whether the quantitative thresholds regarding active end users and active business users for the designation of gatekeepers are met, which is contained in an Annex to this Regulation, in respect of further specifying the additional elements of the methodology not falling in that Annex for determining whether the quantitative thresholds regarding the designation of gatekeepers are met, and in respect of supplementing the existing obligations laid down in this Regulation where, based on a market investigation, the Commission has identified the need for updating the obligations addressing practices that limit the contestability of core platform services or are unfair, and the update considered falls within the scope of the empowerment set out for such delegated acts in this Regulation.

(98) When adopting delegated acts under this Regulation, it is of particular importance that the Commission carries out appropriate consultations during its preparatory work, including at expert level, and that those consultations be conducted in accordance with the principles laid down in the Interinstitutional Agreement of 13 April 2016 on Better Law-Making[19]. In particular, to ensure equal participation in the preparation of delegated acts, the European Parliament and the Council should receive all documents at the same time as Member States' experts, and their experts systematically have access to meetings of Commission expert groups dealing with the preparation of delegated acts.

[19] OJ L 123, 12.5.2016, p. 1.

(99) In order to ensure uniform conditions for the implementation of this Regulation, implementing powers should be conferred on the Commission to specify measures to be implemented by gatekeepers in order to effectively comply with the obligations under this Regulation; to suspend, in whole or in part, a specific obligation imposed on a gatekeeper; to exempt a gatekeeper, in whole or in part, from a specific obligation; to specify the measures to be implemented by a gatekeeper when it circumvents the obligations under this Regulation; to conclude a market investigation for designating gatekeepers; to impose remedies in the case of systematic non-compliance; to order interim measures against a gatekeeper; to make commitments binding on a gatekeeper; to set out its finding of a non-compliance; to set the definitive amount of the periodic penalty payment; to determine the form, content and other details of notifications, submissions of information, reasoned requests and regulatory reports transmitted by gatekeepers; to lay down operational and technical arrangements in view of implementing interoperability and the methodology and procedure for the audited description of techniques used for profiling consumers; to provide for practical arrangements for proceedings, extensions of deadlines, exercising rights during proceedings, terms of disclosure, as well as for the cooperation and coordination between the Commission and national authorities. Those powers should be exercised in accordance with Regulation (EU) No 182/2011.

(100) The examination procedure should be used for the adoption of an implementing act on the practical arrangements for the cooperation and coordination between the Commission and Member States. The advisory procedure should be used for the remaining implementing acts envisaged by this Regulation. This is justified by the fact that those remaining implementing acts relate to practical aspects of the procedures laid down in this Regulation, such as form, content and other details of various procedural steps, to practical arrangements of different procedural steps, such as, for example, extension of procedural deadlines or right to be heard, as well as to individual implementing decisions addressed to a gatekeeper.

(101) In accordance with Regulation (EU) No 182/2011, each Member State should be represented in the advisory committee and decide on the composition of its delegation. Such delegation can include, *inter alia*, experts from the competent authorities within the Member States, which hold the relevant expertise for a specific issue presented to the advisory committee.

(102) Whistleblowers can bring new information to the attention of competent authorities which can help the competent authorities detect infringements of this Regulation and enable them to impose penalties. It should be ensured that adequate arrangements are in place to enable whistleblowers to alert the competent authorities to actual or potential infringements of this Regulation and to protect the whistleblowers from retaliation. For that purpose, it should be provided in this Regulation that Directive (EU) 2019/1937 of the European Parliament and of the Council[20] is applicable to the reporting of breaches of this Regulation and to the protection of persons reporting such breaches.

(103) To enhance legal certainty, the applicability, pursuant to this Regulation, of Directive (EU) 2019/1937 to reports of breaches of this Regulation and to the protec-

[20] Directive (EU) 2019/1937 of the European Parliament and of the Council of 23 October 2019 on the protection of persons who report breaches of Union law (OJ L 305, 26.11.2019, p. 17).

tion of persons reporting such breaches should be reflected in that Directive. The Annex to Directive (EU) 2019/1937 should therefore be amended accordingly. It is for the Member States to ensure that that amendment is reflected in their transposition measures adopted in accordance with Directive (EU) 2019/1937, although the adoption of national transposition measures is not a condition for the applicability of that Directive to the reporting of breaches of this Regulation and to the protection of reporting persons from the date of application of this Regulation.

(104) Consumers should be entitled to enforce their rights in relation to the obligations imposed on gatekeepers under this Regulation through representative actions in accordance with Directive (EU) 2020/1828 of the European Parliament and of the Council[21]. For that purpose, this Regulation should provide that Directive (EU) 2020/1828 is applicable to the representative actions brought against infringements by gatekeepers of provisions of this Regulation that harm or can harm the collective interests of consumers. The Annex to that Directive should therefore be amended accordingly. It is for the Member States to ensure that that amendment is reflected in their transposition measures adopted in accordance with Directive (EU) 2020/1828, although the adoption of national transposition measures in this regard is not a condition for the applicability of that Directive to those representative actions. The applicability of Directive (EU) 2020/1828 to the representative actions brought against infringements by gatekeepers of provisions of this Regulation that harm or can harm the collective interests of consumers should start from the date of application of Member States' laws, regulations and administrative provisions necessary to transpose that Directive, or from the date of application of this Regulation, whichever is the later.

(105) The Commission should periodically evaluate this Regulation and closely monitor its effects on the contestability and fairness of commercial relationships in the online platform economy, in particular with a view to determining the need for amendments in light of relevant technological or commercial developments. That evaluation should include the regular review of the list of core platform services and the obligations addressed to gatekeepers, as well as their enforcement, in view of ensuring that digital markets across the Union are contestable and fair. In that context, the Commission should also evaluate the scope of the obligation concerning the interoperability of number-independent electronic communications services. In order to obtain a broad view of developments in the digital sector, the evaluation should take into account the experiences of Member States and relevant stakeholders. It should be possible for the Commission in this regard also to consider the opinions and reports presented to it by the Observatory on the Online Platform Economy that was first established by Commission Decision C(2018)2393 of 26 April 2018. Following the evaluation, the Commission should take appropriate measures. The Commission should maintain a high level of protection and respect for the common rights and values, particularly equality and non-discrimination, as an objective when conducting the assessments and reviews of the practices and obligations provided in this Regulation.

[21] Directive (EU) 2020/1828 of the European Parliament and of the Council of 25 November 2020 on representative actions for the protection of the collective interests of consumers and repealing Directive 2009/22/EC (OJ L 409, 4.12.2020, p. 1).

(106) Without prejudice to the budgetary procedure and through existing financial instruments, adequate human, financial and technical resources should be allocated to the Commission to ensure that it can effectively perform its duties and exercise its powers in respect of the enforcement of this Regulation.

(107) Since the objective of this Regulation, namely to ensure a contestable and fair digital sector in general and core platform services in particular, with a view to promoting innovation, high quality of digital products and services, fair and competitive prices, as well as a high quality and choice for end users in the digital sector, cannot be sufficiently achieved by the Member States, but can rather, by reason of the business model and operations of the gatekeepers and the scale and effects of their operations, be better achieved at Union level, the Union may adopt measures, in accordance with the principle of subsidiarity as set out in Article 5 TEU. In accordance with the principle of proportionality, as set out in that Article, this Regulation does not go beyond what is necessary in order to achieve that objective.

(108) The European Data Protection Supervisor was consulted in accordance with Article 42 of Regulation (EU) 2018/1725 and delivered an opinion on 10 February 2021[22].

(109) This Regulation respects the fundamental rights and observes the principles recognised by the Charter of Fundamental Rights of the European Union, in particular Articles 16, 47 and 50 thereof. Accordingly, the interpretation and application of this Regulation should respect those rights and principles,

HAVE ADOPTED THIS REGULATION:

CHAPTER I
SUBJECT MATTER, SCOPE AND DEFINITIONS

Article 1
Subject matter and scope

1. The purpose of this Regulation is to contribute to the proper functioning of the internal market by laying down harmonised rules ensuring for all businesses, contestable and fair markets in the digital sector across the Union where gatekeepers are present, to the benefit of business users and end users.

2. This Regulation shall apply to core platform services provided or offered by gatekeepers to business users established in the Union or end users established or located in the Union, irrespective of the place of establishment or residence of the gatekeepers and irrespective of the law otherwise applicable to the provision of service.

3. This Regulation shall not apply to markets related to:

(a) electronic communications networks as defined in Article 2, point (1), of Directive (EU) 2018/1972;

(b) electronic communications services as defined in Article 2, point (4), of Directive (EU) 2018/1972, other than those related to number-independent interpersonal communications services.

---

[22] OJ C 147, 26.4.2021, p. 4.

4. With regard to interpersonal communications services as defined in Article 2, point (5) of Directive (EU) 2018/1972, this Regulation is without prejudice to the powers and responsibilities granted to the national regulatory and other competent authorities by virtue of Article 61 of that Directive.

5. In order to avoid the fragmentation of the internal market, Member States shall not impose further obligations on gatekeepers by way of laws, regulations or administrative measures for the purpose of ensuring contestable and fair markets. Nothing in this Regulation precludes Member States from imposing obligations on undertakings, including undertakings providing core platform services, for matters falling outside the scope of this Regulation, provided that those obligations are compatible with Union law and do not result from the fact that the relevant undertakings have the status of a gatekeeper within the meaning of this Regulation.

6. This Regulation is without prejudice to the application of Articles 101 and 102 TFEU. It is also without prejudice to the application of:

(a) national competition rules prohibiting anti-competitive agreements, decisions by associations of undertakings, concerted practices and abuses of dominant positions;
(b) national competition rules prohibiting other forms of unilateral conduct insofar as they are applied to undertakings other than gatekeepers or amount to the imposition of further obligations on gatekeepers; and
(c) Council Regulation (EC) No 139/2004[1] and national rules concerning merger control.

7. National authorities shall not take decisions which run counter to a decision adopted by the Commission under this Regulation. The Commission and Member States shall work in close cooperation and coordinate their enforcement actions on the basis of the principles established in Articles 37 and 38.

Article 2
Definitions

For the purposes of this Regulation, the following definitions apply:

(1) 'gatekeeper' means an undertaking providing core platform services, designated pursuant to Article 3;
(2) 'core platform service' means any of the following:
    (a) online intermediation services;
    (b) online search engines;
    (c) online social networking services;
    (d) video-sharing platform services;
    (e) number-independent interpersonal communications services;
    (f) operating systems;
    (g) web browsers;
    (h) virtual assistants;
    (i) cloud computing services;
    (j) online advertising services, including any advertising networks, advertising exchanges and any other advertising intermediation services, provided by an

[1] Council Regulation (EC) No 139/2004 of 20 January 2004 on the control of concentrations between undertakings (the EC Merger Regulation) (OJ L 24, 29.1.2004, p. 1).

undertaking that provides any of the core platform services listed in points (a) to (i);

(3) 'information society service' means any service as defined in Article 1(1), point (b), of Directive (EU) 2015/1535;

(4) 'digital sector' means the sector of products and services provided by means of, or through, information society services;

(5) 'online intermediation services' means online intermediation services as defined in Article 2, point (2), of Regulation (EU) 2019/1150;

(6) 'online search engine' means an online search engine as defined in Article 2, point (5), of Regulation (EU) 2019/1150;

(7) 'online social networking service' means a platform that enables end users to connect and communicate with each other, share content and discover other users and content across multiple devices and, in particular, via chats, posts, videos and recommendations;

(8) 'video-sharing platform service' means a video-sharing platform service as defined in Article 1(1), point (aa), of Directive 2010/13/EU;

(9) 'number-independent interpersonal communications service' means a number-independent interpersonal communications service as defined in Article 2, point (7), of Directive (EU) 2018/1972;

(10) 'operating system' means a system software that controls the basic functions of the hardware or software and enables software applications to run on it;

(11) 'web browser' means a software application that enables end users to access and interact with web content hosted on servers that are connected to networks such as the Internet, including standalone web browsers as well as web browsers integrated or embedded in software or similar;

(12) 'virtual assistant' means a software that can process demands, tasks or questions, including those based on audio, visual, written input, gestures or motions, and that, based on those demands, tasks or questions, provides access to other services or controls connected physical devices;

(13) 'cloud computing service' means a cloud computing service as defined in Article 4, point (19), of Directive (EU) 2016/1148 of the European Parliament and of the Council[1];

(14) 'software application stores' means a type of online intermediation services, which is focused on software applications as the intermediated product or service;

(15) 'software application' means any digital product or service that runs on an operating system;

(16) 'payment service' means a payment service as defined in Article 4, point (3) of Directive (EU) 2015/2366;

(17) 'technical service supporting payment service' means a service within the meaning of Article 3, point (j), of Directive (EU) 2015/2366;

(18) 'payment system for in-app purchases' means a software application, service or user interface which facilitates purchases of digital content or digital services within a software application, including content, subscriptions, features or functionality, and the payments for such purchases;

(19) 'identification service' means a type of service provided together with or in support of core platform services that enables any type of verification of the identity of end users or business users, regardless of the technology used;

[1] Directive (EU) 2016/1148 of the European Parliament and of the Council of 6 July 2016 concerning measures for a high common level of security of network and information systems across the Union (OJ L 194, 19.7.2016, p. 1).

(20) 'end user' means any natural or legal person using core platform services other than as a business user;
(21) 'business user' means any natural or legal person acting in a commercial or professional capacity using core platform services for the purpose of or in the course of providing goods or services to end users;
(22) 'ranking' means the relative prominence given to goods or services offered through online intermediation services, online social networking services, video-sharing platform services or virtual assistants, or the relevance given to search results by online search engines, as presented, organised or communicated by the undertakings providing online intermediation services, online social networking services, video-sharing platform services, virtual assistants or online search engines, irrespective of the technological means used for such presentation, organisation or communication and irrespective of whether only one result is presented or communicated;
(23) 'search results' means any information in any format, including textual, graphic, vocal or other outputs, returned in response to, and related to, a search query, irrespective of whether the information returned is a paid or an unpaid result, a direct answer or any product, service or information offered in connection with the organic results, or displayed along with or partly or entirely embedded in them;
(24) 'data' means any digital representation of acts, facts or information and any compilation of such acts, facts or information, including in the form of sound, visual or audiovisual recording;
(25) 'personal data' means personal data as defined in Article 4, point (1), of Regulation (EU) 2016/679;
(26) 'non-personal data' means data other than personal data;
(27) 'undertaking' means an entity engaged in an economic activity, regardless of its legal status and the way in which it is financed, including all linked enterprises or connected undertakings that form a group through the direct or indirect control of an enterprise or undertaking by another;
(28) 'control' means the possibility of exercising decisive influence on an undertaking, within the meaning of Article 3(2) of Regulation (EC) No 139/2004;
(29) 'interoperability' means the ability to exchange information and mutually use the information which has been exchanged through interfaces or other solutions, so that all elements of hardware or software work with other hardware and software and with users in all the ways in which they are intended to function;
(30) 'turnover' means the amount derived by an undertaking within the meaning of Article 5(1) of Regulation (EC) No 139/2004;
(31) 'profiling' means profiling as defined in Article 4, point (4), of Regulation (EU) 2016/679;
(32) 'consent' means consent as defined in Article 4, point (11), of Regulation (EU) 2016/679;
(33) 'national court' means a court or tribunal of a Member State within the meaning of Article 267 TFEU.

CHAPTER II
GATEKEEPERS

Article 3
Designation of gatekeepers

1. An undertaking shall be designated as a gatekeeper if:

(a) it has a significant impact on the internal market;
(b) it provides a core platform service which is an important gateway for business users to reach end users; and
(c) it enjoys an entrenched and durable position, in its operations, or it is foreseeable that it will enjoy such a position in the near future.

2. An undertaking shall be presumed to satisfy the respective requirements in paragraph 1:

(a) as regards paragraph 1, point (a), where it achieves an annual Union turnover equal to or above EUR 7,5 billion in each of the last three financial years, or where its average market capitalisation or its equivalent fair market value amounted to at least EUR 75 billion in the last financial year, and it provides the same core platform service in at least three Member States;
(b) as regards paragraph 1, point (b), where it provides a core platform service that in the last financial year has at least 45 million monthly active end users established or located in the Union and at least 10 000 yearly active business users established in the Union, identified and calculated in accordance with the methodology and indicators set out in the Annex;
(c) as regards paragraph 1, point (c), where the thresholds in point (b) of this paragraph were met in each of the last three financial years.

3. Where an undertaking providing core platform services meets all of the thresholds in paragraph 2, it shall notify the Commission thereof without delay and in any event within 2 months after those thresholds are met and provide it with the relevant information identified in paragraph 2. That notification shall include the relevant information identified in paragraph 2 for each of the core platform services of the undertaking that meets the thresholds in paragraph 2, point (b). Whenever a further core platform service provided by the undertaking that has previously been designated as a gatekeeper meets the thresholds in paragraph 2, points (b) and (c), such undertaking shall notify the Commission thereof within 2 months after those thresholds are satisfied.

Where the undertaking providing the core platform service fails to notify the Commission pursuant to the first subparagraph of this paragraph and fails to provide within the deadline set by the Commission in the request for information pursuant to Article 21 all the relevant information that is required for the Commission to designate the undertaking concerned as gatekeeper pursuant to paragraph 4 of this Article, the Commission shall still be entitled to designate that undertaking as a gatekeeper, based on information available to the Commission.

Where the undertaking providing core platform services complies with the request for information pursuant to the second subparagraph of this paragraph or where the information is provided after the expiration of the deadline referred to in that subparagraph, the Commission shall apply the procedure set out in paragraph 4.

4. The Commission shall designate as a gatekeeper, without undue delay and at the latest within 45 working days after receiving the complete information referred to in paragraph 3, an undertaking providing core platform services that meets all the thresholds in paragraph 2.

5. The undertaking providing core platform services may present, with its notification, sufficiently substantiated arguments to demonstrate that, exceptionally, although it meets all the thresholds in paragraph 2, due to the circumstances in which the relevant core platform service operates, it does not satisfy the requirements listed in paragraph 1.

Where the Commission considers that the arguments submitted pursuant to the first subparagraph by the undertaking providing core platform services are not sufficiently substantiated because they do not manifestly call into question the presumptions set out in paragraph 2 of this Article, it may reject those arguments within the time limit referred to in paragraph 4, without applying the procedure laid down in Article 17(3).

Where the undertaking providing core platform services does present such sufficiently substantiated arguments manifestly calling into question the presumptions in paragraph 2 of this Article, the Commission may, notwithstanding the first subparagraph of this paragraph, within the time limit referred to in paragraph 4 of this Article, open the procedure laid down in Article 17(3).

If the Commission concludes that the undertaking providing core platform services was not able to demonstrate that the relevant core platform services that it provides do not satisfy the requirements of paragraph 1 of this Article, it shall designate that undertaking as a gatekeeper in accordance with the procedure laid down in Article 17(3).

6. The Commission is empowered to adopt delegated acts in accordance with Article 49 to supplement this Regulation by specifying the methodology for determining whether the quantitative thresholds laid down in paragraph 2 of this Article are met, and to regularly adjust that methodology to market and technological developments, where necessary.

7. The Commission is empowered to adopt delegated acts in accordance with Article 49 to amend this Regulation by updating the methodology and the list of indicators set out in the Annex.

8. The Commission shall designate as a gatekeeper, in accordance with the procedure laid down in Article 17, any undertaking providing core platform services that meets each of the requirements of paragraph 1 of this Article, but does not satisfy each of the thresholds in paragraph 2 of this Article.

For that purpose, the Commission shall take into account some or all of the following elements, insofar as they are relevant for the undertaking providing core platform services under consideration:

(a) the size, including turnover and market capitalisation, operations and position of that undertaking;
(b) the number of business users using the core platform service to reach end users and the number of end users;
(c) network effects and data driven advantages, in particular in relation to that undertaking's access to, and collection of, personal data and non-personal data or analytics capabilities;
(d) any scale and scope effects from which the undertaking benefits, including with regard to data, and, where relevant, to its activities outside the Union;
(e) business user or end user lock-in, including switching costs and behavioural bias reducing the ability of business users and end users to switch or multi-home;

(f) a conglomerate corporate structure or vertical integration of that undertaking, for instance enabling that undertaking to cross subsidise, to combine data from different sources or to leverage its position; or
(g) other structural business or service characteristics.

In carrying out its assessment under this paragraph, the Commission shall take into account foreseeable developments in relation to the elements listed in the second subparagraph, including any planned concentrations involving another undertaking providing core platform services or providing any other services in the digital sector or enabling the collection of data.

Where an undertaking providing a core platform service that does not satisfy the quantitative thresholds of paragraph 2 fails to comply with the investigative measures ordered by the Commission in a significant manner, and that failure persists after that undertaking has been invited to comply within a reasonable time limit and to submit observations, the Commission may designate that undertaking as a gatekeeper on the basis of the facts available to the Commission.

9. For each undertaking designated as a gatekeeper pursuant to paragraph 4 or 8, the Commission shall list in the designation decision the relevant core platform services that are provided within that undertaking and which individually are an important gateway for business users to reach end users as referred to in paragraph 1, point (b).

10. The gatekeeper shall comply with the obligations laid down in Articles 5, 6 and 7 within 6 months after a core platform service has been listed in the designation decision pursuant to paragraph 9 of this Article.

Article 4
Review of the status of gatekeeper

1. The Commission may, upon request or on its own initiative, reconsider, amend or repeal at any moment a designation decision adopted pursuant to Article 3 for one of the following reasons:

(a) there has been a substantial change in any of the facts on which the designation decision was based;
(b) the designation decision was based on incomplete, incorrect or misleading information.

2. The Commission shall regularly, and at least every 3 years, review whether the gatekeepers continue to satisfy the requirements laid down in Article 3(1). That review shall also examine whether the list of core platform services of the gatekeeper which are individually an important gateway for business users to reach end users, as referred to in Article 3(1), point (b), needs to be amended. Those reviews shall have no suspending effect on the gatekeeper's obligations.

The Commission shall also examine at least every year whether new undertakings providing core platform services satisfy those requirements.

Where the Commission, on the basis of the reviews pursuant to the first subparagraph, finds that the facts on which the designation of the undertakings providing core platform services as gatekeepers was based, have changed, it shall adopt a decision confirming, amending or repealing the designation decision.

3. The Commission shall publish and update a list of gatekeepers and the list of the core platform services for which they need to comply with the obligations laid down in Chapter III on an on-going basis.

CHAPTER III
PRACTICES OF GATEKEEPERS THAT LIMIT CONTESTABILITY OR ARE UNFAIR

Article 5
Obligations for gatekeepers

1. The gatekeeper shall comply with all obligations set out in this Article with respect to each of its core platform services listed in the designation decision pursuant to Article 3(9).

2. The gatekeeper shall not do any of the following:

(a) process, for the purpose of providing online advertising services, personal data of end users using services of third parties that make use of core platform services of the gatekeeper;
(b) combine personal data from the relevant core platform service with personal data from any further core platform services or from any other services provided by the gatekeeper or with personal data from third-party services;
(c) cross-use personal data from the relevant core platform service in other services provided separately by the gatekeeper, including other core platform services, and vice versa; and
(d) sign in end users to other services of the gatekeeper in order to combine personal data,

unless the end user has been presented with the specific choice and has given consent within the meaning of Article 4, point (11), and Article 7 of Regulation (EU) 2016/679.

Where the consent given for the purposes of the first subparagraph has been refused or withdrawn by the end user, the gatekeeper shall not repeat its request for consent for the same purpose more than once within a period of one year.

This paragraph is without prejudice to the possibility for the gatekeeper to rely on Article 6(1), points (c), (d) and (e) of Regulation (EU) 2016/679, where applicable.

3. The gatekeeper shall not prevent business users from offering the same products or services to end users through third-party online intermediation services or through their own direct online sales channel at prices or conditions that are different from those offered through the online intermediation services of the gatekeeper.

4. The gatekeeper shall allow business users, free of charge, to communicate and promote offers, including under different conditions, to end users acquired via its core platform service or through other channels, and to conclude contracts with those end users, regardless of whether, for that purpose, they use the core platform services of the gatekeeper.

5. The gatekeeper shall allow end users to access and use, through its core platform services, content, subscriptions, features or other items, by using the software application of a business user, including where those end users acquired such items from the relevant business user without using the core platform services of the gatekeeper.

6. The gatekeeper shall not directly or indirectly prevent or restrict business users or end users from raising any issue of non-compliance with the relevant Union or national law by the gatekeeper with any relevant public authority, including national courts, related to any practice of the gatekeeper. This is without prejudice to the right of business users and gatekeepers to lay down in their agreements the terms of use of lawful complaints-handling mechanisms.

7. The gatekeeper shall not require end users to use, or business users to use, to offer, or to interoperate with, an identification service, a web browser engine or a payment service, or technical services that support the provision of payment services, such as payment systems for in-app purchases, of that gatekeeper in the context of services provided by the business users using that gatekeeper's core platform services.

8. The gatekeeper shall not require business users or end users to subscribe to, or register with, any further core platform services listed in the designation decision pursuant to Article 3(9) or which meet the thresholds in Article 3(2), point (b), as a condition for being able to use, access, sign up for or registering with any of that gatekeeper's core platform services listed pursuant to that Article.

9. The gatekeeper shall provide each advertiser to which it supplies online advertising services, or third parties authorised by advertisers, upon the advertiser's request, with information on a daily basis free of charge, concerning each advertisement placed by the advertiser, regarding:

(a) the price and fees paid by that advertiser, including any deductions and surcharges, for each of the relevant online advertising services provided by the gatekeeper,
(b) the remuneration received by the publisher, including any deductions and surcharges, subject to the publisher's consent; and
(c) the metrics on which each of the prices, fees and remunerations are calculated.

In the event that a publisher does not consent to the sharing of information regarding the remuneration received, as referred to in point (b) of the first subparagraph, the gatekeeper shall provide each advertiser free of charge with information concerning the daily average remuneration received by that publisher, including any deductions and surcharges, for the relevant advertisements.

10. The gatekeeper shall provide each publisher to which it supplies online advertising services, or third parties authorised by publishers, upon the publisher's request, with free of charge information on a daily basis, concerning each advertisement displayed on the publisher's inventory, regarding:

(a) the remuneration received and the fees paid by that publisher, including any deductions and surcharges, for each of the relevant online advertising services provided by the gatekeeper;
(b) the price paid by the advertiser, including any deductions and surcharges, subject to the advertiser's consent; and
(c) the metrics on which each of the prices and remunerations are calculated.

In the event an advertiser does not consent to the sharing of information, the gatekeeper shall provide each publisher free of charge with information concerning the daily average price paid by that advertiser, including any deductions and surcharges, for the relevant advertisements.

Article 6
Obligations for gatekeepers susceptible of being further specified under Article 8

1. The Gatekeeper shall comply with all obligations set out in this Article with respect to each of its core platform services listed in the designation decision pursuant to Article 3(9).

2. The gatekeeper shall not use, in competition with business users, any data that is not publicly available that is generated or provided by those business users in the context of their use of the relevant core platform services or of the services provided together with, or in support of, the relevant core platform services, including data generated or provided by the customers of those business users.

For the purposes of the first subparagraph, the data that is not publicly available shall include any aggregated and non-aggregated data generated by business users that can be inferred from, or collected through, the commercial activities of business users or their customers, including click, search, view and voice data, on the relevant core platform services or on services provided together with, or in support of, the relevant core platform services of the gatekeeper.

3. The gatekeeper shall allow and technically enable end users to easily un-install any software applications on the operating system of the gatekeeper, without prejudice to the possibility for that gatekeeper to restrict such un-installation in relation to software applications that are essential for the functioning of the operating system or of the device and which cannot technically be offered on a standalone basis by third parties.

The gatekeeper shall allow and technically enable end users to easily change default settings on the operating system, virtual assistant and web browser of the gatekeeper that direct or steer end users to products or services provided by the gatekeeper. That includes prompting end users, at the moment of the end users' first use of an online search engine, virtual assistant or web browser of the gatekeeper listed in the designation decision pursuant to Article 3(9), to choose, from a list of the main available service providers, the online search engine, virtual assistant or web browser to which the operating system of the gatekeeper directs or steers users by default, and the online search engine to which the virtual assistant and the web browser of the gatekeeper directs or steers users by default.

4. The gatekeeper shall allow and technically enable the installation and effective use of third-party software applications or software application stores using, or interoperating with, its operating system and allow those software applications or software application stores to be accessed by means other than the relevant core platform services of that gatekeeper. The gatekeeper shall, where applicable, not prevent the downloaded third-party software applications or software application stores from prompting end users to decide whether they want to set that downloaded software application or software application store as their default. The gatekeeper shall technically enable end users who decide to set that downloaded software application or software application store as their default to carry out that change easily.

The gatekeeper shall not be prevented from taking, to the extent that they are strictly necessary and proportionate, measures to ensure that third-party software applications or software application stores do not endanger the integrity of the hardware or operating system provided by the gatekeeper, provided that such measures are duly justified by the gatekeeper.

Furthermore, the gatekeeper shall not be prevented from applying, to the extent that they are strictly necessary and proportionate, measures and settings other than default settings, enabling end users to effectively protect security in relation to third-party software applications or software application stores, provided that such measures and settings other than default settings are duly justified by the gatekeeper.

5. The gatekeeper shall not treat more favourably, in ranking and related indexing and crawling, services and products offered by the gatekeeper itself than similar services or products of a third party. The gatekeeper shall apply transparent, fair and non-discriminatory conditions to such ranking.

6. The gatekeeper shall not restrict technically or otherwise the ability of end users to switch between, and subscribe to, different software applications and services that are accessed using the core platform services of the gatekeeper, including as regards the choice of Internet access services for end users.

7. The gatekeeper shall allow providers of services and providers of hardware, free of charge, effective interoperability with, and access for the purposes of interoperability to, the same hardware and software features accessed or controlled via the operating system or virtual assistant listed in the designation decision pursuant to Article 3(9) as are available to services or hardware provided by the gatekeeper. Furthermore, the gatekeeper shall allow business users and alternative providers of services provided together with, or in support of, core platform services, free of charge, effective interoperability with, and access for the purposes of interoperability to, the same operating system, hardware or software features, regardless of whether those features are part of the operating system, as are available to, or used by, that gatekeeper when providing such services.

The gatekeeper shall not be prevented from taking strictly necessary and proportionate measures to ensure that interoperability does not compromise the integrity of the operating system, virtual assistant, hardware or software features provided by the gatekeeper, provided that such measures are duly justified by the gatekeeper.

8. The gatekeeper shall provide advertisers and publishers, as well as third parties authorised by advertisers and publishers, upon their request and free of charge, with access to the performance measuring tools of the gatekeeper and the data necessary for advertisers and publishers to carry out their own independent verification of the advertisements inventory, including aggregated and non-aggregated data. Such data shall be provided in a manner that enables advertisers and publishers to run their own verification and measurement tools to assess the performance of the core platform services provided for by the gatekeepers.

9. The gatekeeper shall provide end users and third parties authorised by an end user, at their request and free of charge, with effective portability of data provided by the end user or generated through the activity of the end user in the context of the use of the relevant core platform service, including by providing, free of charge, tools to facilitate the effective exercise of such data portability, and including by the provision of continuous and real-time access to such data.

10. The gatekeeper shall provide business users and third parties authorised by a business user, at their request, free of charge, with effective, high-quality, continuous and real-time access to, and use of, aggregated and non-aggregated data, including personal data, that is provided for or generated in the context of the use of the relevant core platform services or services provided together with, or in support of, the relevant core platform services by those business users and the end users engaging with the products or services provided by those business users. With regard to personal data,

the gatekeeper shall provide for such access to, and use of, personal data only where the data are directly connected with the use effectuated by the end users in respect of the products or services offered by the relevant business user through the relevant core platform service, and when the end users opt in to such sharing by giving their consent.

11. The gatekeeper shall provide to any third-party undertaking providing online search engines, at its request, with access on fair, reasonable and non-discriminatory terms to ranking, query, click and view data in relation to free and paid search generated by end users on its online search engines. Any such query, click and view data that constitutes personal data shall be anonymised.

12. The gatekeeper shall apply fair, reasonable, and non-discriminatory general conditions of access for business users to its software application stores, online search engines and online social networking services listed in the designation decision pursuant to Article 3(9).

For that purpose, the gatekeeper shall publish general conditions of access, including an alternative dispute settlement mechanism.

The Commission shall assess whether the published general conditions of access comply with this paragraph.

13. The gatekeeper shall not have general conditions for terminating the provision of a core platform service that are disproportionate. The gatekeeper shall ensure that the conditions of termination can be exercised without undue difficulty.

Article 7
Obligation for gatekeepers on interoperability of number-independent interpersonal communications services

1. Where a gatekeeper provides number-independent interpersonal communications services that are listed in the designation decision pursuant to Article 3(9), it shall make the basic functionalities of its number-independent interpersonal communications services interoperable with the number-independent interpersonal communications services of another provider offering or intending to offer such services in the Union, by providing the necessary technical interfaces or similar solutions that facilitate interoperability, upon request, and free of charge.

2. The gatekeeper shall make at least the following basic functionalities referred to in paragraph 1 interoperable where the gatekeeper itself provides those functionalities to its own end users:

(a) following the listing in the designation decision pursuant to Article 3(9):
- (i) end-to-end text messaging between two individual end users;
- (ii) sharing of images, voice messages, videos and other attached files in end to end communication between two individual end users;

(b) within 2 years from the designation:
- (i) end-to-end text messaging within groups of individual end users;
- (ii) sharing of images, voice messages, videos and other attached files in end-to-end communication between a group chat and an individual end user;

(c) within 4 years from the designation:
- (i) end-to-end voice calls between two individual end users;
- (ii) end-to-end video calls between two individual end users;

(iii) end-to-end voice calls between a group chat and an individual end user;
(iv) end-to-end video calls between a group chat and an individual end user.

3. The level of security, including the end-to-end encryption, where applicable, that the gatekeeper provides to its own end users shall be preserved across the interoperable services.

4. The gatekeeper shall publish a reference offer laying down the technical details and general terms and conditions of interoperability with its number-independent interpersonal communications services, including the necessary details on the level of security and end-to-end encryption. The gatekeeper shall publish that reference offer within the period laid down in Article 3(10) and update it where necessary.

5. Following the publication of the reference offer pursuant to paragraph 4, any provider of number-independent interpersonal communications services offering or intending to offer such services in the Union may request interoperability with the number-independent interpersonal communications services provided by the gatekeeper. Such a request may cover some or all of the basic functionalities listed in paragraph 2. The gatekeeper shall comply with any reasonable request for interoperability within 3 months after receiving that request by rendering the requested basic functionalities operational.

6. The Commission may, exceptionally, upon a reasoned request by the gatekeeper, extend the time limits for compliance under paragraph 2 or 5 where the gatekeeper demonstrates that this is necessary to ensure effective interoperability and to maintain the necessary level of security, including end-to-end encryption, where applicable.

7. The end users of the number-independent interpersonal communications services of the gatekeeper and of the requesting provider of number-independent interpersonal communications services shall remain free to decide whether to make use of the interoperable basic functionalities that may be provided by the gatekeeper pursuant to paragraph 1.

8. The gatekeeper shall collect and exchange with the provider of number-independent interpersonal communications services that makes a request for interoperability only the personal data of end users that is strictly necessary to provide effective interoperability. Any such collection and exchange of the personal data of end users shall fully comply with Regulation (EU) 2016/679 and Directive 2002/58/EC.

9. The gatekeeper shall not be prevented from taking measures to ensure that third-party providers of number-independent interpersonal communications services requesting interoperability do not endanger the integrity, security and privacy of its services, provided that such measures are strictly necessary and proportionate and are duly justified by the gatekeeper.

Article 8
Compliance with obligations for gatekeepers

1. The gatekeeper shall ensure and demonstrate compliance with the obligations laid down in Articles 5, 6 and 7 of this Regulation. The measures implemented by the gatekeeper to ensure compliance with those Articles shall be effective in achieving the objectives of this Regulation and of the relevant obligation. The gatekeeper shall ensure that the implementation of those measures complies with applicable law, in par-

ticular Regulation (EU) 2016/679, Directive 2002/58/EC, legislation on cyber security, consumer protection, product safety, as well as with the accessibility requirements.

2. The Commission may, on its own initiative or at the request of a gatekeeper pursuant to paragraph 3 of this Article, open proceedings pursuant to Article 20.

The Commission may adopt an implementing act, specifying the measures that the gatekeeper concerned is to implement in order to effectively comply with the obligations laid down in Articles 6 and 7. That implementing act shall be adopted within 6 months from the opening of proceedings pursuant to Article 20 in accordance with the advisory procedure referred to in Article 50(2).

When opening proceedings on its own initiative for circumvention pursuant to Article 13, such measures may concern the obligations laid down in Articles 5, 6 and 7.

3. A gatekeeper may request the Commission to engage in a process to determine whether the measures that that gatekeeper intends to implement or has implemented to ensure compliance with Articles 6 and 7 are effective in achieving the objective of the relevant obligation in the specific circumstances of the gatekeeper. The Commission shall have discretion in deciding whether to engage in such a process, respecting the principles of equal treatment, proportionality and good administration.

In its request, the gatekeeper shall provide a reasoned submission to explain the measures that it intends to implement or has implemented. The gatekeeper shall furthermore provide a non-confidential version of its reasoned submission that may be shared with third parties pursuant to paragraph 6.

4. Paragraphs 2 and 3 of this Article are without prejudice to the powers of the Commission under Articles 29, 30 and 31.

5. With a view of adopting the decision under paragraph 2, the Commission shall communicate its preliminary findings to the gatekeeper within 3 months from the opening of the proceedings under Article 20. In the preliminary findings, the Commission shall explain the measures that it is considering taking or that it considers the gatekeeper concerned should take in order to effectively address the preliminary findings.

6. In order to effectively enable interested third parties to provide comments, the Commission shall, when communicating its preliminary findings to the gatekeeper pursuant to paragraph 5 or as soon as possible thereafter, publish a non-confidential summary of the case and the measures that it is considering taking or that it considers the gatekeeper concerned should take. The Commission shall specify a reasonable timeframe within which such comments are to be provided.

7. In specifying the measures under paragraph 2, the Commission shall ensure that the measures are effective in achieving the objectives of this Regulation and the relevant obligation, and proportionate in the specific circumstances of the gatekeeper and the relevant service.

8. For the purposes of specifying the obligations under Article 6(11) and (12), the Commission shall also assess whether the intended or implemented measures ensure that there is no remaining imbalance of rights and obligations on business users and that the measures do not themselves confer an advantage on the gatekeeper which is disproportionate to the service provided by the gatekeeper to business users.

9. In respect of proceedings pursuant to paragraph 2, the Commission may, upon request or on its own initiative, decide to reopen them where:

(a) there has been a material change in any of the facts on which the decision was based; or
(b) the decision was based on incomplete, incorrect or misleading information; or
(c) the measures as specified in the decision are not effective.

Article 9
Suspension

1. Where the gatekeeper demonstrates in a reasoned request that compliance with a specific obligation laid down in Article 5, 6 or 7 for a core platform service listed in the designation decision pursuant to Article 3(9) would endanger, due to exceptional circumstances beyond the gatekeeper's control, the economic viability of its operation in the Union, the Commission may adopt an implementing act setting out its decision to exceptionally suspend, in whole or in part, the specific obligation referred to in that reasoned request ('the suspension decision'). In that implementing act, the Commission shall substantiate its suspension decision by identifying the exceptional circumstances justifying the suspension. That implementing act shall be limited to the extent and the duration necessary to address such threat to the gatekeeper's viability. The Commission shall aim to adopt that implementing act without delay and at the latest 3 months following receipt of a complete reasoned request. That implementing act shall be adopted in accordance with the advisory procedure referred to in Article 50(2).

2. Where suspension is granted pursuant to paragraph 1, the Commission shall review its suspension decision every year, unless a shorter interval is specified in that decision. Following such a review the Commission shall either wholly or partly lift the suspension, or decide that the conditions in paragraph 1 continue to be met.

3. In cases of urgency, the Commission may, acting on a reasoned request by a gatekeeper, provisionally suspend the application of a specific obligation referred to in paragraph 1 to one or more individual core platform services already prior to the decision pursuant to that paragraph. Such a request may be made and granted at any time pending the assessment of the Commission pursuant to paragraph 1.

4. In assessing the request referred to in paragraphs 1 and 3, the Commission shall take into account, in particular, the impact of the compliance with the specific obligation on the economic viability of the operation of the gatekeeper in the Union as well as on third parties, in particular SMEs and consumers. The suspension may be made subject to conditions and obligations to be defined by the Commission in order to ensure a fair balance between those interests and the objectives of this Regulation.

Article 10
Exemption for grounds of public health and public security

1. The Commission may, acting on a reasoned request by a gatekeeper or on its own initiative, adopt an implementing act setting out its decision, to exempt that gatekeeper, in whole or in part, from a specific obligation laid down in Article 5, 6 or 7 in relation to a core platform service listed in the designation decision pursuant to Article 3(9), where such exemption is justified on the grounds set out in paragraph 3 of this Article ('the exemption decision'). The Commission shall adopt the exemption decision within 3 months after receiving a complete reasoned request and shall provide a reasoned

statement explaining the grounds for the exemption. That implementing act shall be adopted in accordance with the advisory procedure referred to in Article 50(2).

2. Where an exemption is granted pursuant to paragraph 1, the Commission shall review its exemption decision if the ground for the exemption no longer exists or at least every year. Following such a review, the Commission shall either wholly or partially lift the exemption, or decide that the conditions of paragraph 1 continue to be met.

3. An exemption pursuant to paragraph 1 may only be granted on grounds of public health or public security.

4. In cases of urgency, the Commission may, acting on a reasoned request by a gatekeeper or on its own initiative, provisionally suspend the application of a specific obligation referred to in paragraph 1 to one or more individual core platform services already prior to the decision pursuant to that paragraph. Such a request may be made and granted at any time pending the assessment of the Commission pursuant to paragraph 1.

5. In assessing the request referred to in paragraphs 1 and 4, the Commission shall take into account, in particular, the impact of the compliance with the specific obligation on the grounds in paragraph 3, as well as the effects on the gatekeeper concerned and on third parties. The Commission may subject the suspension to conditions and obligations in order to ensure a fair balance between the goals pursued by the grounds in paragraph 3 and the objectives of this Regulation.

Article 11
Reporting

1. Within 6 months after its designation pursuant to Article 3, and in accordance with Article 3(10), the gatekeeper shall provide the Commission with a report describing in a detailed and transparent manner the measures it has implemented to ensure compliance with the obligations laid down in Articles 5, 6 and 7.

2. Within the deadline referred to in paragraph 1, the gatekeeper shall publish and provide the Commission with a non-confidential summary of that report.

The gatekeeper shall update that report and that non-confidential summary at least annually.

The Commission shall make a link to that non-confidential summary available on its website.

Article 12
Updating obligations for gatekeepers

1. The Commission is empowered to adopt delegated acts in accordance with Article 49 to supplement this Regulation with regard to the obligations laid down in Articles 5 and 6. Those delegated acts shall be based on a market investigation pursuant to Article 19 that has identified the need to keep those obligations up to date in order to address practices that limit the contestability of core platform services or that are unfair in the same way as the practices addressed by the obligations laid down in Articles 5 and 6.

2. The scope of a delegated act adopted in accordance with paragraph 1 shall be limited to:

(a) extending an obligation that applies only in relation to certain core platform services, to other core platform services listed in Article 2, point (2);
(b) extending an obligation that benefits certain business users or end users so that it benefits other business users or end users;
(c) specifying the manner in which the obligations laid down in Articles 5 and 6 are to be performed by gatekeepers in order to ensure effective compliance with those obligations;
(d) extending an obligation that applies only in relation to certain services provided together with, or in support of, core platform services to other services provided together with, or in support of, core platform services;
(e) extending an obligation that applies only in relation to certain types of data to apply in relation to other types of data;
(f) adding further conditions where an obligation imposes certain conditions on the behaviour of a gatekeeper; or
(g) applying an obligation that governs the relationship between several core platform services of the gatekeeper to the relationship between a core platform service and other services of the gatekeeper.

3. The Commission is empowered to adopt delegated acts in accordance with Article 49 to amend this Regulation with regard to the list of basic functionalities identified in Article 7(2), by adding or removing functionalities of number-independent interpersonal communications services.

Those delegated acts shall be based on a market investigation pursuant to Article 19 that has identified the need to keep those obligations up to date in order to address practices that limit the contestability of core platform services or that are unfair in the same way as the practices addressed by the obligations laid down in Article 7.

4. The Commission is empowered to adopt delegated acts in accordance with Article 49 to supplement this Regulation in respect of the obligations in Article 7 by specifying the manner in which those obligations are to be performed in order to ensure effective compliance with those obligations. Those delegated acts shall be based on a market investigation pursuant to Article 19, which has identified the need to keep those obligations up to date in order to address practices that limit the contestability of core platform services or that are unfair in the same way as the practices addressed by the obligations laid down in Article 7.

5. A practice as referred to in paragraphs 1, 3 and 4 shall be considered to limit the contestability of core platform services or to be unfair where:

(a) that practice is engaged in by gatekeepers and is capable of impeding innovation and limiting choice for business users and end users because it:
    (i) affects or risks affecting the contestability of a core platform service or other services in the digital sector on a lasting basis due to the creation or strengthening of barriers to entry for other undertakings or to expand as providers of a core platform service or other services in the digital sector; or
    (ii) prevents other operators from having the same access to a key input as the gatekeeper; or
(b) there is an imbalance between the rights and obligations of business users and the gatekeeper obtains an advantage from business users that is disproportionate to the service provided by that gatekeeper to those business users.

Article 13
Anti-circumvention

1. An undertaking providing core platform services shall not segment, divide, subdivide, fragment or split those services through contractual, commercial, technical or any other means in order to circumvent the quantitative thresholds laid down in Article 3(2). No such practice of an undertaking shall prevent the Commission from designating it as a gatekeeper pursuant to Article 3(4).

2. The Commission may, when it suspects that an undertaking providing core platform services is engaged in a practice laid down in paragraph 1, require from that undertaking any information that it deems necessary to determine whether that undertaking has engaged in such a practice.

3. The gatekeeper shall ensure that the obligations of Articles 5, 6 and 7 are fully and effectively complied with.

4. The gatekeeper shall not engage in any behaviour that undermines effective compliance with the obligations of Articles 5, 6 and 7 regardless of whether that behaviour is of a contractual, commercial or technical nature, or of any other nature, or consists in the use of behavioural techniques or interface design.

5. Where consent for collecting, processing, cross-using and sharing of personal data is required to ensure compliance with this Regulation, a gatekeeper shall take the necessary steps either to enable business users to directly obtain the required consent to their processing, where that consent is required under Regulation (EU) 2016/679 or Directive 2002/58/EC, or to comply with Union data protection and privacy rules and principles in other ways, including by providing business users with duly anonymised data where appropriate. The gatekeeper shall not make the obtaining of that consent by the business user more burdensome than for its own services.

6. The gatekeeper shall not degrade the conditions or quality of any of the core platform services provided to business users or end users who avail themselves of the rights or choices laid down in Articles 5, 6 and 7, or make the exercise of those rights or choices unduly difficult, including by offering choices to the end-user in a non-neutral manner, or by subverting end users' or business users' autonomy, decision-making, or free choice via the structure, design, function or manner of operation of a user interface or a part thereof.

7. Where the gatekeeper circumvents or attempts to circumvent any of the obligations in Article 5, 6, or 7 in a manner described in paragraphs 4, 5 and 6 of this Article, the Commission may open proceedings pursuant to Article 20 and adopt an implementing act referred to in Article 8(2) in order to specify the measures that the gatekeeper is to implement.

8. Paragraph 6 of this Article is without prejudice to the powers of the Commission under Articles 29, 30 and 31.

Article 14
Obligation to inform about concentrations

1. A gatekeeper shall inform the Commission of any intended concentration within the meaning of Article 3 of Regulation (EC) No 139/2004, where the merging entities or the target of concentration provide core platform services or any other services in the digital sector or enable the collection of data, irrespective of whether it is notifiable to the

Commission under that Regulation or to a competent national competition authority under national merger rules.

A gatekeeper shall inform the Commission of such a concentration prior to its implementation and following the conclusion of the agreement, the announcement of the public bid, or the acquisition of a controlling interest.

2. The information provided by the gatekeeper pursuant to paragraph 1 shall at least describe the undertakings concerned by the concentration, their Union and worldwide annual turnovers, their fields of activity, including activities directly related to the concentration, and the transaction value of the agreement or an estimation thereof, along with a summary of the concentration, including its nature and rationale and a list of the Member States concerned by the concentration.

The information provided by the gatekeeper shall also describe, for any relevant core platform services, their Union annual turnovers, their numbers of yearly active business users and their numbers of monthly active end users, respectively.

3. If, following any concentration referred to in paragraph 1 of this Article, additional core platform services individually meet the thresholds in Article 3(2), point (b), the gatekeeper concerned shall inform the Commission thereof within 2 months from the implementation of the concentration and provide the Commission with the information referred to in Article 3(2).

4. The Commission shall inform the competent authorities of the Member States of any information received pursuant to paragraph 1 and publish annually the list of acquisitions of which it has been informed by gatekeepers pursuant to that paragraph.

The Commission shall take account of the legitimate interest of undertakings in the protection of their business secrets.

5. The competent authorities of the Member States may use the information received under paragraph 1 of this Article to request the Commission to examine the concentration pursuant to Article 22 of Regulation (EC) No 139/2004.

Article 15
Obligation of an audit

1. Within 6 months after its designation pursuant to Article 3, a gatekeeper shall submit to the Commission an independently audited description of any techniques for profiling of consumers that the gatekeeper applies to or across its core platform services listed in the designation decision pursuant to Article 3(9). The Commission shall transmit that audited description to the European Data Protection Board.

2. The Commission may adopt an implementing act referred to in Article 46(1), point (g), to develop the methodology and procedure of the audit.

3. The gatekeeper shall make publicly available an overview of the audited description referred to in paragraph 1. In doing so, the gatekeeper shall be entitled to take account of the need to respect its business secrets. The gatekeeper shall update that description and that overview at least annually.

CHAPTER IV
MARKET INVESTIGATION

Article 16
Opening of a market investigation

1. When the Commission intends to carry out a market investigation with a view to the possible adoption of decisions pursuant to Articles 17, 18 and 19 it shall adopt a decision opening a market investigation.

2. Notwithstanding paragraph 1, the Commission may exercise its investigative powers under this Regulation before opening a market investigation pursuant to that paragraph.

3. The decision referred to in paragraph 1 shall specify:

(a) the date of opening of the market investigation;
(b) the description of the issue to which the market investigation relates to;
(c) the purpose of the market investigation.

4. The Commission may reopen a market investigation that it has closed where:

(a) there has been a material change in any of the facts on which a decision adopted pursuant to Article 17, 18 or 19 was based; or
(b) the decision adopted pursuant to Article 17, 18 or 19 was based on incomplete, incorrect or misleading information.

5. The Commission may ask one or more national competent authorities to assist it in its market investigation.

Article 17
Market investigation for designating gatekeepers

1. The Commission may conduct a market investigation for the purpose of examining whether an undertaking providing core platform services should be designated as a gatekeeper pursuant to Article 3(8), or in order to identify the core platform services to be listed in the designation decision pursuant to Article 3(9). The Commission shall endeavour to conclude its market investigation within 12 months from the date referred to in Article 16(3), point (a), In order to conclude its market investigation, the Commission shall adopt an implementing act setting out its decision. That implementing act shall be adopted in accordance with the advisory procedure referred to in Article 50(2).

2. In the course of a market investigation pursuant to paragraph 1 of this Article, the Commission shall endeavour to communicate its preliminary findings to the undertaking providing core platform services concerned within 6 months from the date referred to in Article 16(3), point (a). In the preliminary findings, the Commission shall explain whether it considers, on a provisional basis, that it is appropriate for that undertaking to be designated as a gatekeeper pursuant to Article 3(8), and for the relevant core platform services to be listed pursuant to Article 3(9).

3. Where the undertaking providing core platform services satisfies the thresholds set out in Article 3(2), but has presented sufficiently substantiated arguments in accordance with Article 3(5) that have manifestly called into question the presumption in Article 3(2), the Commission shall endeavour to conclude the market investigation within 5 months from the date referred to in Article 16(3), point (a).

In such a case, the Commission shall endeavour to communicate its preliminary findings pursuant to paragraph 2 of this Article to the undertaking concerned within 3 months from the date referred to in Article 16(3), point (a).

4. When the Commission, pursuant to Article 3(8), designates as a gatekeeper an undertaking providing core platform services that does not yet enjoy an entrenched and durable position in its operations, but which will foreseeably enjoy such a position in the near future, it may declare applicable to that gatekeeper only one or more of the obligations laid down in Article 5(3) to (6) and Article 6(4), (7), (9), (10) and (13), as specified in the designation decision. The Commission shall only declare applicable those obligations that are appropriate and necessary to prevent the gatekeeper concerned from achieving, by unfair means, an entrenched and durable position in its operations. The Commission shall review such a designation in accordance with the procedure laid down in Article 4.

Article 18
Market investigation into systematic non-compliance

1. The Commission may conduct a market investigation for the purpose of examining whether a gatekeeper has engaged in systematic non-compliance. The Commission shall conclude that market investigation within 12 months from the date referred to in Article 16(3), point (a). Where the market investigation shows that a gatekeeper has systematically infringed one or more of the obligations laid down in Article 5, 6 or 7 and has maintained, strengthened or extended its gatekeeper position in relation to the requirements set out in Article 3(1), the Commission may adopt an implementing act imposing on such gatekeeper any behavioural or structural remedies which are proportionate and necessary to ensure effective compliance with this Regulation. That implementing act shall be adopted in accordance with the advisory procedure referred to in Article 50(2).

2. The remedy imposed in accordance with paragraph 1 of this Article may include, to the extent that such remedy is proportionate and necessary in order to maintain or restore fairness and contestability as affected by the systematic non-compliance, the prohibition, during a limited period, for the gatekeeper to enter into a concentration within the meaning of Article 3 of Regulation (EC) No 139/2004 regarding the core platform services or the other services provided in the digital sector or enabling the collection of data that are affected by the systematic non-compliance.

3. A gatekeeper shall be deemed to have engaged in systematic non-compliance with the obligations laid down in Articles 5, 6 and 7, where the Commission has issued at least three non-compliance decisions pursuant to Article 29 against a gatekeeper in relation to any of its core platform services within a period of 8 years prior to the adoption of the decision opening a market investigation in view of the possible adoption of a decision pursuant to this Article.

4. The Commission shall communicate its preliminary findings to the gatekeeper concerned within 6 months from the date referred to in Article 16(3), point (a). In its preliminary findings, the Commission shall explain whether it preliminarily considers that the conditions of paragraph 1 of this Article are met and which remedy or remedies it preliminarily considers necessary and proportionate.

5. In order to enable interested third parties to effectively provide comments, the Commission shall, at the same time as communicating its preliminary findings to the

gatekeeper pursuant to paragraph 4 or as soon as possible thereafter, publish a non-confidential summary of the case and the remedies that it is considering imposing. The Commission shall specify a reasonable timeframe within which such comments are to be provided.

6. Where the Commission intends to adopt a decision pursuant to paragraph 1 of this Article by making commitments offered by the gatekeeper pursuant to Article 25 binding, it shall publish a non-confidential summary of the case and the main content of the commitments. Interested third parties may submit their comments within a reasonable timeframe which shall be set by the Commission.

7. In the course of the market investigation, the Commission may extend its duration where such extension is justified on objective grounds and proportionate. The extension may apply to the deadline by which the Commission has to issue its preliminary findings, or to the deadline for adoption of the final decision. The total duration of any extension or extensions pursuant to this paragraph shall not exceed 6 months.

8. In order to ensure effective compliance by the gatekeeper with its obligations laid down in Articles 5, 6 and 7, the Commission shall regularly review the remedies that it imposes in accordance with paragraphs 1 and 2 of this Article. The Commission shall be entitled to modify those remedies if, following a new market investigation, it finds that they are not effective.

Article 19
Market investigation into new services and new practices

1. The Commission may conduct a market investigation for the purpose of examining whether one or more services within the digital sector should be added to the list of core platform services laid down in Article 2, point (2) or for the purpose of detecting practices that limit the contestability of core platform services or that are unfair and which are not effectively addressed by this Regulation. In its assessment, the Commission shall take into account any relevant findings of proceedings under Articles 101 and 102 TFEU concerning digital markets as well as any other relevant developments.

2. The Commission may, when conducting a market investigation pursuant to paragraph 1, consult third parties, including business users and end users of services within the digital sector that are being investigated and business users and end users who are subject to practices under investigation.

3. The Commission shall publish its findings in a report within 18 months from the date referred to in Article 16(3), point (a).

That report shall be submitted to the European Parliament and to the Council and, where appropriate, shall be accompanied by:

(a) a legislative proposal to amend this Regulation in order to include additional services within the digital sector in the list of core platform services laid down in Article 2, point (2), or to include new obligations in Chapter III; or
(b) a draft delegated act supplementing this Regulation with regard to the obligations laid down in Articles 5 and 6, or a draft delegated act amending or supplementing this Regulation with regard to the obligations laid down in Article 7, as provided for in Article 12.

Where appropriate, the legislative proposal to amend this Regulation under point (a) of the second subparagraph may also propose to remove existing services from the list of core platform services laid down in Article 2, point (2), or to remove existing obligations from Article 5, 6 or 7.

CHAPTER V
INVESTIGATIVE, ENFORCEMENT AND MONITORING POWERS

Article 20
Opening of proceedings

1. Where the Commission intends to open proceedings with a view to the possible adoption of decisions pursuant to Articles 8, 29 and 30, it shall adopt a decision opening a proceeding.

2. Notwithstanding paragraph 1, the Commission may exercise its investigative powers under this Regulation before opening proceedings pursuant to that paragraph.

Article 21
Requests for information

1. In order to carry out its duties under this Regulation, the Commission may, by simple request or by decision, require from undertakings and associations of undertakings to provide all necessary information. The Commission may also, by simple request or by decision, require access to any data and algorithms of undertakings and information about testing, as well as requesting explanations of them.

2. When sending a simple request for information to an undertaking or association of undertakings, the Commission shall state the legal basis and purpose of the request, specify what information is required and fix the time limit within which the information is to be provided, as well as the fines provided for in Article 30 applicable for supplying incomplete, incorrect or misleading information or explanations.

3. Where the Commission requires undertakings and associations of undertakings to supply information by decision, it shall state the legal basis and purpose of the request, specify what information is required and fix the time limit within which the information is to be provided. Where the Commission requires undertakings to provide access to any data, algorithms and information about testing, it shall state the purpose of the request and fix the time -limit within which it is to be provided. It shall also indicate the fines provided for in Article 30 and indicate or impose the periodic penalty payments provided for in Article 31. It shall further indicate the right to have the decision reviewed by the Court of Justice.

4. The undertakings or associations of undertakings or their representatives shall supply the information requested on behalf of the undertaking or the association of undertakings concerned. Lawyers duly authorised to act may supply the information on behalf of their clients. The latter shall remain fully responsible if the information supplied is incomplete, incorrect or misleading.

5. At the request of the Commission, the competent authorities of the Member States shall provide the Commission with all necessary information in their possession to carry out the duties assigned to it by this Regulation.

Article 22
Power to carry out interviews and take statements

1. In order to carry out its duties under this Regulation, the Commission may interview any natural or legal person which consents to being interviewed, for the purpose of collecting information, relating to the subject-matter of an investigation. The Commission shall be entitled to record such interviews by any technical means.

2. Where an interview pursuant to paragraph 1 of this Article is conducted on the premises of an undertaking, the Commission shall inform the national competent authority of the Member State that is enforcing the rules referred to in Article 1(6) and in whose territory the interview takes place thereof. If that authority so requests, its officials may assist the officials and other accompanying persons authorised by the Commission to conduct the interview.

Article 23
Powers to conduct inspections

1. In order to carry out its duties under this Regulation, the Commission may conduct all necessary inspections of an undertaking or association of undertakings.

2. The officials and other accompanying persons authorised by the Commission to conduct an inspection are empowered to:

(a) enter any premises, land and means of transport of undertakings and associations of undertakings;
(b) examine the books and other records related to the business, irrespective of the medium on which they are stored;
(c) take or obtain in any form copies of or extracts from such books or records;
(d) require the undertaking or association of undertakings to provide access to and explanations on its organisation, functioning, IT system, algorithms, data-handling and business practices and to record or document the explanations given by any technical means;
(e) seal any business premises and books or records for the duration of, and to the extent necessary for, the inspection;
(f) ask any representative or member of staff of the undertaking or association of undertakings for explanations of facts or documents relating to the subject-matter and purpose of the inspection, and to record the answers by any technical means.

3. To carry out inspections, the Commission may request the assistance of auditors or experts appointed by the Commission pursuant to Article 26(2), as well as the assistance of the national competent authority of the Member State, enforcing the rules referred to in Article 1(6) in whose territory the inspection is to be conducted.

4. During inspections the Commission, auditors or experts appointed by it and the national competent authority of the Member State, enforcing the rules referred to in Article 1(6) in whose territory the inspection is to be conducted may require the undertaking or association of undertakings to provide access to and explanations on its organisation, functioning, IT system, algorithms, data-handling and business conducts. The Commission and auditors or experts appointed by it and the national competent authority of the Member State, enforcing the rules referred to in Article 1(6) in whose territory the inspection is to be conducted may address questions to any representative or member of staff.

5. The officials and other accompanying persons authorised by the Commission to conduct an inspection shall exercise their powers upon production of a written authorisation specifying the subject matter and purpose of the inspection and the fines provided for in Article 30 applicable in the event that the production of the required books or other records related to the business is incomplete or where the answers to questions asked under paragraphs 2 and 4 of this Article are incorrect or misleading. In good time before the inspection, the Commission shall give notice of the inspection to the national competent authority of the Member State enforcing the rules referred to in Article 1(6) in whose territory it is to be conducted.

6. Undertakings or associations of undertakings are required to submit to an inspection ordered by a Commission decision. That decision shall specify the subject matter and purpose of the inspection, set the date on which it is to begin and indicate the fines and periodic penalty payments provided for in Articles 30 and 31 respectively, and the right to have that decision reviewed by the Court of Justice.

7. Officials of, and the persons authorised or appointed by, the national competent authority of the Member State enforcing the rules referred to in Article 1(6) in whose territory the inspection is to be conducted shall, at the request of that authority or of the Commission, actively assist the officials and other accompanying persons authorised by the Commission. To this end, they shall enjoy the powers set out in paragraphs 2 and 4 of this Article.

8. Where the officials and other accompanying persons authorised by the Commission find that an undertaking or association of undertakings opposes an inspection ordered pursuant to this Article, the Member State concerned shall afford them the necessary assistance, requesting, where appropriate, the assistance of the police or of an equivalent enforcement authority, so as to enable them to conduct their inspection.

9. If, according to national rules, the assistance provided for in paragraph 8 of this Article requires authorisation from a judicial authority, the Commission or the national competent authority of the Member State enforcing the rules referred to in Article 1(6) or officials authorised by those authorities shall apply for it. Such authorisation may also be applied for as a precautionary measure.

10. Where authorisation referred to in paragraph 9 of this Article is applied for, the national judicial authority shall verify that the Commission decision is authentic and that the coercive measures envisaged are neither arbitrary nor excessive having regard to the subject matter of the inspection. In its control of the proportionality of the coercive measures, the national judicial authority may ask the Commission, directly or through the national competent authority of the Member State, enforcing the rules referred to in Article 1(6), for detailed explanations in particular on the grounds the Commission has for suspecting infringement of this Regulation, as well as on the seriousness of the suspected infringement and on the nature of the involvement of the undertaking concerned. However, the national judicial authority may not call into question the necessity of the inspection nor demand that it be provided with the information in the file of the Commission. The lawfulness of the Commission decision shall be subject to review only by the Court of Justice.

Article 24
Interim measures

In case of urgency due to the risk of serious and irreparable damage for business users or end users of gatekeepers, the Commission may adopt an implementing act ordering interim measures against a gatekeeper on the basis of a *prima facie* finding of an infringement of Article 5, 6 or 7. That implementing act shall be adopted only in the context of proceedings opened with a view to the possible adoption of a non-compliance decision pursuant to Article 29(1). It shall apply only for a specified period of time and may be renewed in so far this is necessary and appropriate. That implementing act shall be adopted in accordance with the advisory procedure referred to in Article 50(2).

Article 25
Commitments

1. If, during proceedings under Article 18, the gatekeeper concerned offers commitments for the relevant core platform services to ensure compliance with the obligations laid down in Articles 5, 6 and 7 the Commission may adopt an implementing act making those commitments binding on that gatekeeper and declare that there are no further grounds for action. That implementing act shall be adopted in accordance with the advisory procedure referred to in Article 50(2).

2. The Commission may, upon request or on its own initiative, reopen by decision the relevant proceedings, where:

(a) there has been a material change in any of the facts on which the decision was based;
(b) the gatekeeper concerned acts contrary to its commitments;
(c) the decision was based on incomplete, incorrect or misleading information provided by the parties;
(d) the commitments are not effective.

3. If the Commission considers that the commitments submitted by the gatekeeper concerned cannot ensure effective compliance with the obligations laid down in Articles 5, 6 and 7, it shall explain the reasons for not making those commitments binding in the decision concluding the relevant proceedings.

Article 26
Monitoring of obligations and measures

1. The Commission shall take the necessary actions to monitor the effective implementation and compliance with the obligations laid down in Articles 5, 6 and 7 and the decisions taken pursuant to Articles 8, 18, 24, 25 and 29. Those actions may include, in particular, the imposition of an obligation on the gatekeeper to retain all documents deemed to be relevant to assess the implementation of, and compliance with, those obligations and decisions.

2. The actions pursuant to paragraph 1 may include the appointment of independent external experts and auditors, as well as the appointment of officials from national competent authorities of the Member States, to assist the Commission to monitor the obligations and measures and to provide specific expertise or knowledge to the Commission.

Article 27
Information by third parties

1. Any third party, including business users, competitors or end-users of the core platform services listed in the designation decision pursuant to Article 3(9), as well as their representatives, may inform the national competent authority of the Member State, enforcing the rules referred to in Article 1(6), or the Commission directly, about any practice or behaviour by gatekeepers that falls within the scope of this Regulation.

2. The national competent authority of the Member State, enforcing the rules referred to in Article 1(6), and the Commission shall have full discretion as regards the appropriate measures and are under no obligation to follow-up on the information received.

3. Where the national competent authority of the Member State, enforcing the rules referred to in Article 1(6), determines, based on the information received pursuant to paragraph 1 of this Article, that there may be an issue of non-compliance with this Regulation, it shall transfer that information to the Commission.

Article 28
Compliance function

1. Gatekeepers shall introduce a compliance function, which is independent from the operational functions of the gatekeeper and composed of one or more compliance officers, including the head of the compliance function.

2. The gatekeeper shall ensure that the compliance function referred to in paragraph 1 has sufficient authority, stature and resources, as well as access to the management body of the gatekeeper to monitor the compliance of the gatekeeper with this Regulation.

3. The management body of the gatekeeper shall ensure that compliance officers appointed pursuant to paragraph 1 have the professional qualifications, knowledge, experience and ability necessary to fulfil the tasks referred to in paragraph 5.

The management body of the gatekeeper shall also ensure that such head of the compliance function is an independent senior manager with distinct responsibility for the compliance function.

4. The head of the compliance function shall report directly to the management body of the gatekeeper and may raise concerns and warn that body where risks of non-compliance with this Regulation arise, without prejudice to the responsibilities of the management body in its supervisory and managerial functions.

The head of the compliance function shall not be removed without prior approval of the management body of the gatekeeper.

5. Compliance officers appointed by the gatekeeper pursuant to paragraph 1 shall have the following tasks:

(a) organising, monitoring and supervising the measures and activities of the gatekeepers that aim to ensure compliance with this Regulation;
(b) informing and advising the management and employees of the gatekeeper on compliance with this Regulation;
(c) where applicable, monitoring compliance with commitments made binding pursuant to Article 25, without prejudice to the Commission being able to appoint independent external experts pursuant to Article 26(2);
(d) cooperating with the Commission for the purpose of this Regulation.

6. Gatekeepers shall communicate the name and contact details of the head of the compliance function to the Commission.

7. The management body of the gatekeeper shall define, oversee and be accountable for the implementation of the governance arrangements of the gatekeeper that ensure the independence of the compliance function, including the division of responsibilities in the organisation of the gatekeeper and the prevention of conflicts of interest.

8. The management body shall approve and review periodically, at least once a year, the strategies and policies for taking up, managing and monitoring the compliance with this Regulation.

9. The management body shall devote sufficient time to the management and monitoring of compliance with this Regulation. It shall actively participate in decisions relating to the management and enforcement of this Regulation and ensure that adequate resources are allocated to it.

Article 29
Non-compliance

1. The Commission shall adopt an implementing act setting out its finding of non-compliance ('the non-compliance decision') where it finds that a gatekeeper does not comply with one or more of the following:

(a) any of the obligations laid down in Article 5, 6 or 7;
(b) measures specified by the Commission in a decision adopted pursuant to Article 8(2);
(c) remedies imposed pursuant to Article 18(1);
(d) interim measures ordered pursuant to Article 24; or
(e) commitments made legally binding pursuant to Article 25.

That implementing act shall be adopted in accordance with the advisory procedure referred to in Article 50(2).

2. The Commission shall endeavour to adopt its non-compliance decision within 12 months from the opening of proceedings pursuant to Article 20.

3. Before adopting the non-compliance decision, the Commission shall communicate its preliminary findings to the gatekeeper concerned. In those preliminary findings, the Commission shall explain the measures it is considering taking or that it considers that the gatekeeper should take in order to effectively address the preliminary findings.

4. Where it intends to adopt a non-compliance decision, the Commission may consult third parties.

5. In the non-compliance decision, the Commission shall order the gatekeeper to cease and desist with the non-compliance within an appropriate deadline and to provide explanations on how it plans to comply with that decision.

6. The gatekeeper shall provide the Commission with the description of the measures that it has taken to ensure compliance with the non-compliance decision.

7. Where the Commission decides not to adopt a non-compliance decision, it shall close the proceedings by a decision.

Article 30
Fines

1. In the non-compliance decision, the Commission may impose on a gatekeeper fines not exceeding 10 % of its total worldwide turnover in the preceding financial year where it finds that the gatekeeper, intentionally or negligently, fails to comply with:

(a) any of the obligations laid down in Articles 5, 6 and 7;
(b) measures specified by the Commission in a decision adopted pursuant to Article 8(2);
(c) remedies imposed pursuant to Article 18(1);
(d) interim measures ordered pursuant to Article 24; or
(e) commitments made legally binding pursuant to Article 25.

2. Notwithstanding paragraph 1 of this Article, in the non-compliance decision the Commission may impose on a gatekeeper fines up to 20 % of its total worldwide turnover in the preceding financial year where it finds that a gatekeeper has committed the same or a similar infringement of an obligation laid down in Article 5, 6 or 7 in relation to the same core platform service as it was found to have committed in a non-compliance decision adopted in the 8 preceding years.

3. The Commission may adopt a decision, imposing on undertakings, including gatekeepers where applicable, and associations of undertakings, fines not exceeding 1 % of their total worldwide turnover in the preceding financial year where they intentionally or negligently:

(a) fail to provide within the time limit information that is required for assessing their designation as gatekeepers pursuant to Article 3 or supply incorrect, incomplete or misleading information;
(b) fail to comply with the obligation to notify the Commission according to Article 3(3);
(c) fail to notify information or supply incorrect, incomplete or misleading information that is required pursuant to Article 14;
(d) fail to submit the description or supply incorrect, incomplete or misleading information that is required pursuant to Article 15;
(e) fail to provide access to data, algorithms or information about testing in response to a request made pursuant to Article 21(3);
(f) fail to supply the information requested within the time limit fixed pursuant to Article 21(3) or supply incorrect, incomplete or misleading information or explanations that are requested pursuant to Article 21 or given in an interview pursuant to Article 22;
(g) fail to rectify within a time limit set by the Commission, incorrect, incomplete or misleading information given by a representative or a member of staff, or fail or refuse to provide complete information on facts relating to the subject-matter and purpose of an inspection, pursuant to Article 23;
(h) refuse to submit to an inspection pursuant to Article 23;
(i) fail to comply with the obligations imposed by the Commission pursuant to Article 26;
(j) fail to introduce a compliance function in accordance with Article 28; or
(k) fail to comply with the conditions for access to the Commission's file pursuant to Article 34(4).

4. In fixing the amount of a fine, the Commission shall take into account the gravity, duration, recurrence, and, for fines imposed pursuant to paragraph 3, delay caused to the proceedings.

5. When a fine is imposed on an association of undertakings taking account of the worldwide turnover of its members and that association is not solvent, it shall be obliged to call for contributions from its members to cover the amount of the fine.

Where such contributions have not been made to the association of undertakings within a time limit set by the Commission, the Commission may require payment of the fine directly by any of the undertakings whose representatives were members of the decision-making bodies concerned of that association.

After having required payment in accordance with the second subparagraph, the Commission may require payment of the balance by any of the members of the association of undertakings, where necessary to ensure full payment of the fine.

However, the Commission shall not require payment pursuant to the second or the third subparagraph from undertakings which show that they have not implemented the decision of the association of undertakings that infringed this Regulation, and either were not aware of its existence, or have actively distanced themselves from it before the Commission opened proceedings under Article 20.

The financial liability of each undertaking in respect of the payment of the fine shall not exceed 20 % of its total worldwide turnover in the preceding financial year.

Article 31
Periodic penalty payments

1. The Commission may adopt a decision imposing on undertakings, including gatekeepers where applicable, and associations of undertakings periodic penalty payments not exceeding 5 % of the average daily worldwide turnover in the preceding financial year per day, calculated from the date set by that decision, in order to compel them:

(a) to comply with the measures specified by the Commission in a decision adopted pursuant to Article 8(2);
(b) to comply with the decision pursuant to Article 18(1);
(c) to supply correct and complete information within the time limit required by a request for information made by decision pursuant to Article 21;
(d) to ensure access to data, algorithms and information about testing in response to a request made pursuant to Article 21(3) and to supply explanations on those as required by a decision pursuant to Article 21;
(e) to submit to an inspection which was ordered by a decision taken pursuant to Article 23;
(f) to comply with a decision ordering interim measures taken pursuant to Article 24;
(g) to comply with commitments made legally binding by a decision pursuant to Article 25(1);
(h) to comply with a decision pursuant to Article 29(1).

2. Where the undertakings, or associations of undertakings, have satisfied the obligation which the periodic penalty payment was intended to enforce, the Commission may adopt an implementing act, setting the definitive amount of the periodic penalty payment at a figure lower than that which would arise under the original decision. That implementing act shall be adopted in accordance with the advisory procedure referred to in Article 50(2).

Article 32
Limitation periods for the imposition of penalties

1. The powers conferred on the Commission by Articles 30 and 31 shall be subject to a 5 year limitation period.

2. Time shall begin to run on the day on which the infringement is committed. However, in the case of continuing or repeated infringements, time shall begin to run on the day on which the infringement ceases.

3. Any action taken by the Commission for the purpose of a market investigation or proceedings in respect of an infringement shall interrupt the limitation period for the imposition of fines or periodic penalty payments. The limitation period shall be interrupted with effect from the date on which the action is notified to at least one undertaking or association of undertakings which has participated in the infringement. Actions which interrupt the running of the period shall include in particular the following:

(a) requests for information by the Commission;
(b) written authorisations to conduct inspections issued to its officials by the Commission;
(c) the opening of a proceeding by the Commission pursuant to Article 20.

4. Each interruption shall start time running afresh. However, the limitation period shall expire at the latest on the day on which a period equal to twice the limitation period has elapsed without the Commission having imposed a fine or a periodic penalty payment. That period shall be extended by the time during which limitation is suspended pursuant to paragraph 5.

5. The limitation period for the imposition of fines or periodic penalty payments shall be suspended for as long as the decision of the Commission is the subject of proceedings pending before the Court of Justice.

Article 33
Limitation periods for the enforcement of penalties

1. The power of the Commission to enforce decisions taken pursuant to Articles 30 and 31 shall be subject to a limitation period of 5 years.

2. Time shall begin to run from the day on which the decision becomes final.

3. The limitation period for the enforcement of penalties shall be interrupted:

(a) by notification of a decision varying the original amount of the fine or periodic penalty payment or refusing an application for variation; or
(b) by any action of the Commission or of a Member State, acting at the request of the Commission, designed to enforce payment of the fine or periodic penalty payment.

4. Each interruption shall start time running afresh.

5. The limitation period for the enforcement of penalties shall be suspended for so long as:

(a) time to pay is allowed; or
(b) enforcement of payment is suspended pursuant to a decision of the Court of Justice or to a decision by a national court.

Article 34
Right to be heard and access to the file

1. Before adopting a decision pursuant to Article 8, Article 9(1), Article 10(1), Articles 17, 18, 24, 25, 29 and 30 and Article 31(2), the Commission shall give the gatekeeper or undertaking or association of undertakings concerned the opportunity of being heard on:

(a) preliminary findings of the Commission, including any matter to which the Commission has taken objection; and
(b) measures that the Commission may intend to take in view of the preliminary findings pursuant to point (a) of this paragraph.

2. Gatekeepers, undertakings and associations of undertakings concerned may submit their observations to the Commission concerning the Commission's preliminary findings within a time limit set by the Commission in its preliminary findings which may not be less than 14 days.

3. The Commission shall base its decisions only on preliminary findings, including any matter to which the Commission has taken objection, on which gatekeepers, undertakings and associations of undertakings concerned have been able to comment.

4. The rights of defence of the gatekeeper, undertaking or association of undertakings concerned shall be fully respected in any proceedings. The gatekeeper, undertaking or association of undertakings concerned shall be entitled to have access to the Commission's file under terms of disclosure, subject to the legitimate interest of undertakings in the protection of their business secrets. In the case of disagreement between the parties, the Commission may adopt decisions setting out those terms of disclosure. The right of access to the file of the Commission shall not extend to confidential information and internal documents of the Commission or the competent authorities of the Member States. In particular, the right of access shall not extend to correspondence between the Commission and the competent authorities of the Member States. Nothing in this paragraph shall prevent the Commission from disclosing and using information necessary to prove an infringement.

Article 35
Annual reporting

1. The Commission shall submit to the European Parliament and to the Council an annual report on the implementation of this Regulation and the progress made towards achieving its objectives.

2. The report referred to in paragraph 1 shall include:

(a) a summary of the Commission's activities including any adopted measures or decisions and ongoing market investigations in connection with this Regulation;
(b) the findings resulting from the monitoring of the implementation by the gatekeepers of the obligations under this Regulation;
(c) an assessment of the audited description referred to in Article 15;
(d) an overview of the cooperation between the Commission and national authorities in connection with this Regulation;

(e) an overview of the activities and tasks performed by the High Level Group of Digital Regulators, including how its recommendations as regards the enforcement of this Regulation are to be implemented.

3. The Commission shall publish the report on its website.

Article 36
Professional secrecy

1. The information collected pursuant to this Regulation shall be used for the purposes of this Regulation.

2. The information collected pursuant to Article 14 shall be used for the purposes of this Regulation, Regulation (EC) No 139/2004 and national merger rules.

3. The information collected pursuant to Article 15 shall be used for the purposes of this Regulation and Regulation (EU) 2016/679.

4. Without prejudice to the exchange and to the use of information provided for the purpose of use pursuant to Articles 38, 39, 41 and 43, the Commission, the competent authorities of the Member States, their officials, servants and other persons working under the supervision of those authorities and any natural or legal person, including auditors and experts appointed pursuant to Article 26(2), shall not disclose information acquired or exchanged by them pursuant to this Regulation and of the kind covered by the obligation of professional secrecy.

Article 37
Cooperation with national authorities

1. The Commission and Member States shall work in close cooperation and coordinate their enforcement actions to ensure coherent, effective and complementary enforcement of available legal instruments applied to gatekeepers within the meaning of this Regulation.

2. The Commission may consult national authorities where appropriate, on any matter relating to the application of this Regulation.

Article 38
Cooperation and coordination with national competent authorities enforcing competition rules

1. The Commission and the national competent authorities of the Member States enforcing the rules referred to in Article 1(6) shall cooperate with each other and inform each other about their respective enforcement actions through the European Competition Network (ECN). They shall have the power to provide one another with any information regarding a matter of fact or of law, including confidential information. Where the competent authority is not a member of the ECN, the Commission shall make the necessary arrangements for cooperation and exchange of information on cases concerning the enforcement of this Regulation and the enforcement of cases referred to in Article 1(6) of such authorities. The Commission may lay down such arrangements in an implementing act as referred to in Article 46(1), point (l).

2. Where a national competent authority of the Member States enforcing the rules referred to in Article 1(6) intends to launch an investigation on gatekeepers based on national laws referred to in Article 1(6), it shall inform the Commission in writing of the first formal investigative measure, before or immediately after the start of such measure. This information may also be made available to the national competent authorities enforcing the rules referred to in Article 1(6) of the other Member States.

3. Where a national competent authority of the Member States enforcing the rules referred to in Article 1(6) intends to impose obligations on gatekeepers based on national laws referred to in Article 1(6), it shall, no later than 30 days before its adoption, communicate the draft measure to the Commission stating the reasons for the measure. In the case of interim measures, the national competent authority of the Member States enforcing the rules referred to in Article 1(6) shall communicate to the Commission the draft measures envisaged as soon as possible, and at the latest immediately after the adoption of such measures. This information may also be made available to the national competent authorities enforcing the rules referred to in Article 1(6) of the other Member States.

4. The information mechanisms provided for in paragraphs 2 and 3 shall not apply to decisions envisaged pursuant to national merger rules.

5. Information exchanged pursuant to paragraphs 1 to 3 of this Article shall only be exchanged and used for the purpose of coordination of the enforcement of this Regulation and the rules referred to in Article 1(6).

6. The Commission may ask national competent authorities of the Member States enforcing the rules referred to in Article 1(6) to support any of its market investigations pursuant to this Regulation.

7. Where it has the competence and investigative powers to do so under national law, a national competent authority of the Member States enforcing the rules referred to in Article 1(6) may, on its own initiative, conduct an investigation into a case of possible non-compliance with Articles 5, 6 and 7 of this Regulation on its territory. Before taking a first formal investigative measure, that authority shall inform the Commission in writing.

The opening of proceedings by the Commission pursuant to Article 20 shall relieve the national competent authorities of the Member States enforcing the rules referred to in Article 1(6) of the possibility to conduct such an investigation or end it where it is already ongoing. Those authorities shall report to the Commission on the findings of such investigation in order to support the Commission in its role as sole enforcer of this Regulation.

Article 39
Cooperation with national courts

1. In proceedings for the application of this Regulation, national courts may ask the Commission to transmit to them information in its possession or its opinion on questions concerning the application of this Regulation.

2. Member States shall forward to the Commission a copy of any written judgment of national courts deciding on the application of this Regulation. Such copy shall be forwarded without delay after the full written judgment is notified to the parties.

3. Where the coherent application of this Regulation so requires, the Commission, acting on its own initiative, may submit written observations to national courts. With the permission of the court in question, it may also make oral observations.

4. For the purpose of the preparation of their observations only, the Commission may request the relevant national court to transmit or ensure the transmission to the Commission of any documents necessary for the assessment of the case.

5. National courts shall not give a decision which runs counter to a decision adopted by the Commission under this Regulation. They shall also avoid giving decisions which would conflict with a decision contemplated by the Commission in proceedings it has initiated under this Regulation. To that effect, the national court may assess whether it is necessary to stay its proceedings. This is without prejudice to the possibility for national courts to request a preliminary ruling under Article 267 TFEU.

Article 40
The high-level group

1. The Commission shall establish a high-level group for the Digital Markets Act ('the high-level group').

2. The high-level group shall be composed of the following European bodies and networks:

(a) Body of the European Regulators for Electronic Communications;
(b) European Data Protection Supervisor and European Data Protection Board;
(c) European Competition Network;
(d) Consumer Protection Cooperation Network; and
(e) European Regulatory Group of Audiovisual Media Regulators.

3. The European bodies and networks referred to in paragraph 2 shall each have an equal number of representatives in the high-level group. The maximum number of members of the high-level group shall not exceed 30.

4. The Commission shall provide secretariat services to the high-level group in order to facilitate its work. The high-level group shall be chaired by the Commission, which shall participate in its meetings. The high-level group shall meet upon request of the Commission at least once per calendar year. The Commission shall also convene a meeting of the group when so requested by the majority of the members composing the group in order to address a specific issue.

5. The high-level group may provide the Commission with advice and expertise in the areas falling within the competences of its members, including:

(a) advice and recommendations within their expertise relevant for any general matter of implementation or enforcement of this Regulation; or
(b) advice and expertise promoting a consistent regulatory approach across different regulatory instruments.

6. The high-level group may, in particular, identify and assess the current and potential interactions between this Regulation and the sector-specific rules applied by the national authorities composing the European bodies and networks referred to in paragraph 2 and submit an annual report to the Commission presenting such assessment and identifying potential trans-regulatory issues. Such report may be accompanied by recommendations aiming at converging towards consistent transdisciplinary approaches and synergies

between the implementation of this Regulation and other sectoral regulations. The report shall be communicated to the European Parliament and to the Council.

7. In the context of market investigations into new services and new practices, the high-level group may provide expertise to the Commission on the need to amend, add or remove rules in this Regulation, to ensure that digital markets across the Union are contestable and fair.

Article 41
Request for a market investigation

1. Three or more Member States may request the Commission to open a market investigation pursuant to Article 17 because they consider that there are reasonable grounds to suspect that an undertaking should be designated as a gatekeeper.

2. One or more Member States may request the Commission to open a market investigation pursuant to Article 18 because they consider that there are reasonable grounds to suspect that a gatekeeper has systematically infringed one or more of the obligations laid down in Articles 5, 6 and 7 and has maintained, strengthened or extended its gatekeeper position in relation to the requirements under Article 3(1).

3. Three or more Member States may request the Commission to conduct a market investigation pursuant to Article 19 because they consider that there are reasonable grounds to suspect that:

(a) one or more services within the digital sector should be added to the list of core platform services laid down in Article 2, point (2), or
(b) one or more practices are not effectively addressed by this Regulation and might limit the contestability of core platform services or be unfair.

4. Member States shall submit evidence in support of their requests pursuant to paragraphs 1, 2 and 3. For requests pursuant to paragraph 3, such evidence may include information on newly introduced offers of products, services, software or features which raise concerns of contestability or fairness, whether implemented in the context of existing core platform services or otherwise.

5. Within 4 months of receiving a request pursuant to this Article, the Commission shall examine whether there are reasonable grounds to open a market investigation pursuant to paragraph 1, 2 or 3. The Commission shall publish the results of its assessment.

Article 42
Representative actions

Directive (EU) 2020/1828 shall apply to the representative actions brought against infringements by gatekeepers of provisions of this Regulation that harm or may harm the collective interests of consumers.

Article 43
Reporting of breaches and protection of reporting persons

Directive (EU) 2019/1937 shall apply to the reporting of all breaches of this Regulation and the protection of persons reporting such breaches.

CHAPTER VI
FINAL PROVISIONS

Article 44
Publication of decisions

1. The Commission shall publish the decisions which it takes pursuant to Articles 3 and 4, Article 8(2), Articles 9, 10, 16 to 20 and 24, Article 25(1), Articles 29, 30 and 31. Such publication shall state the names of the parties and the main content of the decision, including any penalties imposed.

2. The publication shall have regard to the legitimate interest of gatekeepers or third parties in the protection of their confidential information.

Article 45
Review by the Court of Justice

In accordance with Article 261 TFEU, the Court of Justice has unlimited jurisdiction to review decisions by which the Commission has imposed fines or periodic penalty payments. It may cancel, reduce or increase the fine or periodic penalty payment imposed.

Article 46
Implementing provisions

1. The Commission may adopt implementing acts laying down detailed arrangements for the application of the following:

(a) the form, content and other details of notifications and submissions pursuant to Article 3;
(b) the form, content and other details of the technical measures that gatekeepers shall implement in order to ensure compliance with Article 5, 6 or 7;
(c) operational and technical arrangements in view of implementing interoperability of number-independent interpersonal communications services pursuant to Article 7;
(d) the form, content and other details of the reasoned request pursuant to Article 8(3);
(e) the form, content and other details of the reasoned requests pursuant to Articles 9 and 10;
(f) the form, content and other details of the regulatory reports delivered pursuant to Article 11;
(g) the methodology and procedure for the audited description of techniques used for profiling of consumers provided for in Article 15(1); when developing a draft implementing act for this purpose, the Commission shall consult the European Data Protection Supervisor and may consult the European Data Protection Board, civil society and other relevant experts;
(h) the form, content and other details of notifications and submissions made pursuant to Articles 14 and 15;
(i) the practical arrangements of the proceedings concerning the market investigations pursuant to Articles 17, 18 and 19, and proceedings pursuant to Articles 24, 25 and 29;
(j) the practical arrangements for exercising rights to be heard provided for in Article 34;
(k) the practical arrangements for the terms of disclosure provided for in Article 34;

(l) the practical arrangements for the cooperation and coordination between the Commission and national authorities provided for in Articles 37 and 38; and
(m) the practical arrangements for the calculation and extension of deadlines.

2. The implementing acts referred to in paragraph 1, points (a) to (k), and point (m) of this Article shall be adopted in accordance with the advisory procedure referred to in Article 50(2).

The implementing act referred to in paragraph 1, point (l), of this Article shall be adopted in accordance with the examination procedure referred to in Article 50(3).

3. Before the adoption of any implementing act pursuant to paragraph 1, the Commission shall publish a draft thereof and invite all interested parties to submit their comments within a time limit, which may not be less than one month.

Article 47
Guidelines

The Commission may adopt guidelines on any of the aspects of this Regulation in order to facilitate its effective implementation and enforcement.

Article 48
Standardisation

Where appropriate and necessary, the Commission may mandate European standardisation bodies to facilitate the implementation of the obligations set out in this Regulation by developing appropriate standards.

Article 49
Exercise of the delegation

1. The power to adopt delegated acts is conferred on the Commission subject to the conditions laid down in this Article.

2. The power to adopt delegated acts referred to in Article 3(6) and (7) and Article 12(1), (3) and (4) shall be conferred on the Commission for a period of 5 years from 1 November 2022. The Commission shall draw up a report in respect of the delegation of power not later than 9 months before the end of the five-year period. The delegation of power shall be tacitly extended for periods of an identical duration, unless the European Parliament or the Council opposes such extension not later than 3 months before the end of each period.

3. The delegation of power referred to in Article 3(6) and (7), and Article 12(1), (3) and (4) may be revoked at any time by the European Parliament or by the Council. A decision to revoke shall put an end to the delegation of the power specified in that decision. It shall take effect the day following the publication of the decision in the *Official Journal of the European Union* or at a later date specified therein. It shall not affect the validity of any delegated acts already in force.

4. Before adopting a delegated act, the Commission shall consult experts designated by each Member State in accordance with the principles laid down in the Interinstitutional Agreement of 13 April 2016 on Better Law-Making.

5. As soon as it adopts a delegated act, the Commission shall notify it simultaneously to the European Parliament and to the Council.

6. A delegated act adopted pursuant to Article 3(6) and (7), and Article 12(1), (3) and (4) shall enter into force only if no objection has been expressed either by the European Parliament or by the Council within a period of 2 months of notification of that act to the European Parliament and to the Council or if, before the expiry of that period, the European Parliament and the Council have both informed the Commission that they will not object. That period shall be extended by 2 months at the initiative of the European Parliament or of the Council.

Article 50
Committee procedure

1. The Commission shall be assisted by a committee ('the Digital Markets Advisory Committee'). That committee shall be a committee within the meaning of Regulation (EU) No 182/2011.

2. Where reference is made to this paragraph, Article 4 of Regulation (EU) No 182/2011 shall apply.

Where the opinion of the committee is to be obtained by written procedure, that procedure shall be terminated without result when, within the time limit for delivery of the opinion, the chair of the committee so decides or a simple majority of committee members so request.

3. Where reference is made to this paragraph, Article 5 of Regulation (EU) No 182/2011 shall apply.

4. The Commission shall communicate the opinion of the committee to the addressee of an individual decision, together with that decision. It shall make the opinion public together with the individual decision, having regard to the legitimate interest in the protection of professional secrecy.

Article 51
Amendment to Directive (EU) 2019/1937

In Point J of Part I of the Annex to Directive (EU) 2019/1937, the following point is added:

'(iv) Regulation (EU) 2022/1925 of the European Parliament and of the Council of 14 September 2022 on contestable and fair markets in the digital sector and amending Directives (EU) 2019/1937 and (EU) 2020/1828 (Digital Markets Act) (OJ L 265, 21.9.2022, p. 1).'

Article 52
Amendment to Directive (EU) 2020/1828

In Annex I to Directive (EU) 2020/1828, the following point is added:

'(67) Regulation (EU) 2022/1925 of the European Parliament and of the Council of 14 September 2022 on contestable and fair markets in the digital sector and amending Directives (EU) 2019/1937 and (EU) 2020/1828 (Digital Markets Act) (OJ L 265, 21.9.2022, p. 1).'

Article 53
Review

1. By 3 May 2026, and subsequently every 3 years, the Commission shall evaluate this Regulation and report to the European Parliament, the Council and the European Economic and Social Committee.

2. The evaluations shall assess whether the aims of this Regulation of ensuring contestable and fair markets have been achieved and assess the impact of this Regulation on business users, especially SMEs, and end users. Moreover, the Commission shall evaluate if the scope of Article 7 may be extended to online social networking services.

3. The evaluations shall establish whether it is required to modify rules, including regarding the list of core platform services laid down in Article 2, point (2), the obligations laid down in Articles 5, 6 and 7 and their enforcement, to ensure that digital markets across the Union are contestable and fair. Following the evaluations, the Commission shall take appropriate measures, which may include legislative proposals.

4. The competent authorities of Member States shall provide any relevant information they have that the Commission may require for the purposes of drawing up the report referred to in paragraph 1.

Article 54
Entry into force and application

This Regulation shall enter into force on the twentieth day following that of its publication in the *Official Journal of the European Union*.

It shall apply from 2 May 2023.

However, Article 3(6) and (7) and Articles 40, 46, 47, 48, 49 and 50 shall apply from 1 November 2022 and Article 42 and Article 43 shall apply from 25 June 2023.

Nevertheless, if the date of 25 June 2023 precedes the date of application referred to in the second paragraph of this Article, the application of Article 42 and Article 43 shall be postponed until the date of application referred to in the second paragraph of this Article.

This Regulation shall be binding in its entirety and directly applicable in all Member States.

Done at Strasbourg, 14 September 2022.

For the European Parliament	*For the Council*
The President	*The President*
R. METSOLA	M. BEK

ANNEX

A. 'General'

1. This Annex aims at specifying the methodology for identifying and calculating the 'active end users' and the 'active business users' for each core platform service listed in Article 2, point (2). It provides a reference to enable an undertaking to assess whether its core platform services meet the quantitative thresholds set out in

Article 3(2), point (b) and would therefore be presumed to meet the requirement in Article 3(1), point (b). Such reference will therefore equally be of relevance to any broader assessment under Article 3(8). It is the responsibility of the undertaking to come to the best approximation possible in line with the common principles and specific methodology set out in this Annex. Nothing in this Annex precludes the Commission, within the time limits laid down in the relevant provisions of this Regulation, from requiring the undertaking providing core platform services to provide any information necessary to identify and calculate the 'active end users' and the 'active business users'. Nothing in this Annex should constitute a legal basis for tracking users. The methodology contained in this Annex is also without prejudice to any of the obligations laid down in this Regulation, notably in Article 3(3) and (8) and Article 13(3). In particular, the required compliance with Article 13(3) also means identifying and calculating 'active end users' and 'active business users' based either on a precise measurement or on the best approximation available, in line with the actual identification and calculation capacities that the undertaking providing core platform services possesses at the relevant point in time. Those measurements or the best approximation available shall be consistent with, and include, those reported under Article 15.

2. Article 2, points (20) and (21) set out the definitions of 'end user' and 'business user', which are common to all core platform services.
3. In order to identify and calculate the number of 'active end users' and 'active business users', this Annex refers to the concept of 'unique users'. The concept of 'unique users' encompasses 'active end users' and 'active business users' counted only once, for the relevant core platform service, over the course of a specified time period (i.e. month in case of 'active end users' and year in case of 'active business users'), no matter how many times they engaged with the relevant core platform service over that period. This is without prejudice to the fact that the same natural or legal person can simultaneously constitute an 'active end user' or an 'active business user' for different core platform services.

B. 'Active end users'

1. The number of 'unique users' as regards 'active end users' shall be identified according to the most accurate metric reported by the undertaking providing any of the core platform services, specifically:
   a. It is considered that collecting data about the use of core platform services from signed-in or logged-in environments would prima facie present the lowest risk of duplication, for example in relation to user behaviour across devices or platforms. Hence, the undertaking shall submit aggregate anonymized data on the number of unique end users per respective core platform service based on signed-in or logged-in environments, if such data exists.
   b. In the case of core platform services which are also accessed by end users outside signed-in or logged-in environments, the undertaking shall additionally submit aggregate anonymized data on the number of unique end users of the respective core platform service based on an alternate metric capturing also end users outside signed-in or logged-in environments, such as internet protocol addresses, cookie identifiers or other identifiers such as radio frequency identification tags, provided that those addresses or identifiers are objectively necessary for the provision of the core platform services.
2. The number of 'monthly active end users' is based on the average number of monthly active end users throughout the largest part of the financial year. The notion

'the largest part of the financial year' is intended to allow an undertaking providing core platform services to discount outlier figures in a given year. Outlier figures inherently mean figures that fall significantly outside the normal and foreseeable figures. An unforeseen peak or drop in user engagement that occurred during a single month of the financial year is an example of what could constitute such outlier figures. Figures related to annually recurring occurrences, such as annual sales promotions, are not outlier figures.

C. 'Active business users'

The number of 'unique users' as regards 'active business users' is to be determined, where applicable, at the account level with each distinct business account associated with the use of a core platform service provided by the undertaking constituting one unique business user of that respective core platform service. If the notion of 'business account' does not apply to a given core platform service, the relevant undertaking providing core platform services shall determine the number of unique business users by referring to the relevant undertaking.

D. 'Submission of information'

1. The undertaking submitting to the Commission pursuant to Article 3(3) information concerning the number of active end users and active business users per core platform service shall be responsible for ensuring the completeness and accuracy of that information. In that regard:
   a. The undertaking shall be responsible for submitting data for a respective core platform service that avoids under-counting and over-counting the number of active end users and active business users (for example, where users access the core platform services across different platforms or devices).
   b. The undertaking shall be responsible for providing precise and succinct explanations about the methodology used to arrive at the information and for any risk of under-counting or over-counting of the number of active end users and active business users for a respective core platform service and for the solutions adopted to address that risk.
   c. The undertaking shall provide data that is based on an alternative metric when the Commission has concerns about the accuracy of data provided by the undertaking providing core platform services.
2. For the purpose of calculating the number of 'active end users' and 'active business users':
   a. The undertaking providing core platform service(s) shall not identify core platform services that belong to the same category of core platform services pursuant to Article 2, point (2) as distinct mainly on the basis that they are provided using different domain names, whether country code top-level domains (ccTLDs) or generic top-level domains (gTLDs), or any geographic attributes.
   b. The undertaking providing core platform service(s) shall consider as distinct core platform services those core platform services, which are used for different purposes by either their end users or their business users, or both, even if their end users or business users may be the same and even if they belong to the same category of core platform services pursuant to Article 2, point (2).
   c. The undertaking providing core platform service(s) shall consider as distinct core platform services those services which the relevant undertaking offers in an integrated way, but which:

(i) do not belong to the same category of core platform services pursuant to Article 2, point (2); or

(ii) are used for different purposes by either their end users or their business users, or both, even if their end users and business users may be the same and even if they belong to the same category of core platform services pursuant to Article 2, point (2).

E. 'Specific definitions'

The table below sets out specific definitions of 'active end users' and 'active business users' for each core platform service.

Core platform services	**Active end users**	**Active business users**
Online intermediation services	Number of unique end users who engaged with the online intermediation service at least once in the month for example through actively logging-in, making a query, clicking or scrolling or concluded a transaction through the online intermediation service at least once in the month.	Number of unique business users who had at least one item listed in the online intermediation service during the whole year or concluded a transaction enabled by the online intermediation service during the year.
Online search engines	Number of unique end users who engaged with the online search engine at least once in the month, for example through making a query.	Number of unique business users with business websites (i.e. website used in commercial or professional capacity) indexed by or part of the index of the online search engine during the year.
Online social networking services	Number of unique end users who engaged with the online social networking service at least once in the month, for example through actively logging-in, opening a page, scrolling, clicking, liking, making a query, posting or commenting.	Number of unique business users who have a business listing or business account in the online social networking service and have engaged in any way with the service at least once during the year, for example through actively logging-in, opening a page, scrolling, clicking, liking, making a query, posting, commenting or using its tools for businesses.

Core platform services	Active end users	Active business users
Video-sharing platform services	Number of unique end users who engaged with the video-sharing platform service at least once in the month, for example through playing a segment of audiovisual content, making a query or uploading a piece of audiovisual content, notably including user-generated videos.	Number of unique business users who provided at least one piece of audiovisual content uploaded or played on the video-sharing platform service during the year.
Number-independent interpersonal communication services	Number of unique end users who initiated or participated in any way in a communication through the number-independent interpersonal communication service at least once in the month.	Number of unique business users who used a business account or otherwise initiated or participated in any way in a communication through the number-independent interpersonal communication service to communicate directly with an end user at least once during the year.
Operating systems	Number of unique end users who utilised a device with the operating system, which has been activated, updated or used at least once in the month.	Number of unique developers who published, updated or offered at least one software application or software program using the programming language or any software development tools of, or running in any way on, the operating system during the year.
Virtual assistant	Number of unique end users who engaged with the virtual assistant in any way at least once in the month, such as for example through activating it, asking a question, accessing a service through a command or controlling a smart home device.	Number of unique developers who offered at least one virtual assistant software application or a functionality to make an existing software application accessible through the virtual assistant during the year.
Web browsers	Number of unique end users who engaged with the web browser at least once in the month, for example through inserting a query or website address in the URL line of the web browser.	Number of unique business users whose business websites (i.e. website used in commercial or professional capacity) have been accessed via the web browser at least once during the year or who offered a plug-in, extension or add-ons used on the web browser during the year.

Core platform services	Active end users	Active business users
Cloud computing services	Number of unique end users who engaged with any cloud computing services from the relevant provider of cloud computing services at least once in the month, in return for any type of remuneration, regardless of whether this remuneration occurs in the same month.	Number of unique business users who provided any cloud computing services hosted in the cloud infrastructure of the relevant provider of cloud computing services during the year.
Online advertising services	For proprietary sales of advertising space: Number of unique end users who were exposed to an advertisement impression at least once in the month. For advertising intermediation services (including advertising networks, advertising exchanges and any other advertising intermediation services): Number of unique end users who were exposed to an advertisement impression which triggered the advertising intermediation service at least once in the month.	For proprietary sales of advertising space: Number of unique advertisers who had at least one advertisement impression displayed during the year. For advertising intermediation services (including advertising networks, advertising exchanges and any other advertising intermediation services): Number of unique business users (including advertisers, publishers or other intermediators) who interacted via or were served by the advertising intermediation service during the year.

Index

Bold numbers refer to chapters, normal ones to margin numbers.